Sustainable
Urban
Neighbourhood

BUILDING THE 21ST CENTURY HOME

David Rudlin and Nicholas Falk

Architectural
Press

An illustration by Squint Opera of URBED's master plan for West Bar in Sheffield. This was developed for a joint venture between Castlemore Securities and Sheffield Council and was granted planning permission in 2008.

Architectural Press
An imprint of Elsevier

Sustainable Urban Neighbourhood

BUILDING THE 21ST CENTURY HOME

David Rudlin and Nicholas Falk

Architectural Press is an imprint of Elsevier
Linacre House, Jordan Hill, Oxford OX2 8DP
30 Corporate Drive, Suite 400, Burlington, MA01803.USA

First published 1999

British Library Cataloguing in Publication Data
A catalogue record for this book is available from the British Library

Library of Congress Cataloguing in Publication Data
A catalogue record for this book is available from the Library of Congress

ISBN 9780 7565 633 7

Designed by David Rudlin
Printed and bound in Great Britain

Contents

PART 3: THE SUSTAINABLE URBAN NEIGHBOURHOOD

Case studies

The book is dedicated to Luca and Jonah
and the city in which they have grown up

The authors

Both David Rudlin and Nicholas Falk head the two parts of URBED, an innovative consultancy and design practice that has its roots in London's Covent Garden of the mid 1970s. Today there are two arms to URBED. The Manchester URBED (Urbanism, Environment and Design) is run by David Rudlin and specialises in masterplanning, consultation and sustainability. URBED (Urban and Economic Development) is headed by Nicholas Falk in London and focuses on economic regeneration and community empowerment.

Both sides of URBED have always combined research with consultancy and have published a wide range of reports. This book brings together much of this work with our experience of practical consultancy to set out our philosophy. While the book focuses mainly on the Sustainable Urban Neighbourhood it draws upon many aspects of URBED's work as well, of course, as more than 30 years experience working on the frontline of urban regeneration in the UK.

David Rudlin BA MTP: A planner by training David started his career with Manchester City Council with responsibility for the early stages of the redevelopment of Hulme. He was also secretary of the Homes for Change housing cooperative, responsible for commissioning one of the flagship buildings of the Hulme Redevelopment and co-wrote the Hulme guide to development. He joined URBED in 1990 to manage the award-winning Little Germany Action project in Bradford. Since then he has managed a range of high profile consultancy projects and master plans such as Temple Quay 2 in Bristol, The New England Quarter in Brighton and the Oldham Beyond vision commissioned after the riots in the town.

He is the author of a number of research reports including '21st Century Homes' for the Joseph Rowntree Foundation, 'Tomorrow a peaceful path to urban reform' for Friends of the Earth and 'But would you live there?' for the Urban Task Force. He is chair of BEAM in Wakefield and has been a member of the CABE design review committee, a trustee of CUBE (the Centre for the Understanding of the Built Environment) in Manchester and a Policy Council member of the TCPA. He is also a founder Academician of the Academy for Urbanism in the UK.

Dr. Nicholas Falk BA MBA: An economist and strategic planner with over thirty years experience of urban regeneration and local and economic development. He has degrees from Oxford, Stanford Business School and the London School of Economics and worked in marketing for Ford Motor Company before founding URBED in 1976. He is the principal author of a number of reports for the UK government including, *Vital and Viable Town Centres, Town Centre Partnerships* and *Partners in Urban Renaissance* – the report of the 24 Towns and Cities Initiative. He has been responsible for many major studies, from large cities such as Birmingham and Bristol to smaller towns such as Cirencester and Ely. Area regeneration studies have included award-winning schemes for Exeter Riverside, and Birmingham's Jewellery Quarter.

He has been a member of the Department of the Environment's Property Advisory Group and the Planning Research Advisory Group. He is an Honorary fellow of the RIBA, Visiting Professor at the School of the Built Environment at the University of the West of England and a member of the Academy for Urbanism and the UK government's Eco-Towns Panel.

Acknowledgements

This book draws upon the ideas of many people too numerous to mention here. It pulls together our research and consultancy work over many years and we are grateful for everyone who has contributed.

Worthy of particular mention are our colleagues at URBED. The book draws heavily on previous work for the Joseph Rowntree Foundation, Friends of the Earth as well as for Hulme Regeneration and through the Environmental Action Fund. Particularly important roles have been played either as clients or associates by (Lord) David Sainsbury, (Lord) Richard Best and John Low of the Joseph Rowntree Foundation, Simon Festing formerly of Friends of the Earth, Charlie Baker and Sarah Hughes formerly of Build for Change and now with URBED, George Mills and Ian Beaumont of MBLC Architects, Jon Rowland, David Levitt, John Doggart, Joe Ravetz, David Lunts, Barbara McLoughlin, Greame Russell and David Birkbeck.

We are also indebted to clients who have allowed us to put these ideas into practice including Chris Gilbert of QED who developed the Brighton New England Quarter, Chris Brown and David Roberts of Igloo, Patrick Power and Eric Hall of Castlemore and Andy Dainty of URBO.

Direct inputs have also been made to the text by Jonathan Brown, Grace Manning-Marsh, David Malcolm and Christina Swensson (who did the initial work on the case studies). We are also indebted to the knowledge and commitment brought by Nick Dodd on the sustainability sections.

Help with design has come from Jason Crouch of M15 Design, additional illustrations have been provided by Vibeke Fussing and many of the drawings are based on photography by Anne Worthington or Charlie Baker.

Thanks also go to Cecile and Vincent in Bordeaux for providing a refuge and a source of inspiration for the completion of the final part of the book. Most important of all has been the role played by Hélène as a critic and confidante without whom very little would have been written.

Preface

To the Second Edition - David Rudlin

This book was completed 10 years ago and was written in the 5 years before that. It was produced as a polemic, targeted at changing the way that people feel about cities, just as the late Jane Jacobs had done thirty years earlier. We were never going to match the rhetorical power of Death and Life of Great American Cities, as a number of reviewers have kindly pointed out. However the feedback since publication suggests that our book has had an impact. A developer friend claims that it is the only book on planning that he has ever read cover to cover and revels in quoting sections back at us when we he feels we are deviating from its precepts in our plans for him. A reader review on Amazon described it as 'one of those books which change the way you look at the world' – which is nice, because that was the idea. It has been taught in schools of the built environment in the UK, the US, Canada and Australia and has even been published in Chinese.

The irony is that the eloquence of Jane Jacobs had virtually no impact on the cities of her time. Death and Life was first published in the late 1960s at a time when the aspects of city life that she so cherished were being swept away. Her heartfelt cry went largely unheeded. Thirty years later, our experience has been very different. Many of the things that we predicted and argued-for in this book at the end of the 1990s have come to pass. Not that we can claim much of the credit – it is more a case of pushing against an open door – and not being alone in doing the pushing.

The seeds that we and others were sowing in the late 1990s fell on fertile ground. For some the suburban dream had turned sour, in the ignominy of the housing crash of the late 1980s. People had started to see the great formless housing estates that had grown like a cancer around every city, town and village in the UK for what they were – soulless, alienating and undermining of civil society. We were not alone in arguing for change – indeed there was a huge coalition of interests embracing everyone from urbanists to countryside campaigners. The former were concerned about the revival of towns and cities, the latter about the loss of rural England under a sea of tarmac and starter homes. The breadth of these concerns meant that the issue united the political right and left. However in the mid 1990s the possibility of change still seemed remote. Indeed while the UK government was starting to talk about reform, most of the groups with power over the built environment, the developers, planners, highways engineers, architects and the police were dead set against it. When this book was first published the battle continued to rage but the outcome was far from certain.

Over the last decade the cities of the UK were transformed from lost causes to engines of economic growth, bristling with tower cranes. Huge problems remain, not least in smaller industrial towns and in the disparities of wealth within the large cities. There are of course also worries in the depths of another housing crash and credit crunch. Can progress can be sustained or will policy-makers panic and overturn the reforms of recent years that have created a UK urban renaissance in an attempt to kick start the housing market? Time will tell, however our sense is that a corner has been turned and that the future for cities in the 21st century will be much more positive that the rather sorry story of the 20th century city that we tell in the first part of this book.

Looking back over the first edition of this book it seems frozen at a point in time. It was written at a time when the outcome of the trends that we described were still far from clear. It is difficult when producing a book on current urban policy to write something that lasts; the government report that seemed so important has long been forgotten, the example that seemed so apt now seems irrelevant or worse still has turned out to be a failure. Some of the assertions that we made have turned out to be untrue. In the late 1990s for example the great issue was the ghettoisation of social housing while we suggested that private housing somehow seemed insulated from decline. How wrong we were, as housing market failure across large parts of northern England in the early 2000s illustrated. This book has therefore been comprehensively rewritten and updated. We have not however erased our mistakes. Instead in this updated version we describe what we said in the first edition before correcting and updating ourselves. The 1990s edition of this book was a first draft of a period of history that we believe will be seen in the future as a turning point in the life of the UK's towns and cities. This book is a second draft and takes the story forward but more drafts will be needed before the entire story can be told.

David Rudlin
2008

Preface

To the First Edition – David Rudlin

My first experience of the city was as a child in Birmingham. I grew up in Hall Green, a respectable suburb in the south of the city, and could look out of my bedroom window across treetops and rooftops to the city centre on the far horizon. My earliest memories of Birmingham were of peering through rain splattered bus windows at the lights of a city as we travelled home on dark winter evenings along the Stratford Road. Indeed much of our life seemed to revolve around the Stratford Road. My family lived near the Stratford Road, as had my grandparents; my dad worked at a factory and my mum in a shop both also on the Stratford Road. It was where we did our shopping, where the family went to church, where the library, swimming baths, police station and cinema were to be found and where my sisters and I were to go to school. To me it represented the city far more than the distant city centre.

Millions of people will know the Stratford Road. It runs from Digbeth on the southern edge of the city centre through Sparkhill and Sparkbrook, Moseley, Hall Green and Shirley to the countryside on the edge of the city, a distance of some twelve miles. It is lined almost continuously by shops, public buildings, pubs, cinemas (now sadly closed) and churches. When I go home to visit my parents I still travel along

the road. When I do I am pleased to see that it remains largely intact and indeed is thriving with activity and life when ten years ago it seemed to be on the brink of terminal decline. To a small child it seemed to be the essence of the cosmopolitan city with its Asian shops and Irish pubs and side streets which led into a warren of terraced housing with corner shops and more pubs. I was not to know that I was travelling along a tenuous thread of urban activity running through largely dull and lifeless residential areas. To me the city seemed to go on forever in all directions and was at once frightening and exciting. This part-imagined city was the territory that I populated in my dreams and which provided the setting for the stories of my childhood, be it Oliver Twist or Mary Poppins. This mixture of fear and excitement seems to me a typical reaction to the urban life.

My other main memory of growing up in Birmingham was the fact that it was being transformed. The city centre in the 1960s was a perpetual building site with the construction of the inner ring road, the Bull Ring and the maze of flyovers and underpasses which were to encircle the city. It was all so modern and confident, and my parents and their friends seemed to agree that it was a change for the better. I am too young to remember the Birmingham which predated this great transformation – the Victorian city of a thousand trades – and find it difficult to mourn its loss. However I do remember the pride of Birmingham people in the new city that was emerging. Visiting friends and relations would be taken to see the Rotunda and the other modern buildings just as today they are taken to see Chamberlain Square and the new convention centre. It is less easy to remember when disillusionment set in but, set in it did. It did not take long for the concrete and steel of the flyovers and high-rise buildings to lose its sheen. We seemed to go less and less into the centre of town, preferring to go to Solihull which itself had not entirely escaped the attention of the planners. Somewhere in the early 1970s the municipal planners and architects fell from grace and nowhere was this more obvious than in the pages of the local paper, the *Birmingham Evening Mail*, which revelled in holding the city and the council up to ridicule.

It seems to me now that what happened to Birmingham is a microcosm of what has happened to all cities in Britain to a greater or lesser extent over the last forty years. The city fathers along with their planners, architects and engineers who transformed Birmingham in the 1960s did not do so out of malice or spite. They believed passionately in what they were doing just as those of us who seek to shape cities today believe that what we are doing is right. They were also, on the whole, supported by the community to a degree which is often forgotten. However something went horribly wrong. The areas that they created, which looked so appealing bathed in sunlight and populated with contented people in the artists' impressions, looked so different on wet grimy winter evenings, strewn with the litter of shoppers and clogged with traffic. The public esteem of the urban professions has never really recovered from this sorry period of our history. A bond of trust has been broken and we are no longer confident that we have all the answers. If we are to regain this trust and confidence we must understand what it was that went wrong, which is what we try and do in the first part of this book.

In the late 1970s I moved to Manchester to study town planning. It is the city where I have made my home and which has provided a constant source of material and examples for this book. Manchester is a city which was fortunate enough to experience its boom in the Victorian period when at least they built decent buildings. The plans of Manchester's city fathers in the 1950s were no less radical than those in Birmingham. Manchester however was in decline. The city has lost a third of its population since 1961 and its industrial base has been decimated. It therefore lacked the resources to realise its dreams so that, with the exception of Piccadilly Plaza and the Arndale Centre, its centre, at least, came through the 1950s, 60s and 70s largely unscathed.

Jane Jacobs in her book *The Economy of Cities* has a section entitled 'efficient Manchester, inefficient Birmingham'. In this she contrasts the great mills of the former with their large compliant workforces with the thousands of small inefficient workshops in Birmingham. She suggests however that this diversity of economic activity was the basis for Birmingham's growth as a great city in the 20th century at a time when northern cities like Manchester were declining. It is in such small enterprises, Jacobs argues, that innovation and new business is generated. This is what made Birmingham such an ideal location for the car industry with its need for large numbers of component manufacturers. One need only compare the engineering sections of the Birmingham and Manchester Yellow Pages to see that there are still vastly more small manufacturing firms in the former.

However to me as a young student Manchester was so much more exciting and inviting as a city. You could walk around on real streets thronging with people rather than being forced underground in dark subways which felt, and often were, dangerous. This may explain why in the 1990s Manchester has managed to reinvent itself. It is now service and knowledge based industries rather than manufacturing which are becoming the backbone of urban economies and these creative industries seem to thrive more in the lively traditional streets of Manchester. The city has managed to reverse its decline and to find a new confidence. It is significant that an important part of this renaissance is based upon an urban vision for the planning of the city.

I started studying planning at a time of great uncertainty, an interregnum when the certainties of the 1960s were being questioned but nothing had emerged to take their place. We knew that system-built estates such as Hulme, where many of us as students lived, had been a mistake but were still taught many of the principles which lay behind such developments. Indeed we were taken on a field trip to admire the Southgate Estate in Runcorn which has since been demolished as a failure. It still amazes me that I spent five years studying planning and was never required to read the *Death and Life of Great American Cities*. It is true that we were taught urban design and studied the great medieval cities of Europe. But this was history and seemed to have no connection to the practical projects that we were set to design housing estates or town centres. Here the driving force was logic, the zoning of uses, the separation of vehicles and pedestrians and the promotion of open space. If any of us had dared to suggest a layout based on Siena or even Bath we would certainly have been failed.

I nevertheless left university a committed urbanist and got a job in the City Planning Department in Manchester. This was a large well-resourced department with a good reputation but was no place for an urbanist, at least outside the city centre. Urban design meant listed buildings, conservation areas and street furniture. It was not the concern of a frontline planning officer dealing with planning applications. Indeed, like my university projects, the planning system left no room for the urban design principles that I had learnt in the pages of Bacon's *Design of Cities* or Kevin Lynch's *Townscape*. Issues such as density, permeability, enclosure and a mix of uses, far from being promoted were the reasons we used to refuse planning applications. Of course we used different names – density became overdevelopment, mixed uses became incompatible uses, and enclosure became overlooking. It was however inescapable that the planning orthodoxies that we worked by, which in themselves were perfectly logical, when taken together were profoundly anti-urban. At first I thought that I had been naïve in wanting to promote urban principles as a planner and set about changing my ways. However I soon became disillusioned and came to believe that planning was the enemy of the city not its saviour. I effectively left the profession by joining my co-author Nicholas Falk at the urban regeneration consultants URBED in the early 1990s.

It was at this time that my interest in planning and to some extent my faith in the profession were restored. A friend of mine, Charlie Baker, had been asked to prepare an urban design code as part of the City Challenge sponsored redevelopment of the Hulme estate in Manchester where he and I lived. He asked me to help and we started going back to all of our half-forgotten urban design text books. We were emboldened by the emerging Urban Villages movement and stories that were starting to emerge about the New Urbanism movement in America. We soon realised that while urbanism had seemed dead from the coalface of planning and architectural practice it lived on elsewhere and even seemed to be making a comeback. We assembled our own set of urban principles for the rebuilding of Hulme based partly on our reading but mostly on our experience of what we liked about urban areas.

Our research cannot have been that thorough because, I am ashamed to say, at the time we were not aware of the work coming out of what was then Oxford Polytechnic. It was therefore with a mixture of relief and disappointment that we realised that the urban framework that we have developed for Hulme and thought so original had been published in an almost identical form and a great deal more detail by Bentley a few years earlier. However while our principles for Hulme were nothing new or radical, what was new was the fact that they were taken seriously by politicians and council officers. We can take no credit for this. It was, after all, the council which had commissioned us to write an urban design guide and we did little more than put meat on an urban vision that had already been adopted. The *Hulme Guide to Development* was adopted by the council and subsequently revised for adoption as supplementary planning guidance covering the whole of the city, a process that we describe in Chapter 13.

The process of developing the urban design guide for Hulme and watching its subsequent application to the redevelopment of the area and the planning of the wider city was the impetus for this book. What started with the politicians' wish to make Manchester more like the European cities that they had visited as part of the city's bid to stage the Olympics, seemed to end up questioning some very fundamental assumptions behind the way that we plan and build within cities. Urban design principles which had been accepted for years, in theory at least, were being applied to the messy business of planning a city and everything was turned on its head. Everyone involved seemed to support the principles but when it came to implementation the resistance from developers, housebuilders, the police, investors, planners and engineers was concerted and fierce. This caused many of us to question why ideas that had such a wide currency, like permeability, were so threatening and radical when put into practice. This book is an attempt to provide some answers and to develop a rationale for the further development of these ideas in the 21st century.

This book will no doubt be seen as part of the new urbanism movement, as indeed it should be. But it is hopefully more than this. It is based on experience of living and working in cities and from a frustration at the harm that has been done. At how, with the best of intentions, we seem to have created the worst of all worlds. My co-author, Nicholas Falk has been dealing with these issues for far longer than I. Together we wanted to get to the root of why things have gone wrong and to look at how they can change. This book is therefore about far more than a new aesthetic for urban areas – it is about a new vision for urban Britain.

David Rudlin
June 1998

Introduction

If the typical 19ᵗʰ century home was the urban terrace and the 20ᵗʰ century home was the suburban semi, where will we be living in the 21ˢᵗ century? Places that one generation regard as normal and even inevitable can very quickly be seen as inappropriate for subsequent generations with different needs. It is the contention of this book that just such a change is taking place at present and the housing which has dominated our towns and cities in the 20ᵗʰ century will fail to meet our future needs. We argue that a revolution will take place, is already taking place, which is comparable to the switch from the predominantly urban society of the Victorian age to the suburban society which dominated the 20ᵗʰ century.

There is something remarkable about a century. It is as if revolutions in technology and values take place as one century passes into the next. The Industrial revolution is something that we think of as being confined to the 19ᵗʰ century whereas many of the the key developments took place in the 18ᵗʰ century. The advent

of a new century is, however, a time for reflection and a reassessment of values and priorities. Such was the case at the beginning of the 20ᵗʰ century when the garden city pioneers succeeded in transforming the British view of the ideal home. At the turn of the century people tend to look forward and New Year resolutions are writ large on the national consciousness. If this happens at the end of a century, how much more would it be the case at the end of a millennium. This was the question that we asked at the end of the 1990s when we produced the first edition of this book. Working now in 2008 on this updated edition we are mid way through the change that we predicted. The way towns and cities in the UK are planned and the way that housing is built has changed remarkably in the last ten years. In this new edition we try to document this change and to assess whether it is as fundamental as the birth of the suburban age at the start of the 20ᵗʰ century.

When we plan our towns and cities, when we build housing, we should be thinking

What will be the 21ˢᵗ century home? A change as radical as that from the 19ᵗʰ century terrace to this century's suburban close is likely to take place in the 21ˢᵗ century

at least 100 years ahead, something that we have manifestly failed to do in the recent past. Successful places are those that stand the test of time, that are built to last. It is ironic that prefabs built as a temporary solution to housing shortages after the war have remained popular and some have even been listed, yet council housing built in the optimism of the 1960s and 1970s when we though we were building a new world, has been demolished. Huge mistakes have been made in the way that we have planned our towns and cities and built our housing. This represents a profligate waste of resources, not only in terms of the money wasted, or indeed the materials and energy which have been squandered, but, most importantly, in terms of the blighted lives of thousands of people forced to live in someone else's flawed Utopia. Those who care about housing need to follow Ruskin's advice: 'When we build let us think that we build for ever'. This is a test that we have too often failed in the 20th century, a failure that we must not repeat in the future.

At the start of the 19th century the population of the UK was booming and dwellings were required in huge numbers to house the expanding industrial workforce. At the start of the 20th century there was also a major housing shortage due to the stagnation of private building. More significantly there was an overwhelming feeling after the First World War that standards had to be improved to provide 'homes fit for heroes'. This translated into a huge increase in housing output, the creation of council housing and the birth of private suburbia. At the end of the 20th century the debate was also about housing numbers, as a result not so much of population growth but household growth. As the nuclear family declined in importance and household structures fragmented, governments projections foresaw the need to house 4.4 million new households between 1996 and 2016[1]. While these projections have fluctuated in the years since 1996, the figure has never dropped below 4.1 million homes and actual household formation rates have in fact run slightly ahead of these projections. This has been the real impetus for change at the turn of the millennium, all the more potent because it unites the political Left, concerned about cities and the Right concerned about protecting the countryside and the interest of the home owner.

The debate raged in the 1990s about where new housing should be built and the balance between green field and urban development. There was however less discussion about what we should be building and the sort of towns and cities that we should be creating. Having had our fingers burnt badly when we last thought seriously about these issues in the 1960s there was initially little appetite for innovation and a feeling that housing design should be left to the market. The result was a last rash of truly awful suburban housing estates in the 1990s, many built on brown field sites and some for social housing. The suburban design of these estates was ill suited to the urban environment in which many were built. The response was to turn the estates inwards so that high back garden walls fronted the surrounding streets. In the most extreme cases they became gated communities.

We and many others were horrified by these schemes and the impact that they were having on the environmental quality, safety and social cohesion of urban areas. If we were

Flawed Utopias: Never again should we force people with no other choices to live in someone else's flawed Utopia

This plan, and the three plans on the following pages was produced
for an exhibition called Organic Cities at the CUBE Gallery in
Manchester. It shows the four ages of the city. This plan is from
1774, just at the dawn of the Industrial revolution when Manchester
remained a small market town.

to accommodate more housing in urban areas there was a need to rethink the way that housing was built, just as the garden city reformers did at the end of the 19th century. This was the challenge that we addressed in the first edition of this book. It has also been a challenge taken up by the UK government through its Urban Task Force[2]. The Task Force was followed by an Urban White Paper[3] and subsequently by the Sustainable Communities Plan[4] and a wholesale revamp of national planning policies. It also led to the establishment of the Commission for Architecture and the Built Environment[5] (CABE) in England and its equivalents in Wales and Scotland.

This all represents a huge change in policy since we first wrote this book and it has had a major impact on the ground. Today most new housing in the UK is built in urban areas (77% in 2007) and the average density of this housing has almost doubled from 23 units per hectare in the early 1990s to 44 units per hectare today[6]. This creates an enormous opportunity to reshape the UK's towns and cities for the new millennium, to turn away from US-inspired low-density sprawl and towards a more European urban model. The question is whether this really is a millennial shift that will change forever Britain's towns and cities or a ten year interlude that will revert back to the underlying suburban trend as soon as the government's attention is distracted or changes.

The pressure for change

In order to understand the potential scale of the change that we are living through we must recognise the shift that is taking place in the population profile of Britain. Household growth represents as huge challenge. 4.4 Million additional households compares to just 2.8 million households living in Greater London. The entire new town programme after the war only accommodated around 1 million households and if we were to accommodate projected household growth through new town building we would have to build more than forty cities the size of Milton Keynes. That is before we even start thinking about replacing the existing housing stock much of which is Victorian in its origin, poorly built and energy inefficient. A study for the Joseph Rowntree Foundation estimated that at current rates of replacement the average house in the UK was going to have to last for a thousand years[7].

All this means that we need to build a lot of housing. The government has set a target of building 240,000 new homes a year by 2016 of which 70,000 will be social houses[8]. The last time we achieved this was in the 1960s and early 1970s. Indeed housing output peaked at just over 350,000 homes a year in the late 1960s. This was achieved through system-built and high-rise estates and the scars that this building boom left on cities as well as its impact on deprived communities remain with us today.

We are nowhere near achieving the government's targets at present. Indeed in recent years housing completions have in fact slumped. It is ironic that this slump dates back to the initial anxiety over the scale of the household projections. What happened was that government concern to protect green fields led to policies to limit green field housebuilding and to increase the percentage of housing on brown field sites. Housebuilders took time to respond to this and by 2001 housing output had fallen to less than 130,000 a year, well below the level needed to accommodate household growth. Since that time the numbers have crept up as housebuilders have responded and housing markets have boomed. However the housing completion figure in 2006 was still only 180,000 homes, a long way below the government target. As we write in 2008 the situation has suddenly become much worse. As a result of the 'credit crunch' housing output has slumped to under 150,000 with private housing output falling by almost 30%. The first great planning issue of the millennium is therefore how to build enough homes. Our failure to do this in the last ten years has led to housing shortages and an unstable and over-inflated housing market.

The second great planning issue is where and how we build all of these homes.

This map is from 1824 and shows the growth
of the city in the first 50 years of the Industrial revolution, after
the arrival of the canals but before the railways. In this time the city
largely grew within its boundaries. Indeed the site occupied by the
town hall is still a field (marked with an *). This is Peters Field in fact
that had been the site of the Peterloo Massacre in 1819, in part a
result of the tensions of industrialisation. So bad did the conditions
become that within a few years the first suburbs would be planned.

Housing is the main ingredient in towns and cities so that the where and the how questions have a huge impact on the way that towns and cities look, feel and operate. We must learn our lessons from the mistakes made in the housing boom years of the 1960s and make sure that the projected 4.4 million homes has a positive effect on the UK's towns and cities.

If we assume that household growth in the 21st century continues at the same pace as it has done in the 20th century and that we are successful in accommodating this growth through house building, we will have built 19 million new homes by 2100. If we assume that we also replace 15 000 existing homes a year, the total housing stock in the year 2100 would be just over 38 million, more than half of which are yet to be built. Decisions made at the turn of the millennium about the future shape of housing will therefore have a fundamental effect on the future of towns and cities and the well-being of a large proportion of the population. If we had chosen to accept the 20th century trends of dispersal and population drift to the south, we would be facing the continued and probable irreversible decline of urban areas, the loss of valued countryside, a huge growth in car use and a fundamentally unsustainable settlement pattern. To avoid this our task was nothing less than a complete rethink, almost from first principles, of UK planning policy which is what we argued for in the first edition of this book

The Policy Shift

These two great planning issues, how to build enough homes and where to put them have created a remarkable political consensus in the UK. The political Right are concerned about the countryside and the workings of the housing market while the Left are concerned about urban areas and housing shortages. This consensus has led to a wholesale revamp of urban policy in the UK. This started under the Conservative government of the early 1990s. The incoming Labour government in 1997 were initially sceptical because of worries about cramming too many homes into urban areas.

However in reality the Labour government were just as concerned about the suburbs and the housing market as the Conservatives, so that when countryside lobby took to the streets of London in early 1998 the Labour government had a change of heart.

This can be traced back to a statement to Parliament in February 1998[9] by John Prescott, the Deputy Prime Minister. He committed the government to the target of accommodating 60% of new housing in urban areas. This had originally been proposed under the previous Conservative government and had been opposed by Labour. Prescott however abandoned the 'predict and provide' approach to planning housing. This had meant that housing was allocated to areas with the greatest levels of population growth. Of course building new homes also caused population growth so that the policy just exacerbated population dispersal. In place of this the government introduced the radical notion that we should make a conscious decision about where to build new homes rather than just facilitating the market. In the same statement Prescott announced the establishment of the Urban Task Force under the Chairmanship of the architect Richard Rogers (Lord Rogers of Riverside). The Task Force met through 1998 and 1999, as we were completing the first edition of this book. They asked to see an advanced copy and we subsequently made a presentation to one of their meetings. Their report *Towards an Urban Renaissance* was published in 1999[10] and contained 105 recommendations. The following year as we have said the government published the Urban White Paper[3], established CABE, The Commission for Architecture and the Built Environment and

This plan from 1900 shows the result of the second half of the Industrial revolution. The city exploded as industrial growth sucked in population and terraced housing spread from the historic centre. Conditions remained pretty dire in what came to be the greatest city of the industrial age. The city's first suburbs of Whalley Range *1 and Victoria Park *2 can just be seen on the bottom edge of the plan. When these were built there were fields between them and the city centre.

announced the first Urban Regeneration Companies in Liverpool, Sheffield and Manchester. Subsequently the *Sustainable Communities Plan* was published in 2003[4] and the *Northern Way*[11] in 2004. All of this comes very close to the complete rethink of UK planning policy that we argued for in the first edition of this book, something that has come to be known as Urban Renaissance. This sets the UK apart from the situation in the US where the equivalent Smart Growth movement has garnered widespread support but has as yet failed to impact on policy other than in certain local areas.

The attractive city

There has been a great deal of heat in this debate. The 'radical' notion of directing housing growth to existing urban areas rather than allowing the market free reign, raised many questions about the ethics and practicality of government dictating where people should live. Wasn't this where we went wrong in the 1960s? Was it really such a good idea to use planning as a tool for social engineering by shifting population back to urban areas which have been losing population for much of the 20th century? Was it even more foolish to promote the sort of high-density housing that people had rejected so conclusively in the past? Whatever the benefits may be, wouldn't it mean forcing people to live where they clearly do not wish to? Such a policy was described as 'Stalinist'[12] but a more pertinent charge was that it was simply unrealistic. Population shifts, it was argued, are part of wider economic trends such as the increase in home ownership, the growth of the middle classes and the decline of manufacturing industry. Jobs and economic activity had moved out of cities and those with resources to do so had followed. This, combined with a clearly expressed preference in most of the surveys of house buyers for the sort of physical environment that suburbs offer, made the task of attracting people back to cities seem almost impossible.

The problem was that the alternative to doing this in the 1990s was unacceptable. Hard-pressed housing developers in all sectors seemed to be catering for the short-term needs of the market and pressures to meet pressing housing needs by producing housing which looked to the past rather than the future and reinforced trends which were no longer sustainable. We and many others, such as David Page[13], feared that a short-sighted approach was causing social housing developers to create suburban 'sink' estates while private developers were creating peripheral enclaves cut off from society. These patterns of housing development were inextricably linked to the growth in car use, to environmentally unsustainable patterns of life, to the increasing polarisation of society, and to the decline of our cities.

However well justified it might be, the repopulation of UK cities was never going to be achieved through regulation. If urban areas were to be repopulated it had to be through attraction rather than coercion. The task was to create urban environments able to attract people back to towns and cities. This is the task that we set ourselves in Part 3 of this book and in the years since it was first published the sceptics who said that it could be never be done have been proven wrong in part at least. City centres have been transformed by the development of apartments that have become a residential aspiration for a considerable proportion of young adults and many inner city neighbourhoods have been redeveloped with a mix of houses and apartments that have proved as popular. Towns and cities may not yet have been transformed, its been less than 10 years after all, however the models have been created and we now know that Urban Renaissance is possible.

In creating these attractive urban

This is the plan from the year 2000 showing the disintegration of the city that too place in the 20th century. This was in part due to the fact that more than half of the population left the city, and partly because it was comprehensively messed up by planners, engineers and architects. The first of an emerging new structure for the city can be seen in the Hulme neighbourhood 1* which is described as an extended case study in Chapter 13

models we are shaping the 21st century home. If this is to be successful the key issues relate not so much to the individual home, important as this is. What matters far more is the location of housing, its layout, its relationship to different uses, to transport systems and to open space. In short we are talking about the shape of our towns and cities. Housing is the predominant urban land use in the UK so that no discussion about the future of urban areas can ignore the issue of housing. The reverse is also true and no discussion of housing can ignore its effect on the wider health of urban areas. The results of this can be seen on the sequence of plans of Manchester that show the disintegration of the city's structure as a result of bad housebuilding. Through models such as the *Sustainable Urban Neighbourhood* our hope is that we can repair this shattered urban structure as can be seen on the fourth plan through the emerging Hulme neighbourhood.

A divided society

For much of the 20th century the housing debate focused not on the impact of housing development on cities but on improving conditions for the tenants of social housing. This led professionals to postulate in bricks and mortar (and concrete and steel), what was good for people, what would promote their health, communities, family life and comfort. Over-simplistic theories and inappropriate values were applied to housing that blighted the lives of thousands of the people least able to cope with the consequences. However the operation of communities and the way people live did not yield easily to such logical analysis. The designation on a plan of a play area does not mean that children will play there. 'Defensible space' means little if it is not defended. Designers have been constantly thwarted by 'difficult' residents who do not live their lives in the way that was intended and fail to share the middle-class values of the designer and developer.

Indeed the middle classes, able to choose where and how they live, were largely able to avoid the attentions of the housing

professions architects and planners. Working through private developers they created what Robert Fishman has called their own 'Bourgeois Utopia'[14] – The middle-class suburb that changed hardly at all through the 20th century. The suburb has many detractors but is undoubtedly the most enduring and successful housing form created in the 20th century. The suburb with its curving tree-lined streets, semi-detached housing and gardens front and back was, more than any of the utopias developed by architects and housing thinkers, the real 20th century housing success. While its origins can be traced back to the garden city pioneers, its success is based upon the extent to which it met the concerns and aspirations of a large part of the population.

20th century housing therefore gave physical form to the divisions in society. Council housing, originally envisaged as providing for the affluent working classes[15], had by the end of the century become the stigmatised housing of last resort. The problems of council housing and urban areas became synonymous and those with the means to do so abandoned the city to the poor and socially excluded. In the 1990s Will Hutton[16] described a 40:30:30 society based not on wealth but on security. He estimated that 40% of the population are privileged to feel secure, 30% are struggling and insecure and 30% are effectively excluded. The excluded lived in a world of dependency and benefits, often on estates which were a legacy of failed housing ideals. Large parts of our cities had been abandoned to this excluded 30%. Unlike Disraeli's Two Nations, who may have lived separately but at least mixed together on the city's streets, Hutton's three societies increasingly lived separate lives at the end of the 20th century. The middle classes shunned the city not because of industry and pollution but through fear of crime and concerns about their children's education. This was no recipe for a just or a healthy city or indeed a healthy society.

This situation has changed little in the first decade of the 21st century. Indeed the Labour government has been criticised for presiding over a widening of inequalities in society.

THE THREE MAGNETS
FOR THE 21ST CENTURY

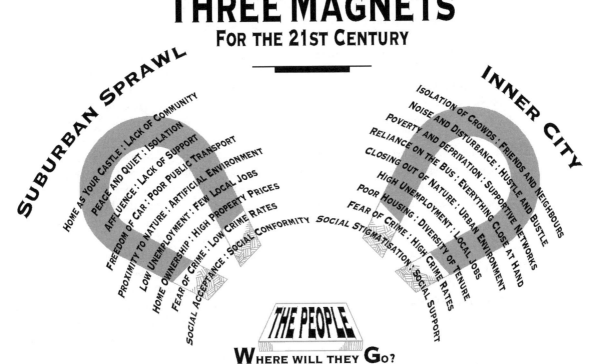

SUBURBAN SPRAWL
HOME AS YOUR CASTLE : LACK OF COMMUNITY
PEACE AND QUIET : ISOLATION
AFFLUENCE : LACK OF SUPPORT
FREEDOM OF CAR : POOR PUBLIC TRANSPORT
PROXIMITY TO NATURE : ARTIFICIAL ENVIRONMENT
LOW UNEMPLOYMENT : FEW LOCAL JOBS
HOME OWNERSHIP : HIGH PROPERTY PRICES
FEAR OF CRIME : LOW CRIME RATES
SOCIAL ACCEPTANCE : SOCIAL CONFORMITY

INNER CITY
ISOLATION OF CROWDS : FRIENDS AND NEIGHBOURS
NOISE AND DISTURBANCE : HUSTLE AND NEIGHBOURS
POVERTY AND DEPRIVATION : SUPPORTIVE NETWORKS
RELIANCE ON THE BUS : EVERYTHING CLOSE AT HAND
CLOSING OUT OF NATURE : URBAN ENVIRONMENT
HIGH UNEMPLOYMENT : LOCAL JOBS
POOR HOUSING : DIVERSITY OF TENURE
FEAR OF CRIME : HIGH CRIME RATES
SOCIAL STIGMATISATION : SOCIAL SUPPORT

THE PEOPLE
WHERE WILL THEY GO?

Where will the people go in the 21st century? It is a hundred years since Ebenezer Howard published his three magnets in *Tomorrow – A peaceful path to real reform*. It has become one of the most potent symbols of 20th century planning. However times have changed and we now need to reverse the polarity of the magnets by developing new models which will attract people back to cities in the 21st century

THE SUSTAINABLE URBAN NEIGHBOURHOOD

PRIVACY : COMMUNITY
URBAN VITALITY : SANCTUARY
A MIX OF CLASSES : CLOSE COMMUNITY
LOCAL SERVICES : EASE OF ACCESS
RICH ENVIRONMENT : URBAN ECOLOGY
MIX OF USES : ECONOMIC OPPORTUNITY
DIVERSITY OF TENURE : BALANCE OF CLASSES AND AGES
SECURE BY DESIGN : SOCIAL INTEGRATION
ENERGY EFFICIENCY : ENVIRONMENTAL AWARENESS

AFTER EBENEZER HOWARD'S THREE MAGNETS
FROM - TOMORROW: A PEACEFUL PATH TO REAL REFORM

However what seems to have happened is that the excluded section of society has become smaller but also more impoverished while the middle section has enlarged and become more secure. The spatial divisions between these groups have also fragmented. It is no longer the case of the poor in the inner city and the middle classes in the suburbs. There are now enclaves of private housing throughout UK cities and the divisions between relatively affluent areas and impoverished areas have been redrawn at the local level. The hope is that this fragmentation represents the start of a process of overcoming these divisions and reinventing urban areas as civilised places that can meet the residential aspirations of a broad cross section of society. This will mean jettisoning the ideological baggage of social housing on the one hand and 'gentrification' on the other to develop urban neighbourhoods capable of housing those with and without a choice over where they live.

Structure of this book

The first part of this book is devoted to the forces which shape housing and the pattern of settlements. Chapter 1 explores the way that towns and cities have developed in Britain and the effect that this has had on our perceptions of the type and location of housing that is valued. Chapter 2 deals with the influence of Utopian thinkers on the 20th century home, both as the root of many current attitudes and as a case study of how change is brought about. Chapter 3 describes the legacy of this thinking on the way that settlements have been planned and Chapter 4 shows how these forces have shaped housing over the last two centuries and have led to the housing that we build today. These factors must be understood by anyone seeking to influence future housing.

Part 2 of the book then sets out the four main influences which we believe will shape future housing, the *Four Cs* as we call them; climate change, choice, community and cost. These factors have, to a greater or lesser extent, always shaped housing. The change, for example, from the extended Victorian family to the self-sufficient nuclear family fundamentally affected housing choices and ideas of community. The predicted future growth in single and childless households may have an equally significant affect on housing preferences.

In Part 3 we describe the sort of housing and urban areas that could result from these trends. We argue that the Four Cs point to the need for housing which is denser, contains a mix of uses, house types and tenures, reduces car use and supports good public transport, is robust and safe, and promotes a sense of community. In short we argue that housing must become more urban and that the *sustainable urban neighbourhood* should be developed as a model that can compete with the attractions of the suburb.

Throughout the book we use the short-hand 'towns and cities' to describe settlements in the UK. Some of the people who looked through the early drafts assumed that we are talking solely about large cities. This is not the case. The processes and attitudes that we describe – which have led to suburbanisation and dispersal – apply, to a greater or lesser extent, to the majority of settlements in the UK from the largest city to the smallest town. This is not to say, of course, that all towns are the same. Suburbanisation has taken place to a much lesser extent in traditional places such as market towns and even historic cities such as Cambridge and Chester. However the conclusions and lessons that we draw are, we believe, relevant to the majority of UK settlements and probably to those elsewhere in the world that have followed the English model, notably the US and Australia.

We have also been accused of putting forward our own Utopia, as unrealistic and dangerous as those of the past. The ideas that we set out are however nothing new; they were advocated by the urban design profession for much of the 20th century, if rarely put into practice. In the last ten years they have become central to planning policy in the UK and are accepted by most local authorities. The principles are also starting to appear in development on the ground. This was initially just a few enlightened schemes, but today most new housing schemes at least pay lip service to this urban design thinking, even if it is not always well understood. What we seek to do is to draw these strands together in the context of the changing trends described in the first part of this book both to document and contribute to the emerging movement – 'New Urbanism' as it has been called in the US.

We are concerned not only with the way that housing is designed but where it is built. Chapter 9 explores the location of housing and the government's attempts to accommodate a greater percentage of housing growth within urban areas. This is important not just as a means of protecting the countryside and providing the homes that we need but as an opportunity to promote the renaissance of our towns and cities. This calls for new models of development. In the early 1990s when urban development did take place the resulting housing, for want of more appropriate models, often ended up aping its suburban cousins. In an over-reaction to the mistakes of the past the curving cul-de-sac and semi-detached starter home started to appear in the heart of towns and cities. This was at its most extreme in Liverpool where the militant

Labour administration argued that what was good enough for the middle classes was what they should be building for 'their people' leading to a rash of low density suburban schemes in the very heart of the city. Our concern was that this type of suburban development was damaging to the grain, diversity and heritage of urban areas, not that these arguments carried much weight against the cry of 'give the people what they want'. More important was the affect of such low-density development on the economy of towns and cities, on their community life and sustainability, and their ability to meet the aspirations of new households.

Our argument is that there is a need for new models of urban development to stand alongside the tried and tested suburban models. These new models need to embrace more than the design of the new housing, they need be based on an understanding of urbanism, to embody sustainable development principles and ideas of community and how people live together. These are the subjects of Chapters 10, 11 and 12 of this book.

The changing face of urban housing: For want of more appropriate models the suburban semi is colonising the very heart of our cities and is as inappropriate as much of the high-rise housing that it has replaced

A number of new urban models did emerge in the 1990s including the Urban Village in Britain and the Pedestrian Pocket in the US. These models however were intended, initially at least, for new settlements. In this book we seek to bring together urban design thinking, the urban policy agenda and the sustainability debate to create a model for redevelopment and urban infill in existing towns and cities. Our aim is to create a model for urban areas that can rank alongside the best parts of our historic cities and successful continental cities.

Over the last thirty years we have been closely involved in these issues through our practice URBED. We have undertaken consultancy work and strategies for local authorities and master plans for private developers, the first of which is now built (see the New England Quarter case study on Page 282). This book is based on the discussions that we have had as part of this work with local authorities, developers, professionals and residents across the country.

Sometimes this can seem like a 30 year-long argument, one that was at its most vociferous in the 1990s when we were working on the first edition of this book. It was generally the case that when we discussed the ideas of urbanism in broad terms there was relatively little disagreement. They were seen as common sense or in some cases a statement of the bleedin' obvious. This is due in part to the images that people conjure up when thinking about urban areas – the historic market town, Georgian Bath, or the vibrant continental towns that they visit on holiday. However when we took the discussion to the next level, the way in which these ideas affect what is built, the reaction was often very different and much more hostile. Private developers claimed that urban housing would never sell, housing associations said that it could not be built within cost limits and would create ghettos, highway engineers complained that urban layouts would be unsafe and planners worried that there would be conflicts of use and town cramming. Everyone wanted to create better urban environments but few were willing to concede their unfettered right to use and park their car. The usual response was 'I support the principles but do have a few detailed concerns'. Yet too often the sum of these 'minor concern's' undermined the basic principles.

In the 1990s the outcome of these arguments was far from certain. We devote Chapter 13 to an extended case study of Manchester, from the redevelopment of the Hulme neighbourhood to the adoption of

urban design guidance for the city as a whole. We do this partly because it is the city that we know best. However it is also because the city has long been at the forefront of these issues. The world's first industrial city which spawned the world's first suburb, it is appropriate that it should have taken a lead in the renaissance of the UK's cities. In Chapter 13 we document the process of change in Manchester, the leadership that was required, the arguments that took place and the victims who lost their jobs as a result. These arguments, having been won in Manchester, were then re-enacted in towns and cities across the UK and are still rumbling on today. The renaissance of cities like Manchester does however mean that they are much easier to win now than they were in the 1990s. In a sense this book is our rebuttal to all the arguments that we have had over the years.

The experience of implementing these ideas has made clear to us that it is not sufficient to describe the physical form of the *Sustainable Urban Neighbourhood*. We must also explore the processes by which it can be built. Otherwise there is a tendency for developers and authorities to accept the ideas but misapply them on the ground. In the concluding chapter we therefore explore the process by which urban areas are created and the way in which an understanding of this process can be used to create the *Sustainable Urban Neighbourhood*.

This book argues that housing and urban planning are going through a change as dramatic as that caused by the Industrial revolution. We are delighted that ideas that were still fiercely contested when we produced the first edition of this book are now widely accepted by mainstream developers and policy makers in the UK. Many of the predictions that we made have come true, some far exceeding our expectations. In this new edition we update the arguments and document the progress that has been made. We are half way through the fundamental change that we predicted and advocated. Progress has been good but it is too early to proclaim victory. UK towns and cities have been reborn over the last ten years and the signs are promising for a much more urban and sustainable 21st century. This however could still be undone by a change of policy, possibly prompted by panic over a recession. We need to keep our nerve and build on the achievements of the last ten years. Just as the first edition of this book played a small part in kick starting the UK's urban renaissance, we hope that this new edition will help maintain its momentum.

Part 1

THE ORIGINS

Any attempt to shape the future of housing must be based upon an understanding of how we have got where we are today. Our attitudes towards new development are shaped by perceptions of what has and has not worked in the past and the cultural baggage which has become associated with the home and its place in towns and cities. In the first part of this book we therefore seek to chart the way that social and economic trends along with Utopian theories and urban reformers have shaped the pattern of housing and the attitudes of developers and residents that we have today.

'If we would lay a new foundation for urban life, we must understand the historic nature of the city'

Lewis Mumford - The City in History , Secker and Warburg 1961

Europe at night:
A satellite image of Europe
showing the extent of
urban areas. This illustrates
a sharp contrast between the
land covered by Paris, Madrid
and Barcelona, for example,
compared to the sprawling
conurbations of Britain. The
reasons for this difference
are explored in this chapter

Chapter 1

The flight from the city

Why is it that in Britain and America there has been such a deep enmity towards the city? Why is it that we celebrate continental cities while, for most of the 20th century, British and US cities have been reviled and even feared? If it is true that without cities we have no civilisation, what has our attitude towards cities told us about the state of our society? It is important that we reinvent the city and to do this we must understand the reasons for the Anglo-American city's fall from grace.

The golden age of cities

This was not always the case. There was a time when the builders of cities were glorified. Cities were the centre of civilisation, the places where the arts, government and commerce thrived. The design of cities was a noble pursuit attracting leading creative minds, from Vitruvius to Michelangelo, Baron Haussmann to John Nash. The building of great cities was the concern of emperors and kings, from Pope Sixtus V's remodelling of Rome as the capital of Christendom, Peter the Great's commissioning of St. Petersburg as his capital and Napoleon III's redevelopment of Paris as a city of boulevards and squares. It was in the cities of Mesopotamia and the Nile Valley that civilisation first flowered. It was in the cities of the Greek and Roman empires that European civilisation was shaped and in the cities of northern Italy where it was rediscovered through the renais-

sance. Cities, as centres for religion, trade and culture, lie at the foundation of modern society. Whilst academics may argue about which came first, whether cities gave birth to civilisation or whether civilisation necessitated the building of cities[1], the two are inextricably linked.

Many of the cities which predate the Industrial revolution and the motorcar, retain their appeal today. These pre-industrial cities exhibit all of the urban qualities that we prize today and on which much modern urban design thinking is founded. Perhaps the most enduring image of this pre-industrial city is the Italian hill town of Siena which has been endlessly analysed and plundered for inspiration. Indeed it is argued[2] that the Commission for the European Union's ideas for the 'compact city'[3] are based more upon the unattainable ideal of the Italian hill town than the rather messier urban realities of most European cities today.

The medieval city was typically small, mixed-use, and based upon travel by foot. At the height of its powers the city state of Florence had a population of just 50 000 which is little bigger than Barnsley or Basingstoke. Yet Florence was one of the largest cities of the renaissance and was almost twice the size of cities like Vienna, Prague and Barcelona[4]. The medieval city was also dense, covering a fraction of the land area of a modern town of similar size. This compactness of built form created the tight urban streets and crowded buildings that we enjoy in historic towns such as Chester and York. The density was partly the result of city walls which restrained growth. But as Hoskins[5] has shown, even unwalled towns and cities with no constraints on growth were remarkably dense. It has been suggested[6] that this density resulted from the needs of travel by foot which undoubtedly played a role in the compactness of great cities like London. It may also have been that compact development was driven by a need to conserve the surrounding agricultural land on which the city relied for its food. These arguments have all been explored at length but they do not hold the whole answer. Most pre-industrial cities were built at far greater densities than can be explained by physical constraints, the needs of travel by foot or the protection of agricultural land. There were other forces at play which go to the heart of the nature of cities and our inability to recapture their character today – this is what we explore in this book.

Why is it that the most remote farm-house is built so that it abuts directly onto the only road for miles? Why is it that remote settlements surrounded by acres of seemingly unused land are built so that their houses almost fall over each other? It seems that historically there was something deep within the human consciousness which sought companionship and security. We could imagine this dating back to the earliest encampments clustered around the communal campfire. Is it too far-fetched to imagine the tents becoming permanent shelters and the camp fire becoming the town square? Once the unseen dangers of the surrounding wilderness had been overcome the pattern of human settlement had been established.

However the need for human contact does not entirely explain the density of early settlements. Whilst fear of the wilderness may have been the initial motive this would soon have been combined with economic and political forces. It is likely that, in those early encampments, the tents nearest the fire would have been occupied by the chief and the most important members of the community. Here they would

The ideal compact city?
Siena is the archetypal compact city. Despite the fact that it was built entirely without the aid of planners and urban designers it has been mined for inspiration by generations of urban professionals

be close to the warmth of the fire and to the focus of community life and decision making. The lower status members of the community would have been relegated to the outskirts of the camp, vulnerable to attack and cut off from the seat of power and status. Since humans have always aspired to improve themselves, it is reasonable to assume that the citizens of those early encampments would have aspired to be near the camp fire, both for the benefits that it would bring but also as a symbol of their status and position.

It is not hard to imagine this process transferred to the earliest cities. As Robert Fish-man has described in *Bourgeois Utopia*[7], the dynamic of the pre-industrial city meant that the centre of the town was the place to be. The richer you were, and the more status and power you had, the nearer to the centre you sought to live and work. The elite of the town, the merchants, nobles, church men and administrators would jostle for the best locations at the centre of town, much as the prime retailers like Marks & Spencer do in modern shopping centres. Just as in a shopping centre,

this demand for the best location would have increased land values so that central areas also became the most expensive and the most profitable. The density of the pre-industrial city is the result of this demand for central sites. The competition for land meant that every available site would be developed to its maximum potential so that buildings became higher and more closely packed. Remember that in these early cities the merchants generally lived over their business, as indeed did many of their employees, so that pressures were intense. An extreme example of this can be seen in the 2 000 year old high-rise buildings in the Yemen.

In these ancient towns there was a gradation in social status as one moved away from the centre. The poorest people and the dirty or marginal uses were pushed to the edge of the town, often outside the protection of the city walls. Indeed the term 'suburb' was originally coined as a disparaging expression meaning literally 'less than urban'. Wherever they lived the citizens were united by a desire to move closer to the centre of city and thus the focus of power and commerce. The poorest denizen

The shatter zone:
A figure ground plan of Barnsley in Yorkshire today. This shows the structure of a dense medieval town surrounded by a zone of ill-defined space which separates it from the surrounding residential development. This space has been described by Llewelyn-Davies as a 'shatter zone' where considerable capacity exists for new development

of the suburb would covet the neighbourhoods within the city walls. The artisans within the walls would covet the middle-class areas nearer the centre and the middle classes would aspire to a location on or near the town square. What is more, this would happen in towns where one could walk from the centre to open countryside in less than twenty minutes.

In Manchester there is a sign on a building on the southern edge of the city centre which proclaims the 'Boundary of the Township of Manchester'. Beyond this is the Gaythorne area, an old industrial quarter – now converted to housing – that for many years was an arc of old industry encircling much of the city centre. Such industrial areas can be found in many modern towns and cities such as on the plan of Barnsley (above). They mark the line of the original poor suburbs. They now lie sandwiched between the town centre and the inner city and yet have a quite different character. These are areas that have always been impoverished and have often been swept aside as the line of least

resistance for railways and ring roads.

This is not to say that suburban trends did not exist in the pre-industrial city. As early as Elizabethan times there was concern about merchants moving out to the country, no doubt aping the landed gentry. However this was often based on single houses well beyond the poor suburbs and the houses tended to be used as weekend retreats. This is similar to the 'dacha' tradition still common in many eastern European countries. In some cases these weekend retreats would be transformed over time into the main family residence with the merchant commuting into town for business. This trend however remained relatively insignificant until the advent of the Industrial revolution.

The industrial city

The picture of growth in the pre-industrial city is a mirror image of modern Anglo-American settlements. The Industrial revolution placed such intense pressures on the traditional city that it reversed the polarity of settlements. In the modern Anglo-American city, status is measured not by how close to the centre you live, but by the distance that you can put between yourself and the perceived squalor of urban life. In the modern Anglo-American city (we will turn to the continental experience in a short while) the pressure for development is not in the centre but at the periphery. This has been the case with housing development for many years but in the last part of the 20th century it became true of all manner of activity. Town centre shopping declined as we switch our allegiance to the suburban supermarket or out-of-town shopping centre. The newspaper industry has largely abandoned Fleet Street for Docklands. Staff in central office districts have been decanted to peripheral business parks and urban cinemas have succumbed in the face of the multiplex.

Many reasons have been put forward for this dispersal of activity. It has been attributed to increasing mobility, initially due to commuter railways but more recently and more potently to the private car. It has been put down

to changing retail and business needs which cannot be accommodated in congested urban areas, to the workings of the land market, and to demographic change. All have played their part; however at its heart this trend of 'counterurbanization' is driven by the same forces which drove urbanisation in the early cities, it is just that today these forces are working in the opposite direction.

Fishman suggests that perhaps the first true suburb was Clapham in London where the Evangelicals, led by Wilberforce, sought to protect their families from the evil influence of the city in the latter half of the 18th century. Clapham was a development of the earlier 'dacha' trend but was conceived from the outset as a suburb around Clapham Common intended to provide the main family residence for its occupants. It represents an important step in the separation of home and family from work and commerce. As such it was an influential model for Victorian family life which was to take such a hold later in the century.

The next step in Fishman's history of the suburb – or Bourgeois Utopia as he called it – took place in Manchester. This is significant, because whereas the Evangelicals were escaping from the traditional city, in Manchester the traditional city was being swamped by the Industrial revolution and something quite different was happening. Before the Industrial revolution the form of Manchester was similar

The pre-industial city: Green's map of Manchester from 1794. The structure of the pre-industrial city in Britain was similar to the Italian cities that we admire today

23

to many medieval towns, as can be seen from Green's map of the city (above previous page) published in 1794. The dense form of pre-industrial Manchester was the result of the same forces of concentration which shaped the Italian hill town. For the early years of Manchester's industrialisation it maintained this traditional shape with density increasing towards the centre and the most affluent merchants living in areas like Moseley Street, Fountain Street, King Street and St. Anne's Square in the heart of the city. However the cotton mills which came to dominate the city required large amounts of labour and the city attracted rural migrants in vast numbers. As H. G. Wells said, this process turned cities like Manchester into 'great surging oceans' of humanity as documented by the plans in the introduction to this book.

The terrible conditions in the early industrial cities have been well documented elsewhere. Our concern here is the catalytic effect that the Industrial revolution had on the British city. The phenomenal growth of population and industry in cities like Manchester, Leeds, Liverpool and Sheffield stretched the capacity of the traditional city beyond breaking point. The industrial city came to be seen not as the chalice of civilisation but as the receptacle for all

Remnants of the early suburbs: Many inner city areas are characterised by large villas dating from the mid-19th century when the areas were developed as early suburbs. Designed for large households with servants, many have been converted to bedsits or institutional uses

that is wrong with society. In the words of one commentator, 'Civilisation works its miracles, and civilised man is turned back almost into a savage'. Cities had limited sanitation, were over-crowded, dangerous and characterised by pollution, crime and congestion. In 1841 the average life expectancy in Manchester was just 24 years and thousands, from all classes, were killed in the great cholera epidemics of 1832, 1848 and 1866[8]. In the other great textile town, Bradford, conditions were, if anything, worse with life expectancies of 19 years and an environment described by one German visitor as 'like being lodged in no other place than with the devil incarnate'. These images of the industrial city have coloured our perception of the city ever since. The potent image of the dark, dangerous city described by Dickens and Conan Doyle along with the paintings of L. S. Lowry have created a stereotypical bad image for the city which has outlasted the conditions it portrayed.

The great escape

As the industrial city boomed an exodus was beginning. The first escapees may have been the London Evangelicals but in Manchester it was Samuel Brookes, a wealthy banker who first broke ranks, moving from his Moseley Street address and leapfrogging the poor suburbs to establish the city's first suburb on sixty acres of agricultural land three miles or so south of the city. He called the area Whalley Range after his home town in Lancashire. He laid out streets, built a college and a church, as well as a fine house for himself and his family. The remainder of the area was marked out as plots for the development of 'substantial residences'. There is in Manchester some dispute about whether Whalley Range was the first suburb, with some arguing that the much grander Victoria Park was built a few years earlier. However it is clear that both were being planned at around the same time and represented the start of an important trend. The great escape had begun. Throughout the country in areas like Manningham in Bradford, Edgbaston in Birmingham,

Sefton in Liverpool or Stoke Newington and Islington to the north of London the merchants and factory owners were setting up residence away from the smoke and the teeming masses of the overcrowded city. These early suburbs provided the foundations for many of the attitudes which have shaped towns and cities ever since.

The first of these attitudes is the idea that the city is bad and the countryside is good so that people who can should move as far away as possible from the city. For Samuel Brookes, dependent upon his horse for transport, this distance may not have been great, but there was open countryside between Whalley Range and the city (a low boggy area known as Moss Side). With modern transport the quest to escape the city can strike deeper and deeper into the countryside until it penetrates the most isolated rural areas.

The second attitude is that high density is bad and low density is good so that people should not only distance themselves from the city but also from each other. As Muthesius[9] has described, this led many of the early suburbs to be surrounded by high walls and protected by toll gates. It also meant that houses were set within landscaped grounds with high walls and curving driveways to hide the house from the street and neighbours. Echoes of these elements of early suburbia can still be seen in the modern suburb.

The third attitude is that home and work should be separated heralding the birth of the first commuter in Clapham. Commuting was initially by horse-drawn carriage but subsequently, with the development of buses, trams and railways, travel became possible to ever more distant suburbs and urban dispersal became possible, if not inevitable. The difficulty and expense of commuting protected the early suburbs from the 'lower classes' even when they were very close to the centre of the town. However as public transport developed these suburbs became vulnerable and the middle classes were forced to move further away from the town to protect their tranquillity.

The fourth and possibly the most significant attitude led to the reversal of the polarity of cities. The richer and more successful people started to measure their status not by how close they lived to the town square but by the distance that they could put between themselves and the centre. In the 20th century the suburban flight of the merchants was followed by the middle classes as public transport networks were established, and eventually even by the working classes as they were decanted from the urban 'slums' to overspill estates and new towns. Whether this migration was by choice or by coercion the reason was the same – the city is bad for you. The result was that the city's role as a home for a cross section of society was undermined and urban populations became dominated by those groups least able to escape. The predominant residential aspiration of British people became the leafy suburb. Negative perceptions of the city were thus reinforced as the problems of the urban poor came to be seen as one and the same as the problems of the city.

This desire of people to escape the city is well documented by market research[10]. Survey after survey has shown that for the majority of people the countryside is their desired place of residence and that urban areas are places from which they desire to escape. The main reasons are that towns are dirty, noisy, stressful and overcrowded. This illustrates an interesting interplay of perceptions and reality. Census information shows that the central parts of most UK cities lost population much of the last century. In relative terms they are anything but overcrowded, yet in people's minds they clearly still appear that way. Of course most people who desire to live in the country end up in the suburbs. It is a matter of speculation whether they see the suburb as an option of second choice or whether suburban life is really able to offer the rural benefits which they desire.

The effects of these attitudes can be seen in the population distribution in England as charted by census data[11]. This shows a consistent movement of population since 1945

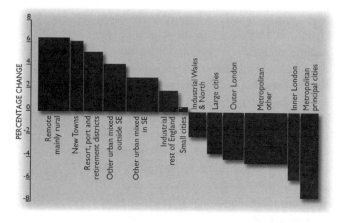

Above – Urban depopulation:
This shows a clear correlation between the urbanity of different types of area and the rate of population loss in the latter part of the 20th century.
Source: OPCS 1992 from Blowers 1993

Below – The lost urban jobs:
The loss of employment from urban areas took an identical path.
Source: NOMIS

from London and other metropolitan areas to smaller urban areas and rural districts. Indeed the largest gains have been in the 'remote largely rural' category. This suggests, as Peter Hall predicted, that the trend is more than suburbanisation but rather the counterurbanisation of settlement patterns in Britain.

It is true that in the last 15 years this trend has slowed and in some cases reversed. In the first edition of this book we remarked on the early signs of renaissance with a small increase in London's population and government household projections predicting an increase in the other cities. Since that time London has boomed, reaching 8 million people for the first time since the 1930s. In most of the other large cities population loss has just about stopped as the rapid repopulation of central areas has started to outstrip the continuing flow of people to the suburbs[12]. However we get ahead of

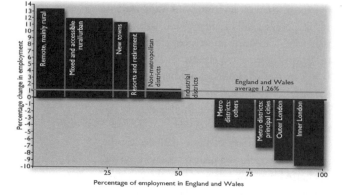

ourselves, here our concern is to tell the story of the second half of the 20th century.

During this time the exodus of people was followed by an exodus of investment and jobs. The city had always thrived on the need for proximity between people and activities. Indeed the growth of the early suburbs, based as they were on public transport, tended to reinforce town and city centres which remained the points of greatest accessibility. If you lived on a suburban railway line then you had little choice but to go into the centre for employment, shopping and other services. However with the growth in the private car this was no longer the case. As society became more mobile and advances were made in electronic communications, city locations became seen as a hindrance rather than a necessity for commercial activity. Industry and warehousing were the first to leave to the new industrial estates and distribution parks such as Team Valley in Newcastle or Trafford Park in Manchester. Offices followed to business parks, and retail activities to out-of-town shopping malls. Bustling cities became conurbations with sprawling commercial and residential suburbs surrounding a shrinking city centre.

Research undertaken as part of URBED's *Vital and Viable Town Centres* report for the UK government[13] charted the loss of employment in cities in the 1980s and 90s. Manufacturing employment declined across the board, but to a much greater extent in cities. Factories closed or relocated and major inward investors such as Japanese car plants would only consider out-of-town sites. However in the 1990s cities were also losing jobs in the service sector to small towns and rural areas (a trend which has also since been reversed). The same was true of retail development as work by Hillier Parker as part of the same research illustrated. In the development boom of 1987–90, 66% of all new retail floor space was out-of-town of which 51% was in retail parks. Even committed town centre retailers like Marks & Spencer started to build out-of-town stores and the development of major out-of-town centres like Meadowhall in Sheffield posed a major threat to traditional town centres. It is estimated for example that Sheffield City Centre lost 30% of its trade to Meadowhall and that many shops only remained because they were tied into leases. Similar trends were seen in entertainment and leisure. Whilst cinema audiences have grown this was largely due to multi-screen out-of-town centres and urban cinemas continued to decline. Even pub and restaurant chains were tending to direct their new investment to out-of-town sites. In the first edition of this book the whole of this paragraph was written in the present tense – it is a measure of the progress that has been made that it can now largely be consigned to the past tense. A potent combination of government policy and some of the trends that we discuss in this book have led to a resurgence of town centres and restrictions on out-of-town development. But back to the 1990s...

The inner city

The flip side of urban dispersal and suburban growth has been inner city decline. As the suburbs grew, large areas of cities were deserted by the middle classes, businesses and investors. These areas were, and largely still are, characterised by poverty, dereliction and a range of social problems. This gave rise to the classic form of the Anglo-American city with an embattled centre surrounded by decline and an outer ring of prosperous suburbs. Perhaps the most extreme example of this is Washington DC where the centre, dominated by government buildings, is surrounded by some of the worst deprivation in the US. Until 2000 the tendency had been for the inner city to expand at the expense of the city centre fringes and inner suburbs. However since that time there have been signs of remission as city centres have extended into the inner city and gentrification has nibbled at its outer fringes.

The recognition of these problems in Britain dates from the mid 1970s and in particular the Labour government's 1976 Inner City Act. A Fabian pamphlet in 1975, co-authored by Nicholas Falk[14], brought together available evidence to show that the problems of multiple deprivation could not be solved without widening economic opportunities in areas which had lost their traditional role. Since that time, a great deal has been written about problems of the inner city and a range of reasons have been put forward to explain the problem. This has given rise to an alphabet soup of initiatives to address the problem, particularly following the riots of the early 1980s. Work has been done to provide training, promote small businesses, tackle housing and environmental problems and improve access. However these initiatives addressed the symptoms of the problem rather than the root causes. As a result they have had little impact and in some cases have made the problem worse. As research for the Department of the Environment by Brian Robson[15] in the 1990s illustrated, despite the billions spent on the inner city, all of the indicators of deprivation and other social problems were the same or worse in the 1990s than they had been in the 1970s.

This is not, on the whole, because the initiatives were a failure. Many were very successful in creating jobs, giving people skills, improving the environment and housing conditions and addressing social problems. However the result was to empower certain people within the inner city to do what people with such power have been doing for a hundred years, namely to move out to the suburbs. Take the example of a major local employer in a deprived inner city area in one of Britain's larger cities. The company was given permission to expand onto council-owned land on the condition that the jobs created went to local people. This they did, but two years later a survey of the workforce showed that virtually none lived locally. Doubt was cast on the reliability of local people or the commitment of the employer. However the reality was that the local employees had used their new-found earning power to move to a less stigmatised area, perhaps to buy a home, certainly to send their children to better schools. In another case the headteacher of an inner city school commented on the fact that an increasing number of Afro-Caribbean pupils were doing very well academically. The reason she suggested was that they saw education as a ticket out of the area.

It could even be suggested that initiatives to improve access by building new roads in the inner city have conspired with this process. Far from improving access for businesses coming into the area they have made it easier for local people to live elsewhere and commute to local jobs.

A society where most of the people living in cities are those without the capacity to escape will always be a divided society. While this remains the case there is never likely to be a solution to the inner city problem or to social exclusion no matter how much money is thrown at it. What is more, whilst the problem remains unsolved the real and perceived problems of the inner city will cast a shadow over attempts to revitalise cities. This remains as true today

as it was when this book was first published. Indeed, while the inner city may have shrunk marginally, the social divisions have arguably got much worse. The only real hope for the inner cities is a reversal of the forces of dispersal by creating attractive neighbourhoods where people want to stay when they find work and which will persuade others to return to the city. This has started to happen but, to date, the renaissance of cities has left most of the inner city untouched.

Inner city problems were not confined to run-down housing estates. Similar forces were at work in commercial areas, as much of URBED's urban regeneration work demonstrated. Most cities in Britain have traditional industrial and commercial areas which have declined as companies have closed or moved out to industrial estates. These included areas like Little Germany in Bradford, the Lace Market in Nottingham, the Jewellery Quarter in Birmingham and Ancoats in Manchester. The issues here were quite different to housing estates. All of these areas are of significant architectural and historic importance, yet they had become anachronisms since the buildings and narrow streets which give them their character were unable to accommodate the modern needs of industry. Instead they became home to marginal businesses, attracted by low rents which were insufficient to maintain the built fabric. The importance of these areas meant that their continued decline was not seen as an acceptable option. However if regeneration was to happen it was seen as necessary to reverse the exodus of activity by developing new economic

Inner city decline did not just affect housing areas: Commercial activity also abandoned cities, leaving historic areas like Little Germany in Bradford without the economic activity to sustain its fine built fabric. Built by German worsted merchants in the last century, the area covers just 20 acres yet contains 53 listed buildings, a third of which were vacant by the mid 1980s. These areas have often been the subject of successful regeneration initiatives such as the project managed by URBED in Little Germany. This attracted commercial activity back into the area, promoted tourism and has eventually created a residential community. Such areas were the first to be regenerated because of their attractive environment but other areas have since followed their lead.

roles. In some areas this has been achieved as buildings have been colonised by creative industries. However more often regeneration has been achieved through residential conversions. Indeed so powerful has the residential market in these areas become that there is concern that it is now housing that is pushing out business.

American experience

Through these trends the modern Anglo-American city was born. In the late 1990s we held up the US situation as a warning about where the UK could be heading. It is in the US where the extremes of urban sprawl and the social and ethnic divisions that it creates can be seen at their worst. An article about Eight Mile Road in Detroit in the Observer[16] in 2006 includes some startling statistics. The piece describes the death of a rapper – a friend of Eminem – on the street made famous in Eminem's 2004 film 8 Mile. Eight Mile Road divides the city of Detroit – 82% Black with an unemployment rate more than double the national average – from the suburb of Oakland – 83% white and average incomes are twice those in the city. In the 1950s Detroit was home to more than 2 million people but lost hundreds of thousands of whites after the race riots in the 1960s and is now home to just 900 000. Yet on the other side of the road Oakland is a 'land of office parks and strip malls – it is a country of Starbucks and car parks and tidy lawns and white picket fences'.

The dispersal of many American cities has led to town centres which are little more than islands surrounded by desolate inner cities and outer rings of peripheral growth characterised by Joel Garreau as 'edge cities'[17]. Indeed younger American cities like Los Angeles have developed without a clearly defined centre. Such sprawling suburban cities based on the accessibility of the private car are the natural conclusion of suburban trends which started with the Evangelicals of Clapham.

There has been widespread concern about the effects of this urban sprawl in the US. In March 1995 the Bank of America in con-junction with a range of other agencies released a manifesto entitled 'Beyond Sprawl'. This listed the social and economic costs of sprawl and argued for compact and efficient growth. Since that time the 'Smart Growth' movement has gathered pace. States such as Oregon have established growth boundaries around its cities and many states have introduced tax incentives and funding mechanisms to encourage more development within existing urban areas by preventing further development on the edge. The results can be seen in cities such as Portland, Oregon which, unlike Detroit, grew from 366 000 people in 1980 to 529 000 people in 2001.

In the UK the principles of Smart Growth (where it is called Urban Renaissance) have become government policy. In the US Smart Growth has been adopted by the Democrats but, with Republicans in the White House until recently, the movement has had only a limited impact. Indeed suburbanisation in the US seems to be accelerating. In the early 2000s sprawl in the US was spreading at a rate of 2 million acres a year and cities such as Phoenix, Atlanta and Georgia were spreading by one acre an hour. The US may have the space to enable this level of growth – something that is less true in the UK. However the economic costs are enormous and it is estimated that the average American family spends 500 hours a year commuting and that traffic delays costs $72 billion in wasted fuel and productivity. The 2004 film *The End of Suburbia*[18] documents the vulnerability of this rampant suburban sprawl in the age of 'Peak Oil' when the energy consumption that it implies will become untenable.

Continental experience

The troubles of the American city can be vividly contrasted with experience on the continent. Here the Industrial revolution created the same pressures as in England. In Paris this led to suburban growth in the early 1800s which, like London, was originally based on weekend retreats. It is likely that, given time, Paris would have followed the British experience. However

this was not allowed to happen because of the transformation brought about by Haussmann's plans for the city. Olsen in *The City as a Work of Art* [19] describes Napoleon's vision for Paris, which Haussmann was charged with implementing. Napoleon saw Paris as the capital of a great empire and wanted the physical form of the city to reflect this. Haussmann achieved this by cutting great boulevards through the cramped medieval city. These boulevards were to be bounded by buildings of at least six storeys and the only use with the potential to fill the volume of buildings implied by this was housing. Indeed to fund the quality of building desired, this had to be middle-class housing.

Yet the development of such large amounts of middle-class housing was inconceivable if the middle classes continued to move out of the city to the suburbs. Incentives were therefore introduced through the tax system to make the new apartment blocks financially attractive and the National Bank channelled national savings into the grand projects. This had the effect of stopping middle-class suburbanisation in its tracks. Within a remarkably short period the spacious urban apartment became established as the residential aspiration of the French middle classes at a time when their English equivalents were switching their aspirations to the suburban villa.

There are lessons here for the UK government which has also been seeking to channel housing back into cities. Napoleon's great success was not to control suburbanisation but to make urban housing more financially attractive. French middle-class aspirations have survived the intervening 150 years more or less intact. True Paris now has affluent suburbs but it is still common for well-to-do families to live in the heart of the city. It is something of a culture shock to visit a busy street in Paris full of shops and cafés. A door between the shops will give access to a staircase and caged lift or perhaps a gateway leading to a secluded courtyard. On the first and second floors there are likely to be solicitors, dentists and other small businesses. On the top floor there may be small inexpensive

flats but in between will be the apartments of middle-class families. These apartments are as spacious as many English villas and many would originally have had servant's quarters. However they are still lived in today by families with children who would be considered eccentric by their English counterparts but who are still seen as quite normal in France.

In Paris the suburb has a very different connotation to the English suburb. There are affluent suburbs, particularly in satellite towns like La Varenne St. Hilaire. However the term suburb or 'banlieu' refers to the municipal housing estates and poor working-class areas on the edge of the city. Paris's inner city problems are on its periphery (as demonstrated by the extensive rioting in late 2005) and are all the more intractable and divisive because they are so remote. This does however mean that, in general terms, Paris has retained the traditional pre-industrial pattern of growth, dispersal has been far less pronounced and its character as a great city is intact. Indeed residential densities in central Paris are four times those of London.

Paris is significant because it was a profound influence on the Emperor Franz Joseph when he embarked on the replanning of Vienna

in the second half of the 19th century. Together Paris and Vienna provided a model for other continental cities and indeed for those of South America. This influence extended not only to architects and planners but also to the general public and the middle classes in particular who aspired to the Parisian ideal of the urban apartment. This is not just confined to major cities. It can be seen in towns of all types and sizes on the continent including industrial towns.

In terms of urban growth the developed world can therefore be broadly divided into two traditions: the Anglo-American model that can also be seen in Australia, and the French model which characterises most of Europe, Latin America and to a lesser extent Canada. (This dichotomy serves our purpose here because it serves to illuminate the UK situation. There are of course other models that, world-wide, are just as influential such as the Islamic city or the Asian city – particularly in China. However even here the great division is between places where the pressure is to be in the centre and those where people seek out the edge.)

This explains why continental towns have retained their form, density and vitality to a far greater extent than British towns and cities.

The continental model: The grand boulevards of Paris as laid out by Haussmann (far left). The Ringstrasse, Vienna (above) which was modelled on Paris. The apartment block, often containing a mix of uses, became the predominant building type in continental cities

An Urban Renaissance: Cities like Manchester
and Glasgow underwent an unprecedented revival
in the 1990s and 2000s. It would once have been
inconceivable that grey, wet northern cities would develop
a thriving café culture

32

One need only look at similar cities such as Marseille and Liverpool or Milan and Birmingham to see the impact of these trends. This is not to say that continental towns have all the answers. They too suffer from urban problems and in recent years have not been immune from the dispersal of people and investment. However if we in Britain are seeking to rediscover the benefits of urban life there is much that we could learn from continental models. Yet it must be understood that the differences between British and continental towns are not superficial and cannot be overcome with a few street cafés. They go to the very heart of the urban forces which shape our towns and cities. It is unlikely that we can ever put the clock back 150 years to redirect these forces. The task instead is to draw upon continental and British models to create successful British urban models which can meet the needs of the 21st century.

The UK Urban Renaissance

There have been times in the 20th century when the city has seemed to be dying. Indeed when you visited a city like Liverpool at the end of the 1980s that rattled around in the husk of a once great metropolis, it was difficult to be optimistic. However the predictions of the death of the UK city have been much exaggerated. Over the last 10–15 years there has been a remarkable renaissance in many British cities. The decline of urban populations has almost been stemmed (although problems remain in smaller cities like Hull and industrial towns like Stoke and Burnley). Despite the advent of seemingly anti-urban trends such as home working, teleshopping and computer conferencing, many British towns and cities have found new roles. The heavy industry and overcrowding which gave rise to the flight from the city no longer exist and are fading from people's perceptions. Whilst there are problems of traffic pollution and urban crime it is clear that many parts of British towns and cities can provide attractive environments in which to live and work.

This resurgence of urban areas has become known as the Urban Renaissance. The first edition of this book was being written at a time when this Urban Renaissance was still part formed and we hopefully played a small part in its shaping. At about the time of its publication the government was convening the Urban Task Force, chaired by the architect Richard Rogers (Lord Rogers of Riverside). We became advisors to the Task Force presenting our work on urban capacity described in Chapter 9 and working with MORI on a report into attitudes to urban living called 'But would you live there?[20]'

The Urban Renaissance is the result of a remarkable confluence of political interests, economic trends, demographic change and environmental concern that caused many people to question the sustainability of the trends of dispersal that we have described in this chapter. As we described in the introduction, The Urban Task Force Report published in 1999[21] was followed in 2000 by an Urban White Paper[22] and subsequently by important policy documents such as the Sustainable Communities Plan in 2003[23] and the Northern Way in 2004[24]. Meanwhile Planning Policy Guidance Notes have been progressively tightened with PPG3 (now PPS3) leading to a drastic reduction in green field housing (far more than intended) and PPG(S)6[25] effectively putting an end to new out-of-town shopping.

In 2006 the Urban Task Force reconvened to assess progress[26] and Michael Parkinson of Liverpool University published a major review of the state of British cities[27]. The consensus of these reports is that huge progress has been made but there is much to be done. The reconvened Task Force lamented the slow progress made in areas such as the design of housing while a minority view by Peter Hall struck a note of caution that far from moving too slowly, the process had gone too far with too many one-bed apartments being built in town centres and not enough family housing. The *State of the Cities* report again pointed to the progress made but highlighted that, despite all of these improvements, the northern cities still lagged far behind those in the south or indeed on the continent.

London is the only British city which would meet Jane Jacobs' criteria for a great city. In the 1990s we wrote that, having boomed in the 1980s, London's growth had stalled as a result of the property crash and the lack of city-wide government. We predicted that this would change with the election of a London Mayor and under the two terms of Ken Livingstone, this did indeed happen. London now has a coherent plan[28] that, for the first time in its history seeks to encourage and accommodate growth rather than to constrain and redirect it. Its population has exceeded 8 million for the first time since the 1930s and it has achieved pre-eminence as one of three world cities (with New York and Tokyo) eclipsing other European capitals. This success is sucking in more people, particularly through immigration so that London is now one of the most racially diverse cities in the world. Success will hopefully be cemented by the staging of the Olympics in 2012 which is part of a major extension of the city to the East into the Thames Gateway.

The provincial cities have also boomed in the last 15 years. This has been led by Manchester, Leeds and Glasgow but the trend has spread to embrace all of the cities and many of the larger towns. This has been led by the development of city centre apartments. Huge amounts of development have taken place, initially for owner-occupation but increasingly for the private rented market. With the poor performance of the Stock Market, private investors and personal pension funds have poured money into property. The city centre populations of most UK cities have rocketed from virtually nothing to tens of thousands. This residential investment has mirrored the growth of city economies, particularly in services, the creative industries and the knowledge sectors linked to the urban universities. There has even been a resurgence of many city centre retail markets which have upped their game to respond to the threat of out of town centres.

It would be easy to conclude that, in stark contrast to the US, the trends of dispersal in the UK described earlier in this chapter have

been reversed. This would however be too hasty. For all the vitality of city centre markets, they are but a small nucleus at the centre of very large conurbations. In Manchester, the population of the city centre has risen to around 25 000 which is just 1 % of the population of Greater Manchester. Less than half a mile from the new apartments blocks in cities like Manchester, Newcastle and Liverpool there are inner city neighbourhoods that have experienced catastrophic decline and abandonment. Indeed the process of population dispersal to the edges of these cities (and indeed London) has not reversed – and may not even have slowed. All that has happened is that city centre apartments and

inner city redevelopment has started to replace some of the people who are leaving. The result is a dynamic balance in which the population of most of the northern cities is now stable but not yet growing.

The most severe urban problems have slipped down the urban hierarchy and are now to be found not in the cities but in the small and medium-sized industrial towns of the north. Like the cities these towns have lost their traditional industries. However unlike their larger neighbours they have struggled to generate new economic activity. Without universities in a world where the government wants 50% of young people to go to higher education, these towns are losing their most able young people to cities, often never to return. Some with good transport links have become commuter towns. However others, such as the industrial towns of East Lancashire, Staffordshire, Yorkshire and the North East have struggled with declining populations, failing shopping centres and a deteriorating environment.

The Dynamics of Change

This book is about the reversal of the polarity of British cities, written as part advocacy and part prediction. Ten years after its initial publication the predictions are coming true. It is too early to proclaim victory, but there is a real sense that UK urban areas have diverged from their US cousins and that, perhaps, the Anglo-American/French dichotomy has been undermined. The reasons for the success of the Urban Renaissance in the UK, compared to the US are complex. It is partly a result of government policy but this would not have been successful had it not been swimming with the currents of demographic, economic and social change that we describe in part two of this book. It is possible to characterise the drivers of this Urban Renaissance as follows:

Policy Drivers: As we have said the issues that have driven public policy include concern on the political Right about the loss of countryside to urban sprawl and, what has often been portrayed as, an attack by urban elites on rural communities (such as the ban on hunting). On the political Left issues have included concern about urban decline and the social exclusion of urban communities while both have been galvanised by the demographics of falling household size, increasing household numbers and the predicted 4 million extra households. Another political influence has been sustainability that has increasingly been linked to the urban agenda, particularly through transport and the need to get people out of their car and onto public transport or their bikes.

Social drivers: These policy drivers have been effective because they have corresponded with a range of economic, social and demographic trends. The first of these is transport. While the car has been responsible for urban depopulation, towns and cities remain important transport hubs with mainline railway stations, motorway connections and airports. They have also benefited from investment in public transport such as the tram system in Newcastle, Sheffield and Manchester. Political concerns to get people out of their cars have started to coincide with social concerns about congestion and the amount of time wasted commuting. An important driver behind urban housing demand is people's recognition that they no longer wish to waste the best years of their life sitting in a traffic jam trying to get to work.

Cities have also benefited from the growth of service industries and cultural and knowledge industries. While these activities are based on modern telecommunication and therefore theoretically freed from locational constraints, the reality is that they feed off face-to-face contact, the ability to attract talented people and the activity produced by dense urban populations. It is difficult to imagine a rural stock exchange, bank or national newspaper. It is equally hard to picture a thriving fashion or music industry which was not able to feed on the street-life of a large city.

Linked to this is the importance of higher education both to the life of cities and to

The historic structure of London: London is the only UK city which would pass Jane Jacobs' test of a great city

their economies. In Manchester the Knowledge Capital Initiative, spurred by the merger of the city's two largest universities, is set to create 300 000 jobs. Whilst there are universities on isolated campuses, they have struggled to compete with the urban universities that can offer culture and night-life to attract students. In the best cities students tend to stay on after their courses, contributing their skills and energy to the city and its economy. This can be seen in cities as diverse as Liverpool and Sunderland which benefit greatly from high student stay-on rates. Former art students account for the fact that Sunderland, despite its size and location, was the Arts Council City of Visual Arts in the 1990s and is the base for the Artists Newsletter, UK's leading national magazine for artists.

The 1980s have seen the emergence of a new urban middle class providing a fresh source of demand for services. As Peter Hall noted in the late 1990s 'the arrival of the yuppies, those suburban-born children of the emigres from the city of the 1940s and 1950s, is creating a boom in consumer-led service employment and in associated construction, which may at last provide the basis for broad-based economic revival with jobs for a wide spectrum of skills and talents'. The 'Friends' generation has, for the first time in three generations, begun to see the city and urban living as a desirable state.

Economic Drivers: Cities have also started to recognise the economic potential of diversity. The American academic Richard Florida developed this idea in his book *The Rise of the Creative Class*[29]. In this he argues that the success of the modern city is based on diversity. Those cities with the greatest numbers of ethnic minorities, gay people and 'counter-culturalists' will be perceived as diverse, tolerant and cool and will thus attract creative, skilled, talented people. These are just the sort of people businesses need so that 'cool' cities and 'cool' people drive economic development. These people also tend to be urban

dwellers and to use cultural facilities. The growth of this 'creative class' is therefore a powerful force reinforcing city growth. This can be seen in the success of ethnic quarters such as Brick Lane and Liverpool's China Town and the phenomenally successful Gay Village in Manchester.

These trends have reawakened the forces that created the great cities of the UK and could lead to their long-term renaissance. This capacity to mobilise the skills and energies of large numbers of people is the factor which has always sustained cities. The city is like a magnifying glass, it focuses and concentrates human activity both positive and negative. It is no accident that cities house the worst excesses of crime and poverty, but also the best of the arts, learning, sports and commerce. If cities did not exist we would not have great art galleries, libraries and theatres; we would not have a subculture to feed and sustain mainstream culture; we would not have a venue for great public events and a focus for regional power and even in the days of the electronic office we would lose the catalyst for economic growth. The magnifying glass works because of the concentration of people who live and work in cities. Human nature requires face-to-face interaction and it is the city, not the suburban close or the motorway service station, where the density of people exists to sustain the creativity of human contact. As Jane Jacobs argued in the *Economy of Cities*[30] it is only in cities that new work is added to existing activities. This, she suggests, is the engine for human and economic growth. It is this basic truth which has saved the city from extinction and which sustains and nourishes its renaissance. As more people are attracted back to the city, and despite the complaints of gentrification and colonisation, there are signs that the traditional role of the city as a marketplace is re-emerging. It may be that our antipathy to the city is waning and that the dispersal trends that date back to the Industrial revolution are reversing. This is certainly our hope.

Chapter 2
Lost Utopias

If we are to shape the form of housing in the the 21st century it is important to understand the way that the design of housing has been shaped in previous centuries. The urban trends described in the last chapter help to explain the impetus behind the development of different forms and locations of housing. They do not however explain how the 19th century terrace evolved into the 20th century semi-detached house or indeed the high-rise block and how this might transform into the 21st century home. This is the task of this and the following two chapters. We must first explore some of the concepts of housing and its place within towns and cities that have dominated the 20th century. In doing this we need to go back to the visionaries who shaped the 20th century home.

The great shapers of the 20th century home were the utopian thinkers[1]. No book on the subject would be complete without Ebenezer Howard's three magnets or Le Corbusier's Ville Radieuse. These and other visionaries reacted against the evils of the industrial city whilst embracing the opportunities of the industrial age. Their ideas have had a lasting effect on modern town planning. At the end of the 20th century new visions are required which respond not so much to the technological opportunity of the modern age but to the unsustainable patterns of development that technology has produced. In doing this it is important to learn from the 20th century visionaries and the way that they have influenced housing and urban development.

The garden city pioneers

The early visionaries were the enlightened industrial philanthropists, people like Robert Owen who developed New Lanark in 1800 to provide better conditions for his workers and to defuse political unrest. He was followed by industrialists such as Titus Salt in Bradford (Saltaire 1853), George Cadbury in Birmingham (Bournville 1879), and William Hesketh Lever in Birkenhead (Port Sunlight 1888) as well as Joseph Rowntree's development of New Earswick in York (1902). These developments combined a genuine concern for the well-being of workers, with a degree of self aggrandisement, and sound commercial sense. They varied

An ancestor of the Garden City: Bournville Village in Birmingham developed by George Cadbury in 1879

greatly in their form, structure, the degree of communal provision and common ownership that they incorporated. However together they provided many of the elements which crystallised at the turn of the century into the garden city movement.

It is just over 100 years since the garden city idea was first proposed by Ebenezer Howard in his book *Tomorrow: A peaceful path to real reform* in 1898[2], republished in 1902 as *Garden Cities of Tomorrow*. Howard recognised that the city had many advantages: social opportunity, employment, well-lit streets and 'palatial edifices'. However there were also many disadvantages such as the 'closing out of nature… the isolation of crowds… foul air and murky skies… slums and gin palaces'. He also saw the countryside as having a balance of advantages and disadvantages and proposed the garden city as a means of combining the advantages of both town and country without the disadvantages.

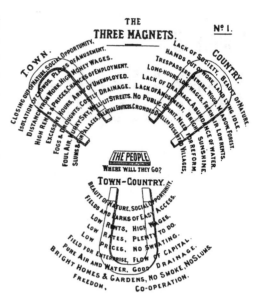

Above – The Three Magnets: Developed by Ebenezer Howard a century ago the diagram has taken on almost iconic status

Below – The Social City: A network of garden cities providing a framework of development encompassing both urban and rural uses

This equation was illustrated with a picture of three magnets which has since featured in virtually every book written on town and country planning. Howard's vision was to reform the organisation of towns, the pattern of settlements and indeed the wider organisation of society. He advocated new towns with a population of 32 000 on 6 000 acres with the majority of land used for agriculture. These towns were to be part of a network of garden cities across the countryside which Howard called the 'Social City'. This abolished the distinction between town and country since agricultural and urban uses were incorporated within a common framework. Land was to be owned co-operatively with everyone paying rents to service debt and to generate a surplus to cover services, health care and pensions.

The form of the garden city was illustrated in a series of diagrams which are almost as famous as Howard's magnets. The garden city was to be organised in concentric rings around a central park surrounded by a covered glass arcade containing shops and services. Be-

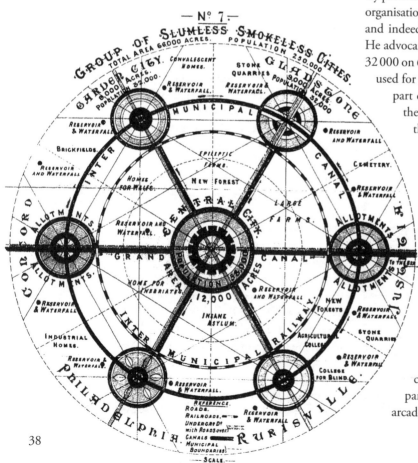

yond this were rings of housing separated from the outer ring of industry by a grand avenue. Many of these features find echoes in modern towns, the covered glass-roofed shopping centres, the tree-lined avenues and the zoning of uses. Howard sought to build his utopia with the formation of the Garden City Pioneer Company in July 1902. The first true garden cities were Letchworth designed by Parker and Unwin in 1903, and then in 1919 Welwyn Garden City designed by Louis De Soissons.

The garden city movement gave birth to the British new town movement and still lies at the heart of the philosophy of the Town and Country Planning Association which Howard helped to found. However our interest here is in the wider influence that the garden city has had on housing development. Here it is not so much the concept of the garden city but the designs for the first developments which have had a lasting effect. The most influential designers at the time were Louis de Soissons who designed Welwyn Garden City and Barry Parker and Raymond Unwin who designed New Earswick, Letchworth and Hampstead Garden Suburb, the latter with Sir Edwin Lutyens. Through

these schemes they developed the form of the garden city which was subsequently to have such an influence on 20th century suburban planning. Raymond Unwin described his philosophy in two influential books, *The Art of Building a Home* and *Town Planning in Practice*[3]. His vision was of wide frontaged semi-detached houses and short terraces at densities of twelve units to the acre (30/ha) in a landscaped setting with plenty of vistas – influenced by Sitte's street pictures. Another important influence was the revival of organic vernacular and Gothic forms through the arts and crafts movement and particularly the work of John Ruskin and William Morris. Parker and Unwin believed that the disposition of housing should be guided by the topography of the site rather than street patterns. This led to the use of 'closes' of houses set away from the road. In New Earswick these were initially served by footpaths. However with the growth in car use these closes evolved into cul-de-sacs which were first seen in Letchworth and Hampstead Garden Suburb. The latter which, due to Lutyens' influence, is more formal than the other garden cities, is probably the finest example of Parker and Unwin's work.

The suburban environment:
The hedges and trees of Hampstead Garden Suburb still represent, to many people, the ideal suburban environment

**The first
cul-de-sac?**

Louis de Soissons'
designs for Welwyn
Garden City (below),
one of the first to make
extensive use of the
cul-de-sac (above)

However Victorian by-laws, designed to prevent the unwholesome yards which had character-ised London slums, specified the development of wide through roads. The narrow roads, closes and cul-de-sacs of Hampstead therefore required a special Act of Parliament to make them possible. Concerns about traffic conges-tion led to a stipulation that housing densities be reduced to eight houses to the acre. Unwin argued that, with the growing number of cars, closes and cul-de-sacs would create a quiet residential environment as well as reducing the land area devoted to roads. However his main concern was to avoid the housing layout being dictated by the road network which, he felt, led to monotonous grids and ribbon development. The closes and cul-de-sacs therefore allowed far greater variety of form which in Unwin's hands led to a streetscape of enduring quality. However as with many visionaries the concepts

have not fared so well on the drawing boards of less talented designers where the results are more often clutter and confusion.

Some of the most enthusiastic ex-ponents of the ideas of the garden city move-ment were the newly created council housing departments in the years after the First World War. One of the most influential of these was the Greater London Council which undertook developments such as the Old Oak Estate in Hammersmith. Another very influential development was Wythenshawe, developed by Manchester City Council on the outskirts of the city in 1930. This was designed by Barry Parker and has been described by Peter Hall[4] as the third garden city. However, unlike the other garden cities, Wythenshawe has remained a predominantly poor working-class area. It is tempting to look at somewhere like Letchworth or Hampstead Garden Suburb which remain popular and to believe that our problems would be less if only all housing were built like this. Yet Wythenshawe is almost identical in design and, as work by URBED[5] in the 1990s showed, the social and economic problems of parts of Wythenshawe, such as Benchill, can be as bad and in some cases worse than Manchester's most notorious inner city areas. How much this is due to the physical design of the area is unclear, but the isolation of the area from the city which is compounded by the disorientating nature of the street layout undoubtedly plays its part. There is a lesson here for those who would argue that the wholesale replacement of high-rise estates with suburban housing will solve the problems of the inner city.

Parker's designs for Wythenshawe in-corporated two further ideas which were to have a lasting influence. The first was the concept of the neighbourhood unit served by local facilities and surrounded by arterial roads. The second was the parkway, an arterial road set within parkland which ran between these neighbourhoods. Prin-cess Parkway, the southern part of which is now the M56 motorway, remains a major arterial route out of Manchester and the concept of setting the road within a linear park can be seen not just in

Wythenshawe but also in the much later development of Hulme, of which we will hear more later. The concept of the neighbourhood unit and the parkway were subsequently to coincide with the ideas of the modernist movement as we will see in the next chapter.

As with all visionaries Howard's ideas and the designs of Parker, Unwin and Louis de Soissons have suffered in less enlightened hands. Forgotten are the ideas for social reform and the organisation of uses and settlements. Lost is the respect for topography and the understanding of how housing can be arranged in a landscaped setting. In superficial terms the modern suburban housing estate owes much to the early garden city designs but rarely have they achieved the same level of quality and character.

The housing designs which emerged from the garden city movement have also become firmly embedded in the public consciousness. The suburban ideal has become a seem-ingly universal aspiration of UK households. It has exerted a powerful influence on municipal housing – alongside the modernist movement – and has become the stock-in-trade of private housebuilders who, for much of the century, have built little else. Ebenezer Howard would, no doubt, shudder to be called the father of the modern suburb but this is perhaps his greatest legacy.

The modernist reformers

The garden city pioneers were not the only utopians to influence the 20th century home and town planning. Another group of visionaries were equally concerned to sweep away the worst excesses of urban squalor but sought to do this, not by turning to the countryside for inspiration, but to art and science. The modernist movement sought to bring order and logic to the confusion and muddle of the city. Tony Garnier and Le Corbusier in France

The Cité Industrielle: One of Tony Garnier's evocative illustrations of his utopian city based on maximising daylight

and the Bauhaus in Germany were the leading exponents of these ideas and, like Ebenezer Howard, their aim was no less than to reinvent the city.

Tony Garnier first produced his plan for the ideal industrial town in 1904 just as Howard started to develop Letchworth. Garnier's ideas were published as *Une Cité Industrielle*[6] in 1917. He envisaged a town of segregated uses with a residential zone, a train station quarter and an industrial zone. The town was to promote social justice through common ownership and, so widespread would social harmony be, Garnier saw no need for the town to include a police station, courts or churches. In an echo of the issues which will concern us in the 21st century, the town was to be energy self-sufficient. Development was sited in relation to the sun and wind and would draw all of its energy from a hydroelectric dam. Residential quarters were to be laid out in east-west blocks allowing all housing to face south. Narrow streets were not to have trees, with wider streets only being allowed trees on the southern side to avoid shading. This is one of the first attempts at passive solar design although at the time the motivation was the health-giving properties of sunlight rather than energy efficiency.

Garnier's Cité Industrielle was never built although echoes of some of his ideas can be seen in the Tony Garnier Estate in Lyon, not least because in recent years a series of enormous murals of Garnier's drawings have been created on the gable ends of the blocks[7]. The architectural style of Garnier's buildings is remarkably contemporary and more accessible than the later proposals of Le Corbusier largely because they are human in scale. His high-density residential quarters are similar to the urban development of the 1990s described later in this book. However in other respects Garnier's legacy is more damaging to the modern city. He was one of the first to develop the idea of zoning uses as well as the modernist concept of buildings as objects within a landscape rather than the 'walls of urban streets'. Garnier's other legacy is his influence on Le Corbusier and it is through Le Corbusier that the ideas were largely transferred to Britain and America.

Le Corbusier, born in 1887 as Charles Edouard Jeanneret, published his utopian vision in two books *The City of Tomorrow* in 1922 and *La Ville Radieuse* in 1933[8]. Whilst these were a development of Garnier's ideas they were less of a reaction to the problems of the industrial city and more of a response to the opportunities of the industrial age. Le Corbusier's vision was based on mechanisation and new technology. It exploited the potential of the car and aeroplane, as well as the new building technologies which allowed for high-rise building and mass production. However the influence of the machine went deeper still into Le Corbusier's vision. He believed that, just as science was ordering nature, so it could order the city. His city is rational, efficient and ordered. Its plan can be read as a diagram of its functions but it makes few if any concessions to the complexity of urban life.

Le Corbusier's aims in developing La Ville Radieuse are similar to those of Howard and to many subsequent planners in the 20th century. He sought to decongest the centre of cities, increase mobility and increase the amount of parks and open space. However he differed

The city in landscape:
Le Corbusier's vision of blocks built on stilts so as not to interrupt the flow of the landscape

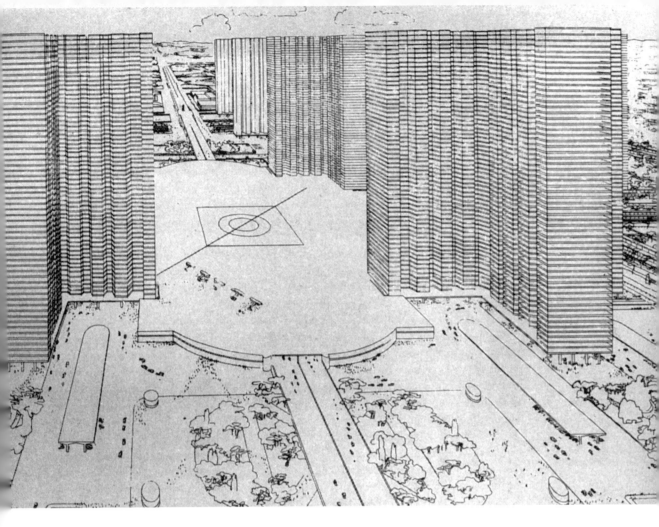

The Ville Radieuse:
Le Corbusier's ordered and rational urban Utopia, dominated by technology as witnessed by the pride of place given to the airport

in one important respect. Unlike the garden city builders and most of modern planning, he wanted to increase urban densities to around 1 200 inhabitants to the acre, almost ten times the average density of Paris at the time. The overcrowding of cities had long been seen as one of the drivers of reform. However far from wishing to reduce densities, Le Corbusier saw higher densities as a prerequisite for mechanised production so that he concentrated on finding technological solutions to overcome the density problem. This he achieved by building upwards and proposing high-rise blocks accommodating not just housing but all of the services required for modern life: schools, shops, services and employment. This liberated 95 % of the land area within the large urban blocks that he proposed for open space and parks.

Le Corbusier has been credited, or condemned, as the father of the high-rise blocks.

Again, like all visionaries, this is largely due to the way in which his ideas have been interpreted by lesser architects. The schemes that he completed, most notably Unité d'Habitation in Marseilles, remain successful. However the influence of his ideas is equally significant in terms of the organisation of cities which, with the exception of Chandigarh in the Punjab, were never built. He saw no place in his plans for the street which he condemned thus: 'The corridor street should be tolerated no longer, for it poisons the houses that border it'. Such streets were seen as incapable of accommodating the swift movement of goods in the quantities required for industrial production. These sentiments echoed the thinking of Barry Parker in Wythenshawe and, as we will see, subsequent planners like Abercrombie with his concern to eliminate muddle. La Ville Radieuse was therefore the first city plan to include a hierarchy

43

of roads but no streets. Subterranean routes were to be created for heavy traffic linked to a network of loading bays. Ground level roads were to be used to get around the city above which, free flowing highways, the precursors of modern elevated motorways, would cater for longer journeys. The roads would be straight and junctions spaced at 400 yards to reduce congestion. This distance determined the scale of urban blocks. However there is little mention of the pedestrian in Le Corbusier's writing and it is clear that the scale of his proposals is based around the needs of the car rather than travel by foot.

The influence of these ideas on post-war commercial and residential development hardly needs spelling out. The vertical separation of uses and movement, with underground loading, elevated motorways and housing on 'streets in the sky', can be seen throughout the country and has blighted town centres and residential estates alike. The dominance of the motor car at the expense of the pedestrian who is relegated to the subway or elevated walkway, the use of mechanised production, and the infamous high-rise estates which by 1980 housed an estimated 1 in 4 UK households[9], can all be traced back in part at least to Le Corbusier. It is tempting to think that Le Corbusier's ideas are dead. However they are still being taught with reverence in many planning schools, appealing as they do to the planner's wish for control and order. His highway engineering ideas, transmuted as we will see through various reports and government guidance, still influence modern practice.

A further influence on housing design came from the Bauhaus in Germany. Here housing design was approached with the same systematic, functional discipline that the Bauhaus sought to apply to all elements of design. While this was on a much smaller scale than Garnier and Le Corbusier it shared a design philosophy focused on industrial production. The Bauhaus was concerned with art, product design and architecture rather than the planning of cities. However the ideas for residential design developed by the Bauhaus were to have a profound influence on the modernist movement. The experimental *Haus am Horn* built for the Bauhaus Exhibition in 1923 was intended as a showcase for modern household products and

The Bauhaus model:
Ideas for a multi-storey housing settlement developed by Ludwig Hilberseimer at the Bauhaus around 1930

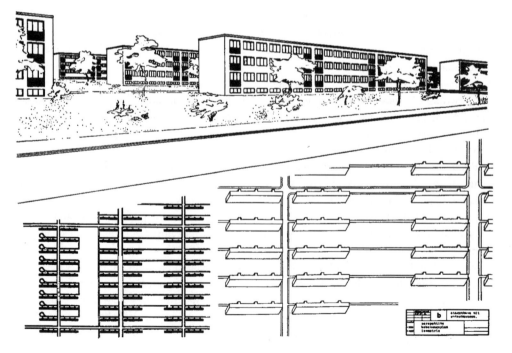

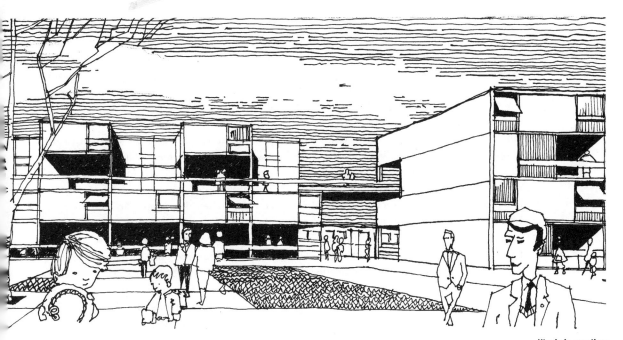

Utopia in practice:
One of the early 'art-
ists' impressions' of
Hulme in Manchester
illustrating how the
planning ideas of the
pioneers were put
into practice

attracted considerable interest. It reflected the rejection by the Bauhaus of the arts and crafts philosophy that had dominated its earlier years and the embracing of technology to create a *Wohnmaschine* or living machine. The house was of steel frame and concrete construction and its design reflected this – form followed function. It was simple, sparse, and logical, perfectly matched to its function if not to the more traditional notions of home. As Walter Gropius, the director of the Bauhaus, said: 'To build means to shape the activities of human life. The organism of a house derives from the activities which take place within it... The shape of a building is not there for its own sake'[10]. There were plans to develop a Bauhaus housing estate. While these were dropped, work was done by Ludwig Hilber-seimer at the Bauhaus on the design of estates where he advocated mixing high-rise and single-storey dwellings. This, he said, means that... 'a development would not only become freer but also achieve a spatial arrangement which results directly from the requirements and which... does not have to rely on decorative trimmings for its urban design'[11].

Paradise lost

The work of Garnier, Le Corbusier and the Bauhaus must be seen in the context of the emerging modernist movement. Just as Howard, Parker and Unwin drew upon the arts and crafts movement, the modernists interpreted the ideas emerging from painters like Mondrian and applied them to the development of housing and the organisation of cities. Both movements held a strong appeal to planners and architects in Britain. Opportunities to implement these ideas were created by the housing shortages and need for reconstruction after the two world wars which led to huge building programmes. After the First World War it was the garden city which held sway. But the modernists came to the fore in the 1920s and 30s and it was they who most swayed the hearts and minds of planners and architects after the Second World War. The modernists did not however supplant the ideas of the garden city pioneers and the two approaches have existed side by side for much of the century. Whilst the modernist school came to dominate planning in cities, the garden city movement's influence has thrived in the new town, the overspill estate and the suburb. What is more when it comes to the organisation of towns and cities, as we will see in the next chapter, the ideas of the two movements are very similar and have been mutually reinforcing.

As we approached the end of the century it was clear that the influence of the modernists on town planning (although not architecture) was rapidly waning. The failure of many of the redevelopment schemes of the 1960s and 1970s was all too apparent and there were few people who would hold up Le Corbusier as a model for future urban development. However the fall of modernists left only the garden city as a tried and tested philosophy for the design of cities. Whilst this may have been appropriate for new settlements and suburbs it was of less value when considering the redevelopment and repopulation of urban areas. This left a void for those seeking solutions to our towns and cities pointing up a pressing need for new urban models.

In seeking to develop such models we can learn a great deal from the 20th century visionaries. They illustrate that through published work, a small number of demonstration projects and, no doubt, a great deal of luck, it is possible to profoundly alter the course of housing development and town planning, if not always in the way that was originally envisaged. It may well be that as young professions, housing and planning in the 20th century were particularly susceptible to new ideas. The visionaries described in this chapter provided an ideological and philosophical base for these professions at a time when they needed to establish their identities. The same may be more difficult in the future. However the way that so many local councils jumped on the urban village band waggon in the 1990s suggests that new visions have not entirely lost their potency or their capacity for misinterpretation. The effective 21st century utopians must understand the way in which their ideas are translated into practice by the planning and housing professions. It is this that we seek to do in the next two chapters.

Chapter 3
The taming of the city

The Industrial revolution left a legacy of fear and mistrust towards the city in the minds of many people, fuelling the flight to the suburbs in both Britain and America. At the same time the Utopian visionaries in the early part of the century were developing alternatives to the city. In some cases, such as Le Corbusier, they were advocating the wholesale redevelopment of existing towns. Most however confined themselves to new settlements, blank canvases on which towns and cities could be reinvented free of the constraints of history. The planners and other urban professionals who were excited and inspired by these ideas did not have such freedom. They sought to apply Utopian ideas to the great if messy task of reforming existing settlements and eliminating what, in their eyes, was the muddle and confusion of urban life. Their great opportunity to do this came with the need for reconstruction and the introduction of the modern town planning system after the Second World War. The context set by the Utopians in the early part of the century was largely anti-urban and this was reflected in the attitudes of postwar planners. It was not that they wanted to do away with the city, they sought instead to make it more efficient, equitable and healthy, in short to tame and control it. They undoubtedly saw themselves as the saviours of towns and cities but in reality they ended up destroying what they sought to protect. In this chapter we chart this destruction.

The ideas of the urban visionaries were transmitted into practice through a variety of routes. It is tempting to suggest that the garden city predominated in the interwar years but after the Second World War its influence was largely confined to new towns with the architectural modernists coming to the fore in urban areas. However the situation was more complex. In developing the intellectual foundation of modern town planning and postwar social housing, practitioners drew heavily on both the garden city and modernist traditions. Whilst in terms of physical form the two traditions would seem to be poles apart, in terms of their underlying principles there were in fact many similarities. Both thought in terms of neighbourhood units, promoted the benefits of open space, air and sunlight and sought to reorganise settlements to accommodate the motor car. Indeed to many, Le Corbusier's ideas were an application of garden city ideals to high-density urban living.

One of the most important organisations responsible for bringing these ideas together and applying them to the planning of cities was the Congrès International de l'Architecture Moderne (CIAM). Formed in 1928 and including people such as Walter Gropius of the Bauhaus, this group was responsible for popularising and making practical the ideas of the visionaries. Through the Charter of Athens in 1933[1] CIAM created the other great foundation of modern planning to counterbalance

The rebuilding of Coventry: Before German bombing (and British planning) Coventry was a fine medieval city. It was originally seen as one of the great successes of postwar planning. Much of the design philosophy underlying its redevelopment has been discredited yet the quality of the original vision can still be seen in parts of the city centre

Howard's *Peaceful path to real reform*. The Charter of Athens developed Le Corbusier's ideas into a set of practical principles which could be applied to the problems of overcrowding and congestion which characterised the modern city.

An insight into the thinking of CIAM can be found in the report of the 1952 CIAM conference on the Heart of the City[2] which took place in England. The conference proceedings are full of statements such as: 'The study of past and present urban shapes, urban ecological process, and urban health will give material for the urbanist's vision'. The conference stressed

diversity, and encouraged humanitarian cities where spontaneity flourishes, the 'individual is king (and) the pedestrian is his own master'. All things that could come from a modern planning document. The influences that they drew on were also promising – the same Italian piazzas admired by many of today's urban designers. Yet the developments which the conference used to illustrate these ideas were the recently completed pedestrian precincts of Coventry and Stevenage town centres. The City Architect of Coventry told the delegates that their plans represented 'the first time that a central area (had been) analysed in terms of its main uses and a plan drawn up which retained only those necessary to its correct functioning; both industry and housing were excluded'. Looking at Coventry city centre today you can almost capture the vision and excitement of these times particularly in the wonderful Cathedral by Basil Spence. However Coventry also includes reminders of how the high ideals of CIAM and the visionaries from which they drew their inspiration turned into the soulless pedestrian precincts and the ghettoised high-rise council estates which have since so blighted our towns and cities. It is paradoxical that Coventry, one of Britain's greatest medieval cities, should have been so readily sacrificed whereas in Germany cities like Nuremberg have been painstakingly rebuilt on traditional lines. The reason for this lies in a number of principles developed by CIAM which became the foundations, some would say the dogma, on which modern planning was built.

Comprehensive redevelopment

One of CIAM's concerns between the wars was slum clearance because of the correlation between poor housing and ill health. CIAM believed that slum areas could not be improved since the building form was fundamentally flawed. They advocated that areas of poor housing should be swept away to be replaced with modern blocks positioned to receive the sun and surrounded by open space. Whilst they were against overcrowding they viewed low densities

as uneconomic. It was therefore logical to follow Le Corbusier's lead by advocating high-rise blocks. These were to be built in a landscape setting leaving no place for traditional streets. In this way CIAM was to establish a blue print which was to guide much of the slum clearance work in America and Britain. This contrasts sharply with the war-damaged sections of West German cities, despite the German origins of many modernist ideas. German towns and cities were rebuilt with 4 to 5 storey blocks on traditional streets which accommodated rather than separated traffic and pedestrians. Germany and many other parts of Europe have therefore retained the vitality of their urban areas and modernist development, where it has taken place, is confined to the periphery of the town.

BRACKNELL NEW TOWN

In 1950 Bracknell was a small town of 5000 people spread out along a traditional high street with eight pubs, a cattle market, shops, a cinema and a garage. In 1944 Abercrombie's Plan for London identified the need to decentralise population to a series of new and expanded towns around the capital including Bracknell. These were to become the Mark One New Towns included in the 1949 New Towns Act.

Bracknell was originally designated as a new town with a population of up to 25000 and plans were developed for a modest expansion to the town retaining the high street. However in 1961 the planned population was increased to 60000. By then the philosophy of town building had changed radically and traffic was seen as much more of a problem. The vision for the new town centre had the

same aims as a town centre plan would today. The vision was for a lively mixed-use centre to be achieved within an urban structure which was more logical and functional than traditional towns. The key element to this was traffic management and the new town plan stated: 'The needs of motor traffic in the Town Centre are quite different from those of pedestrians, whatever their purpose, each should be provided for separately. Cars and delivery vehicles should have a direct service approach to every building and from whatever direction the town centre is approached car parking should be obvious and adequate. Access for pedestrians from car parks and other approaches to the centre should be direct, safe and of constant interest'. This requirement alone fixed the development form of the centre since it required the vertical separation of cars and pedestrians, the creation of two ring roads and extensive service yards.

Despite the aim of creating a

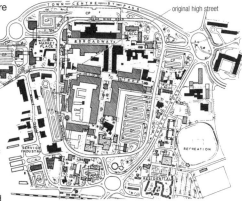

The remnants of the original high street

mixed-use centre, the form of the new town has made this difficult to achieve. There are few restaurants and cafés, fewer pubs than there were on the original high street, and most of the leisure development has been concentrated in a leisure centre on the edge of the centre. In creating a functional centre, the planners over-looked many of the fundamentals which make a town work. Nevertheless the town worked well enough when its new population had little option but to use the centre for shopping and other services. However a more mobile population with greater choice is turning its back on Bracknell as they are many of the new towns. They have neither the convenience and comfort of out-of-town shopping nor the character and charm of historic centres.

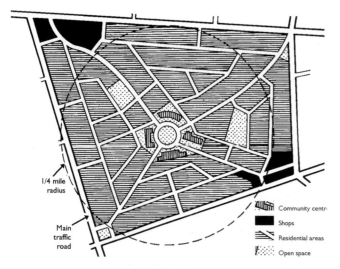

1/4 mile radius

Main traffic road

Community centre
Shops
Residential areas
Open space

The neighbourhood unit: Conceived by Clarence Perry for the New York Plan in the 1920s, the neighbourhood unit is delineated by major routes with community facilities in the centre. However Perry positioned shops at the junctions of the major routes whereas in the UK shops were placed in the centre of the neighbourhood where they were deprived of passing trade

The attitudes of postwar planners in Britain have therefore reinforced the historic differences between British and European towns.

The neighbourhood unit

CIAM also took on board the concept of the neighbourhood unit. As we have seen this played a role in Howard's ideas and was a central part of Barry Parker's proposals for Wythenshawe. It had also been central to Clarence Perry's plan for New York[3] in the 1920s which advocated neighbourhoods of 5 000 people based on the catchment of a primary school with major roads consigned to the edge of each neighbourhood. CIAM developed the neighbourhood unit into the idea of super blocks, each served by a range of local facilities – schools, shops, doctors – and with an allotted area of open space. These blocks were accessible only to the residents. There was however a crucial difference between this and Perry's ideas. Perry placed shopping areas at the junctions of the major roads dividing the neighbourhood units but retained their character as traditional streets. CIAM, by contrast, advocated small district centres at the heart of the neighbourhood keeping the major peripheral roads free of frontage development to ensure the free flow of traffic. This was a direct application of the parkway concept which Parker used in Wythenshawe. Industrial, shopping and commercial areas were similarly to be zoned into blocks to create industrial estates, shopping

centres and commercial districts. These zones were to be separated by swathes of open space within which would run a fast and efficient transport system of roads and motorways.

The free flow of traffic

The great insight of Le Corbusier and the other great visionary not mentioned so far, Frank Lloyd Wright, was to foresee the growth of car use. They saw the car as a liberating force to be accommodated in towns and cities. If this meant that the whole city had to be redesigned then so be it, an attitude which has characterised the approach of most postwar planning. The streets which lay at the heart of traditional urban areas played the dual role of a transport artery and a focus for the surrounding community. They were, as a result, lined with shops and services and bustling with the sort of activity and diversity prized by writers like Jane Jacobs and the visitors to historic towns. However to the tidy mind of the modern planner this 'solidified chaos' in the words of Lewis Mumford[4] was inefficient and was choking the commercial lifeblood of cities and undermining the quality of life of urban communities. Planners and highway engineers therefore sought to reform the system of roads in cities drawing inspiration from Le Corbusier's and Wright's freeways and Parker's parkways. These ideas were developed by H. Alker Tripp, an assistant commissioner in the Metropolitan Police responsible for traffic. In a book entitled *Town Planning and Traffic*[5], which was to influence Abercrombie's plan for London, he advocated that the streets of London should be divided into arterial routes, subarterial routes and local roads. The higher order routes were to be segregated from the highway system, free of frontage development, with widely spaced junctions to reduce congestion.

By the 1960s the emphasis had changed from exploiting the potential of the car to coping with the challenges of congestion. The landmark report *Traffic in Towns* by a group chaired by Sir Colin Buchanan in 1963[6] stared into the abyss that we still face today: 'The potential increase in the number of vehicles is so great that unless something is done conditions are bound to become extremely serious within a comparatively short period of years. Either the utility of vehicles in towns will decline rapidly or the pleasantness and safety of surroundings will deteriorate catastrophically – in all probability both will happen together'. The report goes on to say that these problems concern the form and organisation of urban areas which will become the 'supreme social problem of the future'. To be fair to Buchanan, the arguments in the report are more sophisticated than their subsequent application would suggest. He suggested that in planning for future roads both the economic costs and the environmental costs should be taken into account. If the environmental costs were considered by the community to be unacceptable then traffic restraint rather than road building should be pursued. He therefore put forward maximal and minimal traffic solutions, although it was the maximal solutions which received most interest and which have had the lasting effect. Buchanan has therefore come to

be associated with the network of motorways with grade separated junctions and pedestrian walkways and subways which were so close to the heart of the planners and highway engineers in the 1960s and 70s. While there is now an acceptance of the negative effects of these ideas, the damage has been done. Resources have been wasted, communities divided and isolated and town centres cut off from their hinterland by ring roads which have become the modern equivalent of city walls. Principles such as a hierarchy of distributor routes with frontage development only allowed on minor streets were enshrined in the government's *Design Bulletin 32 – Residential Roads and Footpaths*[7]. This has been a major influence on highway engineers and remained in force until very recently. Design guidance developed by Alan Baxter Associates in 1998 called *Places Streets and Movement*[8] was originally intended to replace DB32 but concerns over liability for accidents (always the most potent argument in the highway engineer's tool box) meant that it was downgraded to

The High Street: Traditional streets such as the Stratford Road in Birmingham serve the dual function of a major traffic route and a community focus. Many of these routes have been transformed into free-flowing traffic arteries free of frontage development and devoid of urban character. However recent improvements to the Stratford Road show how traffic flow can be maintained while retaining vitality. This has been done by creating a single lane of traffic in each direction uninterrupted by parking or turning lanes. This has allowed pavements to actually be widened while traffic flow has been eased

guidance on how to interpret DB32 more flexibly. It was not until March 2007 that DB32 was finally replaced, 30 years after its publication by *Manual for Streets* drawn up by a team led by WSP[9].

The benefits of open space

Underlying much of modern planning is the idea that open space is good. One of the problems with the overcrowded industrial town was that people had little or no public or private open space. The by-law terraces may have been a great improvement on the earlier urban slums but they made little or no provision for recreation or indeed greenery of any kind. It was this which gave impetus to the development of Victorian parks which provided a valuable oasis of open space in areas where trees were rare, play areas unheard of and many people did not even have access to a back yard. However such was the belief in the quality of life-enhancing aspects of open space, that Le Corbusier's assertion that 95% of the land area should be given over to open space was seen as a valid aspiration by many planners. Great deserts of grassland with lollipop trees and the occasional forlorn playground have therefore come to dominate many parts of our cities. Even in the 1970s and 80s large parts of the London Borough of Southwark were blighted by Abercrombie's vision of new parks and riverside walkways in pursuit of which the council continued to buy up and clear large areas of housing and workshops.

The development of buildings in a landscape is common to the garden city and modernist movements. In the garden city, however, most of the land was in gardens. The open space was therefore largely 'privatised' so that it was used and maintained by the residents. In the modernist vision, by contrast, open space was communal and part of the public domain. Some of it may have been used as playgrounds or sports pitches but most lacked any function other than providing a buffer to traffic noise and a 'pleasant' outlook to residents. What use someone living on the tenth floor of a tower block was supposed to make of the formless grassland in which the block is set was not clear. The reality was that this space was unused, dangerous and a burden on public authorities responsible for maintenance.

Yet planners still insist on lavishing their plans with great swathes of open space while architects designate 'landscaping' with no discernible function or generator of activity. Indeed local plans today still often treat open space as a land use in its own right regardless of function or usefulness. They fail to recognise why the open space is spurned by ungrateful residents, has not created value and has harmed the vitality of surrounding areas. This can be seen with many areas of open space such as Burgess Park in Southwark or Mile End Park in Tower Hamlets. Far from being great assets for the community these have quickly come to be seen as problems, little used by local people and with a reputation for crime.

The curse of overcrowding

One of the issues to have sowed most confusion in postwar planning is the issue of density. This is linked to the issue of open space but has more commonly been driven by concern about overcrowding, something which had been recognised as the curse of working-class areas since Victorian times. Overcrowding has been linked to ill health, poverty and crime and was one of the main targets of slum clearance programmes. However the issue of overcrowding – the number of people per room – has consistently been confused with the issue of density – the number of dwellings or people per acre. High-density areas need not be overcrowded and conversely it is quite possible to have a low-density area in which overcrowding is a problem if houses are overoccupied. The visionaries discussed in the previous chapter sought to reduce overcrowding; however, with the exception of Le Corbusier, they failed to recognise this point and their objective became the reduction of densities.

The concern to lower densities can perhaps be traced back to Raymond Unwin's book, *Nothing gained by overcrowding* published

The density myth: It is often argued that the problem of the high-rise estates of the 1960s was that densities were too high. However as these plans of Hulme illustrate, this was far from the case. The plan on the left is from the 1930s when the area was built to around 150 dwellings/hectare. The right-hand plan shows the redevelopment of the 1960s which was just 37 dwellings to the hectare (15 dwellings to the acre). This is the density proposed by Ebenezer Howard for the Garden City. These estates contrive to feel dense (see overleaf) without having sufficient people to sustain facilities and street life

in 1912[10]. This argued that if sufficient open space was provided, the savings in land area to be gained from higher densities were marginal and out-weighed by the benefits of lower density development. He suggested an ideal density of twelve houses to the acre, a target which became the norm for garden city development even though it was lower than the fifteen homes to the acre suggested by Ebenezer Howard. This target was also adopted by the influential Tudor-Walters report of 1918[11] and became the standard density of most interwar development in both the public and private sectors.

In the more recent past the prejudice against density was reinforced by research on rats by Calhoun published as the *Behavioural Sink* in 1962[12]. Indeed this research was still being quoted in questions by members of the House of Commons Environment Select Committee in 1998 as part of their enquiry into housing! Calhoun showed that if a rat colony becomes too large its social structure breaks down. This was equated to the problems in high-density housing areas. However subsequent work has shown that social breakdown is a result of the size of the colony not its density and the situation is not improved by making the enclosure larger. Yet problems are avoided if the colony is fenced off into smaller enclosures even if densities are not reduced.

With the redevelopment of tightly packed urban areas after the Second World War it was felt that the garden city density targets were unrealistic even with the decanting of a large part of the population to overspill estates. The aim in cities was therefore to accommodate higher densities whilst avoiding the problems of overcrowding. Following Le Corbusier's lead this was achieved by building upwards to allow for generous amounts of open space. There was also a trend in the 1970s to develop high-density low-rise estates based around a warren of alleyways.

However even at these higher densities these new developments were built at substantially lower densities than the terraced areas that the new development replaced. Indeed, as Alice Coleman[13] has pointed out, the scale of high-rise estates gives the impression of high densities, an impression often shared by residents who feel that the area is overcrowded. Yet in terms of the number of houses to the acre, these estates were often built to relatively low densities. They therefore achieved the worst of both worlds – the impression of high density without any of the benefits. Hulme in Manchester, for example, was once home to 130 000 people not to mention countless small factories, pubs, shops and public buildings. The redevelopment of the 1960s swept this diversity away to create 5 000 flats in six deck-access estates housing around 12 000 people. Similarly the Five Estates in Peckham were developed at a fraction of the density that had once existed in the area. This however was achieved by building at relatively high densities on part of the site and using the rest to create Burgess Park which became a vast and poorly-used area of open space. It also resulted in many of the local shops on Rye Lane which was once known as the 'Golden Mile' closing for lack of trade. Yet consultants' reports up to the late 1990s continued to suggest that one of the area's problems was the fact that it was too dense. The obvious solution was to build on part of the park to reduce its scale and increase supervision. However such is the hold that lower densities and open space have on professionals and politicians that this was seen as sacrilege.

Jane Jacobs reports a conversation that she had with a planner about the West End in Boston in the 1960s[14]. The planner was ashamed to admit that an area with 275 dwellings to the acre still existed in the city and indicated that, when resources allowed, it would be redeveloped. However he also admitted that the area scored well on indices such as delinquency, disease and infant mortality and even confessed that he enjoyed the street life of the area. The West End may have been unique and there were certainly many dense working-class areas where disease, poverty and crime were the norm. Jacobs' point however was that the blanket use of density as an indicator of such problems is rarely justified.

Densities still exerts a hold on planners. In the 2000s this has been evident in the plans to redeveloped terraced housing areas in Northern England through the Housing Market Renewal Programme. The failure of the housing market in these areas was in part ascribed to their density and the solution, in the early days of the program at least, was seen as 'thinning-out' the housing to create more open space or redeveloping a lower densities.

True, since the first publication of this book there have also been pressures to increase densities. In London the redevelopment of council estates has been funded by releasing land for new private housing. The aim was to provide enough social rented homes for the existing population and enough private housing to fund the development, thus increasing density markedly. The other area where there has been pressure to increase density has been the boom in city centre apartments which in places has come close to recreating the densities in the West End that gave the Boston planners of the 1960s sleepless nights (but somehow without creating vitality). This has led to more howls of protest that we are creating the slums of tomorrow. The objections relate to the size of the units, the lack of open space and the inappropriateness of the accommodation for families. It remains to be seen whether this age-old cry of the planning establishment against density is justified. There are certainly city centre apartment schemes that give density a bad name. Some have been bought by buy-to-let investors and populated with transitory and inappropriate tenants and are exhibiting all of the signs of degenerating into slums. But let us not extrapolate from the worst excesses of the apartment boom and decide that density and social ills remain automatic bedfellows. Many apartment schemes were sold to young childless professionals, remain successful and contribute hugely to the vitality of town and city centres.

Planned and organic towns:
Figure ground plans of Devizes (right) and Yate (left). The towns are roughly the same size and the plans are the same scale. They show a stark contrast between a dense traditional town and one planned in the 1950s applying the principles of postwar planning

Postwar plan making

These various influences came together in the rash of town and city plans developed after the Second World War. The most influential was the plan for the postwar reconstruction of London developed by Patrick Abercrombie with J. H. Forshaw, the chief architect for London County Council, produced in 1944[15] and published as a Penguin special edited by Arno Goldfinger. This plan brought together many of the ideas described in this chapter. London's arterial routes were to become parkways through landscaped strips, bounding inward-looking neighbourhoods arranged around pedestrianised shopping precincts. Much of the development was to be new with the Victorian housing areas which survived the blitz being cleared to create modern, zoned areas of development.

Even at a time of postwar reconstruction, the structure of London's local government, financial constraints and the complexity of the city largely defeated the planners so that Abercrombie's plan was only partly realised. This was not the case in the provincial cities, in small towns due for expansion and of course in the rash of new towns planned after the war. The plans which emerged for these towns took a lead from Abercrombie and, what is more, strong provincial councils were far more able to put them into practice. The 1949 plan for Manchester[16] conceded to the retention of only a handful of city centre buildings. Even Waterhouse's town hall was to be demolished! The radial routes were to be replanned as parkways sweeping away hundreds of shops on formerly bustling streets such as Oldham Road and Rochdale Road to the North of the city. Even greater 'progress' was made in places like Birmingham, Coventry and Stevenage, and even quite small towns like Yate to the north of Bristol or Hemel Hempstead to the north of London. Here existing centres were razed or new towns built to create comprehensively planned centres surrounded by a wilderness of ring roads and parking.

The lost urban vision

The effect of these policies on the vitality and life of cities is best summed up by Jane Jacobs in her tirade in the introduction to the *Death and Life of Great American Cities*[14]. She summarises the ideas which are taken for granted in orthodox planning thus: 'The street is bad as an environment for humans; houses should be turned away from it and faced inward, towards sheltered greens. Frequent streets are wasteful, of advantage only to real estate speculators who measure value by the front foot. The basic unit of city design is not the street but the block, and more particularly the super-block. Commerce should be segregated from residences and greens. A neighbourhood's demand for goods should be calculated "scientifically", and this much and no more commercial space allocated. The presence of many other people is, at best, a necessary evil and good city planning must aim for at least an illusion of isolation and suburban privacy.'

It is hard to better this and the eloquence of Jacobs' argument for the importance of cities. The visionaries and their followers described in this and the previous chapter made the mistake of thinking that towns, cities and the human society that they accommodate are like machines, that they can be described entirely in terms of uses, functions, movement and systems. True such concepts have an analytical value in describing existing settlement patterns. They are however fatally flawed as tools for future planning. First of all towns and cities exist in all of their complex glory. Ordering this complexity requires resources far beyond that which was available even in the building boom after the war. Simplistic Utopias applied to existing urban areas are therefore bound to be compromised and undermined. Thus compromised they are unlikely to work as envisaged and are destined to fail.

However even when there is not the complexity of an existing town to deal with, the application of Utopian visions to a new town is fraught with difficulties. It is almost impossible for a master planner to conceive, on paper, a town which works as well as a traditional town, which is the result of centuries of evolution. This is not unlike the attempts in robotics to replicate the complexity of the human body. Artificial towns, like robots, may be more efficient and many businesses and residents may find this attractive, but they lack the diversity, vitality and character of their older cousins. Also as Jacobs said in the conclusion to *The Economy of Cities*[17]: '...bureaucratised, simplified cities, so dear to present-day city planners and urban designers, and familiar also to readers of science fiction and Utopian proposals, run counter to the processes of city growth and economic development. Conformity and monotony, even when they are embellished with a froth

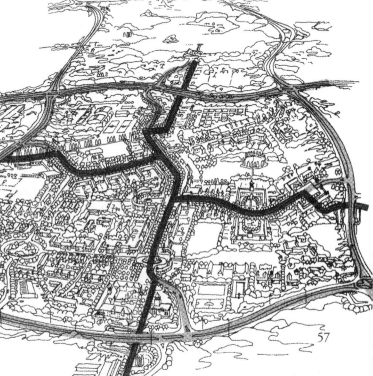

Milton Keynes: An illustrative section of the master plan for Milton Keynes showing the supergrid of major routes which are free of frontage development and the neighbourhood developments within the grid. The city is perhaps the purest expression of much of the philosophy of postwar planning

57

The suburban conspiracy:
Modern planning policies would no longer allow the creation of historic urban areas such as Bradford upon Avon (above). Instead a suburban conspiracy has threatened our cities in which inappropriate housing turns its back on to the streets to which they should be giving life as in Moss Side, Manchester (below right)

of novelty, are not attributes of developing and economically vigorous cities'. This is why town planning at its best is an art rather than a science and why successful urban development is organic rather than mechanistic.

Of course artificial towns can still work. It is instructive to be asked, as we were in the 1990s[18], to advise on the revitalisation of the centre of a new town like Milton Keynes, which incorporates many of the principles of modern town planning. Milton Keynes remains the fastest-growing city in the UK and is based upon a 'supergrid' of streets bounding neighbourhood units with a town centre based around boulevards and a covered shopping centre. It is generally popular with residents even if they do sometimes yearn for areas like Covent Garden where people can be seen throughout the day. However most recognise that the town is convenient and meets their every need. Milton Keynes remains probably the best example in Britain of the sort of urban environment envisaged by postwar planners. However for every Milton Keynes there are countless examples of areas where the application of this conventional

wisdom has created not popular environments, but alienating places devoid of identity, character and life. Once people have satisfied their basic needs for food and shelter they yearn for higher things such as human contact, cultural expression, community, hustle and bustle, and a sense of continuity. People do not miss these things until they are deprived of them, a loss which may be manifested as 'new town blues' or the alienation of people on peripheral estates. Older towns may be less efficient but they undoubtedly meet these human needs more effectively than many modern settlements.

Much of the legacy of 20th century visionaries is therefore negative and over the last twenty years or so has increasingly been recognised as such, particularly in the case of the modernists. Some may argue that this is because many of the ideas have been 'bastardised' by lesser architects and planners to justify development which the visionaries and early planners would have abhorred. However a philosophy which has destroyed the life of large parts of our cities must be questioned in terms of its conception rather than just its implementation. In the 21st century we will continue to struggle with the momentous task of reforming our cities. We are however increasingly dealing not with the exhausted fabric of the Victorian city but with the legacy of 20th century mistakes. Yet can we be sure that we are not repeating the same mistakes? While we may have thrown out many of the most damaging ideas of 20th century planning many of the dogmas remain,

something that in the late 1990s we called the suburban conspiracy.

The suburban conspiracy

An enmity towards the city is shared by many of those involved with the planning and development of housing and urban areas. In an effort to sanitise and tame the city they managed to throw out the baby with the bath water and destroyed what they sought to preserve. The underlying ethos of most professions and investors concerned with the urban environment has been, and largely still is, anti-urban. Indeed all of the urban professions (with the exception of urban design) have been brought into existence to tame the city and to regulate human activities. There is no Anglo-American equivalent of the European 'urbaniste'.

Many of these negative attitudes live on in the minutiae of urban policy. This has started to change with the incorporation of urban design principles into national policy guidance such as *By Design*[19]. Back in the 1990s it was still common for planners to seek to protect housing from noise and traffic by making it turn away from the very streets to which it should relate. Rather than creating a sense of enclosure on streets that were attractive places to be, buildings were set back behind landscape buffers and streets became desolate traffic routes. There are still places where this happens today although national policy discourages it. However planning policies such as privacy distances, parking standards, building lines,

controls on 'over development', the zoning of uses and open space requirements all remain central parts of planning ideology.

If planning is changing slowly, the pace of change in highway engineering is glacial. This is still based upon the eradication of congestion and the reduction of accidents. Who can argue against a policy which saves the lives of children, even if it does make life miserable for pedestrians who are isolated on pavements dominated by traffic noise, and hemmed in by fences? Road hierarchies (with limited access from distributor roads), parking requirements, turning heads, visibility splays, curb radii and opposition to crossroads all make it difficult to recreate today many of the historic urban environments that we so prize. Such are the constraints imposed by modern highway engineers that it is no longer possible to build the medieval streets of York, the Georgian crescents of Bath or even the early 20th century developments like Hampstead Garden Suburb.

So whilst many of the tenets of 20th century planning theory may appear to have been discredited the tenacity of their hold over the urban professions should not be underestimated. The modernists may have fallen from grace but our towns and cities are still threatened by a suburban conspiracy. The conspirators include planners, highway engineers, investors, and, as we will see in the next chapter, the housebuilding industry and residents who have bought into the suburban ideal. Government policy in the early 2000s and the impact of some of the trends described in this book mean that progress has been made, however the conspiracy is still strong and the battle far from won.

New planning disasters

There is perhaps another lesson that we can learn from the 20th century attempts to tame the city. In this chapter we have questioned the philosophy of 20th century planning but it may also be that there is something inherently flawed with the idea of imposing a conventional land-use plan on the complexity of urban life. The

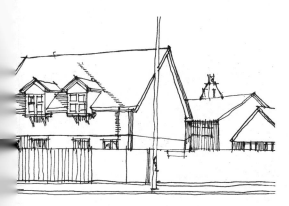

best and most enduring of places seem to have grown organically over time within a planning framework rather than to have sprung from the inspired hand of a single masterplanner. Yet in Britain we have been obsessed with grandiose end-state plans. The town centres and housing estates conceived on the drawing boards of the 1960s looked fine on the architect's blue prints. But these bore little relation to the situation on the ground within a few short years. This is a lesson that we have not yet learned. Architects are once more producing plans for the redevelopment of housing estates to sweep away the mistakes of the past. Is there any more chance that they will get it right this time or is the very process of conceiving a neighbourhood on paper and building it over a few short years a recipe for failure?

However the people with the real power to undertake comprehensive development at the beginning of the 21st century were not weak under-funded councils but private developers. Far from being able to impose its will on the city the modern planning system has struggled to control a booming property market in the early 2000s. Commercial schemes like Brindley Place in Birmingham that have created a sense of place are the exception. More often the private sector created urban business parks, shopping malls, office developments and apartment schemes that have undermined the quality of urban life. Policy changes may mean that they now need to be located within urban areas and have a veneer of urban design thinking. However in their conception and organisation they bear many similarities to the schemes of the 1960s and 70s. Like their forbears, these developments also sought to tame the city by recreating it in safe, comfortable, sanitised environments. They attracted car-borne customers and created large profits for the financial institutions that funded them. While public sector professionals may have failed the city in the 20th century there is little evidence that the private sector is able to do any better.

The future city? Modern shopping developments whether in-town or out-of-town, based upon American models such as this are creating new sanitised environments to tame the rough edges of the city

Chapter 4

The shaping of the English home

How have the forces of urban decentralisation, Utopian thinking and town planning shaped the sort of housing that we have built over the last 200 years? At the end of the millennium the predominant type of housing built in Britain appeared to have changed little since the great suburban boom of the 1920s – as if the Ford Motor Company was still selling the Model T. This type of low-density, detached and semi-detached development somehow seemed to be a natural, even an inevitable part of British life. However, as the history of housing over the last two centuries illustrates, major design changes can take place over relatively short periods of time, prompted by social and economic trends, legislative change and the influence of reformers. These trends continue to influence housing of the future and in this chapter we chart the way that they shaped the housing of the 19th and 20th centuries and how they may shape the housing of the future.

The 19th century home

The traditional image of the 19th century home is of drab uniform rows of terraced housing in the shadow of 'dark satanic mills'. This housing is associated with the subjugation and exploitation of the working classes by the unfettered growth of capitalism in the Industrial revolution, and the concentration of Britain's population in metropolitan centres. It is an image that has been fuelled by the accounts of the 19th century reformers such as Peter Gaskell's who wrote in *Manufacturing Population of England* (1833) : 'The housing of great numbers of the labouring community in the manufacturing districts present many of the traces of a savage life. Filthy, unfurnished, deprived of all the accessories to decency or comfort, they are indeed but too truly an index of the vicious and depraved lives of their inmates'.

The true picture is more complicated. As John Burnett[2] points out, such accounts describe the worst housing of the time as if it were the average. In fact, as Friedrich Engels wrote in 1844; 'Houses of three or four rooms and a kitchen form throughout England, some parts of London excepted, the general dwellings of the working class'[3]. The worst housing conditions were largely confined to overcrowded cellars, lodging houses and older tenements graphically

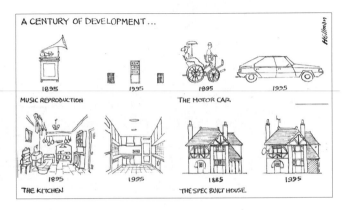

A CENTURY OF DEVELOPMENT...

Hellman

1895 / 1995 — MUSIC REPRODUCTION

1895 / 1995 — THE MOTOR CAR

1895 / 1995 — THE KITCHEN

1885 / 1995 — THE SPEC BUILT HOUSE

described in books such as Jack London's *Edge of the Abyss*. The back-to-back terrace, so universally condemned from the mid-19th century onwards, was in fact relatively desirable since it was self-contained and afforded a degree of privacy to a family.

Bylaw housing:
While bylaw housing was a great improvement on previous working-class housing it created drab, monotonous environments

The development of the 'through' terrace represented even greater progress. This allowed for a back yard with an individual privy which could be cleared by night soil men from the back alley. The greater size of dwell-

ings enabled the separation of living, cooking and sleeping activities as well as meeting those great concerns of reformers for ventilation and day light. Most importantly the terrace started to change the nature of urban life. The early residents of the industrial city, out of necessity if not choice, had lived a very communal life, sharing space, sanitation, and services. This life had taken place in back courts largely hidden from the rest of the city. The Victorians viewed this communal life as a breeding ground for vice, dirt and disease and sought to counter this by promoting the nuclear rather than the extended family. The through terrace allowed the separation of private family life from the public life of the street. The lace curtained parlour and the polished front step created an impenetrable barrier for all but invited guests. This also marked the beginning of the separation of the sexes in which women became housewives responsible for the respectability of the home whilst men went out to work. The through terrace can therefore be seen as the birth place of a number of trends, the natural result of which was the suburbia of the 1900s.

By the second half of the 19th century the through terrace had become the norm. This was spurred not so much by changes in the housing market but by public health reforms, in particular the by-laws which were introduced

locally from 1840 onwards and nationally in 1877. By-law terraces have been widely condemned for their monotony of row upon row of treeless streets with little or no open space. Builders may have built to the lowest standards allowable but these standards were considerably higher than those of earlier decades. By-law terraces were more sanitary, less dense, more airy and light, and internally they were better built, with larger windows, higher ceilings and improved materials. In terms of layout the effect was to create the familiar gridiron layout with regularly spaced streets and occasional cross streets. This however was far more open and easy to understand and police than the warren of yards and back courts of the early part of the century. Whilst large areas of by-law terracing were demolished in the slum clearance programmes of the 1960s and 70s, the areas that were spared have often outlasted the 20th century redevelopment schemes meant to replace them. Only in the closing years of the century did some of the terraced housing areas of northern England start to fail, and even then the quality of the housing was only one of a number of complex causes. Elsewhere passage of time has often seen these by-law neighbourhoods develop into desirable districts that have become 'gentrified' by the middle classes.

Middle-class suburbs

Another important trend in the middle of the 19th century was the emergence of the middle-class suburb. Censuses of the Victorian period show that perhaps three million out of a population of eighteen million could be

considered as middle-class. As we saw from Chapter 1, whilst this class was the product of the wealth generated by the Industrial revolution it was also repelled by the conditions that it created, and sought to construct a way of life which was insulated from the 'evils' of the industrial city. This life centred around Christian values, polite behaviour, privacy, order, and taste. The symbol of this way of life was the middle-class home or villa.

As Stefan Muthesius[4] has described, for much of the 19th century these middle-class aspirations were achieved in terraced housing. This housing was grander, in some cases far grander, that the homes of the working classes but the form was essentially the same. Indeed Muthesius has described how the frontage width of even the grandest terraces was not vastly greater than its more modest cousins. Larger houses were built upwards, sometimes to six storeys, and plots became deeper with coach houses and servants' quarters facing onto the rear alley. Terraces of such houses were made to look like palaces particularly in areas like Grosvenor Square in London and Bath with classical columns and central pediments. Often

Middle-class housing: The housing of the middle classes was also terraced and high-density although on a much grander scale

these urban houses served as second homes for families 'up for the season' who also had country houses from which they derived their status and sense of identity.

In the early part of the 19th century these middle-class terraces became so popular that they were favoured over the detached villa. However as the century progressed the middle-class aspirations for privacy, order and godliness found increasing expression in more suburban housing forms. Donald Olsen[5] argues that the physical form of Victorian development was a deliberate response to what were seen as immoral Georgian values that had emphasised street life

(the promenade) and public pleasures (the spa and the subscription rooms where dances were held). The Georgians were less concerned with the need to separate classes or to celebrate the family and their towns like Bath or Cheltenham excelled in what we now think of as a continental way of life. Early precursors of the Victorian era like Belgravia in London and Victoria Park in Manchester represented a very different view of civic life. They erected walls and gates to protect them from 'lower-class' districts but as time went on gates were not enough and the middle classes sought geographical separation and the outward expansion of the city gained

MIDDLE-CLASS HOUSING IN LONDON

The development of middle-class housing in London is illustrated by looking at four estates as chronicled by Olsen[6], in Primrose Hill, Dyos[7], in Camberwell, Gillian Tyndall[8] in Kentish Town and Linda Clarke[9] in Somers Town. The precarious nature of residential development at the time meant that Primrose Hill and Camberwell remained 'desirable' while, Somers Town became a slum.

These areas were developed speculatively with four-storey housing. A plan would be commissioned by the land owner setting out the roads, the class of houses to be erected together with amenities such as churches, shops and public houses. The classes of home were controlled through the London Building Act of 1774 which divided houses into four 'rates', and stipulated their height in relation to the width of roads as well as the details of their construction. Thus the Eton Estate, which owned Primrose Hill,

The four rates of house specified in the 1774 London Building Act

limited the number of mews, because it knew these frequently degenerated into slums, and sought a balance between the 'higher class' houses along Regent's Park Road and the 'lower class' behind them.

Once approved, leases were sold to small builders so that streets developed incrementally. The builders in turn, sold the houses to small tradesmen who rented them out to provide an income before the days of pensions. The Paving Commissioners laid out the pavements and infrastructures. There was however a major difference between landowners like the Bedford Estate, who thought in terms of long-term value, and those who went in for short-term gains, as in Somers Town.

Somers Town was started in 1773 by the architect Leroux under an agreement with Lord Somers. Leroux's finance came from brick making rather than development values and the 'ring of fire' from brick making put off investors. Pressure to build quickly caused standards to fall and the houses were small, or were tenements dressed up to look like Georgian houses.

By contrast on the neighbouring estate Lord Southampton's direct control meant that a generous layout was retained without 'back streets nor any of so retired a kind as to be

liable on that account to be improperly occupied and to injure the reputation of the district'. The development was protected by gates and designed to 'have as few communications as possible with Somers Town'.

By 1800 Somers Town was characterised by dust hills and dung heaps and proximity to the canal encouraged industry. The tenements became overcrowded and the gardens were built upon, further increasing densities. When the estate was sold in 1802, control was further fragmented. By 1831 it was 'dingy with smoke and deprived almost entirely of gardens and fields'. With 8.4 persons per house it was not surprising that cholera broke out. Many of the houses were demolished as the railways were cut through the worst parts of the area, the remainder being replaced by public housing in the 1930s.

Why is it that such places deteriorate into slums whilst others which outwardly appear very similar succeed? The factors include short-term profiteering from land sales, insufficient public space, air pollution, the loss of social balance, overcrowding, poor standards and neglected maintenance. The lesson is that developers need to retain control and to take a long-term view otherwise grand plans can end up as slums.

Middle-class sanctuary:
Many cities retain districts of spacious housing dating from the middle of the 19th century like Whalley Range in Manchester

pace. Separation from poorer neighbourhoods was however not sufficient. The Victorian family sought sanctuary from unplanned encounters with neighbours not just of different classes but also their own. The detached villa was therefore favoured, surrounded by a high wall and with a sweeping drive to block views from the street. Thus the middle classes were able to recreate their own miniature version of the country estate yet remain within reach of their employment in the city.

As is so often the case the lower middle classes, uncertain in their newly acquired position, were all the more concerned to adopt middle-class values. Unable to afford a detached villa the solution was the semi-detached villa complete with porch and boot scraper. Burnett

cites the first example of semi-detached villas in 1794 and the revolutionary idea was further developed by Nash alongside the grand terraces and detached villas of Regent's Park. However by the end of the century the semi-detached house had made the benefits of suburbia available to a much larger part of the middle class and the foundations of 20th century housing development were being set. As Dyos and Reeder have said: 'The middle class suburb was an ecological marvel… it offered an arena for the manipulation of social distinctions to those most conscious of their possibilities and most adept in turning them into shapes on the ground; it kept the threat of rapid social change beyond the horizon of those least able to accept its negative as well as positive advantages[10].'

The development of flats

Throughout the great boom of urban population in the 19th century it is remarkable that people in England and Wales remained so attached to the individual home on its own plot of land. In Scotland and on the continent the response to overcrowding had been to build upwards – possibly encouraged by a different legal system which allowed 'flying freeholds'. In England and Wales this rarely happened, with occasional exceptions such as the two storey Tyneside flat and the London mansion block often used as bachelor flats. In 1849 the *Builder* published an article which argued that 'the time has now arrived when the expansion and growth of this city [London] must be upwards in place of outwards – when "houses" must be reared above each other… instead of straggling miles farther and farther away from the Centre'[11]. The only developers to take up this call were the housing societies which started to emerge in London and to a lesser extent provincial cities like Leeds. The early associations such as the Society for Improving the Conditions of the Labouring Classes were joined by the Peabody Trust in 1862 and the Guinness Trust in 1890. From the start these societies concentrated on building flats as demonstration projects to show that quality working-class housing could generate a return for investors. By 1870 Peabody had produced more than 5 000 flats in dense six-storey blocks, something which had never before been seen in England. The flats were accessed by wrought iron balconies around internal courts. These models were to influence the earliest council housing in London, Leeds and Manchester such as Victoria Square in Manchester (left). Were it not for the Tudor-Walters Report, such flats could have become the predominant housetype in the 20th century with far-reaching effects on our towns and cities. A further constraint on the development of flats was lack of finance on a sufficiently large scale, unlike Paris where Napoleon III set up a national bank to fund Haussmann's apartment blocks.

However despite the development of middle-class suburbs and flats the 19th century home remained the terraced house. In 1911 only 10% of houses were detached or semi-detached and only 3% were flats[12]. The vast majority of housing was the terrace that had become as ubiquitous in the 19th century as the 'semi' would become in the twentieth.

The 20th century home

As we have seen, major improvements were being made to the standard of housing in the second half of the 19th century. The growth of middle-class housing and the introduction of by-laws had largely overcome the worst problems of the early Industrial revolution at least for new housing. However this did little to address the legacy of substandard housing from the early 19th century which still dominated most industrial towns at the turn of the century. There were for example still 42 000 back-to-backs in Birmingham in 1914.

The next major development in housing was to come about at the end of the First World War when there was the prospect of a severe housing shortage as millions were 'demobbed' at a time of widespread unemployment. The major house building programme launched by the Lloyd George government sought to both address the housing shortage and create jobs. However in doing this the government was also keen to rethink the sort of housing that was produced. The 'Homes Fit for Heroes' campaign turned for inspiration to the garden city movement. The vehicle for

Early council housing in Manchester: In the background, Victoria Square, the first flats to be built in the city. The street in the foreground was originally called Sanitary Street after the council committee which commissioned the housing. The 'S' and 'ry' have since been dropped at the request of the residents of what is now called Anita Street

this was a committee chaired by Sir John Tudor-Walters (and including Raymond Unwin) which published its report *Dwellings for the working classes* in 1918[13]. The recommendations of the committee were incorporated in their entirety in the Local Government Board's *Manual on the preparation of state-aided housing schemes* published in 1919[14] which established the model for interwar housing development. This model was largely based on the work of Parker and Unwin. The houses recommended by the committee and illustrated on advisory plans were widely adopted by local authorities. The preferred housetypes were semi-detached or short terraces of up to eight units. They had wide frontages and narrow plans to maximise the amount of internal daylight. In terms of layout, Tudor-Walters recommended a mixture of housetypes for different classes of tenants. Cul-de-sacs were suggested for economy and the removal of through traffic, and houses were to be at least seventy feet apart to allow the proper penetration of sunlight.

The Tudor-Walters Report was concerned with public housing and its far-reaching impact was due to the great boom in public housing after the First World War. Indeed council housing did not exist until the Housing of the Working Classes Act of 1890 which gave local authorities the power to build housing. The 1919 Housing Act, for which the Local

Government Board's manual was produced, transformed this power into a duty and the 20th century council house was born. This heralded a great step forward in housing quality and was only made possible because the 1919 Act severed the link between the cost of housing and the rents that could be charged. The government undertook to provide the majority of the funds whilst rents were to be set independently in line with the wartime rent controls. Quality could therefore be improved without the costs being passed on to tenants. As a result housing built in 1920 typically cost four times more than the housing of 1914. The alarm that this caused resulted in new approvals being halted in 1921. However when council house building was resumed in 1924 by the incoming Labour government the standard had been set by Tudor-Walters, and despite lower levels of subsidy and less regulation, standards remained high.

The 30 years between 1890 and 1920 therefore saw a radical change in ideas about housing. This provides a valuable lesson for those seeking to promote an equally significant change into the 21st century. The Utopian ideas of Ebenezer Howard were first translated, some would say compromised, into demonstration schemes such as Letchworth and Hampstead Garden Suburb. These received widespread attention in the professional press and in policy-making circles. As a result, when

The suburban ideal:
This illustration and the one on the following page are taken from the handbook of the Building Employers Federation 1932

a major increase in housing output was planned by councils with little or no experience in house-building the garden city model was enthusiastically adopted, first through an official report and then through government guidance. In this way the model for working-class housing was completely transformed over a relatively short period of time.

The Tudor-Walters Report was to have an equally significant impact on private house-building which is another 20th century phenomenon. In the 19th century virtually all housing was privately rented. The only exceptions were the upper echelons of the middle classes and the working-class building clubs (which could be seen as precursors of today's self-build co-operatives). This however changed after 1918 and, of the four million or so homes built in the interwar years, around two-thirds were for owner-occupation. There are many reasons for this, the growth of the middle classes, the provision of state subsidy in the 1923 Chamberlain Act, the opening up of cheap land through the construction of suburban railways and roads and the development of building societies to provide mortgages. The building societies which, like the co-operative movement, grew up in northern towns to help the working classes improve their conditions, ended up reinforcing middle-class ideals of the desirable home.

This expansion in owner-occupation took place in the suburbs where the image of the Victorian villa was combined with the practicalities of Tudor-Walters to create the ubiquitous semi which was to come to dominate private housing provision. It is however debatable whether the demand for owner-occupation created the suburb or whether the suburb made owner-occupation possible. Suburbs grew around most British industrial cities as a consequence of commuter railway lines in the latter half of the 19th century and electric tram lines and buses towards the end of the century. This opened up great swathes of cheap land for development. As a result house and land prices fell in relation to average incomes to an all time low in the 1930s[15]. Home ownership therefore became a real option for most of the middle classes and for the upper sections of the working classes. This growth in owner-occupation is perhaps the most influential trend in the 20th century. Whilst professionals and academics have spent their time debating housing, their ideas have been applied almost exclusively to council housing. Meanwhile private developers and their customers have been quietly working to create a much more practical and enduring Utopia in the suburbs. Unconcerned by the scorn of professionals and designers, private housing has evolved slowly in stark contrast to the grand innovations and disasters in the public sector.

Housing since 1945

Since the Second World War housing has been through a rollercoaster of change unprecedented in the previous 150 years. The pendulum swung first to an almost total reliance on the public sector and then to a similar reliance on the private sector. Housing became, for a period, the prime concern of architects, sociologists, academics and politicians before falling out of favour and becoming once again a largely technical and financial issue.

The situation immediately after the last war had many parallels to the aftermath of the First World War. There was, once again, a severe housing shortage due to wartime damage and a commitment, as in 1918, to improve conditions for the returning troops. In this postwar climate the Labour government swept to power and housing was seen as a central plank of the new welfare state. Indeed political parties vied over how many houses they could build. As in 1918 there was also an influential report, the Dudley report of 1944[16], which set the standard for postwar development. The Dudley Report was very much a progression and updating of Tudor-Walters. It further increased internal space standards as well as considering the layout of housing to overcome the monotony which had been seen as a problem of interwar housing. As with Tudor-Walters, the Dudley recommendations were incorporated into government manuals but were soon being undermined by economic pressures.

A further attempt to increase standards came with the Parker Morris Report[17] of 1961 which updated Dudley in line with changing social trends and was, for a time, mandatory for council housing. Since that time the trend has been to move away from prescriptive standards. The RIBA/Institute of Housing, Homes for the Future Group[18] sought to set standards in 1983 but these were purely advisory and were not taken up by government. In 1994 the Joseph Rowntree Foundation inquiry into housing standards[19] concluded that housing standards were no longer politically acceptable and published instead a consumer guide to help residents to exercise choice more effectively. The withdrawal of standards caused the quality of new public and private housing to decline markedly over the last 20 years of the century. This has caused the Housing Corporation to reintroduce mandatory scheme standard for new social housing and English Partnerships have also introduced their Millennium standards which they have made mandatory on land in their control.

However our concern here is not so much with housing standards but with the effect that they have had on the design and layout of housing. Here the crucial issue is the interac-

The future is bright: An artist's impression of a proposed council high-rise block in Sheffield in the 1960s. It captures some of the excitement and idealism that must have attracted the architects and councillors of the time

tion between the costs imposed by compliance with the standards and the finance available to build the housing. In 1918 the Tudor-Walters Report led to a huge increase in the cost of new housing, after the Second World War this could not happen because budgets were capped. It is estimated that Parker Morris's recommendations would have added 8–15% to the cost of a home had budgets not been fixed so that commensurate savings had to be found elsewhere. In order to comply with the recommendations of Dudley and Parker Morris within their budgets, councils opted for standardisation, system-built construction, and higher densities to reduce land costs. The drive to increase internal standards is therefore at least partly to blame for the high-rise development of the 1960s.

However immediately after the war the concern was not so much with urban development as with overspill. Council minutes from Liverpool after the war show that the intention was to build self-contained houses with a minimum of terraces and flats of no more than three storeys[20]. This was possible because the majority of new housing and displacement from slum clearance was to be accommodated in overspill estates like Kirby and later the new town of Skelmersdale. The most influential element of policy in the immediate postwar period was the constellation of new towns which was launched by the 1946 New Towns Act. There were initially twelve new towns with planned populations of 50 000 to accommodate overspill from London. A second round of ten larger Mark Two new towns was launched in the 1960s for populations of up to 250 000, included Milton Keynes, Cumbernauld and Warrington/Runcorn. In many respects these new towns represented the fulfilment of Howard's garden city vision, if in practice they bore little relation to the original concept. They were important because they provided great laboratories for public housing development. They attracted the best designers and planners and provided an opportunity to put into practice many of the concepts propagated by CIAM and others between the wars. Because they had a blank canvas on which to work, the new town planners could implement the ideas of neighbourhood units, pedestrian vehicle separation and open space described in the previous chapter. Through extensive coverage in the professional press they had a far-reaching impact on new housing throughout the country.

However by 1982 only two million people or 4% of the population lived in new towns[21]. The vast majority of population growth was accommodated through suburban expansion and the development of overspill estates. Indeed the vast new town building programme accommodated less than half of the projected growth that is projected in the number of households over the next twenty years.

In the early years after the war overspill development took the pressure off urban areas. However in 1951 the incoming Conservative government enacted a number of measures which radically altered the situation. The new

Municipal ambition: Hyde Park in Sheffield was one of the most striking examples of modernist council housing. It was converted as accommodation for the World Student Games although the Neighbouring Park Hill estate is being renovated both physically and in the eyes of potential occupiers

town programme was halted, save for the completion of those which had already been designated. Budgets were reduced, making it difficult to implement Dudley's recommendation and most importantly the Government Regional Offices which had been responsible for managing overspill were abolished. This, together with the introduction in 1955 of the first green belt, made it increasingly difficult for urban authorities to plan for overspill estates. Many had planned to accommodate growth through the expansion of smaller towns by agreement between urban and rural authorities. However two major inquiries about Manchester's plans to expand Knutsford and Birmingham's plans for Wythall were resolved in favour of the rural authorities. Urban authorities were therefore placed in an increasingly difficult situation. Populations were expanding and household sizes were falling yet the overspill option to deal with these pressures was being closed off to them. The need to accommodate families displaced by the slum clearance programme which was reactivated in 1955 potentially made the problem worse. However it also offered a partial solution since it released land for new development.

So by the late 1950s pressures for higher standards and lower costs, household growth and restrictions on overspill created the conditions where Le Corbusier's ideas seemed to make perfect sense. This was reinforced by higher government subsidies for housing over six storeys so that by 1964, 55% of approved tenders were for the development of flats. At this time around 90 000 slum properties were being cleared each year, mostly to be replaced with high-rise and deck-access council housing. Many developments made use of continental prefabricated systems ill suited to UK site practice or weather. This was the period when architects and planners came to the fore and were given the opportunity to apply the ideas taught in planning and architecture schools to

POSTWAR COUNCIL HOUSING IN LIVERPOOL

1945–1954. The council was committed to building self-contained houses. However in the inner city land was scarce and most new housing was three-storey walk-up blocks on clearance or bomb damage sites. These blocks 'standing forlorn in a sea of tarmac open space' became some of the least popular in the city.

1954–1960. Liverpool councillors visited America to study high-rise housing and were impressed. This combined with government subsidy and architectural fashion unleashed 'municipal megalomania'. The housing committee observed that there was 'no reason why the twenty storey mark should not be passed… as important a step in the construction of domestic dwellings as was the breaking of the sound barrier in flight'.

1960–1973. The era of comprehensive neighbourhood policy in which whole sections of the city were razed for redevelopment not only with high-rise housing but also roads, shops, schools and other facilities. During this period Liverpool was building 2 000 houses a year, most of the worst slums in the city were removed and most of today's problem estates built.

1973–1985. The council resolved not to build above five storeys and embarked on a disastrous programme of high-density low-rise development. Eventually it was decided not to build above two storeys. The final phase of council housing in the city which, due to the politics of the city, continued after council house building elsewhere had ceased, was traditional, low-rise and semi-detached.

Liverpool was left with a legacy of unpopular housing which is difficult to let and expensive to maintain. It had also created a hugely unbalanced housing stock, 86% of properties in the south of the city were flats and large parts of the city became mono-tenure council housing.

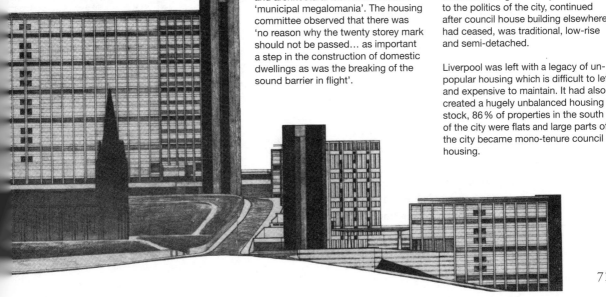

large areas of the city. As Martin Richardson says of the London County Council in the 1960s, 'The whole of the housing division seemed like a giant nursery school whose principal objective was the happiness of the architects'[22]. Architects praised the new megaliths for their exciting contribution to urban form whilst dismissing bland petty suburbia and even suggesting that 'aesthetically pleasing' housing may be difficult to live in. Great problems were seen as requiring great solutions and the bulldozer was king.

The model of walk-up blocks, so common in European towns was largely ignored, perhaps because it was too prosaic or because people were obsessed with technological breakthroughs at a time when Harold Wilson was talking about the 'White heat of technology'. Christopher Booker has summed up the effect of all this on our cities: 'We have seen one of the greatest fantasies of our time burgeon forth from the minds of a few visionaries to make a hell on earth for millions of people ... leaving only what remains of our wrecked, blighted, hideously disfigured cities behind'[23].

The end of high-rise development is normally dated to the 1967 explosion at Rownan Point in London and the ending of additional subsidy for properties over six storeys. However, in practice, the development of deck-access housing continued apace. Much of Hulme in Manchester, including the infamous Crescents, was not completed until the early 1970s. Indeed in Manchester the bulldozer had been particularly effective and the scale of the city's 'achievements' was used to criticise other local authorities.

By the early 1970s the emphasis had changed to low-rise high-density development. This was largely done through standard housetypes so that the main concern of architects became layout. This has been characterised by Bill Hillier[24] as based upon enclosure, repetition and hierarchy to invoke traditional urban courts, squares and greens. Housing would be built in small groups around courts to foster community. In many respects this was the age of social engineering as housing became the

The end of an era: The Byker estate in Newcastle designed by Ralph Erskine in the 1970s. It can be seen both as the last of the great slum clearance schemes which characterised the 1960s and 70s and also the first major example of a more community-based approach to housing development. It was designed from an architect's office based in the heart of the area and involved extensive community consultation. For years it was by far the most successful major council redevelopment, however by the 1990s it had succumbed to many of the same problems

concern of social scientists as much as designers. Oscar Newman's book *Defensible space: People and design in the violent city*[25] published in 1972 was an important influence, as was the idea that the design of housing estates could create close communities. There was still a commitment to pedestrian/vehicle separation and the result was to create a warren of deserted walkways and blind corners. Whilst these estates have received less attention than the earlier high-rise developments the problems, particularly of crime, that they have experienced have been equally severe.

Towards the end of the 1970s it is arguable that council housing departments were starting to get it right. Developments by architects like Darbourne and Dark in London and Ralph Erskine's redevelopment of Byker in Newcastle illustrated the quality of what councils could achieve. They showed that innovation was not incompatible with the creation of successful neighbourhoods. The key to success was often the close involvement of residents in design, something which councils had started to recognise just in time to see their house building programmes curtailed by the incoming Conservative government of 1979.

The private house building industry since 1945 has been almost entirely untouched by the changes in fashion in public housing. In Colquhoun and Fauset's comprehensive review of housing design[26] only one private developer, Span, is deemed worthy of significant mention prior to the 1980s. Span developed innovative private housing in the late 1960s such as New Ash Green – in partnership with the GLC – only to go into liquidation when the GLC failed to take up their allocation. However Span were very much the exception. For most developers there was no need to innovate. Until 1974 mortgages were cheap, building costs were stable and demand outstripped supply. Private developers could therefore sell pretty much anything they were able to build and space standards at the lower end of the market declined markedly[27]. This meant that the differential between private housing and council housing was eroded and eventually reversed so that by the 1970s council housing was generally larger and built to a higher standard than private housing. Private developers therefore sought to differentiate their product and increase its 'kerb appeal' with ornament and suburban frills. Indeed suburban owner-occupation was as much about status as housing requirements. As a participant at a RIBA client focus group on housing[28] stated: 'People are judging a potential new home not on what's inside it, but on what it says about them'. In design terms private housing followed the continuum established between the wars with semi-detached ribbon development and cul-de-sacs at ten houses to the acre.

This period was also marked by an increasing geographical separation between public and private housing. While local authorities may have been forced to build within their administrative boundaries, private developers operated under no such constraints, and in any case urban land was scarce. Private housebuilding therefore took place in the very rural districts which had been so active in opposing council overspill. It is this development that accounts for much of the urban dispersal during the period. There was little or no private housing in the inner city and metropolitan areas increasingly became a monoculture of council housing – at one point 82% of households in Tower Hamlets in London were council tenants. Thus was established the pattern of unpopular high-rise council housing in urban areas and popular low-density private housing in the suburbs and smaller towns. This was partly the result of a desire to escape the city but, as social segregation became more marked, it also became one of the reasons for dispersal. It was no longer just the problems of heavy industry and overcrowding which repelled the suburban emigrants, it was the council estates and poverty which had now come to dominate urban areas.

The history of the last fifty years suggests that this situation is the result of a very specific set of circumstances and by no means inevitable. It is not long ago that urban areas accommodated upmarket housing and there is no reason to believe that they should not do so again.

Private housing since 1980

Alongside the decline in council housing there has been a commensurate increase in home ownership. The private housebuilder has supplanted public authorities as the main provider of new housing despite the two housing market crashs of 1988 and 2008. The private housing sector was pretty stable until the mid 1970s with consistent, but modest rises in values. This came to an end with the slump of 1974 when high interest rates and inflation caused costs to increase while reducing demand. Over the following decade minor recoveries were followed by further slumps. This caused a good deal of self-reflection in the housing industry – as Tom Barron of Christian Salveson stated in 1983: 'The housing industry has at long last accepted that it... must produce the sorts of housing that customers will want to buy and not the sorts of housing it wants to build'[29]. However as the Conservative government's home owning democracy hit its stride and the market accelerated into the boom of the late 1980s, all of this was forgotten. In 1988 the annual rate of housing inflation exceeded 30% and people rushed into home ownership fearing that they would miss the boat if they did not jump. Developers could sell virtually anything they wished to build. With a permissive planning regime, housing estates grew like tumours around Britain's towns and cities – the most notorious of which, Bradley Stoke in Bristol, was soon to become a byword for negative equity being renamed 'Sadly Broke' by its residents. As a result of the boom the percentage of UK owner-occupation rose to 66%[30] by the start of 1988 and personal sector debt, largely devoted to mortgages, rose from 55% of disposable income to 110%[31]. Because of this the housing market and interest rates in particular came to have a major influence on the UK economy. When interest rates rise it reduces disposable income and the economy suffers. This does not happen in other European countries where levels of owner occupation are much lower and is one of the reasons why the UK has found it so difficult to join the Common European Currency.

The housing bubble burst in 1988 when double tax relief on mortgages was abolished and the basic variable mortgage rate started a rise that would take it to 15%. House prices fell by 30% between 1989 and 1992 and the number of transactions fell from 2.1 million to 1.1 million[32]. More than a quarter of a million homes were repossessed and almost a million households fell into negative equity.

The first edition of this book was written in the mid 1990s when the housing market was still in recovery from this crash. The 30% losses in value had been recovered and houseprices had been rising gradually for a few years with even some occasional predictions of a return of the boom years[33]. However the predominant view was summed up by the housing analyst John Wrigglesworth[34] who suggested that 'The typical buyer in the 1990s will be buying for nesting not investing'. The feeling was that with job insecurity, flexible employment patterns and memories of the slump still fresh, people would be more cautious about what they bought and developers more cautious about what they built. We even postulated that we might follow a European model where people buy later and buy for life rather than relying on trading up through the housing ladder citing evidence from Savills Residential Research[35] that the age of the average first-time buyer in the mid 1990s was almost ten years older than their 1980s counterparts. Savills went on to predict that the successful housebuilder of the future would find opportunities in 'unconventional product ranges' which might involve homes for letting and single person households rather than 'bulk estates for mortgage reliant families'. They concluded that 'never before has it been so important to find new markets and break new ground in housing construction'. In this they have been proved right as witnessed by the rise and rise of Urban Splash, the Manchester/Liverpool based developer that

Private sector innovation:
Much of the housing innovation in the 1980s took place in the private sector in areas like London's Docklands

has risen to become a national player by creating flats for young singles.

However as memories of the 1988 crash faded so did the caution of buyers and developers. At the end of the 1990s houseprices once more started to accelerate and 2002 saw price rises which came close to matching those of the late 1980s. In the years that followed there were fluctuations in house price inflation but, despite predictions of doom, the inexorable rise in prices continued until the end of 2007. This was in part due to low interest rates and high levels of employment. However an important reason was scarcity of supply. Low levels of housebuilding (because of planning controls on green field housing) combined with increasing household numbers particularly in the South-east meant that the law of supply and demand prevented prices from falling. The weakness of world stock markets in the early 2000s also meant that investment money was channelled into housing. Many people put their pension money into an apartment that they then let out, leading to a boom in the buy-to-let market in city centres. Indeed housing was such a good investment that many people did not even bother to tenant the flats, relying instead on its rising value to make them money, a trend that became known as 'buy to leave'.

However against this backdrop of rising houseprices a counter trend emerged in Northern England where some housing markets started to collapse. This phenomenon first became apparent at the end of the 1990s. In a study for the Joseph Rowntree Foundation Anne Power documented the abandonment of certain private inner city neighbourhoods in Manchester and Newcastle[36]. What appeared to be happening was that as local authorities became tougher on problem tenants, these

HOUSING MARKET RENEWAL

URBED have been involved in a number of master plans for Housing Market Renewal Areas. One of the first was Werneth in Oldham where a plan (right) was developed with local residents. There was a great deal of pressure to demolish more terraced housing which we and the residents resisted, opting instead to redevelop some of the unpopular council housing in the area. Nevertheless there was a strong local reaction against even this reduced level of demolition and residents staged a number of demonstra-tions to prevent demolition. Much larger demonstrations took place elsewhere culminating in a major victor in the town of Nelson in Lancashire where a consortium of residents and heritage bodies overturned a decision to redevelop a terraced neighbourhood. Following that most of the later Housing Market Renewal plans avoided widespread clearance.

The URBED plan for Werneth (right) is based on the retention of the street pattern of the area with the introduction of new larger homes and more generous open space provision.

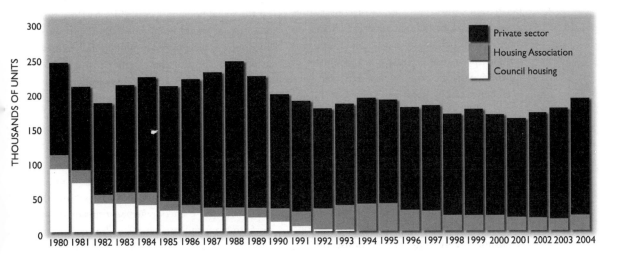

Housing Output:
Housing completions in the UK by sector, Source: *JRF Housing Review 1996/97 updated based on UK government web site 2006*

families were pushed into the private rented sector. Here unscrupulous landlords were only too happy to rent to disruptive families even if they did ransack the house and terrorise the street. The effect of this was to reduce values in the street, allowing landlords to buy up more property to rent out. This process, in just a few months, could turn a successful community in which houses sold for £30 000 or more, into an abandoned, burnt-out shell where houses changed hands in the local pub for less than £1 000. This was happening in many northern cities at a time in the early 2000s when the rest of the housing market was booming.

The UK government acted in 2003, identifying nine Housing Market Renewal 'Pathfinders' to share over £1 billion of funding over 15 years to address their failing housing markets. The nine areas selected had all seen a quarter of house sales in 2003 below £30 000. This however was a blunt measure and the net caught a variety of fish. In addition to the neighbourhoods ravaged by private landlords, there were former mill towns where falling population was causing the abandonment of the least popular stock. In larger cities like Liverpool, Manchester and Sheffield, an oversupply of subsidised private housing had caused certain terraced areas to fall out of favour even though

the overall population of the city had stabilised. In other places with large ethnic populations the problem was not abandonment but overcrowding and the obsolescence of housing due to lack of maintenance. The government's initial impetus had been a return to clearance and the pathfinders were charged with identifying areas for redevelopment. However the variety of Housing Market Renewal areas inevitably meant that a one-size-fits-all approach was never going to work. Extensive redevelopment has taken place in some of the cities, however elsewhere demolition has been thwarted by resident opposition and, in a final ironic twist, by rising house values.

These changes in the workings of the private market had an effect on the design of private housing. Reviews of innovative housing design are now full of private schemes, from the apartment blocks that have spread through the UK's city centres to the Millennium Communities, promoted by the government and delivered by private house builders. Private housing has responded to the issues described in this book, particularly the growth in childless households, and increasingly prefabrication and sustainability issues. However the most important influence on private housing has been government legislation to choke-off the supply of green field housing sites. This together with government design guidance and a good deal of cajoling and persuasion caused even the most conservative developers to look to higher density schemes on infill sites. Much of the private sector's output remains poor, but at least good examples of innovative private housing now exist and have been embraced by buyers.

As we complete this new edition in 2008 the housing market has once again crashed. This was in part due to an old fashioned price bubble, especially with city centre apartments. However the main reason as been the withdrawal of lending from the housing market as a result of the 'Credit Crunch'. In the 12 months to August 2008 housing transactions fell by more than 70 %[37] and the housebuilding industry has virtually shut down. It is too early to judge the effect that this will have on the housing market. Household formation continues apace and some analysts predict that the laws of supply and demand could cause the market to bounce back as credit is switched back on[38]. However confidence has been badly shaken and there are already signs that housebuilders may seek to turn back to 'safer' suburban models in a fragile recovering market.

Social housing since 1980

The period since 1980 has been just as turbulent for the social housing sector. Prior to 1980 the majority of social housing was council with housing associations occupying small niches such as housing for the elderly or those with special needs. After 1980 new council house building effectively stopped dropping to less than 1 000 units a year in the 1980s compared to the hundreds of thousands of council homes built each year in the 1960s. At the same time the existing council stock was eroded as tenants were given the right to buy their homes at discounted values. The losses continued as council's were encouraged to transfer their stock to housing associations. The incoming Labour government in 1996 did nothing to reverse this process. Indeed by introducing a 'Decent Homes Standard' for all social housing they have sealed the fate of many council estates that would be too expensive to improve. Instead these estates, particularly in London are being redeveloped at increased densities. The additional homes are being sold to generate a surplus to pay for the new social housing. Many councils no longer manage any social housing (including the very biggest such as Glasgow)

BLACKBIRD LEYS – OXFORD

Blackbird Leys on the edge of Oxford is typical of the sort of social housing that caused people to question the sustainability of large social housing estates in the early 1990s. The estate is adjacent to a large council estate which was the scene of rioting in the early 1990s. The new estate covers 34 acres and was at the time one of the largest housing association developments in the country with 1 232 social housing units built between 1992 and 1998 in addition to almost 500 private houses.

The scheme was built on open land five miles from Oxford because of the scarcity of housing land within the urban area. However this raised concerns about the number of poor people who were to be housed in an area remote from facilities. As a result a great deal of effort was made by the Council and the developers to ensure that shops, facilities and services were provided.

Approximately £12 million was invested by the Council in infrastructure including a new school, community facilities, play areas, sports facilities and extensive landscaping.

However local shops and employment uses have proved more difficult. It was also difficult in the early phases to provide bus services which had to be subsidised by the council. Therefore while the development of such sites was inevitable in places like Oxford there was great concern that in the early years at least, people would be isolated without access to facilities, employment or transport.

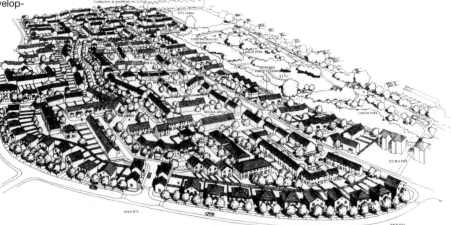

and council housing could soon become a rarity less than 100 years since it became a responsibility of local councils.

Throughout the 1980s and 90s new social housing was built by housing associations at a rate of 20–30 000 units a year. The story of new-build social housing during this period is one of frustration on the part of government that housing associations were ill-suited to this challenge. The largest associations in the 1980s such as North British had less than 30 000 properties – the equivalent of a modest urban council housing department and a quarter the number of homes managed by Glasgow.

In order to encourage housing association new build, their funding mechanism was changed in the 1988 Housing Act. Before that associations had benefited from 95 % grant rates but their rents were controlled to prevent them making a surplus. The 1988 Act transferred development risk to associations, reducing grant rates, removing rent controls, allowing them to borrow money and making them compete for funds. The wind of market forces blew through the social housing world as it had done through many other areas of public life in the 1980s. With all of this in place the amount of money for new housing was doubled to £2 billion by the early 1990s with grant rates falling to just over 50 % allowing a trebling of output.

The response of housing associations was confused – they were delighted at the new freedom and responsibility while being outraged at the cut in grant rates. As Adrian Coles, Director General of the Council for Mortgage Lenders said at the time: 'It is noticeable that each successive reduction in grant rates has been accompanied by dire threats that development will no longer be possible, accompanied by increased competition between housing associations to underbid the new grant rate'[39]. It became a matter of pride for associations to be able to announce that they had developed schemes with as little as 25 % grant[40]. Associations also made great 'strides' in improving value for money by developing partnerships with private developers and ditching their largely architect-designed homes for the

developers' cheapest range of starter units. It was therefore hardly surprising that the government saw the potential for further reductions in grant rates. However by the early 1990s their motivation was not to increase output but to reduce budgets. As a result social housing output fell to its lowest level for 100 years and social housing entered a period of crisis that was to dominate the housing world in the late 1990s. There were two elements to this crisis – the poor quality of new social housing and the social problems on new estates.

The first of these problems was documented by Valerie Karn and Linda Sheridan in research for the Joseph Rowntree Foundation[41]. They concluded that associations were becoming the 'mass providers of poor homes for poor people'. The private developers' standard housetypes being used by associations were designed for under-occupation. A three-bed home consisted of two bedrooms and a box room, the latter included for the sole reason of increasing the prestige and value of the home. It was not expected that anyone would actually live in the third bedroom! Private households would staircase-up to a larger unit via the housing ladder as their housing needs increased. Social tenants had no such option and housing allocation rules meant that the same three-bed home would be let to a family who needed three bedrooms. As a result social housing tenants were being consigned to life squashed into a starter home designed as the first rung on the housing ladder.

The second problem was documented in research by David Page, also for the Joseph Rowntree Foundation[42]. He showed how the lack of new social housing meant that new lettings were prioritised for those in greatest need – often desperate need. In an attempt to meet urgent housing needs, housing associations were filling estates with such concentrations of the poorest tenants that problems were inevitable. Whereas in the general population there was an average of one child to every four adults, in new housing association estates there were often fewer adults than children who were as a result out of control. Combine this with the poor quality and size of the housing, the fact that estates were getting bigger and were often in isolated locations without facilities and there was a recipe for disaster. As a result Page concluded: 'The process of rapid decline of large social housing estates, which some had thought peculiar to council housing, can also apply to the stock of housing associations'. What is more, while council estates had taken years to decline, in some housing association estates decline had taken place in as little as four years.

As with all housing crises, this one passed. Rising houseprices in the early 2000s forced more people to rely on social housing removing some of the stigma. Housing Associations like councils had also learnt to be better managers and were less tolerant of bad behaviour in their tenants. The situation today resembles the position in the 1920s when social housing was for the 'deserving working classes' while the poorest in society were left to the mercy of private landlords. Similarly today, those excluded from social housing have ended up in private rented property where there is little or no management infrastructure to deal with the problems they create.

In the 2000s there remain huge problems with under supply of new social housing. There has been an increase in resources but the emphasis has moved away from housing associations constructing new homes. All but the largest associations have closed down their development department and now rely on private developers to build their new housing. This is secured through the planning system as developers are required to provide a proportion of social housing on all new estates. In the London plan this proportion is 50 % and in many other parts of the south it is 40 %. When grant is not available the cost of this new social housing is borne by the developer becoming essentially a tax on new private housing. The market will not allow the costs to be passed on to buyers so that the effect is to reduce land values and development profits. This is more possible in the buoyant markets of the south than the weaker markets of the north. The effect is therefore to concentrate new social housing in the strongest housing markets.

Towards the 21st century

The history of housing over the last 200 years has seen a progression of problems – mostly poor housing conditions and housing shortages followed by well-intentioned action which often had unforeseen circumstances and led to a further set of problems. At the end of the 20th century innovation in housing had become a dirty word since virtually every housing innovation in the previous 50 years had failed. The response for a time was a return to the private sector housing forms which were seen to have stood the test of time. These harked back to an idealised vision of family life and the golden interwar age of; 'leafy suburbia that apparently, for a great swath of the British middle class, is the ideal home'[43]. The prevalence of advertising images had firmly embedded the suburban ideal in the consciousness and aspirations of the providers and residents of both social and private housing. Inadequate as they may be, the use of suburban housetypes by housing associations, portrays exactly the image that many of their tenants seek. So engrained had the suburban ideal become that it was difficult to imagine any other type of housing dominating the UK market. The fear was that as suburbia come to dominate, the UK would follow a US development model as described in the last chapter.

However the history of housing over the last two centuries shows that these certainties are anything but certain. In the first edition of this book we argued that alternatives to the suburb were necessary if we were going to respond to demographic change and to save our towns and cities, not to mention the planet. We believed that there were forces at work, as described in Part 2 of this book, that could shape a very different type of housing in the 21st century. This is no longer prediction, it has started to happen even if the rate of change is too slow and the prognosis for our towns and cities, even more so for the planet, still uncertain.

THE INFLUENCES

Underlying the sedimentary strata of theory and policy described in Part 1 of this book is a bedrock of influences which has always shaped housing and urban development and is likely to do so in the future. The second part of this book describes these influences and how they are likely to shape the home of the future. These have been characterised as the 'Four Cs': Climate Change, Choice, Community and Cost.

'We continue to build post World War II suburbs as if families were large and only had one bread winner, as if jobs were all downtown, as if land and energy were endless, and as if another lane on the freeway would end traffic congestion'

Peter Calthorpe - The Next American Metropolis: Ecology, community and the American dream, Princeton Architectural Press, 1993

Chapter 5
Climate Change
Environmental pressures on future settlements

The growth in the environmental movement has been one of the most significant influences on government policy and public attitudes in the last three decades. It has developed from a fringe concern of fringe groups into a principle which, whilst not always followed, is at least accepted by a large majority of decision makers. Ever since we ventured into space and were able to look back on the earth it has dawned what a small fragile place it really is. This has continued at an ever-accelerating pace since the first edition of this book was published with the action required to address global warming now widely accepted by government and scientists even if the political will to instigate this action is still sometimes lacking.

Pollution and resources have always been a concern to city dwellers. In the past however these were local concerns about food production, water supply or more recently smog and the disposal of waste. City dwellers of the past were however always able to assume that the capacity of the wider environment – the atmosphere, rivers, land and sea – to absorb pollutants and supply resources was limitless.

The impact of a city on these systems is today known as its Ecological Footprint, a term coined in 1992 by the Canadian ecologist William Rees[1]. It refers to the hypothetical area of land needed to sustain something whether it be a city or an individual. The Ecological footprint of a Medieval City would have covered many hun-

dreds of square miles. Modern cities however are of an entirely different scale. It is estimated that the ecological footprint of London is greater than the entire land area of the UK. It is therefore clear, when you factor in the other 85% of the UK's population, that the UK's ecological footprint is many times its land area. Factor in again the rest of the human race and it estimated that the Earth's ecological footprint covers approximately three planets. These patterns of resource consumption and pollution are heading us towards disaster. The disaster potentially includes, habitat and species loss, acid rain, resource depletion, pollution and over-extraction of drinking water and, overriding everything else, global warming. The real danger is that a combination of these factors triggers a run-away effect in which the ice caps melt causing temperatures and sea levels to rise. If the rain forest were also to be lost, as they might, the build-up of CO_2 in the atmosphere would run out of control potentially making the planet uninhabitable within, if

In tune with the environment: Medieval cities such as Bristol were shaped by the availability of natural resources such as water and were scaled to the needs of travel by foot

principles and lay behind the development of by-law housing as well as the recommendations of the Tudor-Walters committee.

Compared to today's global environmental concerns, these were peripheral issues. To uncover the fundamental trends which have guided development we need to consider the impact of resource consumption. As we have seen, the pre-industrial city was far more compact than today's settlements due largely to the limited availability of resources and the technology with which to exploit and transport them. When the main sources of energy were water and the horse, settlements had to be located on rivers or streams and their scale was determined by distances that people and goods could cover on foot and hoof. With the advent of steam power and canals, locational constraints were not so severe but settlements still had to be sufficiently dense for people to get about on foot and factories had to be multi-storey to allow the efficient use of belt-driven machinery. When workers had no way of commuting other than on foot, it was inevitable that their houses should be tightly huddled around the factories or mills where they laboured.

The dispersal of housing and industry over the last 150 years has been made possible by the harnessing of energy through technology. The development of electricity and gas supplies, the railway system, the trolly car and tram systems and, most important of all, the internal combustion engine, have shaped the way that human settlements have developed in the 20th century. This has largely been unconstrained by the notion that energy is a finite commodity, particularly in the area of transport. The availability of cheap fuel in the first half of the 20th century allowed people to write off energy costs as a locational factor so that settlements were able to disperse.

The same is true of waste; the ability to dispose of human waste and other pollutants has, in the past, been an important constraint on the growth of human settlements. The medieval city was able to use its waste to fertilise the fields outside the city walls but, if cities were to grow,

not our lifetime, then that of our children or grandchildren. There is no greater danger facing humankind and it is now widely accepted that policy should be guided by the 'precautionary principle'. This suggests that the consequences of climate change are so significant that we must act now rather than wait for absolute scientific proof.

The environment and the shape of settlements

It may seem that the influence of the environment on housing and urban development is a relatively recent phenomenon. However, as we saw in Part 1 of this book, certain environmental issues have been a concern of housing reformers for much of the century. Tony Garnier's *Cité Industrielle* in 1917 incorporated careful passive solar design and was self-sufficient in terms of energy through hydroelectric power. His main concern however was the health-giving properties of daylight and fresh air rather than energy efficiency. The same was true for much of the 19th and early 20th centuries when daylight and fresh air were important guiding

more 'sophisticated' means of disposal were required. The city of the Industrial revolution is infamous for its pollution, smogs and the resulting mortality rates of its population . The solution however was not to curtail harmful activities, such is not human nature. Instead technologies were developed to mitigate the environmental effects of growth such as smoke-less fuel, clean electricity and gas, piped water supplies and sewage systems. More importantly for the city, zoning policies were developed to separate the people and their homes from the polluting industry.

It is not the nature of cities to accept external constraints on their growth. There have been cities in history which have disappeared as a result of environmental factors such as drought or pollution but there has never been a city which has averted such disaster by limiting its own growth. Indeed it is doubtful whether the citizens of cities or their governments have the capacity to limit their growth. Jane Jacobs has argued[2] that cities are always 'impractical'. Cities in every age have grown beyond the point where the problems of energy supply, water, food and waste can be easily solved; just as cities today are not practical in terms of car use and congestion. She suggests that this impracticality is part of what makes a city different to other forms of human settlement because it is a spur to technological innovation which in turn drives economic development. London was no more practical in the 17th century as witnessed by the Black Death and the Great Fire than it is today despite being almost a hundredth of the size.

Profligate use of energy has charac-terised much of the 19th and 20th centuries. The first doubts about this came not as a result of the environmental movement but because of the oil crisis of 1974, which led to escalat-ing energy costs and early attempts to reduce energy dependence. The environmental move-ment was able to use this concern to change attitudes through ground-breaking books like Rachel Carson's *A Silent Spring* and *The Limits to Growth* published by the Club of Rome[3]. Since then attitudes have changed and it is no

longer assumed that traditional energy sources and natural resources are infinite, nor indeed the capacity of the environment to deal with the effects of consumption. Growth remains the driving force of world economies and has been synonymous with increased consumption. However environmental considerations can no longer take a back seat and governments in the developed world have been wrestling with the seeming oxymoron of sustainable develop-ment.

Attitudes to resource consumption have been closely linked with the growth of cities in which human activities have become increasingly divorced from nature and natural ecosystems. In modern cities energy is available at the flick of a switch, water is on tap, resources from all over the world can be purchased in supermarkets and waste can be flushed away or left out for collection. The environmental con-sequences of our urban lifestyles are effectively hidden or packaged up and located at a distance. As a result there is little incentive for people in cities to pursue more environmentally-friendly lifestyles because the benefits of this are hidden from them. However as Ulrich Beck in his book *Ecological politics in an age of risk*[4] has argued, this is changing as a result of health scares and climatic disasters. Beck talks about food scares, water quality and air pollution all of which have led to more and more frequent scares in recent years. However the most important events were probably the European heatwave of 2003 that killed 30000 and the 2004/5 hurricane season in the US which culminated in Hurricane Katrina. Such events are uncomfortably close to home compared to droughts in Africa or floods in Bangladesh. They have made the public realise how environmental issues can have a direct effect on them and their families. When we have to ask whether our homes are secure, our food and water are healthy to eat and drink and our air safe to breath, we might increasingly question a system in which these necessities are controlled by distant authorities beyond our control and influence. This, Beck suggests, will increasingly influence public attitudes to the environment.

Cities may no longer belch smoke and pollution as they did in the Industrial revolution. They have however become symbols of our resource-hungry society. They suck in energy and raw materials and spew out waste and pollution in linear systems which are divorced from natural ecosystems. It is partly because of this negative image of cities that many sustainability pioneers have championed an anti-urban back-to-the-land approach to sustainable living. However it was the profligate use of energy and a disregard for environmental consequences that allowed cities to sprawl and it is possible that resource austerity may make this sprawl seem immoral causing a return to more compact settlement forms. Thus transformed the city could come to be seen not as the source of environmental concerns but as a tool to address them. This was certainly the conclusion of the *European Green Paper on the Urban Environment*[5], which postulated a new type of city as the answer to many environmental concerns – the compact, walkable city. In advocating the compact city the European Union referred back to pre-industrial cities such as Siena as a model. The same has happened in the UK and US where models such as the Urban Village[6] and Pedestrian Pocket[7] have been put forward as sustainable settlement forms to promote walking and public transport. Thus the influence of the environment on human settlements could come full circle and the sprawl of the 20th century may come to be seen as a temporary aberration.

The rise of environmental awareness

The growing awareness of environmental issues has resulted in international agreements. One of the first was the United Nations Framework Convention on Climate Change, agreed at the 1992 Rio Summit and the subsequent Kyoto Protocol adopted in 1997. The best definition of sustainable development is still that put forward by the Bruntland Commission[8] – 'Development that meets the needs of the present without compromising the ability of future generations to meet their own needs'. The UK government has summed up the same sentiments using the language of the market: 'Sustainable development means living on the earth's income rather than eroding its capital. It means keeping the consumption of renewable natural resources within the limits of their replenishment. It means handing down to successive generations not only man-made wealth… but also natural wealth, such as clean and adequate water supplies'[9].

Yet defining sustainability is one thing, achieving it is quite another. The fact that agreement was reached in Rio and Kyoto may

A sustainable settlement?
Models like the American Pedestrian Pocket are also based on the needs of travel by foot and public transport

have been remarkable but little or no progress has been made since then. The biggest energy consumer and polluter, the US, did not even sign-up to Kyoto because of concern about the impact on its economy. Policies instead have been driven by crisis management with individual initiatives introduced in response to environmental scares, such as the banning of CFCs in response to the discovery of the hole in the ozone layer. Whilst such individual initiatives can be important (in 2006 scientists suggest that the ozone hole has started to contract), what is needed is a more comprehensive approach to ensure that human activities are more sustainable.

As we write this in 2008 this is starting to happen and a series of responses have emerged. One school of thought is that we must all cut back and accept lower levels of growth. This after all is a small price to pay given the impact on the economy of environmental collapse as set out in the Stern Report[10]. This approach forms the basis for the United Nation's and European Union's[11] thinking with the development of system-orientated approaches that looks at the whole cycle of production, consumption and disposal to systematically reduce resource consumption. A similar concept is BPEO (Best Practical Environmental Option) which suggests that all decisions should be taken to minimise their environmental impact within the constraints at the time of the decision. This approach is an important first step because it provides the tools to assess and reduce environmental impacts. The problem is that as yet no country or company has accepted the goal of lower growth, the market simply does not allow them to do so. The debate has therefore got hung up on the paradox of 'sustainable growth'. Other approaches to sustainable development have therefore concentrated on working with the market to bring about a reduction in resource use. There are a number of ways of doing this; persuading them, compelling them and rewarding them.

The first has been applied with some success in the West at least through environmental campaigns. These have changed the way people consume resources by, for example, flying less, driving more efficient cars, insulating their home. This change in attitudes has in turn persuaded many companies of the importance of their green credentials. Goods labelled as environmentally-friendly sell from supermarket shelves, ethical bank accounts attract new customers and environmental pressure groups attract larger memberships than political parties. A good example is the introduction of a set of ethical and environmental principles by the Co-operative Bank in the UK. This was a sincere attempt by the bank to put environmental and ethical considerations at the heart of its corporate decision making. Yet it was also a very useful marketing tool and helped the bank to establish itself as one of the big players in the UK market. This focus on consumer attitudes certainly does no harm, however it is not clear whether this represents a cultural change in attitudes that will eventually spread to the whole of society. The danger is that it is little more than a public relations necessity for companies and a middle-class fad for concerned consumers who remain a minority in the market.

Consumer action may have its limits but there are other ways in which consumer behaviour can be changed. One is regulation and law making such as the requirement that manufacturers recycle their products, bans placed on environmentally damaging substances or the building regulations for new construction. Laws may not always be popular and there is always the problem of enforcement but at least they do not rely on winning over hearts and minds and so can impact on all of society rather than just the committed few.

Another approach is to work with markets by giving a financial value to environmental impacts. In its simplest form this can be achieved through taxation such as the land fill tax or the reduction in tax on lead-free petrol both of which have had significant impacts in the UK. A good example is the Fossil Fuel Levy on electricity generation. This was introduced in 1989 to make the nuclear industry attractive to private investors. However its real impact was on energy and since 1998 it has been used to transform the market for wind power in the UK. Carbon tax is a similar mechanism, introduced in Sweden as long ago as 1991 and since introduced in Finland, the Netherlands, and Norway. In the UK the nearest equivalent is the Climate Change Levy introduced in 2001 for non-domestic energy use in which companies pay tax on energy use but are able to claim a commensurate reduction on other taxes.

A more sophisticated use of the market involves emissions trading. This involves capping company CO_2 emissions. If they wish to emit more than the cap they must buy carbon credits, however if they reduce their energy use they can also sell their credits. This gives a value to carbon emissions and in theory should allow governments to control emissions through the availability of credits. The initial UK system was introduced in 2002 and the European system at the beginning of 2005. This system is also being explored for nations as part of the implementation of climate change agreements. It is even possible in the future that we will all be given individual carbon budgets that we have to manage by changing our way of life or buying carbon credits from other people.

The market approaches to sustainability give a monetary value to resources. This has the effect of causing people to use/emit less to save money. It also increases the viability of alternative technologies. The technological approach to sustainability is based on a version of Jane Jacobs' 'impossible city' thesis – in other words a crisis will act as a spur to technological innovation. This is happening in many areas including renewable energy which is becoming more efficient and affordable, bio-fuels, hydrogen fuel cells as a replacement for petrol engines and carbon capture and sequestration.

When we produced the first edition of this book many of these agreements and mechanisms were not in place. The world's best hope still seemed to lie in appeals to the consciences of consumers, companies and politicians. This seemed a forlorn hope because those with

consciences susceptible to this type of pressure were probably already convinced and were far from being a majority. Since that time great progress has been made in decision-making as well as market mechanisms and technological innovation. However we are still a very long way from bringing ourselves onto a consumption path which averts future disaster. There is a huge amount to be done and the impact on our towns and cities will be enormous.

The impact of global warming

Of all the issues affecting the environment, by far the most important is global warming caused by the greenhouse effect. The evidence for the impacts of this on society have become overwhelming since the first publication of this book. The ten years to 2004 included nine of the warmest years on record. The European heat wave of 2003 killed more than 30 000 people and in the US, the record hurricane seasons of 2004/5 culminated in the destruction of New Orleans. A NASA study[12] in 2007 found that the Arctic ice sheet had shrunk by 23% in just two years. This could mean that the North Pole may be ice free in Summer within a decade compared to 2070 as current models predict. This raises concerns about the great land-based ice sheet in Greenland. If this were to collapse global sea levels would rise by 5–7m.

The impact has also been seen closer to home in the UK where Spring is arriving earlier and extreme weather conditions and flooding are becoming more common. Climate systems are predicted to move northwards by as much as 200 kilometres so that southern England could acquire the climate of the Loire region in France. The south has become drier and subject to droughts whilst the north has become wetter and prone to flooding[13].

Future predictions become much more extreme. Melting polar ice could cause the Gulf Stream to divert leaving the UK icebound like other countries on the same latitude. The Benfield UCL Hazard Research Centre has shown the impact of rising sea levels. If the Greenland and the West and East Antarctic ice sheets were to melt, global sea levels would rise by 84m leaving England as an archipelago. This may be unlikely but even modest sea level rises will leave large parts of coastal England including London vulnerable to inundation.

For years even much more modest predictions were treated as scare stories. Compelling as the evidence may have been, many people, including decision makers, found it difficult to imagine the loss of large areas of coastal land to rising sea levels, the collapse of agricultural production or the death of the rain forest. This has changed fundamentally. The UN's Inter-Government Panel on Climate Change (IPCC) produced its 4th Assessment Report in 2007[14]. Its conclusion that the evidence for climate change is unequivocal – global temperatures rose by 0.6°C in the 20th century – and that this is 'very likely' (90% certain) due to human activity has been widely accepted even by sceptical governments and finally by the US with the election of President Obama.

The IPCC sets out a number of climate change scenarios which would see global temperature rises of between 1.1 and 6.4°C and sea level rises of between 18 and 59cm by the end of the 21st century. Atmospheric CO_2 levels are currently 380ppm (parts per million) compared to pre-industrial levels of 270ppm. This means that we have the highest level of Atmospheric CO_2 for 650 000 years and much of this increase has taken place in the last twenty years. The tipping point at which global warming runs out of control could be as low 450ppm.

Global warming results from the collection of greenhouse gases in the troposphere which then act like a greenhouse to trap infrared radiation. About 50% of the greenhouse effect is caused by carbon dioxide (CO_2). Other gases such as CFCs and methane are more damaging but are produced in much smaller quantities. In 1990 just under half of UK CO_2 by use came from business with 19% from transport, 22% from housing and the balance from agriculture and public services. Since that time while the government has had some success in reducing

emissions, the domestic share of CO_2 emissions has remained at around 22% while employment emissions have dropped below 40%. Transport emissions have risen to 25% and are projected to account for almost 30% of emissions by 2020[15].

In 1992 the Rio Summit set a global target to reduce CO_2 emissions to 1990 levels by the year 2000[16]. The UK was one of only two Rio signatories to meet this target – the other being Germany. In Kyoto in 1997[17] further targets were agreed for a 5.2% global reduction in CO_2 emissions on 1990 levels over 15 years. The UK's share of this target was a 12.5% reduction in emissions. Developing nations had argued, with some justification, that pegging their emissions at a much lower per-capita level than the established economies of the west would be unfair. The UK for example has 1% of the world's population but produces 2.3% of CO_2 emissions. The protocol therefore sought greater reductions from the developed world, something that caused the US – the world's greatest CO_2 emitter – to refuse to sign the agreement.

The UK had in fact already committed itself to a 20% reduction in CO_2 emissions by

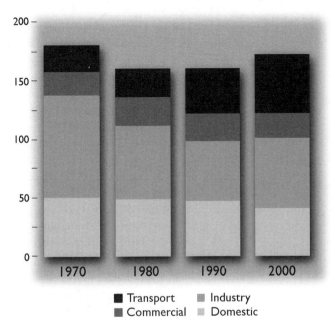

Carbon dioxide emissions by sector: *Source UK government*

2010[18] and had met its Kyoto target by 1999. This however was largely because of the transfer from coal to gas power generation. The UK had also seen a reduction in its manufacturing base as companies relocated factories to cheaper parts of the world, effectively exported our CO_2 emissions. Both of these factors are temporary and in 2003, for example, UK CO_2 emissions rose by 1.4%. The current prediction is that the UK will miss, if not by much, its 20% reduction target by 2010. The agenda has however moved on and the Draft Climate Change Bill published in 2007 proposed binding targets for a 60% reduction in CO_2 emissions by 2050[19]. This is at last getting closer to where we need to be. The 60% target was recommended as long ago as 1996 by the UK government's own scientific panel on global warming[20].

Indeed some commentators suggest that we must go much further. Mayer Hillman of the Policy Studies Institute working with Aubrey Meyer of the Global Commons Institute has promoted the concept of 'Contraction and Convergence'[21]. This is based on equalising per capita CO_2 emissions across the globe, something that would involve a 10% annual reduction in UK emissions every year for 25 years. Hillman suggests that carbon rationing be introduced to enforce this with everyone being given a personal carbon budget covering everything from heating and travel to the carbon emissions of food production. The implications of this level of CO_2 reduction are immense; it would mean the end of air travel and supermarkets. Cars could only be used as a luxury or in an emergency. Indeed any form of mechanised transport would soon leave a hole in your carbon budget so that walking and cycling would become the most common forms of transport. It is difficult to see how cities in their current form could be sustained under such levels of carbon austerity.

A more optimistic view of the implications of these CO_2 targets is set out in a study by the Tyndall Centre for Climate Change for Friends of the Earth[22]. This maps out a route to a future where we reduce our CO_2 emissions by 70% in 30 years, a long way short of Mayer Hillman's target but nevertheless some way ahead of the government's. The first steps by 2010 would see the phasing out of tungsten light bulbs, the introduction of carbon statements on energy bills and an increase in the fuel efficiency of all cars to at least 45 miles per gallon with electric cars becoming more common in towns. By 2030, they suggest, double-decker high-speed trains should have replaced short-haul flights and the total number of cars will have reduced by 10 % leaving town and city centres car free. Many of vehicles will be run on hydrogen or biofuels and the country will have invested in major renewable energy infrastructure such as tidal barrages, wind and wave power. By 2050 hydrogen fuel cells should be producing 25 % of energy much of which will be locally generated. Green industrial hubs will create circular resource systems and petrol stations will have been phased out to be replaced by multi-fuel stations selling hydrogen, electricity and bio fuels

The impact even of this scenario on towns and cities will be profound. One of the implications will be a localisation of energy production. Currently even the most efficient large power stations convert only 30 % of available energy into electricity. Much of the energy is lost as surplus heat, or because the plant must be sized to meet peak demands. Losses are also incurred through the distribution of power over long distances. The solution to sustainable power generation may therefore lie in more local power generation. The Japanese government for example set a target of a million roofs generating photovoltaic power a few years ago as an alternative to building new power plants. In Scandinavia neighbourhood combined heat and power plants are so common that they are no longer deemed worthy of mention in best practice literature. Such solutions are more responsive to demand, avoid distribution losses as well as making it possible to use surplus heat. The experience of continental Europe suggests that we may be on the threshold of major change in the power generation industry. Market intervention by the German government, for example, to reduce the cost of photovoltaic technology is transforming the economics of power generation. Carbon taxes are also being considered by many governments[23] which will increase the costs of fossil fuel generation. It is certain that housing and urban areas in the future will need to be designed for a much less energy-intensive way of life and also to accommodate a range of local power generation technologies. Indeed at the end of 2006 the UK government introduced its Code for Sustainable Homes[24] which will require that all new homes are carbon neutral by 2016.

Other environmental issues

Global warming is a potential extinction issue for the human race: however it is not the only issue that we face.

The Ozone Layer: The other great global environmental issue in recent decades has been the loss of the ozone layer, although this is of less relevance to physical development. Without the ozone layer plants and animal life would be fried by ultra-violet radiation from the Sun. The development of a protective ozone layer has allowed life to develop on earth and without it we would suffer skin cancers, crop failure and massive damage to ecosystems. It was therefore worrying when the British Antarctic Survey identified a 'hole' in the ozone layer over the Antarctic in the 1970s. By the 1990s the hole had grown with another appearing over the Arctic and it was estimated that ozone depletion was running at 8 % per decade in northern latitudes. This was linked to an increase in the incidence of skin cancers and unusual and persistent weather patterns in the winters of 1992 and 1993.

A number of substances are responsible for ozone depletion, the most damaging of which are chlorofluorocarbons (CFCs). These substances are controlled by the 1989 Montreal Protocol, which has been twice updated and sought to phase out these chemicals by 1996. In the short term they are being replaced with less damaging hydro-chlorofluorocarbons (HCFCs) although these too will be phased out by 2030. This will affect household goods such as fridges as well as insulation materials. Recent measurements suggest that this is working and that the ozone hole has started to contract. There are still however concerns about the production of ozone damaging substances in the developing world as well as the disposal of old fridges which contain large reserves of CFCs. Nevertheless this is a heartening illustration that global issues can be addressed by concerted international effort.

Pollution: Another example of this is Acid Rain. In the 1970s 20% of forests and Lakes in Northern England and Scandinavia were damaged by acid rain. Sulphur dioxide emissions from manufacturing and power generation were drifting on the North-westerly winds to fall as rain on forests far to the north. Since 1970 sulphur dioxide emissions in the UK have been reduced by 45% and there is evidence of recovery in many northern forests[25]. This is partly due to industry putting its house in order but is also the result of manufacturing decline. The same cannot be said for China where coal-fired power generation is creating new generations of acid rain damaged forests.

More localised pollution has long been a problem in British cities. As late as the winter of 1953 urban smogs caused 4000 deaths in London, largely as a result of the burning of coal in domestic fires and emissions from industry. The 1953 smogs gave rise to the Clean Air Acts of 1956 and 1968 and the introduction of smokeless fuels meant that smogs became largely a thing of the past. However air pollution remains a problem and domestic heating has been replaced as a cause by transport. Today's pollutants are oxides of nitrogen (NO_x), carbon monoxide, particulates and volatile organic chemicals (VOC). Oxides of nitrogen and VOCs can react with sunlight to create ozone, something which may be of benefit in the upper atmosphere but is damaging to health and plants at ground level. Background ozone levels have doubled in Britain over the last century and we now regularly break World Health Organisation guidelines particularly in hot summers. NO_x is also emerging as a new cause of acid rain as emissions from road transport have risen steadily.

The trend with chemical emissions has therefore been for industry to put its house in order as a result of regulations, but for these gains to be partly cancelled out by the growth in pollution from cars. Here progress has also been made with more efficient engines, catalytic converters and lead-free petrol. Yet while individual cars may be less polluting their numbers and use are growing so that overall pollution continues to increase.

Water and Sewage: Another important issue is water use. In a wet island like Britain it has sometimes been difficult to persuade people that water is a scarce resource. However a number of severe droughts such as the one in 1995 have exploded this perception. In hot summers

reservoirs have run dry and river extraction has caused levels to become dangerously low, endangering wildlife. In the south-east in particular the margin between available rainfall and demand is perilously small and is being eroded by new development. Indeed water companies in the UK have demanded rights of consultation on major planning applications and have predicted that they will be unable to meet the anticipated demand from the projected increase in households in the next twenty years.

Water saving is also important because of the large amounts of energy used in purification and sewage treatment. The quality of water in the UK is very high but having expended so much energy in purification, up to 25% of the water leaks away in the distribution system and once it gets to the home a further third is flushed down the toilet. It then creates problems with disposal and there are coastal areas where sewage is pumped into the sea, something being phased out by European directives. Like power generation the response to these problems has been seen in terms of capital investment and new technology, such as the London ring main. Plans have also been considered to pump water between catchment areas, to develop desalination plants for sea water in the Thames Estuary and to incinerate sewage sludge. All of these will be tremendously expensive both in terms of finance and energy use and yet will do little more than prop up a linear system of resource consumption. A more economic and sustainable option would be to turn this linear system into a circular system by which water is recycled and reused.

Water saving may therefore play an increasing role in future development. The first steps have included the introduction of water metering to give users a financial incentive to save water. Requirements have also been placed on water companies to reduce distribution losses. To go further than this, homes and urban areas in the future will need to be designed to make much more efficient use of water. This might include water collection from roofs, the restoration of grey water (water from sinks and baths) to flush toilets, and composting toilets. At present there are only a few environmental demonstration projects which include such systems. Schemes like Hockerton in Newark and Sherwood include reed beds to recycle water and in Berlin there is even an urban block which purifies waste water through a series of reed tanks down the side of the building. While these may not become a common feature of urban areas, technologies are developing for the local treatment of household sewage. One example is the bioworks developed as part of a regeneration project in Kolding in Denmark (see page 186).

Domestic waste: The UK produces 20 million tonnes of domestic waste a year. In the 1990s only 5% of this was recycled. Since then major progress has been made and the average recycling rate in England is just over 30% of household waste. This however still lags far behind Germany at 57% and Holland at 64%. This represents an enormous waste of energy and natural resources and continues to blight large areas with tipping. Landfill sites also produce methane which contributes to global warming.

In the mid 1990s most UK recycling took place via 'bring sites' and was little more than a middle-class fad. Indeed one piece of

Summary of environmental issues and their impact on urban development

Issue	Impact	Policy context	Implications
Carbon dioxide	Global warming leading to rises in global temperature, a rise in sea levels and extreme weather conditions. There is a danger of a runaway effect that could threaten the future of the planet or at least the human species.	Kyoto targets to reduce global emissions by 6% on 1990 levels by 2008 and European emissions by 8%. The UK government is set to just miss its target of a 20% reduction on 1990 levels by 2010. Current proposals (2006) for a target of 60% reductions by 2050.	30% of CO_2 emissions relate to housing and 23% to transport although the latter is growing rapidly through car-use and air travel. Need to increase energy efficiency and reduce car use
Ozone depletion	A destruction of the ozone layer by up to 8% with an increase in skin cancers and a 15% drop in global food production. In 2006 there are signs of the situation improving.	Montreal Protocol 1989/90/92 and the UK Environmental Protection Act 1990 seeks to phase out CFCs and to reduce HCFCs	The main impact on the building industry has been the phasing out of insulation materials which incorporate CFCs and HCFCs
Rain forest	The destruction of rain forests adding to global warming and reducing natural diversity and a possible source of new drugs	Voluntary industry accreditation systems	The avoidance of tropical hardwoods in buildings such as window frames and plywood
Car use	Has risen in the UK from 219 billion km/year in 1981 to 330 billion km/year in 1990 and just under 400 billion km/yr by 2005.	Government commitment to reducing car use in Sustainable Development – the UK Strategy, PPG 13, reduction in road building, Integrated transport policy.	60% of housing on brown field sites, increased densities, road pricing, limits on out-of-town development, improvements in public transport, restrictive parking policies
Natural resources	The environmental impact of materials in terms of extraction, manufacture, transport, use and disposal	Government policy to ensure sustainable supply through minerals PPGs, alternative sources, more efficient use and recycling	The use of locally sourced materials, timber from managed sources, bricks fired with landfill gas, recycled materials such as PFA
Recycling	Every person in the UK produced 517kg of waste per year up from 397kg/yr in 1984. The recycling rate has increased from 6 – 30% in the decade to 2006. This is wasteful of resources and producing methane contributing to global warming.	EU Directives, National Waste Strategy 2000 and 2007. Landfill Tax Escalator and Landfill Allowance Trading Scheme. Local authority statutory recycling targets.	Domestic and trade waste recycling, segregated collection, local recycling points, segregation of waste within the home
Water	Water use is increasing, leading to droughts and potentially limiting development in the SE. Purification and disposal uses large amounts of energy.	Government regulation of the water companies, targets for the reduction of leakage, domestic water metering.	In an energy-efficient home water bills can be more than all other utility bills. Water capacity may limit development. Greater demand for water saving features.
Ecology	The loss of ecosystems, diversity, and the extinction of species	Government biodiversity Action Plan seeks to protect specific areas and species and increase overall diversity	Protection of habitats limiting green field development. Site ecological surveys, permaculture, planting, gardens, parks, landscape
Acid rain	Acid rain is caused by sulphur dioxide, smoke, and oxides of nitrogen. 20% of UK trees were affected in the 1990s plus northern lakes	Government target of 60% reduction in sulphur dioxide emissions and 30% reduction in nitrous oxide achieved by switching from coal-fired power stations	The main cause of acid rain is now car emissions which will be a further justification for measures to reduce car use

AUTONOMOUS HOUSING

In the 1990s much of the focus on sustainable housing was on autonomous houses such as the house illustrated to the right, designed and lived in by the architects Robert and Brenda Vale. They also designed a scheme hailed as the UK's first genuinely self-sufficient settlement, a group of five autonomous houses at Hockerton in Nottinghamshire. The houses promoted by Nick Martin of the British Earth Sheltering Association produce their own power and water and recycle their waste. The development is partly underground with south-facing sunstores. The plan included 3 000 trees that were planted for shelter, wildlife, and coppicing along with ponds for water supply, sewage treatment and fish farming. A wind turbine provides power and residents farm the surrounding 25 acres for food.

The scheme is on green belt land and despite 'breaking all of the planning rules' was welcomed by the local Newark and Sherwood Council which has since developed the Newark Energy Village on a former colliery site to demonstrate the wider application of these zero carbon principles.

research at the time suggested that the environmental impact of people driving to recycling points outweighed the environmental benefits of the materials recycled. Beyond this recycling was left to the voluntary sector and, where profitable, the private sector. Indeed the major reform of waste collection through compulsory competitive tendering (CCT) that took place in the 1980s had made virtually no provision for segregated waste collection. Instead we switched from dustbins to *wheelie bins* which required equally significant investment in new bins and refuse vehicles. However because the wheelie bins were larger and easier to collect they actually increased the volume of unsegregated waste.

The policy context in the UK has been transformed as a result of EU Directives implemented through National Waste Strategies in 2000 and 2007. Tax incentives have been introduced through the Landfill Tax Escalator and and a Landfill Allowance Trading Scheme creating strong incentives to divert waste from landfill. Local authorities have also been funded to introduce kerbside recycling facilities and waste treatment facilities. These have been combined with statutory recycling targets for every local authority in the country.

When this book was first published segregated collection was confined to a handful of urban areas like Milton Keynes. Since that time it has been introduced in virtually every UK local authority area. There remain however a variety of systems of use, from green box schemes to multiple wheelie bins and communal recycling points.

The impact on development

There are a bewildering range of environmental issues for the would-be environmentally-conscious developer to consider. In the 1990s an increasing number of such developers started to emerge. High profile schemes such as the Hockerton autonomous homes near Newark and later the BedZED scheme in south London attracted huge amounts of attention and column inches. Such schemes drove forward innovation but in doing so they left behind the rest of industry.

Unfortunately most developers and house buyers are not particularly environmentally-conscious. Hard nosed developers were never going to be converted into environmental pioneers by their conscience. Further more whilst the green consumer may have caused toilet roll manufacturers to rethink their product, they have had little impact on house builders. As a survey of house buyers in the 1990s concluded[26]: 'Energy efficiency is said to be important but only when prompted. It is perhaps an aspirational necessity rather than something which will actually influence the decision to purchase'. This has changed little and it is still unclear why people who are concerned about the fuel consumption of their car do not ask the same questions of their home. Why do they care that their washing up liquid is green but not their kitchen?

The problem is that the greenness of housing is not reflected in its value. A few developers such as BioRegional have and successfully marketed green housing at a premium. They remain however the exception and to most developers and buyers the quality of the fitted kitchen is of far greater importance to the value and saleability of a new home. The situation is not much better with social housing. True there have been a number of high profile low-energy housing schemes by developers such as North Sheffield Housing Association and Gwalia in Swansea. However these exceptions disguise the fact that the majority of new social housing is built by private developers and does little more than meet Building Regulations. Energy efficiency is seen as an expensive luxury despite

the benefits to tenants in terms of comfort and running costs.

In as much as the housing industry has started to change it has been because of regulations, fiscal measures and conditions placed on land sales and planning permissions. Part L of UK Building Regulations covers energy use in buildings and the standards required have been increased in 1996, 2000 and 2006. However on many sites developers have had to go beyond this. As government policy has reduced the amount of green field development, developers have found themselves bidding to build on recycled land that is often in public ownership such as hospitals and military sites. Through the bidding process and conditions on the sale of land, government agencies have imposed higher environmental standards and developers have been forced to comply.

One of the vehicles for this has been checklists such as the Building Research Establishment's Environmental Assessment Method,

BedZED – Sutton

Short for the Beddington Zero Energy Development, BedZED was developed in 2003 as a partnership between the the architect Bill Dunster, the BioRegional Development Group and the Peabody Trust on land provided by the London Borough of Sutton at reduced price. The scheme consists of 82 houses, 17 apartments, and just under 1500m² of workspace.

The aim of the scheme was to use only energy from renewable sources generated on site. This was to be achieved partly through energy efficiency with the south-facing blocks profiled to maximise solar gain while workspace is located on the northern side of the blocks. There is extensive use of solar panels and a CHP plant that was to have been fuelled by a gasifier running on council waste (although this has been beset by problems).

The scheme collects rainfall for reuse and appliances were chosen to be water-efficient and use recycled water when possible. The scheme included a 'Living Machine' system of recycling waste water but this also is not currently operating.

The houses are built from sustainable materials sourced from within 35 miles of the site. The scheme also includes a partnership with City Car Club to provide a car-sharing scheme which now includes an electric vehicle.

Monitoring in 2003 found that BedZED had achieved reductions in energy use of 88% for space heating, 57% for hot water, and 25% for electricity (11% of which was produced by solar panels). Water consumption has been reduced by 50% and residents' car mileage by 65%.

and Eco-Homes[27] system. These have provided a useful way of clarifying what is required and what is being achieved. However as with all checklists the focus has sometimes become 'how to I get a good score' rather than 'how do I make the development more sustainable'. Partly in response to this the Code for Sustainable Homes[28] no longer allows developers to play off one issue against another. The intention is to ratchet up performance under this system until all new homes are zero carbon by 2016.

An important development in the UK is the introduction of Energy Performance Certificates as part of a Home Information Pack on all property being sold[29]. The Energy Performance Certificate is similar to the labels that are found on domestic appliances and give the home an energy rating from A to G along with its CO_2 emissions and potential measures to improve its performance. The system applies to all new and second-hand house sales and will for the first time give house buyers information on the energy performance of the home they are thinking of buying. The hope is that this will start to influence housing choices which in turn will give developers an incentive to build high-rated homes. The biggest impact however is likely to be on second-hand homes that are likely to perform poorly compared to new houses. Given that most house sales involve second-hand property it will be interesting to see whether sellers will be forced to improve the efficiency of the house in order to compete in the market. This is something that we recommended in our original 21st Century Homes report for the Joseph Rowntree Foundation in 1995.

The stranglehold of the car

Concentrating on the specification of homes is all well and good but if they are located where they can only be reached by car then superinsulation is something of a false economy. In the late 1990s we predicted that the real environmental villain of the 21st century would be the car not the home. In terms of its impact on towns and cities, the effect of environmental concerns on housing design will be as noth-ing compared to attempts to reduce car use. As well as being the fastest-growing source of CO_2 emissions, road transport is responsible for low-level ozone pollution, acid rain, the use of resources through road building, and carcinogenic particulates.

The situation on road traffic has improved slightly since the 1990s[30]. The total amount of traffic on our roads increased by 84% between 1980 and 2006 (from 277 to 511 billion vehicle kilometres). However most of this growth happened in the 1980s and since 1990 traffic has only increased by just under 25%. Indeed in the year to 2005 car travel actually fell although it has since started growing again. There are many factors affecting traffic growth, the most important being a strong correlation with GDP. The government has been trying to decouple traffic growth from GDP and has had some success as traffic volumes have risen less steeply than national wealth.

This is partly due to spending on roads. More than 9 000 kilometres of new roads were built between 1985 and 1990 in England and Wales and road spending peaked at £6.6 billion in 1991/92 (at today's prices). This had dropped by almost half in 2000 but rose again to £4.4 billion in 2005/06. This reflects the Labour government's attempts to divert spending away from roads and its change of heart when fuel price protests in September 2000 almost brought the nation to a halt. Despite continuing concerns about the price of fuel, the real cost of motoring has not risen in real terms since the 1980s. As a result traffic levels have risen faster than the amount of road space with inevitable consequences for congestion that increased by just over 10% between 2005 and 2007.

Public transport has followed a similar path, declining from 5 billion passenger journeys in 1986 to just 3.8 billion in 1994. This has since recovered to 4.4 billion journeys in 2007 largely because of increased bus usage in London and bus passes for the elderly. This still represents an overall reduction of 12% since 1985. A new element to the mix in this period have been tram and light rail systems.

Controlling the car – Edinburgh

In the 1990s the city of Edinburgh led the way with a series of radical measures to reduce car use. The city aimed to reduce car dependency, congestion and pollution.

Traffic was been rerouted to deter motorists from driving into the centre along with simple measures such as increasing the delay at traffic lights. However the scheme came unstuck when the road-pricing scheme that would have encompassed the whole city was defeated at a referendum in 2005.

The aim had been to create a cordon around the outskirts of the city where motorists would have paid £2. Because the city is relatively compact, and has few entry points with little through traffic it was considered ideal for this scheme but the defeat is a chastening reminder of the difficulty of implementing these schemes.

More successful was the establishment in Edinburgh of one of the UK's first car clubs with a taxi-style booking system to hire communally owned cars parked in reserved spaces. Now run by City Car Club the system has spread to eight cities including Brighton, Bristol and Norwich. In Europe there are now 300 similar schemes, one of the largest being Berlin which has 3000 members of car sharing clubs.

There are now eight systems in the UK including new systems in Croydon, Sheffield, Manchester, Birmingham/Wolverhampton and Nottingham. These systems now account for around 4% of public transport us (179 million passenger journeys).

The last ten years in the UK have therefore seen a partly successful attempt to address road transport. The government accepted the arguments[31] that new roads are as likely to increase car use as to reduce congestion and so make the problem worse. This was picked up by the Labour government which launched its Integrated Transport Policy in 1998[32]. Following the protests over road building schemes in Twyford Down and Newbury in the early 1990s, the strategy was seen as an end to major road building and a change in emphasis to demand reduction. The reality is that the government backed away from this policy in the face of accusations of being anti-car as well as the practical problems of chaos on the railways following rail crashes at Paddington and Hatfield which highlighted the huge under investment in the railway system. Nevertheless the figures show that the policy even in its interrupted rather than integrated form, has had some effect. People in the UK made an average of 1037 trips in 2006 which is actually 4% less than in 1995, even if the total distance that they travelled (7133 miles) rose by 2%[33]. The effect of policy has been to slow the growth trend rather than reverse it. It has also illustrated the political 'difficulty' of the issue.

The other strand to the government's policy, as we will see in subsequent chapters, was to change settlement patterns to reduce the need to travel. Planning Policy[34] sought to concentrate new development in existing settlements to reduce the need to travel and to increase the density of housing so that it was able to support viable public transport. This has had some effect

FREIBURG – GERMANY

Freiburg in Southern Germany has led the way in reducing car-dependency since the 1970s. Its strategy
has included an employment location and density
policy to maintain the traditional urban structure of
the city. A tram network with right of way over cars is
linked to a 'Regio-Ecoticket', a cheap one-far pass
valid on all regional rail, street car and bus routes.
High parking charges and resident-only parking has
been introduced along with a park-and-ride system.
Speed limits throughout the city have been limited
to 30km/hr and roads have been narrowed to reduce
capacity. 400km of cycle routes have been created
along with parking for 700 cycles.

In the late 1980s, while the UK was deregulating
public transport, Freiburg saw public transport use
increase by 30%. Indeed between 1976 and 1989
car-ownership in the city rose by 46% but car use
did not increase at all.

Modal share of trips in Freiburg

	Cars	Public Transport	Bikes
1976	60%	22%	18%
1989	48%	25%	27%
1999	43%	28%	29%
2010	34%	33%	33%

Source: Freiburg City Council publications 2008

Freiburg has also become a model through the 'green' urban extensions of Vauban and Rieselfeld. Because the town is physically
constrained, these new settlements have been carefully designed
to make use of surplus sites. Vauban was designated in 1993 on
former French barracks. It covers 38 hectares and now has a population of 5 000. It is the product of community action having grown
out of opposition to a nuclear power plant. This led the regional
government to ask how energy needs were to be met, which in turn
led to setting up the Vauban Forum in 1994. The municipality is now
committed to zero carbon development on its land.

Rieselfeld (pictured above) started in 1992 with a masterplanning
competition. The population is now 8 000 and planned to grow
to 12 000. The area has been developed in sections along a tram
line, each made up of 6 – 10 blocks so that the style of building is
continually changing while the form is a relatively simple grid. The
sense of place comes from the way 3 – 5 storey buildings are set in
a rich and diverse landscape. The design this space is controlled by
residents who also take on responsibility for maintenance.

but the attachment of people to their cars has proved hard to break. People still sit for hours in traffic jams and car speeds in many towns can be outstripped by a sprightly pedestrian. One of the reasons for this is that mobility is not the only consideration. Public transport use may have increased in recent years but the lack of investment in the 1980s and 90s meant that buses were largely abandoned by the middle classes. Bus deregulation outside London meant that unviable services were cut leaving many dispersed, low-density areas unserved. The development of trams has made a difference by getting people out of their cars but the tram building programme was effectively shelved in 2004 when schemes were abandoned in Leeds and Liverpool and the expansion of existing systems was halted. The existing lines can therefore only serve a small part of their conurbations.

The exception to many of these trends is London where Ken Livingstone as the first mayor between 2000 and 2008 managed to implement a integrated transport policy. This was based on a Congestion Charge introduced in February 2003 that has helped fund improvements in public transport. Today over 85% of people arrive in London at peak hours by public transport. Indeed more Londoners travel to work by public transport than the all the other urban areas of England and Wales combined – 5.9 million passengers a day[35]. Indeed with a third of the country's bus passengers, London is single-handedly responsible for much of the increase in bus use in the UK.

Whether the rest of the UK can follow this lead remains questionable. Edinburgh and Manchester residents voted resoundingly against proposed congestion charging in 2005 and 2008, in Manchester's case despite a promised £3.4 billion investment in public transport. With the deregulation of bus services everywhere outside London it is difficult to see how the London model can be emulated. However it is clear that in the coming century the practicality and social acceptability of driving into town will be greatly reduced. Cities must both respond to this and to the threat that people will abandon town altogether in favour of out-of-town facilities so increasing car use.

It is clear that the first of the 4Cs, climate change, will have a far-reaching effect on future housing and development patterns. This will result partly from public pressure but much more significant will be regulation and financial necessity as governments and markets come to terms with finite resources and the catastrophic effects of climate change.

Chapter 6
Choice Changing household characteristics and the 21st century home

Choice was the mantra of the late 20th century. It was the justification for a raft of legislative change giving the consumer choice in many aspects of their lives, not least housing. It would however be a mistake to assume that policies to increase housing choice did anything of the sort. The only real choice on offer was to move from renting, and in particular the council sector, into owner-occupation. However the choices that we are interested in here relate not to tenure but to design and location. In many respects the late 20th century saw a diminution of choice in these areas. As housing provision became dominated by private builders, so housing design and location was driven by profits from land sales rather than by improving the quality of the product. This meant that the housing stock became increasingly out of step with society's changing needs.

The driving factor in housing provision in the 1980s and early 1990s was market forces. These dictated the location of housing (not in the inner city), its form (avoid flats where possible), its design (detached best, semi-detached good, terraced bad), its layout (cul-de-sacs with large gardens preferred), detailing ('Tudorbethan' trimmings a bonus) and technical specification (clean electric heating!). In other parts of the world such as Scandinavia, North America and Japan a sophisticated house building industry allowed consumers to choose from a catalogue of factory-made high specifica-

tion houses. By contrast in Britain houses were being built in the same chaotic manner as they had been for most of the century. This was possible because the market placed a premium on the sort of traditional suburbia which had come to so dominate the UK in the 20th century.

In the first version of this book we suggested that this was unsustainable and would change radically in the 21st century. This has happened more quickly than we could ever have imagined. In the 1980s only 13% of housing completions were flats. In 2007[1], by contrast, flats and maisonettes made up more than half (51%) of new homes started in England, almost double the combined percentage of semi-detached and detached homes started (28%). This percentage of flats represents a property bubble that as we write in 2008 has burst. The question is whether we have gone too fast too soon in responding to demographic changes in the UK. Whether the boom in apartment construction of recent years is a temporary phenomenon or whether it is, as we predicted in the first edition of this book, the start of a permanent and far-reaching change in the UK housing market and indeed UK society.

Back in the 1990s the preference was still very much for traditional suburbia particularly for people purchasing new houses. A survey in 1995 for the Housebuilder's Federation[2] of 818 households who had recently bought new houses found that 76% rejected the idea of

Town Centre Housing: Such is the ubiquity of city centre apartments that it is difficult to imagine that anyone ever imagined that they could not be developed and no one would want to buy them.

Merchant's City: Glasgow

In Glasgow City Centre over 1 200 housing units were created during the 1980s. Of these 41% involved the conversion of existing buildings, many in Merchant's City. These were made possible by grants which averaged £5 100 per dwelling. The early pilot schemes required grants amounting to 39% of the development costs, plus the value of the buildings gifted by the Council. Later schemes required lower grant levels but it wasn't until the mid 1990s that the first scheme took place without grant. One of the largest early schemes, Ingram Square, involved the renewal of a complete block, including three warehouses, a department store, and a new build block to create 239 dwellings. This was developed in a partnership between the City Council and the Scottish Development Agency each taking a 25% share.

Whitworth Street: Manchester

Between 1986 and 1996 around 2 600 flats were developed along the Whitworth Street corridor in Manchester. Twenty buildings were converted representing investment of over £120 million. The area is characterised by large Victorian commercial buildings, rising to 10 storeys. Two of the developments were undertaken by housing associations for rent, the conversion of India House by Northern Counties Housing Association into 100 flats and a 6-storey new-build scheme by Tung Sing, an association catering for the large local Chinese community. The first residential conversion for sale was Granby House in 1986. This 6-storey, 7 000m² building was converted by Northern Counties Housing Association to 70 flats for sale at a total cost of £1.7 million including a subsidy of £785 000. Even then Northern Counties struggled to raise borrowing for the scheme and had to invest over £400 000 of their own resources. However on completion the flats sold quickly at average prices of £16 000. Within months they appeared on the resale market at double this value. This was a very practical demonstration of the market potential in the city which persuaded other developers, and lenders, to follow the lead.

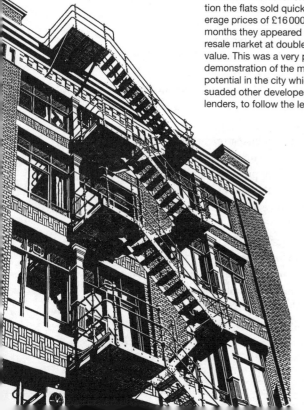

living in urban areas, citing as their reasons hostile environments, traffic, noise, dirt and the poor quality of schools. They were concerned about the 'density' of urban areas, particularly space standards, small gardens and lack of parking, and summed up the attraction of their new home with phrases like: 'it's a nice cul-de-sac, not close to shops or pubs… you're just away from everything'. Indeed these attitudes were most pronounced amongst lower socioeconomic groups and those who had experience of living in urban areas.

The desire to escape into 'your own little world' drove suburban growth for much of the last century. In the 1990s, and one suspects even today if you scratch the surface, many housebuilders believe that this represents the aspirations of the majority of households and that government policy has prevented them from meeting the legitimate aspirations of their customers.

Such attitudes rest on the assumption that the predominant household in the UK is made up of two parents with children, is able-bodied, mobile and in regular employment. This was certainly the view of many of the middle-class housing professionals, estate agents, developers and architects who shaped the housing of the late 20th century. The Housebuilder's Federation survey cited above was of families who had recently bought a brand new home on a suburban housing estate. Even if these people were typical of house buyers (which they were not since nine out of ten house buyers buy 'second-hand' houses) it is hardly surprising that they should express a preference for the sort of housing that they had recently bought. However, more fundamentally, while this group may have been a majority of the UK population in the interwar years they had become a minority by the end of the century.

Another survey at the time that we were preparing the first edition of this book spoke to people who had recently moved into some of the early city centre apartments in Manchester[3] and told a very different story. Of the 170 households surveyed 40% were single people and only five had children. Nearly two-thirds of the households had all of their adults in full-time employment, mostly in professional occupations, and two-thirds of the owner-occupiers were first-time buyers. This of course was as unrepresentative as the Housebuilders Federation survey, but back in the 1990s it represented the start of a city centre apartment market that has become hugely important to the housebuilding industry in the UK in the intervening years.

When the first warehouse in Manchester was converted to housing in 1986 the flats were sold for £16 000, so uncertain were the valuers about the market for this type of housing. When the flats started to change hands for more than £30 000 within a few months it was clear that a market existed and a flood of residential warehouse conversions followed. As in the above survey, the buyers were young professionals without children and 'empty nesters' whose children had left home and who worked in the city centre. At the time they were regarded as a niche market but have grown to dominate the housing market in the centre of most UK cities. Our pridiction that, just as the 19th century home changed in response to the growth of the nuclear family, so the 21st century home would reflect its decline has been realised in less than 10 years.

Changing household composition

It seems reasonable to assume that the design and location of housing should match the characteristics of the households for which it is built – although this can sometimes seem a radical concept in the housing world. As household characteristics change housing should surely also evolve. The trend which has dominated the last two centuries of housing is declining household size and increasing household numbers. As a result the need for new housing has consistently outstripped population growth. In crude terms this can be seen from overcrowding figures which saw a fall from 5 – 11 persons per dwelling in 1861 to an average of 2.97 in 1966[4]. The same trend can be seen with average household size which fell from 4.6 persons in 1901 to 3.1 in 1961 and to just 2.4 in 2000. So, whilst the UK population rose by just over 20% between 1921 and 1961 from 38 to 46 million, household numbers leapt by more than 70% from 8.7 to 14.9 million, an increase of 1.75% per year.

Figures from the Office for National Statistics[5] show this trend is still at work. The nuclear family, made up of a mother and father with children, now makes up just 21% of households, rising to 29% if all households with dependent children are included. Ten per cent of households have grown-up children while

Household composition (Percentages)

	1971	1981	1991	2001	2007
Without Children	49	53	58	61	60
Single households	6	8	11	14	14
Retired	12	14	16	15	15
Couple without children	27	26	28	29	28
Two or more unrelated adults	4	5	3	3	3
With Children	51	47	42	39	40
Couples with children	35	31	25	23	21
Families with grown-up children	12	12	12	9	10
Lone parents	3	5	6	7	7
Multi-family households	1	1	1	1	1
All households (millions)	18.6	20.2	22.4	23.8	24.4

Source: Census, Labour Force Survey, Office for National Statistics

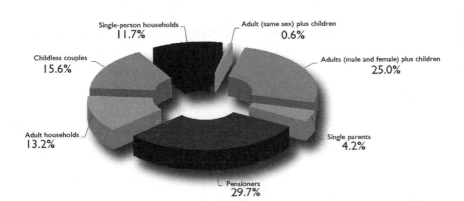

Single-person households
11.7%

Adult (same sex) plus children
0.6%

Childless couples
15.6%

Adults (male and female) plus children
25.0%

Adult households
13.2%

Single parents
4.2%

Pensioners
29.7%

Household Composition:
The diagram to the left dates from our first piece of work on households published in 1995 on the basis of the 1991 census. The table above shows that the trend has continued since then

McCarthy and Stone

The growth of McCarthy and Stone is a good example of the development of new housing forms for emerging demographic groups. The company specialise in the development of blocks of flats near the centre of small towns for people aged over 60. Since 1977 they have built over 45 000.

A typical development is Deans Mill Court 800 yards from the centre of Canterbury. This consists of 43 one and two-bed units with fitted kitchens and bathrooms incorporating mobility features. All flats have telephone entry and 24 hour 'Careline' support from a resident manager. A service charge is made to cover all maintenance and gardening.

The brochure stresses the fact that the scheme is within easy walking distance of shops and facilities such as doctors, dentists and a post office. This means that most schemes are in urban locations which tend to be favoured by elderly households. Whilst privacy and independence are stressed, the schemes create a strong sense of community. A range of communal facilities are provided such as a residents' lounge, a guest suite for visitors and a laundry room. These are however not sheltered housing schemes and the flats in Canterbury went on sale in the 1990s for prices starting from £60 000.

60% are childless including single people, childless couples, retired people and unrelated adults. This trend has continued for many years and yet in the 1990s most new housing continued to be built for families. The reason, it seemed to us, was that most of society's decision makers – developers, investors and politicians – tend to be married with children and fell into the trap of assuming that everyone lived this way (or in the case of politicians, should live this way).

In fact the most important household type is below pensionable age and childless. Of the 45% of households which fall into this category 28% are childless couples, and 14% single people. In the last ten years these groups have fuelled the apartment market (both as buyers and renters). Yet in the 1990s this was still regarded by most of the housing industry as a niche market. It was assumed that most people would buy a family house in anticipation of starting a family and 'settling down'. The reality is that more people have been delaying having a family and enjoying a more affluent lifestyle in their twenties and thirties. During this childless stage of life people are not just families in waiting, saving up and decorating the nursery. It is rather the time when they build up their careers, expand their social horizons and experiment with different lifestyles. Their housing requirements are therefore very different from those of families. While some have been drawn to suburbia, a significant proportion have prioritised activity and vitality over peace and privacy and proximity to facilities and employment opportunities over space and gardens. This is the market which the apartment developers in the big cities have tapped and, as we predicted in the first edition of this book, the demographic figures suggest that it is a far larger market than planners and developers ever believed that it could be. The other great area of household growth is pensioners who make up 30% of all households and are increasingly recognised as an important consumer and political group. Just over 13% of the population were aged over 65 in 1971; this has risen to 16% by 2006 and is projected to reach 21% by 2026.

In the past the reality for many elderly people was that they end up rattling around in the former family home which was only accessible by car. Over the years this became less well-suited to their needs, with the large garden, so good for children, becoming a chore to look after and the peace and quiet, once so welcome, becoming the backdrop to fear and loneliness. Eventually they would become unable to look after themselves and would go into a home. This situation has changed in the last few decades.

People are not only living longer but they are staying healthy and active for longer. This has opened up an entirely new stage of life, what the marketing people call the 'empty nesters'. These are people in their fifties, sixties and well into their seventies whose children have left home and have sufficient income and health to give them a good quality of life. These postwar baby-boomers have been changing the face of Britain throughout their lives and will continue to do so into old age. Many will sell the family home to fund a move to warmer climes, however a significant number have moved into the urban areas. They have become an important element of the demand for urban apartments particularly at the upper end of the market.

As people become older further markets are emerging. The number of people aged over 75 has increased from 2.6 million in 1971 to just over 4.6 million in 2006 and is projected to reach almost 7.5 million by 2026. In the US retirement villages are one of the fastest-growing forms of development. As Andres Duany has pointed out[6], so car-dependent has American society become, that there is a danger of starvation in a suburban housing estate if your car breaks down. Because of this old people have to give up their home when they are no longer able to drive and must spend their life savings to move to a retirement community. Similar trends exist in the UK although the drive is more a search for fellowship rather than the impossibility of living without a car. Developers like McCarthy and Stone have built a very successful business specialising in housing for the elderly. They do not build bungalows or indeed separate retirement communities but rather urban

The Wigan Foyer

Changing demographics have led to new forms of urban housing in the UK. An example of this are foyers which have been developed in many British towns and cities based on a concept imported from France. French foyers are a combination of a youth hostel and a student hall of residence and are targeted at young people. They include a café and are a focus for local social services. In the UK the concept has been developed to include a much greater emphasis on training and employment.

One of the best UK foyers is to be found in Wigan. In the 1990s the council realised that its social housing stock was almost entirely made up of family units. The council resolved to target new housing at groups not served by this stock including the elderly and the young, the latter being served by the foyer. This was to provide short-stay accommodation for 42 young people aged between 16 and 25 along with a communal lounge and a range of resources and facilities to assist them in finding work. The foyer opened in September 1996 as part of a major mixed-use refurbishment of the Coops Building on the edge of the town centre by Grosvenor Housing Association. The building is in three sections: The foyer occupies the left wing, the central section has been converted to 15 000 sq.ft. of managed workspace and the right wing to 11 flats for social letting and 18 for market rent both for single people.

The scheme cost £4.2 million and was financed through a complex cocktail of funding, indicative of the difficulty of developing schemes of this kind. It also requires ongoing revenue support from a variety of sources. Public funding for workspace and housing cannot easily be mixed and schemes like this that blur the boundaries between these uses are difficult to fund. This suggests that funding mechanisms will need to change in recognition of the need for new kinds of housing development.

apartment blocks in smaller towns. Their brochures emphasise not seclusion and privacy but community and access to facilities.

There are other demographic factors which are influencing housing. One is disability, since one in four households will have one of their members disabled in their lifetime[7]. Disability is not therefore a need that can be met with a couple of specially adapted units in the corner of an estate, it relates to all new housing. Since one cannot predict which households will be affected, all housing should be designed with the needs of the disabled in mind. This means that if a household member becomes disabled the home should be sufficiently flexible to prevent the family having to move or have to undertake expensive conversions. The Joseph Rowntree Foundation's Lifetime Homes standards[8] provides practical guidance including level entry to houses and sufficient internal circulation space for wheelchair access. The units do not look any different from normal homes and are lived in by households who are not disabled. Many of these standards have now been incorporated into Part M of the Building Regulations[9].

It is also important to consider ethnic minority households which form a significant proportion of urban populations. 80% of Afro-Caribbean and Bangladeshi and 68% of Indian households are urban dwellers and their household characteristics can differ markedly from the national average. For example 42% of Afro-Caribbean and 67% of Asian households have children compared to a national average of 30%. The Afro-Caribbean population also has a greater proportion of single people and single parents but significantly less pensioners. The Housing Corporation sought to promote ethnic minority housing associations in the early 1990s, both as a means of empowerment and to ensure that housing better reflected the needs of ethnic groups. A good example is Manningham Housing Association in Bradford which has specialised in producing large units for extended Asian families.

The mechanisms of demographic change

The reasons behind household change are varied and complex and have become mixed up with political dogma about traditional family values. The evolution of the large 19th century household to the small 20th century family was driven by two parallel trends. For the middle classes the reduction in household size was not so much a matter of falling birth rates but a reduction in servants and other household members. In the mid 1800s even the lowliest middle-class household – say a bank clerk with an income of £200 per year – would employ a servant, whilst a family with £1 000 per year would have three female servants, a coachman and a footman. Given an average household size of three children plus mother and father this would mean an establishment of ten people[10]. A survey of households in York in 1851 showed that middle-class households were on average one person larger than working-class households and the average middle-class household contained 1.15 servants, 0.42 lodgers, 0.41 relatives and 0.21 resident visitors.

The reduction in the size of middle-class households stems from the gradual loss of these servants and dependants. This was particularly true after the First World War when the returning troops turned their back on domestic service. This is how the ten-person establishment of the 1850s evolved from its rambling gothic villa to the interwar four bedroom detached house with its domestic labour saving appliances.

At the same time the working-class household was also shrinking. In the 1870s 61% of households had more than five live births and 18% had more than ten. However infant mortality was high; in Nottingham, for example, less than 20% of families had more than four surviving children. Initially medical advances would have increased household size by improving infant mortality. However as time went on families had less need to insure against infant deaths with large families so the number of children fell. These trends were reinforced by an increasing availability of contraception.

As housing conditions gradually improved throughout the last century overcrowding was also reduced. Houses which once accommodated a number of families became home to just one. As access to housing became easier extended families found it less necessary to live under the same roof. Unlike middle-class housing, the trend with the working classes was for house size to grow whilst household size decreased.

Household characteristics therefore changed dramatically at the end of the last century as did the housing built to meet their needs. For different reasons both middle-class and working-class households shrunk, heralding the emergence of the nuclear family. As the middle-class home got smaller and the working-class home improved, both evolved into the semi-detached home which came to so dominate the 20th century.

The change from the 20th to the 21st century household is likely to be just as dramatic. As we have seen, the nuclear family which dominated provision in the 1920s has become a minority household type in all but the minds of some traditionalist politicians. This does not however herald the disintegration of family life and all that the traditionalists hold dear. Instead it means that people are spending less of their life in child-rearing. The Victorian family may have had their first child in their early twenties and continued child bearing into their late thirties. This would put them into their dotage before all of their children left home, with perhaps a few years of retirement before their allotted three score years and ten. The modern family by contrast is having a modest brood of children in their thirties and can confidently expect their offspring to have flown the nest, or at least to be living independent lives, by their early fifties. With modern life expectancies they can expect more than thirty years of life ahead of them and for much of this they will be at the height of their earning potential.

Two significant demographic groups have therefore emerged which have transformed the housebuilding industry. In the past people

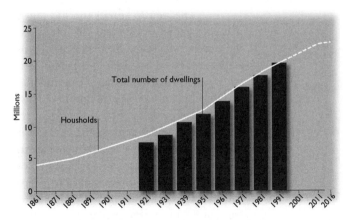

Household growth is nothing new: Historic and projected growth in household numbers compared to the total stock of dwellings. This shows that projected household growth rates are no different from past rates and that housebuilding has actually outstripped household growth
Source: DETR

would have stayed at home until marriage and then fairly quickly started their own family. Today they are living single, or certainly childless lives in their twenties before settling down and having children in their thirties. These 'swinging singles' or 'urban venturers' in the parlance of the marketing industry are an important and growing market with high levels of disposable income. The other group are the parents of these 'swinging singles'. Indeed the number of 'empty nesters' households is growing even more quickly than their absolute numbers because one of the other things that many of them seem to do having got rid of their kids is to divorce each other. Add to this the growing number of single parents and the trend of declining household size and rapidly increasing household numbers becomes even stronger.

Household growth

The big policy headache to emerge from these social trends is household growth and its impact on housebuilding. Government projections[11] in the 1990s predicted a 4.4 million increase in households between 1991 and 2016. This represented a 23% increase from 19.2 million to 23.6 million. Many commentators questioned these figures but in the historical context they were no more dramatic than past household growth. Indeed the most recent household projections[12] from 2006 showed that we had already reached 21.1 million households and the new projections saw this rising to 26.5 million by 2029.

The figures scared the life out of planning authorities up and (mainly) down the country who feared the march of suburbia across precious green belts. But family housing was not what was wanted. Unfortunately the household projections do not break down household growth by the size or age of the household. Instead they project figures for married couples, cohabiting couples, lone parents, multi-person and single-person households. The married couples' category includes people with and without children as well as the elderly. Nevertheless the trend is clear, in the mid 1990s 55% of households were married whereas by 2004 this had fallen to 45% and was predicted to fall to 33% by 2029. This means that while the number of households is increasing the total number of married couples is falling, from 10.5 million in the mid 1990s to 9.5 million today and 8.8 million by 2009.

The recent projections show rises in all other categories including a 65% rise in cohabiting couples but the total numbers remain small (just under 2 million households in 2004). The biggest change however is with single-person households. In the 1990s these were predicted to rise from 3.5 million to 5.1 million households. In 2004 they had in fact already exceeded 6.5 million and were predicted to grow by a further 3.8 million by 2029. We pointed out in the first edition of this book that single-person households made up more than 80% of the net increase in household numbers. This has

happened and yet single-person households are still projected to make up 70% of the new predictions and within a couple of years their numbers will exceed the number of married couples. A large part of this growth will be made up of elderly people. As people live longer, and three-generation households decline, the number of single elderly, particularly elderly women, will increase rapidly. Three in five women over 75 live alone and one in three men.

The average household of the 21st century will therefore be significantly smaller than its 20th century grandparents. But will the 21st century home be smaller? After all working-class housing last century grew whilst household sizes fell. This was the subject of heated debate in the 1990s as certain groups like the Town and County Planning Association feared the debate about household size was being used to roll back a century of improvements in housing standards. Alan Holman[13], for example, argued that there is no evidence to suggest that smaller households would opt for flats rather than houses. He pointed out that elderly widows and widowers tend to remain in their family home and suggested that since most single and divorced people are under 60 and 77% of these live in houses (three-fifths of which have more than three bedrooms) then that is the natural state of things. He was right to suggest that single people were no less affluent than married couples and it was even true in the 1990s that they were buying houses. This however was a self-fulfilling trend. The Housebuilders Federation would argue that figures showing that the majority of housebuilders bought houses meant that houses were what were wanted and more should be built. However in a market where few apartments were being built it was hard to see how they could do otherwise.

Implicit in these arguments was an idea that flat dwellers were second-class citizens and that all right-minded people would opt for a house if they could afford it. England it was suggested was different to the continent where flats (or apartments; a word which has altogether different connotations) have always been per-

The nature of household growth: Projected household growth by household type 2004

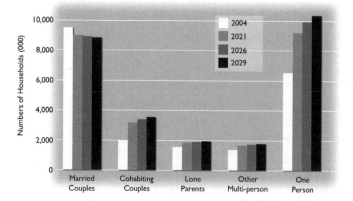

fectly respectable. We argued in response that people should be given a choice. We were not suggesting – as some of our critics accused us of doing – that all childless households should be forced to live in flats. We were simply suggesting that, if given the choice, a proportion, maybe a significant proportion, would. In doing this they would not be sacrificing their living standards to live in a flat as Holman suggests but living in lively urban areas more suited to their needs.

Today these arguments feel as if they come from a different age. As we have said in the last quarter of 2007 the number of new apartments completed in the UK exceeded the number of houses for the first time. Attitudes to apartment living have been transformed and to many twenty-somethings the city centre apartment is now their housing of choice if, that is, they can afford one.

The change in the housing market over the last ten years in the UK has been extraordinary. Traditional housebuilders have transferred their attentions to urban apartments and towns and cities across the country have experienced a huge building boom. Our predictions have been more than fulfilled, but as is so often the case with markets, things have gone too far. There is little doubt that the quality and space standards of many of the apartments built in recent years give the Town and Country Planning Association cause to say 'we told you so'. A significant part of the market has also involved buy-to-let sales. People have found property a better return than other forms of investment and have bought apartments off plan to rent out. At one level this has been healthy as young people have for the first time had access to rental apartments in town centres. However the buy-to-let market had reduced incentives for developers to maintain build-standards and in some cases 'buy-to-leave' investors have found it easier not to let the property but just to ride escalating property prices.

As we write in 2008 this investment boom has popped. This may have been triggered by the 'Credit Crunch' but it was a bust waiting to happen due to oversupply in certain areas and the poor quality of some of the produce. The question for us is whether this crash is a blip in a trend that has seen a transformation of the housing market (as we predicted in the first edition of this book), or whether it will undermine confidence in the market causing it to return to its old 20th century ways. It is too early to say, however the fundamentals of household growth and the dominance of single person households remain the same. An oversupply of apartments in certain city centres also does not change the fact that nationally there is still an under-supply of new homes.

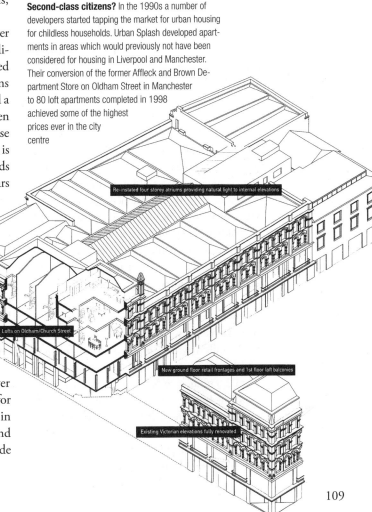

Second-class citizens? In the 1990s a number of developers started tapping the market for urban housing for childless households. Urban Splash developed apartments in areas which would previously not have been considered for housing in Liverpool and Manchester. Their conversion of the former Affleck and Brown Department Store on Oldham Street in Manchester to 80 loft apartments completed in 1998 achieved some of the highest prices ever in the city centre

Re-instated four storey atriums providing natural light to internal elevations

Duplex and triplex Lofts on Oldham/Church Street

New ground floor retail frontages and 1st floor loft balconies

Existing Victorian elevations fully renovated

Changing social and economic trends

As important as demographic change is the influence that social and employment trends will have on future housing. These include the increasing number of women in the workforce, increased leisure time and changes in employment patterns. Just as suburbia developed in response to the nuclear family so it also responded to a particular way of life and set of economic circumstances. As we have seen in previous chapters, suburbia developed with the expansion of the middle classes and the desire to separate the home and work environments. It was based on stable employment to pay the mortgage and an assumption that the family would be a self-sufficient unit with the wife managing the home and the husband bringing in the money.

These assumptions are increasingly open to question. Women are making up an increasing proportion of the workforce, partly because they are having children later in life. In 2000 there were a record 12.5 million women in the UK workforce. This had risen by 843 000 since 1990, while the number of men in the workforce was only 33 000 higher[14]. A report by the Henley Centre for Economic Forecasting[15] highlighted some of the potential effects of this growth in female employment. They suggest that women are less willing to tolerate a long commute to work or other facilities, particularly if they have to juggle working life with the needs of children. They may therefore be attracted to urban areas but are likely to be very choosy and are only likely to be attracted to urban areas capable of providing a high quality of life.

The nature of employment is also changing. Since 1978 manufacturing employment has fallen from just under 7 million people to 3 million while employment in financial and business services has more than doubled from 2.6 million to 5.5 million and the public sector including education and health has put on 2 million jobs[16]. It has been predicted for many years that this change in employment patterns and the advent of new technology would increase leisure time. This certainly happened for the first part of the last century at the beginning of which people worked more than 50 hours a week on average[17]. The working week fell to around 35 hours by the end of the 1970s due to higher productivity. This however came to an end in the 1980s as a result of a shift in employment towards occupations where long hours were expected such as self-employment and managerial and professional jobs. In the early 1990s UK males worked an average of 43.3 hours a week, longer than any other group in Europe. However since then the trend has reversed again and in April 2006, full-time workers averaged 39.5 hours a week. This is partly because of European Working Time Directive. It is also likely to be because the employment market has been more competitive and people have been seeking a more positive work – life balance. It is nevertheless the case that those with the money to enjoy leisure time are probably the ones with least time, while those with time on their hands do not have the resources to enjoy it.

The distribution of wealth in society has also changed since we first produced this book in the 1990s. Then we quoted Will Hutton's analysis of the 40:30:30 society[18] which was the legacy of Thatcherism. Forty per cent of people were in secure employment, working long hours and being well rewarded, 30% were struggling in poorly paid and insecure work while 30% were excluded due to unemployment or incapacity. The biggest change in this equation has been the middle slice. In a strong economy these people have become more secure and better paid and their numbers have been swelled by people pulling themselves up from the bottom 30%. However those left at the bottom of society have been cut adrift as the disparities between the richest and poorest in society have actually grown. Currently more than 44% of young people go to university and the government's target is that this should be 50% by 2010. In broad terms the size of the middle class is growing and the working class is being replaced by the workless class which makes up a small but increasingly impoverished section of society.

The impact on cities

The impact of all this on housing and cities is difficult to predict. In some respect the increase of the middle classes, the availability of mortgages and the strong household growth is similar to the conditions that led to the growth of interwar suburbia. However it is not clear whether the new educated middle class will make the same choices as their equivalents in the 1920s. As we have said they are less likely to have children and more likely to work with their minds rather than their hands. Couples are likely to both be going out to work and may even be working in different towns. Working hours may have fallen but they are still some of the highest in Europe and we may increasingly question spending the most valuable hours of the day travelling to and from work by car. One response to this is home working. There are around 3.75 million self-employed people in

the UK[14] which is about 13% of the workforce. There are also 2.3 million people who tele-work from home, a figure that has doubled since 1997. This has not however had the predicted impact on the design of housing. There was a great deal of interest in live/work accommodation on the 1990s and flexible housing forms that allowed for home working. However all that is really required for most home workers is a desk and a high speed Internet connection so that a spare bedroom or even the dining room table will serve perfectly well.

A more significant impact of information technology and flexible working is on the location of new housing. Richard Florida has explored the locational implications of these trends in his book Who's Your City?[19]. In this he argues that people make three really important decisions in their life; their job, their partner and

Live/work housing

While people argued over the viability and desirability of mixed-use development in the 1990s a few intrepid developers took the concept one step further by mixing uses within units. Live/work units, sometimes called atelier units, are places designed both for living and working behind the same front door.

This is similar to the traditional corner shop although new live/work units owed more to the original New York loft which was a place where people, often artists, both lived and worked. While most UK loft developments had not been designed for working, there was a growth, in London in particular, of live/work loft conversions. Indeed so common did these become in Hackney that the council adopted supplementary planning guidance on the issue. Live/work units were generally found in converted warehousing fitted out to shell standard

and available both to rent or buy. The impetus behind their development was not so much a demand to work from home but local planning policy which prevented residential development in designated employment areas. The cheap buildings in these areas were attractive to housing developers yet they could only get planning permission for live/work units. This meant in theory that everyone was happy, the developers got a residential development and the council could claim to have attracted employment into the area. Whether people did actually work from the unit remained a moot point.

A handful of live/work schemes took this idea a step forward to create a new form of development. The aim was to combine housing with economic regeneration. Schemes were planned in Liverpool, Birmingham, Bolton and London. The best known example was the Westferry scheme (below) developed by the Peabody Trust near Canary Wharf. This is part

of a wider development by Peabody and is aimed at promoting local economic development, particularly in the cultural industries. The courtyard scheme includes nine business units on the ground floor below twenty-seven live/work units on the three upper floors. The live/work units have a floor area of 80m². They have heating, a shower and a basic kitchen but were otherwise left to be fitted out by incoming tenants. They were let on standard business leases on the basis that 60% of the floor area would be used for business and 40% for living.

A common thread to these schemes is that they are targeted at artists and other individuals working in creative industries who are the main market for this type of development. They are often young and unable to afford separate premises to live and work. They work irregular hours and some activities, such as the firing of pottery, require constant attention. As a result many artists work from home and find the bespoke live/work unit more appropriate than the restrictions of the spare bedroom or the kitchen table. These live/work schemes are a good example of innovation in urban development as demographic and economic change creates demand for new types of unit. A comparison with the range of cars now available may suggest that there are other niches to fill.

where they live. Yet, while huge amounts of work have been done on industrial location, there is very little on the locational decisions of people. This is important because urban economies have become dependent on the 'creative class' and the future of these economies will be determined by where these people choose to live. In the US the creative class makes up 30% of the population but account for 50% of wages. These people are attracted to places with a high quality of life and a good environment (traditional suburban characteristics). However they are also attracted to places with 'energy' where they have access to cultural facilities, sports, stimulating employment opportunities and good quality facilities. It is for these reasons that they are often attracted to cities. However they are not just attracted to any city. In the US they are found in places like New York and San Francisco and in the UK in London. The ability of provincial cities in the UK to attract these people will, in large part, dictate their future.

In the 1990s it was predicted that technology would make it possible for creative people to live wherever they wanted – and that, it was suggested, was unlikely to be in cities. However to quote a Google employee introducing a lecture by Richard Florida[20] 'technology makes the world seem boundless and flat, but it isn't that flat, where we live matters'. Indeed Florida suggests that where you live is the most important decision of your life. Part of this is specialisation – you are not going to get very far in film unless you are in Los Angeles. In Britain the same is true of London and financial services as well as many areas of the arts. However it is also because of the wider benefits of urban living. If you want to get on, if you want to make contacts, exploit opportunities and enjoy a full cultural life, you aren't going to get very far in a leafy suburb or a sleepy village, however good your Internet connection. These may be options for people who have already established their career and reputation but its no good on the way up – that is when you need to be in a big city. This has obvious implications for the growth in twenty-something households described earlier in this chapter.

This trend has been reinforced as large employers have increasingly out-sourced activities. Organisations like the BBC, which once carried large workforces, now contract out much of their work often to former employees. These self-employed workers and small businesses rely on networks of contacts to get business and to stay in touch with developments. Whereas a middle manager in a large company could afford to relax in the suburbs this new economy needs cities where there is a market for work and a critical mass of similar businesses.

The effect of information technology on cities could be seen as far back as 1996 when Graham and Marvin[21] charted Internet use in the US. They pointed out that the top fifteen metropolitan core regions accounted for just 4.3% of the national population but for 20% of Internet use. They argued that more, not less, face-to-face contact was required to interpret and harness the huge amount of information on global networks and to respond to increasingly volatile international markets. More than anything else, the commodity that cities deal in is information. Therefore cities are not only being strengthened by the Internet, they are driving its growth. It is in cities that high bandwidth infrastructure is available reinforcing the urban dominance of information technology. Far from leading to the death of the city, information technology has heralded its resurgence.

In this chapter we have reviewed the demographic and social trends which will shape future housing and settlements. These are no less potent than the trends which transformed the city a hundred years ago. Since we first published this book in the late 1990s the impact of these trends has been greater than even we imagined. The UK may still be a suburban society but there is a sense that a corner has been turned. Many UK city centres are thriving and urban populations have started rising for the first time in a century. It is too early to say whether this change is as profound and long-lasting as was the birth of suburbia at the start of the 20th century. However the demographic and social trends described in this chapter give every indication that it could be.

HALL · MARKET

The information city:
London is booming as
global markets and
information technology
increase the need for
the face-to-face
contact that only large
cities can offer

113

Chapter 7
Community Social sustainability in the suburb and city

In the last chapter we looked at how people live together as households. In this chapter we cast the net wider to look at how households live together as communities. The word 'community', like 'choice', is a word which has been devalued by overuse. Because community is generally seen as a good thing the word has become a euphemism to disguise unpopular policies, from care in the community to the community charge. In other contexts the word has become little more than a collective noun for human beings as in the black community or the gay community.

Yet when we talk about community in a geographical sense we still have a fairly clear idea of what we mean. Be it the rough-edged urban communities of Coronation Street or Eastenders or the rural fraternity of the Archers in Ambridge, community implies a sense of belonging and pride, a common bond and shared identity, the willingness to help neighbours and support them in times of need, and perhaps also a suspicion of outsiders. Indeed the community is probably the most basic form of human organisation dating back to the earliest hunting groups.

Community is motherhood and apple pie. No one would suggest that it is a bad thing. This is not, of course, to say that everyone wants to live in a community. To miss-quote Oscar Wilde; 'a community may be a fine institution but who wants to live in an institution?'

Indeed, as we have seen, urban trends over the last hundred or so years have been driven not by the desire of people to live in communities but by a desire for separation. People, while paying lip service to the idea of community, have sought, through the location and design of their home, to reduce contact with others. The basic building block of society in the 20th century became not the local community but the nuclear family. A gap therefore opened up between our idealised notions of community and how we actually chose to live our lives. It is this tension which has shaped our housing and the way that our towns and cities are organised.

However for many people the sustenance offered by the family is no longer enough. As we saw in the last chapter, the family is much less common than it once was and will become even less so in the future. As family members disperse in search of education, employment or a partner, they may find more need of community as an antidote to loneliness. The single person and elderly households of the 21st century may well place more value on community life than did the self-contained nuclear family of the 20th century. The self-employed home worker, the unemployed and retired – deprived of their workplace community – may look to their home environment for support and social contact. In short it is possible that the concept of community will be a potent influence on the 21st century home. It is therefore important that we understand the nature of communities.

The value of community

The existence of a strong community can be the difference between successful and declining urban areas. Which comes first is less clear. Does the existence of a strong community create a successful place, or are communities only able to develop once an area has become successful? Certainly many of the urban areas with severe problems lack a sense of community. Yet estates with a fierce community spirit and pride are not immune to problems whilst other areas without any obvious sense of community do perfectly well.

By all accounts the back-to-backs and courts of the Victorian city fostered strong communities but they are hardly a model for the future. Indeed there is an element in the character of communities which thrives on adversity. This might be a feeling of being 'in this together' or uniting against a common enemy. It is certainly common for tenants' associations to thrive when an area is being ignored only to wither on the vine when their demands are accepted and improvements to the area have been completed.

It does however seem that the existence of a sense of community can help an area to avoid problems and can lessen their impact when they do occur. The reason for this is that a community gives people a reason to care as well as a sense of pride and belonging. This may be one reason why the middle classes seem to have less need of community. In affluent areas people have a keen sense of the value of their property and a strong financial incentive to discourage antisocial behaviour which might affect this value. In social rented housing this does not exist and needs to be replaced with other reasons to care. In the past this may have been a sense of affinity or respect for the council landlord and today it can be provided through structures like co-operatives or estate management boards. However the most effective means of engendering pride is the existence of a strong community.

This works in a number of ways. Communities share a common sense of identity and pride. They also provide a structure to allow peer pressure to control antisocial behaviour and encourage an understanding that community members will support each other. In a strong community people will be more inclined to keep their property in a reasonable state, to pick up litter or at least not to drop it. They are more likely to make the area their long-term home so creating a stable population. They will support their neighbours in small ways such as holding a spare set of keys or feeding the cat. These may be small things but they are the mortar which binds together urban areas and can make the difference between success and failure.

These elements of community are fundamental to many aspects of urban life, not least to the control of crime and social order. In the past a community member challenging antisocial behaviour could do so in the knowledge that they would be backed up by other members of the community. In today's more violent urban environment this may be over-idealistic and we all know of press stories of people accosted or worse for challenging a gang of youths. It is nevertheless still true that perpetrators of antisocial behaviour are likely to feel more vulnerable to challenge in a strong community which is a deterrent in itself. Indeed this is the basis for much of the thinking about 'secure by design' approaches to address crime. Whilst a great deal of attention has been given to surveillance cameras and security guards, the majority of secure by design work depends on surveillance by residents. There is much talk of windows being eyes onto the streets. This however is of no value if the people behind those windows feel no connection with their neighbours and have no incentive to intervene.

To landlords – be they social landlords or the new breed of buy-to-let landlords – communities can also bring very real financial benefits. They make areas easier to manage and mean that problems which would once have been reported to the landlord are dealt with locally. David Page's ground-breaking report for the Joseph Rowntree Foundation in 1993 was called *Building for Communities*[1]. In this he painted a disturbing picture of the problems arising on the housing association estates being build in the early 1990s where communities had not taken root. The reason, Page argued, was that developers were focusing on the cost efficiency of building houses rather than the long-term task of building communities. Indeed the social housing developers of the 1990s seemed to believe that making the area look like a middle-class suburb would avoid the problems of social housing estates. Since this book was first published this has been taken one step further as the majority of social housing is actually now built by private developers as a planning obligation. It remains to be seen whether creating social housing enclaves in the least attractive corner of private development sites is any more conducive to the creation of sustainable communities than were the cheap imitation private estates built for social housing tenants in the 1990s.

Communities are good for you

Recognising the value of community is one thing, understanding how communities work is quite another. Yet without this understanding attempts to create communities can go hopelessly wrong. This is where the paternalism of public authorities has devalued the concept of community and where academic and professional debate has been dominated by some very muddled thinking.

Why does no one agonise about the need to build middle-class communities? Is it that middle-class communities are so strong that they do not need professional help or that middle-class areas do not need strong

---

Suburban or urban communities?

The debate about what sort of communities we should be creating in urban areas has dominated discussions between professionals and local residents as illustrated by the examples of Hallwood Park in Runcorn and, on the following page, the Divis Flats in Belfast and St. Wilfred's in Hulme.

Hallwood Park: Runcorn

The Southgate Estate in Runcorn is familiar to anyone who studied housing and planning in the 1970s and 80s. Designed by James Stirling, it attracted tremendous attention with its external servicing, multicoloured cladding and round windows. The scheme, which included 1100 deck-access flats and 255 three-storey town houses, was a development of the system-built schemes of earlier decades. Yet even as students were being shown around, it was clear that it was not working and residents were campaigning for demolition.

The task of redevelopment fell to Merseyside Improved Homes who developed a scheme of 226 three and four-bedroom homes plus 16 one-

bedroom units and renamed the area Hallwood Park. This was the first part of a two-phase development which was planned to maintain the community by allowing people to stay on the estate. The new development was subject to extensive consultation. Having lived in an architect's vision the community wanted something much more traditional and low density. The resulting scheme is characterised by

traditional semi-detached homes (14 different styles) on cul-de-sacs with front and back gardens.

The new Hallwood Park has certainly fared better than the old Southgate. The developer is proud that they were able to give the community exactly what they wanted, which was to feel like owner-occupiers. This Hallwood Park achieves very effectively.

communities to ensure their success? The debate about community in the 20th century was almost entirely focused on social housing. The reason was that communities came to be seen as 'good for you' rather than just good. There is just a short step from this to the philosophy that 'our idea of community is good for you'.

Inevitably many of the professionals and academics who have debated the value of community over this period have done so while living in the suburbs. In the suburbs what people tend to mean by community is the rich network of voluntary groups such as churches and amateur dramatic societies which thrive in such areas. People may only be on nodding terms with their neighbours but they play an active part in networks of people who share similar interests and values often over quite a wide geographical area. At the same time behaviour is controlled by a milieu of social pressures which ensures that lawns are trimmed and disturbance is minimised.

This is not however the sort of community which has exercised academics and professionals concerned with the inner city and social housing development. Their idea of community has not been the social networks and interest groups that characterise suburban areas but rather a vague notion of conversations over the garden fence, corner shops and being able to leave your front door open while children play on the street. This lies at the heart of the confusion over what we mean by community. We have been seeking to promote a vague and idealised notion of urban community yet we have judged such communities by suburban standards so that we have failed to recognise and value them even where they do exist.

Divis Flats: Belfast

The 800 unit Divis Flats estate was one of the most notorious in Belfast and was redeveloped by the Northern Ireland Housing Executive in the 1990s. As part of this extensive consultation and participation work took place with tenants organised by the Town and County Planning Association. While residents wanted individual homes they opted for a layout of traditional streets and for relatively high densities. This however was not accepted by the authorities and subsequent revisions to the master plan saw the number of units reduced from 562 to 366 and eventually to 244 units developed in a suburban layout based on cul-de-sacs.

St. Wilfred's: Hulme

As part of the development of Hulme in Manchester, North British Housing Association undertook the redevelopment of a system-built estate. The scheme of 215 houses and flats was developed in a close partnership with the local community. The initial scheme involved three cul-de-sacs with a mixture of semi-detached and terraced housing at medium densities. The tenants welcomed the scheme but it was not accepted by the Council who were seeking to promote Hulme as an urban neighbourhood (see Chapter 13). A series of intensive workshops were undertaken by the Hulme Community Architecture Project to look again at the designs for the scheme. This started by going back to memories that people had of the area prior to the original redevelopment in the 1960s. Many of the older residents remembered the terraces and started to develop ideas based on urban rather than suburban ideas of community. As a result they threw out the initial scheme and redesigned the scheme based on a grid of streets with terraced housing and flats. The area remains one of the most successful parts of the Hulme redevelopment.

This is perhaps best illustrated by a personal example from Manchester. I (DR) remember walking around the terraced streets of the Great Western Street area of Moss Side with a group of fellow council officers in the mid 1980s. It was a warm day that could have come from the memoirs of those elderly residents who moan that things were so much better in the old days. Front doors were left open, children were playing in the street, people were chatting on doorsteps, a couple of men were fixing a car propped up on bricks and one particularly blasé dog was snoozing in the middle of the street. The perfect picture of an urban community, one might think. However this was not what my fellow council officers were seeing. What they noticed was the loud music coming from the open doors and the group of youths on the corner who might have been drug dealers. The children playing amongst the parked cars were in mortal danger (not to mention the dog) and were symptomatic of the area's lack of play facilities. The car mechanics were an unauthorised use on the public highway. They noticed the overturned bin, the broken glass, the graffiti and could no doubt have found a syringe or two if they had looked hard enough in the back alleys. In short, what they saw was not a tightknit urban community but a stressed inner city district in need of their help.

This is the way that many professionals view urban communities – through suburban eyes. Most of my fellow council officers commuted in from the leafy suburbs of south Manchester and had a very different idea of community from the people of Moss Side. This is not to say that either idea of community is right or wrong or to suggest that Moss Side's community was perfect. It does however illustrate some of the confusion that muddles the debate about community. The community in many of the older parts of Moss Side has many of the characteristics that professionals and academics have been promoting for years yet when confronted with such a community, warts and all, in a deprived inner city area they either do not recognise it or do not like what they see. Instead they start judging urban areas by suburban standards. This is when attempts to build or engineer communities can go badly wrong.

The ideal urban community? One of our consultation techniques it to get residents to pick out pictures of neighbourhoods where they would like to live. The most popular, by some way is the Moravian Settlement in Ashton built in 1779

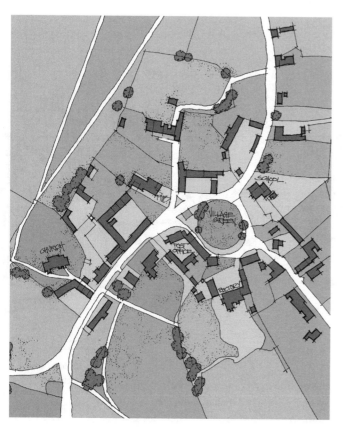

Different types of community

There are different types of community in suburban and urban areas, something which is rarely discussed except by sociologists[2]. To listen to planners and politicians one could be forgiven for thinking that community is a homogeneous concept and local differences are aberrations. This probably means that different groups have spent years talking the language of community and meaning entirely different things. It is therefore important to explore in more detail different ideas of community. The attachment of people to these very different ideas is one of the forces which shapes human settlements.

The first community ideal, which many people think of when visualising a community, is the close-knit village of Miss Marple or James Herriot. A place where everyone knows each other and everyone knows their place. It is a community with a natural focus, the church, pub and local shop which brings people together and allows news (perhaps gossip is a better word) to be shared. The community has clearly-defined boundaries, both in terms of the people who lay claim to membership and the geographical area covered. As such the community is suspicious of strangers and reluctant to embrace newcomers, as many an émigré from the city has found to their cost. The village community is mixed and includes everyone from the squire to the labourer. This is not, of course, on an equal basis, but as part of a strict hierarchy. The village community is guided by unwritten rules which are as rarely stated as they are transgressed. It is an ordered, civil society where people feel at ease and where a certain image of English life has continued undisturbed for centuries. Whether or not such village communities exist is not the point, the ideal exists in people's imagination and shapes their ideas about the ideal community in which they would like to live.

The other community ideal is almost the complete opposite of this. This is the urban street as described by Jane Jacobs. If the village community is a rock pool the urban community is the shoreline washed by the ebb and flow of the tide. In the *Death and Life of Great American Cities*[3], Jane Jacobs recounts an incident on her own street in Greenwich Village which serves to illustrate the qualities of an urban community. She describes how she noticed from her window a small girl being dragged against her will along the opposite sidewalk by a suspicious looking man. Before Jacobs could decide whether to intervene she noticed '…from the butcher's shop had emerged the woman who, with her husband, runs the shop; she was standing within earshot of the man, her arms folded with a look of determination on her face. Joe Cornacchia, who with his son-in-law keeps the delicatessen, emerged at about the same time and stood solidly on the other side. Several heads poked out of the tenement windows, one was withdrawn quickly and its owner reappeared a moment later in the doorway behind the man. Two men from the bar next to the butcher came to the doorway and waited, …the locksmith, fruitman and laundry proprietor had all come out of their shops and the scene was also being surveyed from a number of windows besides ours. The man did not know it but he was surrounded.'

This is very different to the village community, although successful urban communities like Greenwich in New York often come to be known as villages. Yet there were probably more people living on Jane Jacobs' Hudson Street than in the whole of our ideal village. They did not know each other although most of them did, like Jacobs, know Joe Cornacchia and the other shopkeepers. They also quite clearly felt a responsibility for the street but this did not translate into a hostility towards strangers. Indeed the little girl in the story effectively became a co-opted member of the community with full rights of support and protection for the duration of her short walk

down the street with, what turned out to be, her father. The urban community therefore embraces the stranger as someone who enriches it rather than as a threat. Indeed a stranger need only visit the street on an occasional basis to feel part of the community.

Jacobs described how her street changed during the day with the commuters leaving for work in the morning followed by the arrival of the local office workers and the children going to school. Later in the morning mothers with young children and 'bums' tended to dominate followed by the frenetic activity of lunchtime and so on throughout the day. This cycle of activities continues day after day as part of wider weekly and annual cycles so that the constantly changing street scene is accommodated within a regular and unchanging structure. Jane Jacobs was writing in 1961 and she has been accused[4] of sentimentalising

The village in the city: Successful urban communities like Moseley in Birmingham often come to be known as villages. Indeed many were originally villages which were engulfed in the expanding city

121

The suburban community: Roslyn Place in Pittsburgh, the street described by Allen Jacobs

It seems likely that most people's vision of community is at least partly based on one of these two models. While the same may not be true in continental Europe, in the UK it is the village community which has tended to hold sway in the past. Most surveys of housebuyers show that what many still aspire to is the rural ideal even if very few actually achieve it. What they do achieve is the suburban community which is, in many respects, a hybrid form of community – a development of the village in an urban context.

We have already discussed the communities based on networks of interest that thrive in suburban areas. There is however a more local dimension to the suburban community which is more rarely achieved. A good description of such a community is Allen Jacobs' evocation of the street where he once lived in his book *Great Streets*[6]. In this he describes Roslyn Place in Pittsburgh, a short tree-lined cul-de-sac of eighteen detached and semi-detached houses: 'in a small space there are eighteen doors that people walk into and out of so people pass each other and each knows where the other lives… Recognition, discussion, communication, community are encouraged by the nature of the street. On a Saturday morning in Spring, Izzy Cohen, chemist, is screaming at the retired butcher who parked last night where Izzy usually parks… later more intimate discussions of what went on and why will take place in small knots of two or three neighbours. Surely Izzy will want to explain to each group what happened. The butcher doesn't speak. He is a quiet man. Solitude, if you want it, is also possible… people will sweep a walk, others will garden, people will come and go. Maybe a date will be made for coffee later or for a dessert after dinner'.

This is also an idealised vision and is not typical of most suburban areas. As Allen Jacobs points out, the street has no off-street parking so that houses are closer together with uninterrupted sidewalks and the parking of cars provides an endless topic of discussion for Izzy and his neighbours. Whilst the description of street life has overtones of Jane Jacobs, the

urban life. Some question whether such urban communities exist any more or even whether they ever really existed in the past. This again is not the issue. Like the village ideal, the urban community is an idea which inspires many city dwellers. Indeed it can be seen in popular Television programmes like *Friends*. A few years ago when we did some market research with MORI into attitudes to urban living[5] it was clear that the 'Friends lifestyle' had taken a strong grip on the imaginations and aspirations of many young people.

community that Allen Jacobs describes is much more like the village. Everyone knows each other and strangers are not welcomed. There is no sense in the description of the wider urban area, which one feels is probably part of the attraction. However unlike the village this suburban community is not mixed. Its strength is social homogeneity rather than variety. It works, not because it can accommodate different lifestyles but because its residents share similar values.

However not all suburban environments are as supportive as Roslyn Place. Few manage so skilfully to balance the desire for privacy with the need for contact. Indeed as Allen Jacobs points out, a host of regulations would prevent Roslyn Place from being built today. Much suburban development also takes place on a far greater scale. David Popenoe in his book the *Suburban Environment*[7] looks at Levittown, one of the first large private suburban estates in the US started in the late 1940s and including 17 300 single-family homes. Levittown is divided into neighbourhoods which contain not eighteen but 430 homes, each on its own plot. As Popenoe summarises: 'In the early years of Levittown the teenager, the elderly person, the widow or divorced female… the working class women living in tight financial straits and cutoff from relatives, were unfamiliar

---

BENTILEE: STOKE-ON-TRENT

The Bentilee Estate on the outskirts of Stoke-on-Trent is an interesting example of the application of a community ideal. Bentilee is a council estate of some 5000 properties which was developed in the garden city style of the 1950s. Over the years the estate acquired a poor reputation and struggled to achieve a community identity because of its scale and isolated location. In 1996 the opportunity arose to improve the estate through the government's Single Regeneration Budget. The concept behind the scheme was the transformation of the estate into a series of villages in a programme that became known as the the Villages Initiative.

URBED undertook the work to explore the transformation of the estate into a series of eight village centres. By studying the history of the area and building upon local nodes such as shopping parades, pubs and schools, a series of village centres were identified. These were reinforced by creating community halls, and introducing new housing development to create a sense of enclosure and increased density. It

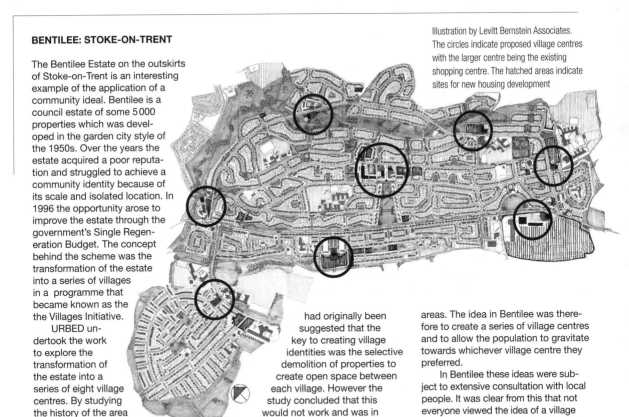

Illustration by Levitt Bernstein Associates. The circles indicate proposed village centres with the larger centre being the existing shopping centre. The hatched areas indicate sites for new housing development

had originally been suggested that the key to creating village identities was the selective demolition of properties to create open space between each village. However the study concluded that this would not work and was in any case based on a model of a village community which was not appropriate for the area. Rather than a rural village a concept was developed based on the villages which exist in urban areas. These are defined by their centre rather than their edge and tend to merge into the surrounding urban areas. The idea in Bentilee was therefore to create a series of village centres and to allow the population to gravitate towards whichever village centre they preferred.

In Bentilee these ideas were subject to extensive consultation with local people. It was clear from this that not everyone viewed the idea of a village community as a positive thing. Indeed young people saw it as somewhere where people stuck their noses into your business and stifled individuality. However the word village still held a strong appeal, particularly to the older members of the community, and the proposals received widespread support.

figures. Today they have become common and the environment is not as congruent with them as it was with their predecessors. For adults in anything but a fully functioning, economically secure family system, Levittown may be an invitation to trouble'. This, again, is an extreme example but it illustrates how mass suburbia, at least in its most extreme form, does little to foster the sort of communities described in this chapter. Such environments can be found around all UK towns and cities. Created for the nuclear family, they are increasingly inappropriate for the demographic groups who are likely to dominate the 21st century.

Here are three very different views of community – the village, the urban street and the suburban hybrid. Each may be rarer than we would like to think but undoubtedly provide valuable models. Each can deliver the benefits that flow from a strong community but will only thrive in a particular context. Indeed none of the models transplant well from one situation to another. The rural village may be a model that many people aspire to but translated, as it was, into the tight courtyard council house developments of the 1970s it was always destined to fail. It is however the suburban model of community which has been most consistently misapplied. It is this type of community, at least as described by Allen Jacobs, that many professionals have been striving to achieve for decades. For ourselves we may strive for the village or urban communities but when planning communities for others it has generally been the tightknit, homogeneous community that we have had in mind. It is however far from clear whether such communities can be created, particularly on a large scale. It is also questionable whether such communities will thrive if the only thing that people have in common is the fact that they are disadvantaged, which is often the case on new social housing estates.

However if, as we have suggested, environmental and demographic trends are pointing towards a more urban society in the future, the question is whether the suburban community can be transplanted to urban areas. This has been achieved by people like the Old Eldonians Housing Co-operative in Liverpool. However generally this type of suburban community is not tolerant of the strangers which are inevitable in cities. This can make it vulnerable to crime and antisocial behaviour which in turn creates pressure for overt security measures. A third of all new housing development in the US is taking place in 'gated communities'[8] separated from the rest of the world by fences, gates and security guards. Is this what we must resort to if we are to preserve the suburban community in the city?

In the 21st century people's ideas about the ideal community, both for themselves and others, will continue to shape the city. However we must recognise that different types of community only thrive in the right context. The village and suburban communities are attractive ideals to which many people aspire. These aspirations will continue to drive suburbanisation as people seek to achieve their ideal of community. These ideals should not however drive urban planning. The village or suburban community transplanted to the city simply will not work. If we are to make cities more popular we need to develop new models of urban communities to complement the suburban communities which will continue to serve large sections of society. Jane Jacobs' description of urban community life may already have been dying out in the early 1960s when she was writing. However it is still a vision which is attractive to a growing section of society. If urban areas are to be revitalised it will be by tapping these very urban ideas of community rather than importing inappropriate models from the suburbs.

It is likely that the notion of community will be an increasingly important influence on the 21st century home. This will require a rethink of our preconceptions about the 'good community' and the development of concepts of community more suited to non-family households and urban living.

Chapter 8
Cost The economy of urban development

The final 'C' stands for cost, a factor which has always influenced housing design more as a constraint on innovation than as a respectable goal like green design, consumer choice or community. Great improvements tend to be made in housing design when cost constraints are less strong, as in the 1920s. However when concerns focus on value for money – as has happened in the recent past – fears are raised that standards are falling and innovation is being stifled. It may be simplistic to suggest that spending more money will always produce a better product but we must raise our sights above the penny-pinching battles which have characterised late 20th century housing. In doing this it would be reckless to ignore the issue of cost.

Innovation and cost

The transformation in housing design which took place at the beginning of the 20th century shows the impact that innovation can have on cost. While Ebenezer Howard devoted large parts of his writings to the economic structures of the garden city, his object was not to show that it could be built as cheaply as the terraced housing which made up the majority of development at that time. When the garden city ideas were first put into practice on a large scale in the council housing of the 1920s the costs increased four-fold over what had been produced before the First World War. The result so alarmed the Conservative government of the time that council house

building was stopped. When it resumed in the mid 1920s efforts were made to reduce costs. However, having seen the future and liked it, councils, their architects and their tenants were not going to go back to prewar standards. Thus a great leap forward in housing standards and a great burst of innovation was accompanied by a huge increase in costs. The new standards also had a profound influence on private production and, whilst private developers undoubtedly built cheaper than councils, they had to match the new public sector standards and therefore also saw a substantial increase in their costs.

In the 1960s something similar happened with the introduction of the Parker Morris space standards for new homes in the UK. It is estimated that these put up construction costs by 15%. Yet the government was not willing to increase the funding per unit given its drive to increase overall housing output. The result was that councils were forced to resort to system building and high-rise blocks to achieve economies of scale.

Today the same is happening as the UK government seeks to improve the standard of new housing in areas such as energy efficiency, disabled access etc. But at the same time is seeking to reduce costs. Research has suggested that achieving Level 6 in the government's Code for Sustainable Homes could cost £30 000 – £50 000 per unit[1]. Yet it was not so long ago that the government was promoting a competition to build the £60 000 home[2]. This circle is to be squared as it was in the 1960s, with prefabrication or modular construction as it is now called. A series of reports into construction efficiency starting with the Latham report in the late 1990s[3] have suggested that construction costs in the UK could be reduced by as much as 30 % based on a reform of the construction industry and greater use of factory-produced modules that can be delivered to site. The problem is that without high volumes, these systems have proved more, rather than less, expensive than current techniques. Indeed UK housebuilders are past-masters at minimising cost and maximising value. The starter home is one product of this optimisation and the double-loaded apartment block (flats built of either side of a central corridor) is another. Both are the modern day equivalent of the system-built flat of the 1960s. There are many in the industry who doubt whether there are 30 % of savings to be found while achieving higher standards no matter how many official reports tell them the contrary.

Continental approaches: Social housing by Herman Hertzberger at Linden Strasse in Berlin. This scheme is widely quoted in housing histories but was always difficult to emulate in the UK because our cost base is so different

Continental approaches to cost

Much of the inspirations for innovations in the UK housing stock come from the continent. This however often ignores the very different housing economics on the continent. In the 1980s German construction costs[4] (excluding land and external works) were £1 200 – £1 500/m². At the time the equivalent figure in the UK was just £450–£600/m². Even in 2007 a typical detached house in the UK at 116m² cost £91 206 to build which is just £786/m². Not only are UK construction costs less than half those in Germany, average floor area of German housing is some 50 % greater. The Germans are by no means unique in this, if anything the Swiss spend more on their housing although it is significant that most of this, even at the top of the market, is for rent rather than sale.

Since the 1980s the gap between UK and continental construction costs has widened as a result of a steady downward pressure on UK housing costs. Part of the greater costs in Europe can be accounted for by higher labour and materials costs, however it is difficult to escape the fact that their housing is much better constructed. This is because of a radical difference in UK and continental views of housing as a long-term investment.

The German people view home ownership very differently from the British. The UK approach has been to struggle onto the first rung of the housing ladder at the earliest opportunity and to rely on rising values to carry you up the ladder in order to achieve the home of your dreams later in life. People will therefore put up with a cramped, substandard house or apartment in their twenties in the hope that it is only a staging post to something better. In Germany, by contrast, a house is an investment made much later in life with the intention that you will live there for a long time and pass it on to your children. People therefore make do with rented accommodation in their twenties or even live with their parents until they have accumulated sufficient capital to invest in a substantial home or they inherit the family home. In Japan this long-term approach is reflected in the introduction of fifty year, inter-generational mortgages.

These attitudes have also influenced German social housing developers who have used private housing as a quality benchmark, as happened in Britain in the 1920s. In Germany social housing is built to last with a view to maintainability, running costs and long-term value. In the UK, by contrast, the attitude is that if the private sector can produce a perfectly saleable starter home for a pittance then social landlords who spend more are clearly being inefficient. As Valerie Karn described in her report for the Joseph Rowntree Housing Standards Committee[5] in the 1990s this meant that housing designed by private developers as the first rung on the housing ladder was being filled to capacity by housing associations with families who have no realistic capacity of moving on as their needs change. In the depressed housing markets of 1990 and 2008 the same fate can befall owner-occupiers as negative equity denies them the ability to 'ladder up' to something more suited to their needs.

Market constraints

Over the years commentators[6] have argued that the UK housing market is becoming more like the continent as people buy for 'nesting not investing'. However this is wishful thinking and whenever the market picks again, housing in the minds of a British people becomes both an investment and a place to live. In 2006 just before the Credit Crunch mortgage lending in the UK topped £1 trillion for the first time while a further £3 trillion of property was owned outright[7]. Mortgage debt represented 70 % of GDP in the UK compared to 24 % in France and 50 % in Germany[8]. Because of this, factors that affect the value of housing in the UK are as important as what people want from their home. Unfortunately the two things do not always line up.

Concern about the value of their home has long been an obsession of the British middle classes. But its impact on new housing is mostly mitigated through the mortgage market. Mortgage providers lend against the value of the house as estimated by a professional valuer.

The mortgage dependent purchaser is not able to pay more than this independent valuation however much they may like the home. This does not happen in any other form of consumer transaction. If you really like a particular car then the finance provider is not going to tell you 'it's not worth what you are paying and therefore I'm not going to lend you the cash'. One of the reasons for this is that the value of the car will fall as soon as it leaves the showroom, whereas the house is expected to increase in value and to provide collateral for the full loan.

The way in which valuations are done therefore has an important impact on housing. If you go to a surveyor and ask how much a house is worth, they will base their valuation on recent house sales in the area, to do otherwise would lay them open to a claim of professional misconduct. The value of anything new is therefore based on the value of what has been sold in the past. Valuing something new that has not been built in the past is therefore really hard, and the response of valuers tends to be to say that it can not be worth very much. This of course stifles innovation.

While there have been surveys[9] that show that people consider energy efficiency to be an important consideration when buying a house, it remains the case that the quality of the kitchen and the property's 'kerb appeal' are much more important to them. This may be because buyers are not being given enough information about savings on running costs, something that will be addressed by the Energy Performance Certificates in Home Information Packs. However even where this information has been given in the past, for example through a National Home Energy Rating, it does not appear to have played a major part in purchasers decisions. The real problem is that energy efficiency is not reflected in the value of the house unlike the fitted kitchen. This means that an energy efficient home will cost more to build but will be worth no more than a bog standard building regulations house. For the purchaser it would make sense to pay more for the house because they would make this back in reduced running costs. However they would have to fund the additional capital costs without the aid of a

mortgage. Because of this developers realistically find they cannot recoup the additional costs of energy efficiency and therefore have no incentive to improve what they build. The classic story that illustrates this relates to the houses built in Milton Keynes, which were so energy efficient that they did not need central heating. Unfortunately they could not be sold[10] because the estate agent, not being able to find the central heating valued them as 'unimproved'.

The same is true of floor areas, which may explain why German and indeed American housing is 50% larger than in the UK. In Germany and America housing is valued by floor area and everyone can, and probably will, tell you the square metreage of their home in the same way as British people will tell you how much it is worth. In the UK housing is valued by the spurious measure of the number of bedrooms. So for example a seventy square metre house will have a greater value if it has three bedrooms than it would with two. No matter that the storage cupboard masquerading as the third bedroom can accommodate nothing other than a single bed, it gets a tick on the valuer's chart and puts the proud home owners a notch above their two-

bedroom neighbours. Another example from that great laboratory of housing design, Milton Keynes, makes the point. Here a private builder developed a number of 200 m² two-bedroom houses intended for affluent couples whose children had left home. Again these units caused headaches for the valuers since as two-bedroom units they should have been starter homes yet clearly they could not be valued as such.

One last example of the influence of mortgages on the housing market comes from Manchester where Urban Splash, responding to government exhortations to promote modular homes, developed their Moho scheme (short for modular home). This was an apartment scheme in which each apartment was factory built and was heralded as an exemplar of good practice. Unfortunately the mortgage lenders would not lend on the property and Urban Splash ended up having to provide their own mortgages.

As long as housing in the UK is viewed as both shelter and investment this situation will continue. With an investment it is safety, not innovation, that counts. For something to be a good investment, you must be sure that other people will accept its value. The further that you move away from the market norm the more you run the risk that this will not be the case especially in a weak market. An example of this is the old rule-of-thumb that an architect-designed home is worth 10% less than an equivalent house of standard design. People buying a home therefore face a dilemma if their idea of the ideal home is different to that of the mass market. Do they maximise the return on their investment or go for the home that they want? The same is true of private builders who need to be sure that what they built will sell quickly and for a good price. It is, of course, possible for market norms to change as developers like Urban Splash have done, but there is an inbuilt conservatism in the market that will always act as a check on innovation.

Location

As the old adage goes in estate agent circles, the three most important factors in property value are location, location and location. Unlike the quality of construction, energy-efficiency, the floor area, or even the attractiveness of the design, the location of the property really does affect its value. One of the problems with the attempts to attract people back to urban areas in the 1990s was that the locations to which estate agents attached the highest values, parts of London excepted, were not urban. Developers argued that this simply reflected where people want to live. However in some cases the market was working to inhibit these preferences. Housing in urban areas cost as much to build as housing in the suburbs, yet surveyors were marking down the values because they had nothing to compare it to.

In Chapter 6 we described the example of the first warehouse apartment conversion on Whitworth Street in Manchester. There were no other city centre apartments on which to base values so that the flats were initially priced at £16000. Within months they were selling for twice this and today one of the apartments would cost more than 10 times that amount. These values, of course, gave surveyors the confidence to increase values and pretty soon developers were piling into the market. The same problem still occurs elsewhere such as the inner city and government-designated Housing Market Renewal areas. Because historic value data is often based on poor quality stock it becomes very difficult to fund new housing.

The development industry

One of the factors to have emerged in the last ten years is the regeneration developer. Until the 1990s most private housing was built by housebuilders rather than developers. This is an important distinction which is worth dwelling on for a moment. Developers will buy a site, commission an architect to prepare a scheme, run an appraisal and if the values stack up they will commission a contractor to build the scheme before renting it or more likely selling it to an investor. Development is a risky business and most developers are relatively conservative people and their appraisals are based on historic valuations as described above.

Housebuilders are quite different. Traditionally they have bought options on land and then put all of their efforts into getting planning permission. If they can do this the value of the land will leap and all they need to do is to put houses on it so that it can be sold in chunks. The houses are not generally designed by architects but are standard housetypes from pattern books. These housetypes have been optimised and the housebuilder's supply chain will be finely tuned to building them as efficiently as possible. In this respect housebuilders are more like car makers than developers. They have also tended to be rather conservative and like to build housing in areas where they can see other housebuilders at work and where values are well-established.

The regeneration developers has a different business model. Pioneers like Roger Zogolovitch in the 1980s and Urban Splash in the 1990s have created a business out of developing in areas where no one else could see the potential. They would buy up land or buildings at knock-down prices in run-down areas, tap all of the available public sector grant and then use marketing to change perceptions of the location thereby increasing values. Urban Splash got to the point where they could increase values just by putting their name on the side of a building so that they could build virtually anywhere because they brought their market with them. Regeneration developers differ from the traditional developer as they are not bound by historic valuations. Indeed their business model is based on challenging historic valuations to find opportunities that the market is blind to. Their valuations are based upon the prices that they believe they can generate through marketing rather than what has been achieved in the past. This type of valuation makes lenders feel uncomfortable so developers like Urban Splash have developed a financing system based on pre-sales. The site is marketed, buyers sign-up, pay a deposit and once enough flats have been sold (proving the valuation) finance can be raised and construction can commence.

This model has changed the house-building industry. Seeing the success of Urban Splash has caused many traditional housebuilders and developers to try and emulate them. Some of their early attempts at urban apartments felt and looked like suburban boxes stacked on top of each other, but they gradually learned lessons about the use of design and marketing to sell a lifestyle. However, no matter how it is dressed up, most housebuilders are still followers not pioneers. Their urban schemes tend to just be new versions of their pattern book with standard apartment types rather than housetypes.

Land value

The reality is that, while the Germans may spend twice as much as we do in the UK on building houses, German homes don't cost twice as much to buy. The difference is accounted for by land value. This again is a result of the way that we assess values in the UK. Developer appraisals are based on the residual valuation method. This means that you estimate the costs of the development, add the developer's profit and subtract the amount that you are able to sell it for. The figure left is what you can pay for the land. Developers will normally assume that they make around 15% profit on a scheme. However the real scope to make money comes from the land. As we have

seen, regeneration developers do this by buying land that no one else wants so that they can raise values through good quality marketing.

The traditional model of housebuilders was to do the same thing through the planning system. Housebuilders would build up large 'land banks' by purchasing sites, or options on sites around the edge of towns and cities in anticipation of getting permission to build on them. Money is made partly by buying sites at the bottom of the market and bringing them forward when houseprices are high. However the real cash comes from getting planning permission for housing on agricultural land which can increase values ten-fold. In the past the government has sought to recover part of this 'unearned' value through Betterment taxes although no system has ever been made to work.

The planning system therefore has a huge influence on the value of land. In the pre-industrial cities that we discussed in Part 1 of this book, the classic land value gradient saw values fall from a peak in the city centre to the lowest values at the edge. This was one reason why higher density development was found in the centre. This started to change with suburbanisation which started to place a premium on peripheral sites. However the real impact came when Green Belt choked off the supply of peripheral sites. The greatest value therefore became attached to the scarcest sites – those with permission for housing on the edge of the conurbation. Perversely to achieve these high values the land had to be developed with low-density housing.

As a result of this system a large proportion of the amount we pay for housing is the price of the land that it is built on. As Colin Ward has pointed out, in 1945 land prices accounted for 5% of the cost of housing. By the 1960s this had risen to 40% and in parts of the south-east today it is as high as 65%[11]. All of that money, which elsewhere is invested in the quality of construction, is sunk into the cost of buying the land.

This has started to change through recent government policy as we will see in the next chapter. By setting targets for the proportion of housing on brown field land and stating that

The Urban Splash Fridge: Early publicity for an Urban Splash scheme in Manchester emphasising the benefits of living in the city centre

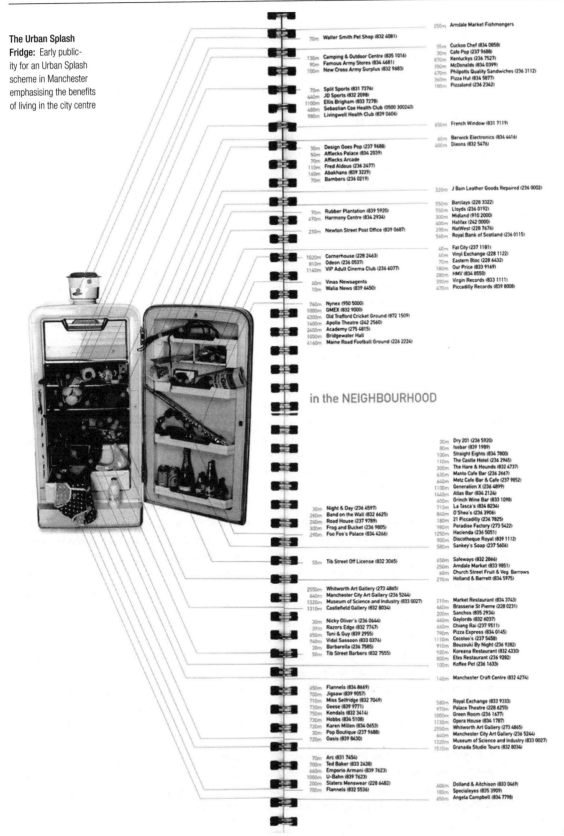

250m Arndale Market Fishmongers

70m Walter Smith Pet Shop (832 4081)

55m Cuckoo Chef (834 0858)
30m Cafe Pop (237 9688)
870m Kentuckys (236 7527)
350m McDonalds (834 0399)
470m Philpotts Quality Sandwiches (236 3112)
360m Pizza Hut (834 5877)
180m Pizzaland (236 2342)

130m Camping & Outdoor Centre (835 1016)
90m Famous Army Stores (834 4681)
100m New Cross Army Surplus (832 9683)

70m Split Sports (831 7374)
440m JD Sports (832 2098)
1100m Ellis Brigham (833 7278)
480m Sebastian Coe Health Club (0500 300240)
980m Livingwell Health Club (839 0606)

650m French Window (831 7119)

40m Berwick Electronics (834 4416)
400m Dixons (832 5476)

30m Design Goes Pop (237 9688)
50m Afflecks Palace (834 2039)
70m Afflecks Arcade
110m Fred Aldous (236 2477)
160m Abakhans (839 3229)
70m Bambers (236 0219)

320m J Bain Leather Goods Repaired (236 0002)

550m Barclays (228 3322)
550m Lloyds (236 0192)
300m Midland (910 2000)
400m Halifax (242 0000)
200m NatWest (228 7676)
568m Royal Bank of Scotland (236 0115)

70m Rubber Plantation (839 5920)
670m Harmony Centre (834 2934)

230m Newton Street Post Office (839 0687)

45m Fat City (237 1181)
40m Vinyl Exchange (228 1122)
70m Eastern Bloc (228 6432)
180m Our Price (833 9169)
280m HMV (834 8550)
390m Virgin Records (833 1111)
470m Piccadilly Records (839 8008)

1920m Cornerhouse (228 2463)
810m Odeon (236 0537)
1140m VIP Adult Cinema Club (236 6077)

60m Vinas Newsagents
10m Walia News (839 6450)

760m Nynex (950 5000)
1000m GMEX (832 9000)
4300m Old Trafford Cricket Ground (872 1509)
1400m Apollo Theatre (242 2560)
2400m Academy (275 4815)
1050m Bridgewater Hall
4160m Maine Road Football Ground (226 2224)

in the NEIGHBOURHOOD

30m Dry 201 (236 5920)
80m Isobar (839 1989)
100m Straight Eights (834 7800)
110m The Castle Hotel (236 2945)
300m The Hare & Hounds (832 4737)
630m Manto Cafe Bar (236 2667)
640m Metz Cafe Bar & Cafe (237 9852)
1130m Generation X (236 4899)
1440m Atlas Bar (834 2124)
600m Grinch Wine Bar (833 1098)
710m La Tasca's (834 8234)
840m O'Shea's (236 3906)
180m 21 Piccadilly (236 7825)
980m Paradise Factory (273 5422)
1250m Hacienda (236 5051)
900m Discotheque Royal (839 1112)
580m Sankey's Soap (237 5606)

30m Night & Day (236 4597)
260m Band on the Wall (832 6625)
260m Road House (237 9789)
300m Frog and Bucket (236 9805)
290m Foo Foo's Palace (834 4266)

650m Safeways (832 2866)
250m Arndale Market (833 9851)
60m Church Street Fruit & Veg. Barrows
270m Holland & Barrett (834 5975)

55m Tib Street Off License (832 3065)

2550m Whitworth Art Gallery (273 4865)
640m Manchester City Art Gallery (236 5244)
1320m Museum of Science and Industry (833 0027)
1310m Castlefield Gallery (832 8034)

210m Market Restaurant (834 3743)
600m Brasserie St Pierre (228 0231)
200m Sanchos (835 2934)
440m Gaylords (832 6037)
660m Chiang Rai (237 9511)
790m Pizza Express (834 0145)
1110m Cocotoo's (237 5458)
910m Bouzouki By Night (236 9282)
920m Koreana Restaurant (832 4330)
800m Efes Restaurant (236 9282)
100m Koffee Pot (236 1633)

30m Nicky Oliver's (236 0644)
39m Razors Edge (832 7747)
650m Toni & Guy (839 2955)
740m Vidal Sassoon (833 0376)
30m Barbarella (236 7585)
50m Tib Street Barbers (832 7555)

140m Manchester Craft Centre (832 4274)

650m Flannels (834 8669)
700m Jigsaw (839 9057)
710m Miss Selfridge (832 7049)
730m Geese (839 9771)
750m Kendals (832 3414)
730m Hobbs (834 5108)
720m Karen Millen (836 0653)
30m Pop Boutique (237 9688)
720m Oasis (839 8430)

580m Royal Exchange (833 9333)
970m Palace Theatre (228 6255)
1060m Green Room (236 1677)
1130m Opera House (834 1787)
2550m Whitworth Art Gallery (273 4865)
640m Manchester City Art Gallery (236 5244)
1320m Museum of Science and Industry (833 0027)
1510m Granada Studio Tours (832 8034)

70m Arc (831 7454)
700m Ted Baker (833 2438)
660m Emporio Armani (839 7623)
1000m U-Bahn (839 7623)
200m Slaters Menswear (228 6482)
700m Flannels (832 5536)

400m Dolland & Aitchison (833 0469)
180m Specialeyes (835 3909)
650m Angela Campbell (834 7798)

green field housing allocations can be revoked, they have changed the traditional housebuilding equation and cast uncertainty over the value of land banks. Builders are increasingly having to bid to public sector organisations like English Partnerships to acquire sites such as former hospitals and collieries. English Partnerships demands higher standards of construction and performance but are also prepared to see a commensurate reduction in the value they receive for the land. This starts to transfer some of the land value into increased spending on the home.

In theory this should happen with all land transactions. If costs rise – for example because of the government's target of carbon free housing by 2016 – this should just be discounted off the value of the land. In practice the system is not so flexible. Land owners have unreasonable expectations. Developers buy up land in advance based on assumptions of what their costs will be and if these costs change they lose money. They also need to be very sure that the additional costs are going to be shared by all developers otherwise they will be outbid for the land. It is also important that the extra costs do not eat away all of the land value as may happen in depressed markets. This would create a negative land value which would halt development altogether.

Cost constraints in social housing

Of course most of the housing innovations in the past have had nothing to do with private housing. In Ian Colquhoun's history of housing design[12] only one private developer, Span, merits a mention prior to the 1980s. Before that virtually all housing innovation took place in social housing – experimenting on the poor as it could be called. Social housing providers, free from the constraints of the market, drove virtually all innovation in the 20th century, from the birth of suburbia in the garden city estates of the 1920s to the council estates of the 1960s.

This came to a grinding halt in the 1980s when council house building was virtually stopped and housing associations took on the mantle of social housing provision. Associations had a proud history of housing innovation and

some like The Peabody Trust, Circle 33 and Manchester Methodist Housing Association (now part of the Great Places Housing Group) have continued to innovate. These are, however, the exception and cost pressures on most of the social housing sector have been as stifling of innovation as in the private sector.

Part of this is because social housing tenants have reacted against innovation. The comments from an RIBA Focus Group in the 1990s are just as relevant today: 'They want Brooksides… ask your average council tenant what they want and you will discover that they want to live in a house that makes them look like an owner occupier'[13]. However, despite the community architecture movement, it is not often that social housing tenants today are asked what they want. In the 1990s cost pressures caused many housing associations to lower their sights to those of the starter home. At first pressure on costs was applied through cost yardsticks imposed by the social housing funder the Housing Corporation. However even when a competitive tender climate made these yardsticks easier to hit, a downward pressure on costs continued to be applied through a drive to reduce grant requirements. Housing associations were forced to bid against each other for grants and the winners were those able to build the most houses with the least public subsidy.

In some respects this was understandable given the acute shortage of social housing. With huge housing pressures and limited resources, it must be right to build three houses with the money which once built two as one London housing association boasted[14]. Yet this process led to a crisis in the social housing sector in the late 1990s. Housing associations bought into the bottom end of the private housebuilder market creating large suburban estates of starter homes on the edge of town. Tenants may have wanted something that made them look like an owner-occupier, and if they were offered a new house after being stuck in a bed and breakfast hostel they were not going to quibble. However once they had moved in and were occupying the house to capacity – as the allocation rules dictated – they soon noticed the lack of space, the dearth of local facilities and the bus which never came. By that time, unless they were lucky enough to be able to buy somewhere, they were stuck.

Of course there were exceptions to this trend and if you look at housing association publicity material you would think that most of their schemes were well-designed and involved tenants. Yet for every flagship scheme in the 1990s there were maybe four or five estates built in peripheral locations in consortium deals with private developers using standard housetypes[15]. Indeed on a site visit organised as part of the Joseph Rowntree Foundation's Housing Standards Committee in the late 1990s the director of a medium-sized housing association was shocked to discover the poor quality of housing being built on some of their less high profile new estates. Here cost, or what was euphemistically called 'value for money', was the name of the game.

The situation today has not changed greatly in its fundamentals. In 2008 most council housing has been transferred away from councils to 'Stock Transfer Housing Associations' or to 'Arms Length Management Organisations'. These new organisations have swelled the size of the housing association sector. Their main concern has been to meet the government's 'Decent Home Standard' which most are required to do by 2010. To achieve this many of the poorest council estates that could not be brought up to the standard at a reasonable cost have been demolished. Typically these estates have been redeveloped in partnership with private developers with densities being increased so that the receipts from private housing can be used to fund replacement social housing.

In terms of new social housing the process of development may have changed but the issues remain the same. In the 1990s housing associations went into partnership with private developers to build for them. In the 2000s it is increasingly rare for associations to develop their own sites. Instead they are taking on property developed by private housebuilders as part of planning gain agreements (known as Section 106 Agreements in England). The London Plan[16] includes a requirement that 50% of all new private housing schemes over a certain size must be social housing. The rate varies across the rest of the country but most planning authorities have a social housing requirement of at least 20%. Research for the Joseph Rowntree Foundation in 2005[17] found that the proportion of social housing provided in this way had grown from a third in 1999 to more than half by 2003.

The standard of social housing provided in this way is regulated through the Housing Corporation's Scheme Development Standards that covers issues such as floor area, disabled access and energy performance. This often means that the social housing elements of new housing schemes are built to a higher standard than the private homes. There is however still a tendency for social housing to be pushed to the back of the site in the least attractive locations.

The cost of these houses is now carried by the development industry rather than the tax payer. In the process that we describe above, this should be netted off the land value. The system does however give control of social housing provision to developers with no incentive to spend more on innovation, nor even a long-term management interest in the property.

The future influence of cost

In both the private and social housing fields there are therefore powerful economic forces at play which limit the scope for innovation and design quality in new homes. In the 1990s these trends served to reinforce both suburban designs and suburban locations and in the 2000s it has also led to poor-quality, high-density apartment schemes.

What will happen in the future is unclear. We have argued that we need to spend more on the construction of housing in order to achieve continental standards. In doing this we would be in good company but how do we square this with the UK government's campaign to promote the £60K house that is surely pulling in the opposite direction? The government were rightly concerned about affordability in the mid 2000s when rising house values had priced even people on an average wage out of the market. However focusing on construction costs may not be the best way to achieve this. Government research into green field housing costs[18] in the early 1990s showed that as little as 30% of the costs of a typical new suburban house was accounted for by construction. This was eclipsed by land costs at 35%, developers' overheads at 19.7% and infrastructure at 12.8%. The situation with apartments is slightly different. Here construction costs are around twice those of houses. Land and infrastructure costs make up a lower proportion of unit costs because they can be spread over a larger number of units. Nevertheless even in apartment schemes up to 40% of costs can be non-construction related. There are a number of strategies that could be used in the future to increase the quality of new housing including lower land values, valuing the right things, reducing infrastructure costs and more efficient construction.

Infrastructure costs: One of the reasons why the infrastructure costs were so high for green field housing in the survey quoted above was that the sites were so poorly served by infrastructure. On green field sites developers have to put in the roads, sewers, street lighting, cabling etc. They may have to pay to increase the capacity of the local sewage works or water pumping station and through planning gain may be asked to build or extend a primary school. To make such investment worthwhile there has been a tendency to look for economies of scale by building ever larger estates.

By contrast there are potential cost savings (as well as environmental benefits) to be

THE MILLENNIUM VILLAGE: GREENWICH

One of the most high profile prefabricated schemes in the UK is the Millennium Village in Greenwich. The scheme by Erskine Tovatt is based on a steel frame prefabricated system clad with factory-made timber panels to which glazing and external finishes are attached. The system uses timber intermediate floors up to eight storeys with concrete floors for higher buildings. Bathrooms and kitchens are factory-made timber pods fully fitted and ready for attaching to services.

The system was designed specially for the project and is targeted to reduce construction times by 5% in year one, rising to 25% over the three years as well as reducing total costs by 15% in the first year and up to 30% over the life of the project. It was also projected to eliminate defects by year three and to reduce accidents from eight per thousand employees to two.

made by building within existing settlements. Here roads and other infrastructure already exist, there is likely to be spare capacity in schools, as well as in services like water and sewage. In URBED's *21st Century Homes* research for the Joseph Rowntree Foundation we sought to test this through a series of demonstration projects. The results were inconclusive[19]. Certainly the land costs for the urban demonstration projects were low and some infrastructural savings were possible. However poor ground conditions caused by back-filled basements cancelled out some of these savings and in other areas contamination may also be a problem. Much of the urban infrastructure is also in need of renewal. Indeed on larger brown field sites the need to provide infrastructure may be greater than on green fields. It is possible that smaller scale infill development would overcome the problems of infrastructural costs, although here developers would not be able to achieve economies of scale and lack of space may increase site costs.

The approach in Germany has been for the public sector to provide infrastructure for large developments such as has also become a model through the 'green' urban extensions of Vauban and Rieselfeld in Freiburg. One of the findings of URBED's report *Beyond Eco-towns*[20] was that this was one of the most important ways in which innovation and higher standards have been secured. In the UK by comparison the developer carries the cost and risk of infrastructure provision. In Germany, by contrast, development can be undertaken by a range of smaller developers with the public sector recouping its costs through land sales.

Housing Values: Affordability issues have meant that there is little appetite for housing values in the UK to rise. Values are, in any case, determined by macro-economic factors as much as by the quality of a particular home. There may however be mechanisms that can be used to influence the way that housing is valued so that quality and innovation are recognised by the valuer.

Attitudes towards valuations have changed markedly in recent years. The Urban

Splash business model that we described above also extends to the design and specification of the apartment. The early housebuilder-promoted warehouse conversions fitted out the apartments as if they were semi-detached houses, with false ceilings, fitted carpets, wall paper, curtains and traditional kitchens. Urban Splash when it started converting warehouses stripped out all of this chintz, leaving the original floorboards and bare walls, thereby saving hugely on fit out costs. Yet by emphasising design, selling an attractive lifestyle and developing their brand they actually managed to increase values. Adverts for city centre apartments are even stating to quote floor areas and the cost per square foot. Yet we still talk about flats as one or two bed units. If we were to move to a point where all homes were sold on floor area then we would start to give a value to larger units.

The Home Information Packs introduced by the UK government in 2007 will hopefully start to do the same for energy efficiency, since energy performance certificates will make clear the running costs of the home. Such measures need not increase the overall cost of homes but can change the factors that influence values, incentivising quality construction.

Efficiency of construction: The other element of the cost equation is the efficiency of construction and the assumption in the UK is that our housing industry is hopelessly inefficient. Compare if you will, the sight of hairy-arsed builders working knee-deep in mud to construct what is supposed to be a technologically sophisticated product with the spotless factory-made houses of Scandinavia or Japan. However the cost base on which those hairy-arsed builders work has been optimised to perfection. Developers know to the pound how much a particular housetype will cost and how long it will take to build. As they will tell you, if there were a way of building the house cheaper they would probably have found it.

There is a degree of confusion in response of policy makers who bemoan the results of this process and yet seek to reduce costs further. Many, like the Urban Task Force under the chairmanship of Richard Rogers[21] made the mistake of thinking that housing is architecture. They seem to suggest that a new neighbourhood should be procured in the same way as one would a concert hall or an office building. Architects should appointed along with engineers, quantity surveyors and service engineers to work their creative magic to produce a design which meets the clients' needs, fits the location and, hopefully, enhances our quality of life. Such a process can produce fine housing developments (although it can also produce disasters). However it is rarely a cost-effective way of building what is our most common form of building in the UK. Indeed it is a bit like a car manufacturer commissioning a team to design each run of a hundred cars coming off the production line. Because architecture is a creative profession it somehow does not feel right for architects to reproduce the same designs for each new scheme they undertake. The tendency is therefore for the wheel to be reinvented on every site with all the extra fee expenditure that this entails.

This is not how the majority of housing is or ever has been built. Most council housing was produced using standard housetypes, a system which dates back to the standard designs in the *Local Government Manual* of 1920. In Man-

chester low-rise housing estates can be dated by the design of their houses from the earliest 'H1' to the 'H6' which were the last council houses built in the city. In Wales, Tai Cymru (the Welsh equivalent of the English Housing Corporation) introduced a mandatory pattern book of sixteen designs to be used for all new housing built with their funding" much to the consternation of Welsh housing associations. When councils were not using standard housetypes they were using building systems, often imported from the continent for the high-rise and particularly the deck-access property of the 1960s and 70s. Then as now, the architect-designed estate was something of a novelty and was confined to flagship developments like the Crescents in Manchester, Hyde Park in Sheffield or the last great council estate, Byker in Newcastle.

The same is true of private production where the architect-designed estate is also a rarity. Here the standard housetype has dominated, albeit with names which are more appealing than the strict numbering system used in Manchester. The private sector has also been more skilful in disguising standard types with exterior decoration which can introduce endless variation into an estate of houses which are basically the same.

Model plans:
A series of standard housetypes designed for Noel Park in London in 1833. In the 19th century pattern books were common, perhaps the most influencial being Banister Fletcher's Model Houses for the Industrial Classes, 1871

The Artizans Labourers' & General Dwellings Estate
at HORNSEY

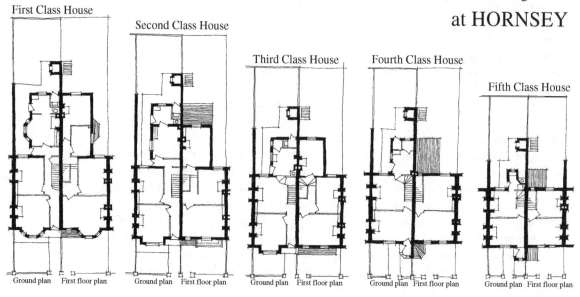

First Class House

Second Class House

Third Class House

Fourth Class House

Fifth Class House

Ground plan   First floor plan   Ground plan   First floor plan   Ground plan   First floor plan   Ground plan   First floor plan   Ground plan   First floor plan

These approaches illustrate the two main solutions to the problem of maintaining standards whilst reducing costs; pattern books of standard housetypes and prefabricated systems. In the UK with the exception of a short period in the 1960s we have tended to prefer standard housetypes, whereas on the continent they have opted for prefabrication. This is why in the UK standard housetypes save money while prefabrication costs more. We do not have the production capacity or production volumes to make prefabrication cost effective – at least not in the housing sector, prefabrication is used extensively for hotels, prisons and even MacDonald's Restaurants. It is therefore strange that organisations like English Partnerships (The Homes and Communities Agency since late 2008) are so against standard housetypes while being so keen on modular construction and prefabrication. In reality standardisation is a perfectly sensible way of reducing design time and therefore fees, increasing cost predictability and allowing the mass production of components. The problem is that standard housetypes are tainted by association with the housebuilder box marketed as 'The Balmoral' in the past. They are seen as leading to monotonous repetition and to a stifling of innovation.

The problem is not the principle of standard housetypes but the miserable selection of types that we have had to choose from in the past. This however is changing and some housebuilders have developed pattern books with a huge variety of units including specials that can be used for example to close an urban corner block or turn an unusual angle. At their best these pattern books collect the experience of the builder. When a site throws up an interesting new design it can be added to the range and used elsewhere, while designs which develop problems or which do not sell can be dropped. If the pattern book is treated as a positive tool, standard housetypes could have an important role to play in reducing costs and allowing the dissemination of good practice without the need to constantly reinvent the wheel. This, after all, is how most houses used to be built. In Georgian and Victorian times only the very grandest houses would

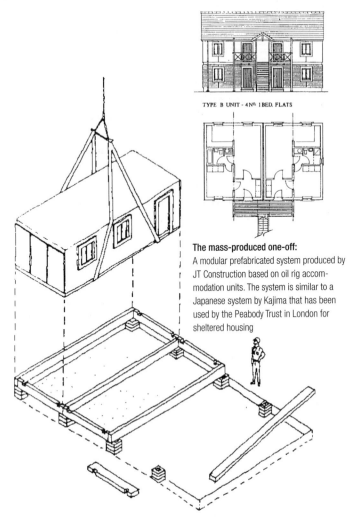

TYPE B UNIT - 4NO. 1 BED. FLATS

The mass-produced one-off:
A modular prefabricated system produced by JT Construction based on oil rig accommodation units. The system is similar to a Japanese system by Kajima that has been used by the Peabody Trust in London for sheltered housing

have been designed by an architect. Most were developed speculatively by small developers who would get the floor plans and elevations from pattern books which they would buy.

Jane Jacobs in the *Economy of Cities*[23] identified three stages of development for manufacturing industry: craft production, mass production and differentiated production. She pointed out in the 1960s that the construction industry was only just emerging from craft production more than a hundred years after most industries had done so. Yet it's attempts at mass production were, on the whole, disastrous and it has since reverted back to craft techniques. The future is however with differentiated production where a product can be produced with endless variations whilst still retaining economies of construction.

This must be the future for the housing industry which is so ill-suited to mass production.

An example of what this might mean can be seen in Japan[24] where the greatest advances in prefabrication have been made. The Japanese housebuilding industry constructs eight times as many new homes a year as we do in Britain, for a population only twice as large, and the largest developer, Seki Sui Heim, produces 70 000 units a year, more than 10 times the largest UK housebuilder. They do this using computer-aided design and computerised manufacture to customise each unit to the resident's requirements. Purchasers can choose a house style from a catalogue or exhibition and then adapt it to suit their own requirements. Japanese companies began research into increased industrialisation of housing production in the 1950s in response to oil price rises, the threat of earthquakes, skills shortages and the need to replace low-quality housing. Heavy investment has been made in marketing and production facilities made possible by the involvement of large companies such as Toyota. A house frame can be erected in as little as 3 hours and from order to completion, design and construction times have been reduced to just 50 days. Companies are able to achieve economies of scale through mass production of some elements while tailoring the product to the varied needs of their customers. The trend has been to move away from timber frame in favour of steel frame construction. This is more reliable in terms of quality. The systems also include pre-made modules such as bathrooms, kitchens and exercise rooms which can be added on to the house or used for extensions at a later date. Such prefabricated systems are by no means confined to the Japanese. They are widely used in Scandinavia, Canada, the US and Europe.

Is this the future for the British 21st century home? It may well be that the British, brought up on the three little pigs, are committed to the brick-built house which will not blow down however hard the wolf huffs and puffs. In our *21st Century Homes* research we concluded that the prefabrication industry in the UK was a graveyard of good intentions and questioned whether it really had any future in the face of market and industry resistance. It may be that we should play to our strengths and focus on getting the most out of standardisation.

While the total amount of money available for new housing in the future will not be very different to the budgets available to us today, this does not mean that we must resign ourselves to building the mean houses which characterise so much of our recent production. We should instead look to the economics of the land and housing market to reduce plot costs and ensure that quality is recognised in valuations. We should also look to the way that housing is procured to ensure that we are getting the full benefits of efficient volume production without the disbenefits of standardisation and monotony. People want their home to be unique as witnessed by the huge sums that people who have bought their council homes will lavish on stone cladding and external decoration. The challenge of the housing industry this century will be to produce what has been called the 'Mass-produced one off'[25] which can economically meet these diverse needs.

Part 3

THE SUSTAINABLE URBA

The 21st century home is evolving and, over coming decades, is likely to bear little resemblance to the suburban product that we became so used to in the 20th century. The influences described in Part 2 of this book are leading to a reversal of the centrifugal forces of dispersal. However while pressure for change is building and progress is being made, we may yet have reached a tipping point and we still lack clear models for new urban development. The principles of suburban development became so institutionalised in the 20th century that they are hard to shake off. They remain inherent to much of the land-use planning system, in detailed planning controls and in high-

'The multifunctional, creative city, which is also the liveable city, is the one that pollutes least'

European Green Paper on the Urban Environment

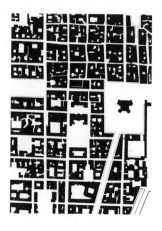

NEIGHBOURHOOD

way standards. They also underlie the workings of the land market, are reflected in public aspirations and have penetrated the very heart of professional philosophy. These are powerful forces which will inhibit change. Furthermore the urban areas to which people might return have been disfigured by years of misguided planning and urban decline. People may initially have fled from the overcrowded industrial city but they now fear to return to cities which they see as ugly, alienating environments, strangled by roads and beset by crime. Today's anti-urban sentiments are a result of what we have done to our cities rather than a rejection of the principle of urban living.

We therefore combine prediction with advocacy. The influences that we have described will only result in people and investors returning to urban areas if urban areas are reformed and are able to provide attractive places to live and work. We will not do this by turning urban areas into counterfeit suburbs or by recycling the outdated Utopias of the 20th century. What is needed are new models for urban development which can create the successful, humane urban areas required by the 21st century to attract people back to towns and cities. Part 3 of this book is devoted to one such model, The Sustainable Urban Neighbourhood.

Chapter 9
Urban repopulation

The most fundamental feature of the Sustainable Urban Neighbourhood is its location – the fact that it is located within existing towns and cities. Unlike past urban visions we do not set out a Utopian vision for new settlements free from the complexity and muddle of existing urban areas. Ours is a reforming vision and we propose the Sustainable Urban Neighbourhood as a building block to regenerate urban areas ravaged by decline and postwar planning. However developing a vision for the reform of urban areas is of little value if people do not want to live there, if developers refuse to build there and if businesses are not prepared to locate there. In the 1990s there were many who argued that activity could not be attracted back to urban areas that it had been abandoning for much of the century simply by placing limits on green field development. People, it was suggested, patently did not want to live in urban areas and in a free market any policy that assumed that they would was doomed. The location of development (in urban areas) was therefore the most difficult and even radical element of our vision in the 1990s. The chapter is therefore devoted to this issue, or urban repopulation as it has become known.

Government policy to stem dispersal
Concern to control the dispersal of British cities has been a feature of British planning policy for more than 50 years. Following the great interwar sprawl of private suburbia, government realised in the 1950s that they needed to act to limit the sprawl of cities. The main tool used to do this was the Green Belt which was wrapped around towns and cities and fiercely guarded from development. In many respects this policy has been hugely successful in preventing the scale of urban sprawl seen in many US cities. It has not however persuaded people or developers to remain within cities but has rather led to what has been called 'counter urbanisation'[1]. People with the means to do so have leapfrogged the green belt to live in smaller towns and remote rural areas. Bibby and Shepherd[2] have shown that between 1981 and 1991, for example, for every hectare of land developed on the fringe of urban areas four were developed in villages, hamlets and more remote rural areas. Green belt policy therefore distorted rather than reversed the trend of urban dispersal. In doing so it inflated land values without benefiting urban areas. Indeed, it could be argued, that the Green Belt was designed, not to prevent urban areas from depopulating, but to protect the countryside from a process of urban depopulation which was seen as inevitable and even desirable.

In recent years this view has changed. The initial impetus for policy was to reduce car use as set out in the 1990 *European Green Paper on the Urban Environment*[3] and echoed in *Sustainable Development: The UK Strategy*[4]. However in recent years the debate has shifted largely as a result of the household projections. In the mid

1990s population projections were released that showed that England needed to accommodate 4.4 million additional households by 2016. This raised the spectre of the housebuilder running rampant across England's green and pleasant land and led a coalition of urban and rural interests to lobby for more urban development in order to protect the countryside. To this was added another, less high profile argument – the regeneration of urban areas. This was put forward by the UK Round Table on Sustainable Development[5] and came to the fore with the election of a Labour government in 1997 with its traditional constituency in urban areas. If it is true that urban areas have declined as a result of population loss so the argument went, urban repopulation must be a prerequisite of their revival.

Each of these arguments has been the subject of considerable controversy. It has been suggested that urban development has little impact on car use, that the loss of green field land is not significant given the land area of the UK, and that, far from regenerating urban areas,

increasing the amount of urban development will lead to 'town cramming' and a decline in the quality of life in towns and cities. We review these arguments later in this chapter. However one of the reasons why these arguments were made so forcibly by the critics of the compact city in the 1990s was their horror that the concept had been largely accepted by government.

The government's enthusiasm for urban development took root under the stewardship of John Selwyn-Gummer, Conservative Secretary of State for the Environment in the early 1990s. This was a reversal of the free market policies under Thatcher that had seen a boom in out-of-town development following the liberalisation of the planning system. Swayed, no doubt, by the views of voters in the shire counties, the John Major government sought to tighten controls over out-of-town development while promoting higher densities, mixed-use development and encouraging more people and activities back into existing towns and cities. This policy shift was based, in part, on work by David Lock[6] into the most sustainable form of development. He

DICKENS HEATH – SOLIHULL

For most of the 20th century new town planning was something done by the public sector. However in the early 1990s private developers spurred on by a shortage of sites, got in on the act. Many private new settlement proposals were hard to distinguish from run of the mill suburban sprawl, and most never managed to chart a course through the planning system. However one that did and was worthy of the title new settlement, was Dickens Heath.

Dickens Heath is a new village built on 126 acres of green fields near Solihull. The plans included for schools, shops and commercial and recreational facilities along with 850 new homes for sale. It was built by a consortium including Solihull Council, Laing Homes, and Bryant Homes.

The scheme was designed by the Barton Willmore Partnership to create a clear identity for the new village with a safe and healthy environment for both residents and pedestrians. The village was

planned with a low-density rural fringe (six houses per acre) which gradually develops into a higher density urban village centre (eighteen houses per acre). The aim was to emulate a traditional village allowing the development of a mix of housing types in different parts of the settlement. The aim was to create a diverse and sustainable com-

munity. A mix of land uses was also planned along with open spaces and a traditional village square to provide a focal point for the community. Sites were also allocated for commercial and retail uses and a community hall/library, primary school and medical centre.

The village was designed so that walking distances were minimised to reduce reliance on the car. There are three main roads through the village and traffic is excluded from parts of the centre and dispersed along a series of residential roads with 20mph speed limits. Footpaths and cycleways run parallel to the roads and in two circular loops around the village.

While it was not as large as schemes like Cambourne, Dickens Heath was one of the largest of the private sector new villages to actually be built. Yet it barely meets the first rung on the sustainability ladder suggested by David Lock.

identified five 'classic' ways in which housing growth could be accommodated; urban infill, peripheral expansion, the expansion of selected villages, the expansion of all villages, and new settlements. Each of these was evaluated against a series of economic, social and environmental criteria. The result was not entirely clear-cut. Urban infill and new settlements achieved the highest scores but scored poorly on certain criteria. However he did suggest three levels of sustainability for settlements:

750–1000 houses: Somewhere which would support a primary school but not jobs, public transport or other amenities. Such settlements, he argued, would be heavily car-dependent.

3000–5000 houses: A place that would support a secondary school and some jobs and amenities but would not be large enough to serve its population or to be considered self-sufficient.

10000 houses: A settlement with a population of 25–30000 people was considered the threshold for sustainability. It would be able to achieve a critical mass of jobs, services and amenities to serve its population and would support a good public transport service so reducing both the need to travel and the reliance on the car. Two possible conclusions were drawn from this work. We should either be building very large new settlements or should be building within existing urban areas. Both have since become strands of policy with the introduction of the Eco-Towns programme in 2007[7]. However in the 1990s the only new settlements being planned were those promoted by the private sector, the largest of which came nowhere near the threshold for sustainability. The inevitable conclusion was that the majority of development would have to take place within existing settlements.

David Lock's work formed the basis for the first version of version of *Planning Policy Guidance Note 13*[8] on transport in 1994. This was described by Lock as having 'such far-reaching effects that it would soon come to be regarded as a major landmark in the evolution of planning and the true start of the journey towards sustainability'. It was indeed one of the first government policy statements to seek to reverse the dispersal of settlements. Amongst other things it sought to prevent out-of-town retail, leisure and commercial development and stated that, where possible, all new housing should be built within existing towns and cities. If this was not possible new development must be served by public transport and new settlements would only be considered if they were likely to reach a population of 10 000 within twenty years. In urban areas it stated that local plans should seek to 'concentrate higher density residential development near public transport centres... and close to local facilities'. In a section entitled Planning at the Neighbourhood Scale, it also promoted the idea of mixed-use development suggesting that '...planning for a variety of uses – shops and restaurants – on the ground floor of developments will help keep streets lively. Attention to preserving or enhancing continuous pavement level streetscapes and the avoidance of blank frontages... can be a major contribution to retaining pedestrian activity, retaining the commercial life of the area and to crime prevention'.

The government thus set down as long ago as 1994 the outline of what we have called the Sustainable Urban Neighbourhood in the unlikely form of a planning circular on transport. However this was just the first of a series of Planning Policy Guidance Notes (now called Planning Policy Statements), notably PPG 1 on local plans, PPG 3 on Housing and PPG 6 on retail development[9].

The focus of government policy then moved to housing, particularly following the 1995 household projections[10] which increased the number of new households projected by 2016 to 4.4 million. This added impetus to government policy since it meant that a policy of locating more housing within existing urban areas would not only reduce transport but also the number of green fields lost to development. The 1995 Housing White Paper[11] set a policy target that half of all new homes should be built in urban areas. This initially went unnoticed by many in the planning world who were still arguing that the household projections were too high (they have since been shown to be right). However the issue came to a head the following year when the government suggested in the Green Paper *Household growth: Where shall we live?*[12] that the target should be increased to 60%. This was based on land-use change data[13] that showed that 49% of all new housing in 1993 had been built on previously developed urban land, in other words that the 50% target was virtually being met.

The Conservatives never had the opportunity to enact this 60% target because in May 1997 the Labour Party swept to power. In opposition they had been cautious about the 60% target for homes built in urban areas, calling it 'aspirational' and suggesting that it was unlikely ever to be achieved. Their suspicion had been that the Conservatives were protecting their suburban and rural support base by cramming housing into cities[14]. Indeed concerns about 'town cramming' were widely heard at the time as the planning profession fought a rear-guard action against urbanisation. Initially the Labour government stuck to the 50% target. However the turning point came in early 1998. In the previous Autumn the government had approved the extension of Stevenage into its green belt. This, together with some unguarded comments by the Planning Minister Richard Cabourn who seemed to suggest that the green belt was 'up for grabs'[15], fuelled a campaign that culminated in the Countryside March of Spring 1998. Thousands of people from rural England converged on London driven by the feeling that the government no longer had their best interests at heart, whether it be plans to ban hunting or a seeming willingness to sacrifice the countryside to build new housing.

The government had however already started to shift its position under the leadership of the Deputy Prime Minister John Prescott. He had been given a 'super department' bringing together planning and transport. While his political background did not suggest that he was a natural supporter of the countryside lobby, he did accept the arguments about urban regeneration and sustainability, representing as he did, the City of Hull that had suffered more than most

from depopulation and decline. In a statement to the House of Commons on 23rd February 1998[16] Prescott accepted the 60% target and signalled a wider change in policy away from a 'predict and provide' approach to accommodating household growth. Up until this point housing had been built in areas where the population was growing. Building new homes, of course caused the population to grow even more leading to more housing allocations and so on... These growth figures were then imposed on local authorities who were under an obligation to allocate sufficient housing land in their plans. Prescott announced that local authorities would henceforth be able to provide for less homes than projected for their area provided that they monitored house prices, homelessness and other indicators to ensure that demand was being met.

The other initiative that Prescott announced was the establishment of the Urban Task Force under the Chairmanship of the architect Richard Rogers (Lord Rogers of Riverside). The Task Force embarked on a year-long programme of visits and discussions drawing heavily on experience from cities like Barcelona. They also commissioned research including a report into attitudes to urban areas that URBED undertook with MORI and which was published as *But would you live there? Shaping attitudes to urban living*[17].

The Task Force Report *Towards an Urban Renaissance* was published in 1999[18] and contained 105 recommendations. This led in the following year to an Urban White Paper *Our Towns and Cities: The Future – Delivering an Urban Renaissance*[19] and subsequently to *The Sustainable Communities Plan – Building for the Future*[20] in 2003 which has formed the basis of government policy ever since. *The Sustainable Communities Plan* has two strands, the accommodation of growth pressures in the south and the revival of the north under the *Northern Way*[21] set up in 2004. The process also led to the establishment of the Commission for Architecture and the Build Environment (CABE) under its first chief executive John Rouse who had been secretary to the Urban Task Force.

It is difficult to know when writing a book such as this which reports will have a lasting impact and which will be forgotten within a year or so. Some of the policies that we thought so important in the first edition are now long forgotten. However the suite of policies and documents driven through by John Prescott between 1998 and 2005 has changed the way that Britain is planned. In its 2005 update[22] the Urban Task Force were able to report that the proportion of new housing being built in urban areas was running at 70% and the average density of new housing had risen from 23 to 40 dwellings per hectare. Indeed for those of us working as urbanists it seems that everything has changed. Housebuilders who once built only on green fields became focused almost entirely on urban areas, be they city centre apartments or new housing for sale in the inner city. The remaining problems, as the Task Force accepts in its review, relate to policy areas beyond the control of the planning system such as the state of inner city schools and the deprivation that still besets many inner city communities.

It may be too early to say, but our belief is that the Urban Task Force will be to the 21st century what the Tudor-Walters report, that we described in Chapter 4, was to the 20th century – the point when the tide turned. The low-water mark when the forces of dispersal that had been pulling cities apart for a century eventually started to recede. It is interesting to compare this to the US where the advocates of Smart Growth remain a pressure group. They have garnered widespread support but have failed so far to reverse the dispersal of US cities. Compared to this the market in the UK has been completely transformed and with it the fortunes of British towns and cities. We believe that this will come to be seen as an object lesson in how public policy can shape urban areas.

The people – where will they go?

The battle ground on which these issues were fought so intensely in the mid 1990s was the 60% housing target. The intensity of this debate has faded from memory. There were however many people who thought that the government had caved in to protests against green field development and were undoing the work of a century of planning that had sought to overcome the problems of urban areas. The 60% target was compared to the high-rise building programme of the 1960s and was seen as an unacceptable imposition of people's freedom to choose where they live.

An important contribution was made by the Town and Country Planning Association which organised a series of major studies and enquiries focusing on the 60% target. These included with *The People – Where will they go?*[23] and the *Urban housing capacity and the sustainable city* programme[24]. While this work aired a broad range of views, the thrust was to question the logic and feasibility of urban infill. As Sir Peter Hall and Michael Breheny stated in an article in *Town and Country Planning*[25]; 'The fashionable logic suggests that, by packing more people into existing urban areas we can both reduce the need to travel – thus reducing fuel consumption and emissions – and minimise loss of open countryside to development'. They go on to state that: 'This raises the critical question of whether sustainability really entails urban compaction or whether – as the TCPA has argued – it is possible to plan new developments, including new communities in ways that are perfectly sustainable'. This reflects the TCPA's traditional advocacy of the garden city as an alternative to urban areas. Their arguments against urban containment are that the benefits of protecting the countryside and reducing car use do not outweigh the problems which include the lack of scope for urban infill, the problems of town cramming and the lack of demand for urban living.

In the middle of this debate URBED were commissioned by Friends of the Earth to rebut these arguments and indeed to test the feasibility of increasing the target from 60% to 75%. Our report, *Tomorrow: A peaceful path to urban reform*[26], paraphrasing as it did the Ebenezer Howard original, was a conscious dig at the Town and Country Planning Association (our differences with the TCPA have since been overcome and I (DR) even served as a policy council member with them for a number of years). The *Tomorrow* report together with our earlier report for the Joseph Rowntree Foundation[27] formed the initial material for this book. In it we enjoyed ourselves by pointing out how ridiculous it was to claim that cities were overcrowded and could not accommodate new housing after a century in which they had been haemorrhaging population. The suggestion that 75% of new housing could be accommodated within urban areas was ridiculed at the time. However the government's land-use change statistics show that in 2005 the figure was 77%[28]. In the remainder of this chapter we review the arguments that we explored in the *Tomorrow* report for and against urban development:

Urban density and gasoline consumption

The original impetus behind the promotion of development within urban areas was sustainability, specifically the reduction of car use. As the *European Green Paper on the Urban Environment*[29] states 'the city offers density and variety (and) the efficient time and energy combination of social and economic functions'. The idea that the city may provide our environmental salvation may initially seem strange since so many of our environmental problems are concentrated in cit-

ies. However, as we saw in Chapter 5, many of the environmental issues that will shape the future city: CO_2 emissions, pollution, damage to the ozone layer and acid rain relate to the private car. What is more, while the domestic and industrial sectors have gradually reduced their environmental impact, these gains have been cancelled out by the growth in transport emissions. Policy to reduce car use has included taxation, restrictions on parking places and investment in public transport. Alongside this, governments across the English-speaking world have also seen the location of new development as an important means of reducing the demand for car use.

This was based on influential research by Newman and Kenworthy in the late 1980s[30] that demonstrated a correlation between per-capita gasoline consumption and population density. They found that US cities have twice the gasoline consumption of Australian cities and four times that of European cities and that there was a direct relationship between this and the compactness of urban form. This research was used to justify urban containment policies in the United States, Australia and Europe.

Newman and Kenworthy's work did not go unchallenged[31]. Its critics suggested that as jobs and services decentralised commuting distances from suburban housing would reduce and also that the findings took insufficient account of income levels and fuel prices. However the main objections related to the acceptability of urban containment. This has been a consistent thread running through the debate about the compact city. The critics of containment have always started from the assumption that living in towns and cities is unacceptable to the majority of the population and have therefore reacted against research which has concluded that this is where they should be forced to live. They argued that holding back the tide of urban expansion would require unacceptable levels of state control on people's freedom to choose where to live. This was always an ideological debate about free market-led decentralisation verses state intervention and had little to do with the environmental impacts of different settlement patterns.

Density and travel:
There is a strong correlation between population density and both total travel distances and the distances travelled by car.
Source: ECOTEC 1993

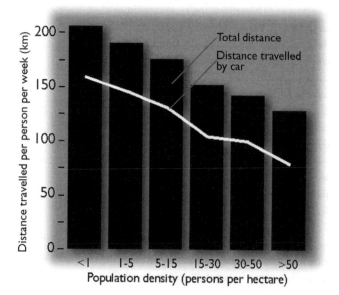

In the UK research by ECOTEC[32] in 1993 reinforced Newman and Kenworthy's findings. They demonstrated that people in the UK living at the lowest densities travelled twice the distance by car per week as the people living at the highest densities. Peter Headicar[33] has also demonstrated that travel distances in rural areas are growing much more rapidly than in larger cities. There is however a problem here as the late Michael Breheny[34], a leading member of the TCPA, pointed out. He calculated that, if all of the UK population were to live at the population densities of metropolitan areas, it would save about 34% of energy used in transport. This, as he pointed out, is impossible and the level of savings achievable even through the most draconian use of planning powers was more likely to be 10–15%. However a better estimate of savings, he argued, can be calculated by looking at the rates of decentralisation in the 30 years to the mid 1990s. If this had not taken place, the transport energy savings would have amounted to just 2.5%. This he suggested was the most that urban containment policies could hope to achieve and did not justify the unpopular policies that would be required to bring it about.

He had a point, increasing the density of cities is not the easiest nor the most sensible way to reduce transport CO_2 emissions. Better to use taxes or congestion charging as has been successful in London. Better still invest in public transport which is another way of shrinking distances.

However this does not mean that the compact city is of no utility in reducing the impacts of transport. Brehemy's argument rests on the assumption that there are major disbenefits to the compact city – the forced repatriation of unwilling suburbanites to the city – that do not justify the modest benefits. If the compact city is not seen as a bad thing then this argument does not hold. If the compact city was a place that is attractive to a range of people as a result of social and demographic change then the disbenefits fall away and a 2.5% reduction in transport emissions is a saving well worth having.

Of course transport is one of the factors that has made urban areas more attractive. As congestion increases and fuel becomes more expensive commuting is increasingly unattractive. As Andreas Duaney[35] has pointed out, the unions in the US fought long and hard to reduce the working week yet these gains have been completely cancelled out as the average American employee now spends more than two hours a day locked in a metal box travelling to and from work. The response to this could be for employers to relocate to the suburbs as has happened in the US and to an extent in the UK. The problem is that suburban employment cannot be served by public transport and few people will live within walking distance. The congestion is therefore just transferred to peripheral roads such as the M25 around London and the problem remains.

Another solution is home working as we have described elsewhere. However, as predicted by the Henley Centre[36] report that we quoted in the first edition of this book, there is also a trend for people (particularly professionals and women) to move back to larger cities which are able to offer a high quality of life. The pressures of juggling family life, work and leisure in households where both partners are working makes it impossible to contemplate the sort of commuting times that men have been accepting for years.

In identifying a correlation between the density of development and car travel, we may therefore have been confusing cause and effect. It may have been that people in high-density cities do not travel less because they live at high densities, they live at high densities because they are fed up of travelling. As personal mobility is constrained by congestion or restrictions on car use, the attractiveness of low-density locations is reduced. Conversely locations with employment and facilities within easy reach on foot or by public transport are becoming more attractive. This is well summed up by hoardings advertising urban housing developments which suggest to passing motorists stuck in traffic that if they bought one of the apartments they could be home by now.

While compact settlement policies may not therefore be the most effective means to reduce car use, measures to reduce car use

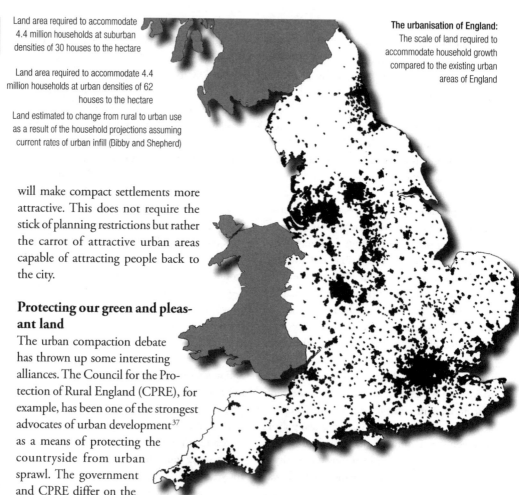

Land area required to accommodate 4.4 million households at suburban densities of 30 houses to the hectare

Land area required to accommodate 4.4 million households at urban densities of 62 houses to the hectare

Land estimated to change from rural to urban use as a result of the household projections assuming current rates of urban infill (Bibby and Shepherd)

The urbanisation of England:
The scale of land required to accommodate household growth compared to the existing urban areas of England

will make compact settlements more attractive. This does not require the stick of planning restrictions but rather the carrot of attractive urban areas capable of attracting people back to the city.

Protecting our green and pleasant land

The urban compaction debate has thrown up some interesting alliances. The Council for the Protection of Rural England (CPRE), for example, has been one of the strongest advocates of urban development[37] as a means of protecting the countryside from urban sprawl. The government and CPRE differ on the amount of countryside that is being lost to development. In the 1990s the government put the figure at around 5 000 hectares a year whereas the CPRE suggested that the figure was more like 11 000 hectares a year. Either way the loss of countryside represented a relatively small proportion of the total countryside area. The total land

area of England is just over 13 million hectares, of which just under 1.4 million hectares or 10.6% is urbanised. Figures from Bibby and Shepherd[38] in the 1990s suggested that the projected 4.4 million increase in households could lead to the loss of a further 169 400 hectares of rural land between 1991 and 2016 which would increase the urbanised area from 10.6% to 12%. While this is not exactly the wholesale destruction of the English countryside, it is a significant area – the equivalent of losing the county of Surrey to development. Since that time the rate of development on green field land has halved from around a third of new housing to just over 15%[28]. However the regional distribution of household growth still means that the loss of countryside is concentrated in southern counties where Bibby and Shepherd suggested that it would be up to

Housing land:
Proportion of new dwellings built on previously-residential, agricultural and vacant or derelict land, 1989 to 2006. *Land Use Change Statistics (England) 2007 – provisional estimates (July 2008)*

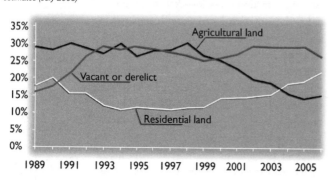

six times the national average, much of it valued by local people. In the south the protection of the countryside therefore remains a compelling case for maximising the amount of development which takes place within existing settlements.

The loss of rural land is of particular concern where it involves areas of natural beauty and ecological importance. However most green belt land falls into neither of these categories – much of it is agricultural land of little ecological or landscape value. In the past there have been concerns about the loss of agricultural capacity. However this has faded as intensive farming techniques and European set-aside subsidies have reduced the area of land in cultivation. Nevertheless land taken out of intensive agriculture should probably be exploited for its ecological rather than its development potential. We should also be moving to less intensive, organic forms of agriculture and reducing food air miles by increasing local production. We may even need to use this land to produce biofuel. There remain good rural protection reasons to minimise the amount of countryside lost to development.

Not all land in rural areas is green and pleasant; almost half of derelict land is to be found in rural areas, representing some 19 000 hectares in the 1990s. This includes mine workings, military dereliction and redundant institutions or industrial sites. This has always created confusion in government statistics because land is categorised by its previous use rather than its location – derelict hospitals or airfields in the heart of the countryside developed for housing would therefore be categorised as an urban brown field development. Indeed in the 2000s some 80 hospital sites as well as many former mine sites are being brought forward for development by English Partnerships – some as 'Carbon Challenge' schemes or Eco-towns. Few of these sites are part of existing settlements and many are hardly the most sustainable location for development. While the most politically sensitive sites tend to be those in the green belt on the edge of existing towns, these sites can at least be functionally linked to existing towns and could be more sustainable than isolated brown field sites.

The regeneration of our cities

The final reason put forward for the development of more housing in urban areas is the need to regenerate urban areas. This was suggested by the UK Round Table on Sustainable Development[5] but received less attention than the reduction in car use and the loss of countryside in the discussions of the 1990s. This has however turned out to be the most compelling reason for urban repopulation. We suggested in Part 1 of this book that the depopulation of urban areas and inner city decline are two sides of the same coin. Those with the power to do so abandoned cities in the late 20th century to the poor, the powerless and the vulnerable. It is therefore hardly surprising that urban areas experienced high levels of unemployment, crime and other social problems. It is also not surprising that the billions of pounds of government money that have been spent to address inner city problems had little or no effect on these levels of deprivation. The problem has been that the people assisted by these initiatives often used their new-found economic power to join the urban exodus. The problems of urban areas has therefore been a combination of population loss and the fact that they have become a sink for poverty.

The only way to address the root cause of these problems is to stem and then reverse the loss of population from Britain's cities. This is something that has been partly achieved in the eight years since we first published this book as we describe in the following pages. Urban environments have been created that have attracted people back to cities and persuaded others not to leave. The results however are patchy and while certain parts of the inner city have been transformed the problems elsewhere remain intractable and disparities of wealth in urban areas have actually increased. The other side of repopulation is gentrification and with it the danger is that rising values squeeze out local people or displace deprivation to other areas. However gentrification goes hand in hand with urban repopulation and without this there is little prospect of revival in the inner cities.

There is not the space

The most fundamental argument against the accommodation of household growth within urban areas has been that the capacity was simply not available. There is no point, it was suggested, arguing that a greater proportion of household growth should be accommodated in urban areas if this was either not possible or would have led to unacceptable conditions in those areas. This has led to a whole new discipline, the measurement of urban capacity – the amount of housing that could be accommodated within any given urban area. Indeed it is a discipline that we could claim to have partly invented. After our Friends of the Earth report was published, we were contacted by the government who were drawing up a new version of PPG3 on housing. This was to include a requirement that all planning authorities had to undertake housing capacity assessments. The idea was that they would measure the capacity of their urban areas and only allocate green fields for the development of housing that could not be accommodated in these urban areas. A number of these studies had been done in the early 1990s many of which seemed to have been designed to prove that capacity did not exist. With a couple of exceptions even the positive studies had come up with capacity estimates below the government's 60% target. Our FOE report had cast the net much more widely in measuring capacity and in the government's view had come up with the 'right' answer. We were therefore asked to review recent capacity studies and to draw up guidance for all future capacity studies. The methodology we developed in our report: *Tapping the Potential*[39] is still in use today.

The lost urban populations: This table illustrates how central urban areas have lost population to a far greater extent than the metropolitan counties.
Source: Office for National Statistics

	1911	1931	1951	1961	1971	1981	1991	2005
Greater London	7 161	8 110	8 197	7 977	7 529	6 806	6 809	7 387
Inner London	4 998	4 893	3 679	3 481	3 060	2 550	2 627	2 644
Outer London	2 162	3 217	4 518	4 496	4 470	4 255	4 263	
West Midlands	1 780	2 143	2 547	2 724	2 811	2 673	2 629	2 578
Birmingham	526	1 003	1 113	1 179	1 107	1 021	1 007	992
Greater Manchester	2 638	2 727	2 716	2 710	2 750	2 619	2 570	2 530
Manchester	714	766	703	657	554	463	439	432
West Yorkshire	1 852	1 939	1 985	2.002	2 090	2 067	2 085	2 095
Leeds		446	483	505	710	749	718	715
South Yorkshire	963	1 173	1 253	1 298	1 331	1 317	1 302	1 272
Sheffield		455	512	513	581	579	548	512
Merseyside	1 378	1 587	1 663	1 711	1 662	1 522	1 450	
Liverpool	746	856	789	741	610	517	481	441
Tyne and Wear	1 105	1 201	1 201	1 241	1 218	1 155	1 130	1 083
Newcastle	112	267	286	292	336	312	384	266

The lost populations

The staring point for our assessment of urban capacity in the *Tomorrow* report was the historic loss of population from cities. If towns and cities had lost so many people, surely they must have huge amounts of urban capacity. It is actually really difficult to get a handle on the population of UK cities. Outside London the quoted population figures are based on administrative areas so that they depend more on the way that boundaries are drawn than the size of the city. Because of this, cities like Manchester and Liverpool appear smaller than they are because large parts of the cities fall within other local authorities. In Manchester, for example, the population of the City Council is 430 000 yet parts of Trafford and Salford stretch to within half a mile of the city centre. We have calculated that the functional city of Manchester – that which lies within the M60 Motorway is around 1 million people while Greater Manchester, including the satellite towns is just over 2.5 Million.

The table to the left shows population change in the UK's urban areas. London is the largest city by some distance, indeed it is now the largest city in Europe and has been growing rapidly since the start of the century. However as the table shows, this is despite the fact that the population of inner London has halved since 1911, largely through the planned dispersal of people through slum clearance.

In the other metropolitan conurbations the population loss in the 20th century was relatively modest. Indeed between 1911 and 1961 each of the six main conurbations continued to gain population. Their populations peaked at 19.7 million in 1961 since when they have lost 7.7 % of their population or about 1.5 million people. The population loss has been concentrated in the inner areas. Manchester has lost a quarter of a million people since its peak in the late 1950s just within its limited geographical area. Liverpool has lost even more and if we were to extend our view we would find that the same is true of Glasgow. Compared to this the other cities have retained their population, indeed Leeds has

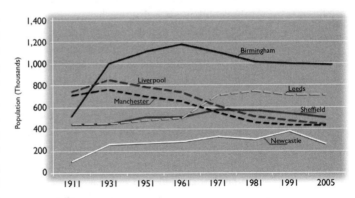

The changing population of UK cities: Based on the table to the left, this graph shows population change in six of the UK's core cities. *Source: Office for National Statistics*

grown. This is in part a statistical anomaly. Much of the population loss has been from the centre to the periphery through population dispersal. Since Leeds and Birmingham contain many of their own suburbs, population dispersal does not register as population loss. However it also reflects wider issues of decline. The old industrial cities have haemorrhaged population since the 1950s as a result of the loss of their economic base.

This we discussed at length in Part 1 of this book. Here our interest is in the recent trend. In Urban Task Force's 2006 update [22] they quote the population increase of Manchester city centre from 90 to 25 000 as evidence of progress. You would think, as most people do, that Manchester's population is therefore growing rapidly. This is not however the case. Since 1991 the population of both Greater Manchester and Manchester City has in fact fallen slightly, despite the boom in city centre housing. The same is true of all of the other cities outside London. The State of the Cities Report published in 2006 [40] tries to unravel what has been happening. The picture is confused by the overall loss of population from the North and West to the South and East of England. There have also been fluctuations with cities gaining population in the 1980s and the late 1990s but with losses in the early 1990s and another dip in the early 2000s. However while the State of the Cities report is able to say that, excluding London, the top 55 cities in England have grown by 8 % between 1997 and 2003, the reality is that this growth is concentrated in the south and in the smaller cities. The best that can be said of the big cities, both the core and the conurbations, is that they have stemmed the haemorrhage of population but they are yet to achieve any consistent population gains.

One process that is at work in these figures is what Tony Champion[41] has called the 'cascade effect' of population loss. There is a process at work in England of population movement down the urban hierarchy from inner urban areas to suburban districts, from suburbs to peripheral areas and from the periphery to rural districts. This process is at work even in cities that are growing. The size of a city depends on the scale of the cascade and the rate of inward migration often into the inner city to replace the people who are leaving. Manchester may have been successful in attracting city centre residents but within a few years they join the cascade, particularly when they start to have children. The big cities have also undertaken huge housing restructuring programmes in the 2000s through the Housing Market Renewal programme. This has involved the clearance of many inner city neighbourhoods in preparation for redevelopment. Stoke, for example, is clearing 15 000 homes in a ten year programme that will eventually see them replaced.

The current situation may be slightly confused, but the fact remains that Britain's inner urban areas have lost huge numbers of people in the last 50 years – Manchester and Liverpool alone have lost half a million people. This loss has occurred through the hollowing-out of these cities leaving them with a physical structure too large for their current population to sustain and therefore surely with huge capacity for repopulation. However this notional housing capacity does not necessarily translate into physical capacity for new homes. While cities may have lost population the land occupied by these people has not remained fallow. It has been redeveloped for housing at lower densities, used, often very wastefully, for road building, or turned over to commercial use. Our urban areas have therefore become crystalised into a low-density pattern of development which is now very difficult to change.

We do however need to find new ways of measuring the housing capacity of these urban areas which is what we tried to do in the *Tomorrow* report and subsequently in the *Tapping the Potential* guidance for the government. The following sections are based on the findings of this work. The research was done in the 1990s when many of our critics argued that the capacity we described was finite, it could be used up once and then would be gone. However it seemed then that the amount of available capacity, be it vacant land, commercial conversions or redevelopment, seemed to remain constant despite being used up – the proverbial bottomless cup. It would be nice to be commissioned to do a proper review of the figures to understand fully what has happened since the original research. In the meantime we have tried where possible to get contemporary figures to compare our original work to the situation in 2008.

Brown field land

Much of the discussion about urban housing capacity has focused on brown field land – land that has previously been developed. In the 1990s almost half of new housing was already built on urban, previously-developed land suggesting a ready supply of brown field sites. However these figures had to be treated with care for three reasons. The first was that they masked huge regional variations from 83 % in London to just above 30 % in the East Midlands and the South West. The second was the fact that urban land was defined by its previous use rather than its location. A significant proportion of 'urban' brown field land may in fact have been in the countryside. The third reason was highlighted by Michael Breheny[42] who pointed out that the percentage rise in the amount of brown field land developed for housing in the early 1990s took place in the context of falling housing output. The area of urban land developed for housing in the early 1990s had actually fallen, the percentage only increased because other categories declined more rapidly. He concluded that the best brown field sites had been used up and that, with the exception of the North West, brown field land

Capacity at net densities of..

Source	Area (ha)	30units/ha	62units/ha
Derelict urban land justifying reclamation	19 759	415 000*1	879 000
Half of all reclaimed derelict land since 1988 in 'soft uses'	1 236	26 000	55 000
Urban land reclaimed since 1988 with no end use	772	16 000	34 000
Vacant urban land which has previously been developed	9 226*2	194 000	411 000
Vacant urban land not previously developed	13 965*3	293 000	621 000
SUB TOTAL	44 958	944 000	2 000 000
Urban land likely to become derelict 1993–2016	19 800*4	416 000	881 000
Urban land likely to fall vacant 1993–2016	9 245*5	277 000	573 000
SUB TOTAL	29 045	693 000	1 454 000
TOTAL	74 000	1 637 000	3 454 000

*1 All capacity figures assume that half of the land will be large sites and therefore subject to gross densities of 12 and 27 units/ hectare rather than net densities. All figures are rounded to the nearest thousand and may not sum to the independently rounded totals
*2 Based on the figure from the 1990 survey of vacant land discounted to take account of reclaimed derelict land
*3 We have assumed that half of the vacant previously undeveloped land could be brought forward for development.
*4 Based on the annual rate of land becoming derelict in urban areas and justifying reclamation between 1982 and 1993
*5 Based on the same rate of increase as that for derelict land

Predicted recycled land capacity 1998: Estimate of potential recycled land available for housing within urban areas. *Source: URBED*

was likely to be exhausted by 2006 at which point the amount of housing that could be built on recycled sites would drop to 30–40%.

This idea that there is a finite stock of brown field land which is rapidly being used up was not however borne out by derelict and vacant land data. The 1993 *Survey of Derelict Land in England*[43] for example identified just under 40 000 hectares of derelict land. This had fallen by 900 hectares since 1988 despite the fact that 9 500 hectares had been reclaimed. While almost half of this land was in rural areas the greatest increases were in general industrial dereliction, much of which was in urban areas. What is more, much of the land that had been reclaimed, had no end use or had been turned into low grade open space that may be available for development.

In addition to this the *National survey of vacant land in the urban areas of England*[44] undertaken in 1990 used Ordnance Survey mapping data to survey all of the urban areas of England with a population of more than 10 000 people. This estimated that there was a national stock of vacant land of around 60 000 hectares; 'an area the size of a small county the size of Cleveland'. However more than half of this is land had never previously been developed.

In our work for Friends of the Earth we struggled to bring together these data sets and to make assumptions about future rates of vacancy and dereliction. The findings are summarised in the table above which estimated that there were just under 45 000 hectares of vacant urban land available for development in England and that this could grow by a further 30 000 hectares by 2016. If all of this land had been developable for housing it would have accommodated 1.6 million homes at garden city densities and twice that at urban densities. You will recall that our task was to explore whether 75% of the 4.4 million extra households could be accommodated within urban areas. If all derelict land had been developed at urban densities this was just about possible although, of course, there were a range of practical and economic reasons why this was very unlikely. The conclusion was that, based on vacant land alone, which was all that most of the urban capacity studies of the time measured, we were going to struggle to achieve even the government's 60%. We needed to find other sources of capacity as described below.

The most up to date information on current levels of vacant land is the *National Land Use Database 2006*[45]. This identified 62 700 hectares of previously developed land in England suitable for housing. Of this 34 900 hectares were derelict or vacant (the balance being sites with existing uses but with redevelopment potential). These figures are not directly comparable to the data quoted above. The 1990 vacant land figure relates just to urban areas and the derelict land figures relate only to land 'so damaged by industrial or other development that it is incapable of beneficial use without treatment'. Only 17 850 hectares of land in the *National Land Use Database* covers land this damaged. This appears to suggest that the amount of brown field land has probably halved since the early 1990s.

It is not surprising that the level has fallen given that we have experienced a ten year development boom. However even in London, where you would think that every acre of vacant land had been sought out and built on, the survey identifies 860 ha of vacant land. The reason for this is that vacant land is part of the development cycle. It is always being created and developed. In times of low development activity vacant land is created more quickly than it is developed while the opposite is true in a buoyant market. The type of vacancy also changes. The rate of industrial restructuring and mine closures that characterised the 1990s may have slowed but urban areas are always evolving and vacant land is

a natural result of this process. Vacant land today is more likely to be the result of institutional closures such as hospitals than industrial closure. Future sources of vacant land are difficult to predict – maybe large format retailing will close as a result of Internet shopping or perhaps car parks will become surplus to requirements due to policies to reduce car use. It is however reasonable to assume that vacant land will continue to characterise urban areas and will continue to provide a source of urban housing capacity.

Other sources of urban housing capacity

Urban housing capacity is an elastic concept. It is difficult to measure because it is so dependent on demand. This is why London, which is already the most intensively developed part of Britain, was able to accommodate more than 98% of new housing on previously developed land or conversions in 2005[28]. People want to live and work there, developers have a market for housing and therefore have an incentive to seek out capacity beyond that which any capacity study could ever identify. This extra housing capacity comes from the following sources:

The redevelopment of council estates: David Hall, writing in Town and Country Planning in 1997[46], suggested that 'it should not be forgotten that there are still many thousands of high-rise flats... which within the timescale of the household growth projections will very likely have to be pulled down'. This has been precipitated by the government's Decent Homes Standard and a massive programme to transfer social rented housing from councils to various forms of independent, financially self-sufficient organisations. Because many estates from the 1960s cannot economically be brought up to the decent homes standard they are indeed being redeveloped.

This however has not happened as David Hall predicted when he said: 'high density housing is the least preferred by people when they have the choice. Thus there will be an "overspill" of population from (the redevelopment of) these estates'. In fact many of these estates were not

Distribution of derelict land in the 1990s: Area of derelict land within urban areas (percentage indicates the proportion of derelict land within the region in urban areas).
Source: Survey of Derelict Land in England 1993 - DOE

5-6,000 hectares
3-4,000 hectares
2-3,000 hectares
1-2,000 hectares
<1,000 hectares

46%
65%
73% 6,285ha
42%
61%
28%
81%
14%
36%

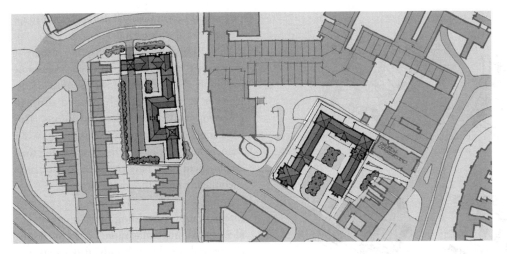

Coventry City Centre: A plan from work by URBED in Coventry to explore the development of under-used city centre car parks for housing. This was part of a council strategy to accommodate 1 000 homes within the ring road, 355 of which could be accommodated on surface car parks

built to particularly high densities, they just felt that way. The Crescents in Hulme in Manchester, for example were built at just 15 units to the acre which is what Ebenezer Howard suggested for the garden city (see illustrations on pages 53 and 54). The problem was that they had the worst of both worlds, looking and feeling overcrowded but accommodating insufficient people to animate public areas, support local services and make them feel safe. It was therefore possible to redevelop Hulme at twice the density of the 1960s development. Indeed across the country the model for the redevelopment of council estates has exploited this density gap by redeveloping high-rise and deck-access estates at between 130% and 200% of their previous densities and selling the 'surplus housing' to help fund the development. The redevelopment of these estates has therefore been a net contributor to housing capacity. Our very conservative estimate of this in the *Tomorrow* report was that the capacity from this source could be around 22 000 extra homes. While we are not aware of research into the real figure it is a safe assumption that this was a huge underestimate.

The development of car parks: In the 1990s surface-level parking was the premium land use in many towns and cities, in other words it was more profitable to demolish a vacant building to create a car park than it was to refurbish or redevelop it. As a result many towns were

surrounded by a wasteland of poor quality parking, much of it underused. We predicted in the 1990s that restrictions on car use were likely to change the financial equation and cause much of this parking to be released for development creating capacity for as many as 200 000 homes. Again this was a significant underestimate since surface car parks have provided much of the land for the development boom that has taken place throughout UK town and city centres. The mechanism has not however been restrictions on car use, but rather rising development values. These have meant that apartments rather than parked cars are now the premium land use. As the amount of parking has reduced the cost of parking has risen. This has made multi-storey car parks more viable so that the result has often been a more intensive use of land for parking rather than a reduction in total parking capacity. Nevertheless expensive parking increases the

The Royal Free Hospital Islington: Former hospitals have become a major source of housing capacity. This housing association scheme accommodates 200 homes at 124/ha

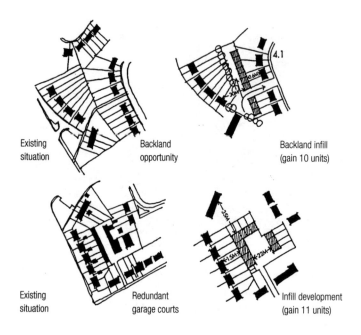

Existing situation   Backland opportunity   Backland infill (gain 10 units)

Existing situation   Redundant garage courts   Infill development (gain 11 units)

Urban intensification: An example of one of the design exercises undertaken by Urban Initiatives in Hertfordshire to assess housing capacity of existing residential areas through intensification

attraction of public transport so that the overall benefit is probably positive.

The conversion of empty commercial space: Capacity need not only exist on cleared sites. There has always been capacity in vacant commercial property. There is a long history of converting historic mills to housing but in the 1990s there was also a trend of converting modern office space to housing because of the lack of office demand and the higher values commanded by apartments. James Barlow[47] estimated in 1992 that 20% of office space in London and 15% in the provincial cities was vacant. Herring Baker Research[48] estimated that there was 500000m^2 of this space in London alone which represented a 'permafrost' layer which would never be let. The subsequent resurgence of London shows how wrong predictions can be. However there were a huge number of residential conversions of office buildings. The capacity study undertaken for London[49] estimated capacity from this source of 54000 homes and we estimated the capacity nationally at 100000. This again may be an underestimate since the National Land Use Database in 2006 estimated[45] that there was capacity for 420000 homes in disused commercial

property although this included space over shops which we deal with separately below.

Until the 2008 credit crunch it remained the case that apartments were more profitable than offices. However most of the transfer to housing has happened through redevelopment rather than conversions. This has happened to such an extent that cities like Manchester, worried that they were losing their employment base, have put specific effort into encouraging new office development.

Intensification of existing housing areas: The idea of accommodating more homes in existing residential neighbourhoods also received a considerable amount of attention in the 1900s. It was the subject of a major study in Hertfordshire[50] which suggested that intensification could produce capacity for 7522 to 16500 new homes in the county. The main opportunities were identified as backlands development of garage courts, back garden development, building on small areas of open space and redevelopment at higher densities. Each of these was contentious and was only seen as attractive in parts of the country where other sources of capacity were scarce. We estimated the national capacity from this source at around 280000 extra homes.

The better use of empty homes: In 1997 three-quarters of a million homes were empty in England[51]. This figure has remained reasonably constant, the figure from the Empty Homes Agency in 2000 was 748778 and in 2007 it remained at 672924[52]. In the 1990s it was assumed that this was partly due to mismanagement by the public sector, something that was only partly true then and is not an issue at all today. Most empty homes are in the private sector, a proportion of which are the result of the natural workings of the housing market. However in the mid 1990s around 250000 homes had been empty for more than a year and at the end of 2007 the Halifax Building Society estimated that 289000 had been empty for more than six months[53]. Some of these have been allowed to fall into disrepair and others will be part of Housing Market Renewal Areas. However a new trend is the buy-to-let market that has gown up with city centre apartments. This has created a development bubble, flooding city centre markets with poor quality apartments. Some buyers, worried about the trouble of tenants and happy to ride on rising values have not even attempted to let the flats in what became the buy-to-leave market.

Living over the shop: The empty homes over shops was also subject to a lot of attention in the 1990s. At one time most shop keepers lived over their premises, but with the decline of independent retailers and the expansion of chain stores much of this accommodation fell vacant. In the 1990s there were just over 400 000 flats over shops[54] and, based on shopping floor area data, we estimated that the capacity could be as much as 1.5 million units. However the impact of programmes run by the Housing Corporation and the government to encourage the use of this space for housing had been limited because the units were small and uneconomic to bring back into use. However one area where progress has been made is housing over supermarkets. In London in particular the major supermarkets have become very interested in the value of the air

space over their stores for housing development. Following early pioneering schemes such as the Tesco/Peabody Trust redevelopment of the Osram Building in Hammersmith that illustrated how technical problems could be overcome, a number of schemes have proceeded across the country (see Brighton New England Quarter case study page 282)

The subdivision of larger houses: The conversion of large houses to flats or multi-occupancy has traditionally been the way that urban areas have mopped up housing capacity, particularly for single people (who make up the majority of household growth). Work by Llewelyn-Davies

Living over the shop: A scheme of six flats in converted space over town centre retail premises in Grantham

---

CIRENCESTER – URBAN INFILL

Proposals developed by URBED for the historic town of Cirencester that explored how a site occupied by a supermarket and associated car parking could be developed for housing and reintegrated into the town. The scheme creates a hundred residential units plus a substantial increase in town centre shopping on a site that would not have been identified in a housing capacity assessment.

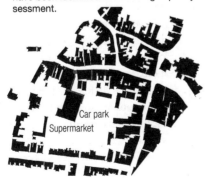

Car park
Supermarket

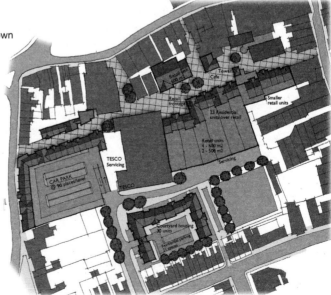

The housing
capacity of urban
areas: Summary
of potential urban
housing capacity
(thousands of units).
Source: URBED

Net densities (units/hectare)	Unconstrained capacity		Policy target	Adjusted capacity	
	30	62		30	62
Current and reclaimed derelict land	457	968	60%	274	581
Previously developed vacant land	194	411	80%	155	329
Vacant urban land not previously developed	293	621	70%	205	435
Land likely to fall vacant 1993–2016	693	1 454	60%	416	872
Redevelopment of large council estates	22	22	100%	22	22
Redevelopment of underused car parks	100	200	80%	80	160
Conversion of industrial buildings and offices	100	100	80%	80	80
Living over the shop	1 000	1 000	40%	400	400
Subdivision of larger under-occupied property*1	1 900	1 900	20%	380	380
Intensification	280	280	80%	224	224
Bringing empty homes back into use	325	325	100%	325	325
TOTALS*2	5 364	7 281		2 561	3 818

*1   To give a realistic figure the capacity from the subdivision of existing property is based upon the 30% of properties which Llewelyn-Davies suggested could get planning permission

*2   Similar estimates of urban housing capacity were made in *Tomorrow's World*, published by Friends of the Earth in 1997. Based on comparable assumptions, and adapted from the UK to England, those figures suggest capacity for approximately 3.5 million dwellings in towns and cities, but propose greater additional potential for the planned regeneration of urban areas towards the end of the household projection period.

Note that figures are rounded and so the columns may not sum exactly.

for LPAC and the Joseph Rowntree Foundation[55] in the 1990s suggested that the potential capacity from subdivision may be up to four times the capacity from brown field sites. Based upon under-occupation data from the Office for National Statistics[56] we estimated that if every under-occupied home were to be subdivided the capacity nationally could be as high as 6 million units. This, of course, would never happen because most home owners will not want to subdivide and the planning authorities in any case would not allow it. Nevertheless, as Llewelyn-Davies stated 'there is significant headroom in the existing stock for the conversion of homes to flats'.

These various sources of urban housing capacity are brought together in the table from the *Tomorrow* report above. We estimated that if all potential capacity were added together and was developed at urban densities the total capacity of urban areas would be just under 7.3 million homes. This however would never happen and we set out policy targets for each of the capacity sources to achieve a target of 75% of all new homes within urban areas. At the time we suggested that even this would never be achieved unless we address the workings of the property market and the planning system. We were also concerned that the greatest housing capacity was in the areas with the lowest levels of household growth and demand. In the growth areas of the south most available land had been developed as is natural in a buoyant urban economy. The greatest potential existed in northern areas which had been losing population and investment for many years. This was where the greatest potential seemed to exist to unlock housing capacity and to stem the decline of these urban areas. The Land use change statistics quoted above show that in 2007 the percentage of homes built from these sources met our 75% target (in 2006 it had been 77%).

However this had not been achieved by developing the huge capacity in the North – the North has in fact lost population to the south. What has happened is that government policy has been very effective at closing off the prospect of green field development. In buoyant urban markets developers have been much more efficient in seeking out capacity than even we were in the *Tomorrow* report. This is despite the fact that our estimates of urban capacity were far higher than any others at the time and were ridiculed for being hopelessly optimistic.

There were two main concerns about our

assumptions. The first was that the development of this urban capacity would lead to town cramming and the second was that there would be no demand to live in these areas. Now that the target has been reached we can ask whether these fears were well founded.

The 'curse' of town cramming

One of the concerns which has permeated the debate about urban repopulation is the fear of town cramming. A good example was Collis, quoted in the *Compact City* who warned that 'settlements could consume themselves from within by eating up the private and public green space that contributes so much to urban quality'[57]. Critics have feared that town cramming will lead to the loss of open space, increased congestion and a lower quality of life for urban dwellers. These issues have a long pedigree. They date back to Victorian concerns about overcrowding

The density gradient: A comparison of densities of different types of development

AREA	Units/Ha	Persons/Ha	Source
Low-density detached – Hertfordshire	5	20	Urban Initiatives
Average net density Los Angeles	15	60	Newman and Kenworthy
Milton Keynes average 1990	17	68	Sherlock
Average density of new development in UK 1981 – 91	22	88	Bibby and Shepherd
Minimum density for a bus service	25	100	Local Government Management Board Sustainable Settlements Guide (assuming that the housing is occupied to capacity)
Private sector 1960s/70s – Hertfordshire	25	100	Urban Initiatives
Interwar estate – Hertfordshire	30	120	Urban Initiatives
Raymond Unwin 1912	30	120	Nothing gained by overcrowding
Tudor-Walters 1919	30	120	Local Government Management Board's Manual on the preparation of state-aided housing schemes
Private sector 1980s/90s – Hertfordshire	30	120	Urban Initiatives
Hulme – Manchester 1970s	37	148	Hulme guide to development
Average net density London	42	168	Newman and Kenworthy
Ebenezer Howard – Garden city 1898	45	180	Tomorrow: A peaceful path to real reform
Minimum density for a tram service	60	240	Local Government Management Board Sustainable Settlements Guide
Abercrombie – Low density	62	247	Greater London Plan 1944
RIBA	62	247	Homes for the future group
New town high-density low-rise – Hertfordshire	64	256	Urban Initiatives
Sustainable urban density	69	275	Friends of the Earth
Hulme – Manchester planned	80	320	Hulme guide to development
Victorian/Edwardian terraces – Hertfordshire	80	320	Urban Initiatives
Abercrombie – Medium density	84	336	Greater London Plan 1944
Central accessible urban density	93	370	Friends of the Earth
Holly Street – London 1990s	94	376	Levitt Bernstein Architects
Holly Street – London 1970s	104	416	Levitt Bernstein Architects
Abercrombie – High density	124	494	Greater London Plan 1944
Sustainable Urban Neighbourhood (maximum)	124	494	URBED
Hulme – Manchester 1930s	150	600	Hulme guide to development
Average net density Islington – 1965	185	740	Milner-Holland
Singapore planned densities 1970s	250	1 000	Scoffham and Vale
Kowloon actual	1 250	5 000	Scoffham and Vale

1. The grey boxes show the source figure from which the density has been calculated
2. An average dwelling size of 4 bedspaces has been assumed throughout this table although it should be noted that this is higher that the average household size in the UK.

Town cramming?
There are many historic environments like Rye which are built to very high densities yet which people regard as attractive places to live

and density which have been a major influence on modern town planning, but how relevant are they to today's city? While the 1990s literature on urban containment was full of concerns about town cramming it was rarely defined nor was the nature or extent of the problem explored. It was almost as if it was an accepted pillar of planning philosophy which was not open to question and as such it cast a shadow over the entire debate.

If town cramming has a relevance to the urban repopulation debate anywhere then it surely must be in London. Parts of London, it is true, seem overcrowded and polluted (although pollution levels have fallen as a result of the Congestion Charge). Looking at central London it is difficult to imagine how it could accommodate more development. When, for example we were working on our master plan for Southall Gas Works (see page 203) we undertook a highway capacity assessment.

Elsewhere in the country it is necessary to show that there is highway capacity to accommodate a new scheme before it can proceed. However in London there is no spare highway capacity and that attitude would mean a moratorium on all new development. Of course this does not happen. Development proceeds (although unfortunately not our Southall scheme) yet somehow the roads do not gridlock, the system adjusts and goes on working. This happens in all cities, even the densest. However London is not a dense city by international standards. Inner Paris, for example, has three times the population density of inner London and yet is not three times more uncomfortable to live in. The profits of town cramming doom forget that cities adjust and regulate themselves and are perfectly capable of absorbing growth. This takes us back to Jane Jacobs' point about cities always being on the verge of impossibility which is what drives innovation and improvements. If this is true of London how much more true is it of northern cities in the UK which rattle around in shells built for much larger populations?

This is part of a long-standing confusion between overcrowding, space standards and density as illustrated by a quote from Professor Alan Hooper[58]: '...an unreflective response which matches smaller households to smaller dwellings at high densities in concentrated urban areas is not likely to result in a sustainable form of development'. The first part of this point is well made, rising incomes make it dangerous to assume that smaller households will opt for smaller units. However to equate this to high-density urban development is to make a mistake that planners have been making for years. There is no reason why large apartments or even houses cannot exist in urban areas at high densities as witnessed in Knightsbridge or St. John's Wood in London, Manhattan in New York or Central Paris.

A useful way of reconciling these confusions has been suggested by Brenda Vale and Ernie Scoffam[59] who make a distinction between the density and the intensity of development. The former is an objective measure of the number of houses, people or rooms to the hectare while the latter is a subjective measure of how crowded a place feels. They point out that the relationship between density and intensity is far from clear. Many intense environments such as high-rise council estates, are actually built to quite low densities whereas many high-density environments, particularly in historic areas, do not feel overcrowded. Alice Coleman made a similar point in *Utopia on Trial*[60] when she said that 'flats certainly cram in more litter, crime and vandalism to the acre... but they do not, in Britain, pack in more dwellings to the acre'.

Scoffam and Vale conclude by suggesting that prescriptions about density are irrelevant since 'the same density can conceal a variety of built forms which both psychologically and physically may be either compact or loose, urban or sub-urban, intense or diffuse'. Problems arise when densities are increased without rethinking the design of housing and the layout of urban areas. If the density of suburban designs are increased, lower space standards are inevitable along with congestion and a lack of open space. These problems can however be avoided if the form of development is changed. The optimum form to maximise density without creating the perception of overcrowding is the three or four-storey terrace around squares and open spaces. This is the traditional way in which the Georgians built within cities and there is no reason why we should not rediscover these forms as Harley Sherlock has suggested[61] to ensure that quality space standards and urban development are both achieved.

It therefore seems that there is a great deal of potential to increase the population of urban areas, particularly in the north, without running the risk of town cramming. This is why we have used the term urban repopulation rather than urban infill because we are advocating the replacement of a proportion of the population that these cities have lost. This does however raise the question of whether people will want to return to these areas.

Will people return to cities?

The other concern about urban repopulation is that it runs counter to what people appear to want, people have, after all, been voting with their feet by leaving urban areas for years. As Michael Breheny suggested: 'Clearly there are groups of people – of particular ages, occupations and levels of income – who may choose high density urban living. Likewise there are high density urban areas – usually historically and architecturally interesting and socially exclusive – that remain popular... However these people and these areas are very much the exception. Many people who do live in high density urban areas.... are more likely to have been trapped than they are to have made a conscious decision to live there'[62]. Behind this statement lurks a series of assumptions, one might say prejudices about high-density urban housing. It is no wonder that the critics of urban repopulation were so outraged if they thought that suburbanites were going to be forced to live in inner city council estates!

Our argument has always been that repopulation can only happen by people making choices to live in urban areas by creating sufficiently attractive urban neighbourhoods – more Chelsea than Millwall. The fact is that this has been happening to an increasing extent over the last ten years. One reason for this is demographic change and the fact that groups of a 'particular age, occupation and income' far from being the exception have made up a major part of the net increase in households – 80% of which has been single people or childless couples. In the mid 1990s there were enough of these people choosing to live in urban areas to refute the assertion that they were an exception. Since that time their numbers have grown to become a significant part of the entire housing market.

In 1999 we were asked by the Urban Task Force to explore attitudes to urban living. With MORI and the University of Bristol we organised a series of extended focus groups to understand how people felt about urban areas. The report published in 1999 as *But would you live there?*[17] concluded that the market for urban living had originally been a niche but was growing to such an extent that it represented a fragmentation of the housing market. The people who initially moved back to city centres were 'pioneers' who had been attracted by the risks of urban living.

This was the niche market and was relatively small. However the pioneers were being followed by 'settlers' who were attracted to the idea of urban living but were more risk averse. In an age when *Friends* was the nation's most popular TV show, there were few people in the focus groups who were not a little bit attracted to urban living. We concluded that if the risks could be ameliorated a significant proportion of these people could be attracted to live in urban areas.

One of the reasons why this market for urban living has not been exploited in the past is the self-fulfilling nature of housing projection as we have described. The planning system tends to reinforce existing trends and created an inbuilt bias against urban areas towards the end of the last century. Few people were building urban housing so few people chose to live in urban areas because the option did not really exist. The assumption was that there was therefore no demand for it. In this way planning did not just responded to residential preferences, it shaped them.

This argument can apply on a number of levels. It has, for example, been argued that household growth itself is dependent on housebuilding and that if houses are not built fewer households will form. At the regional level it has also been argued that the fact that we build more houses in the south than the north is one of the reasons for higher levels of population growth

Playing on urban fears: An advert for Milton Keynes, offering escape from the pressures of life in London

MILTON KEYNES

in the south. At both of these levels the circularity argument has weaknesses. However it becomes much more important at the local level within travel to work areas. We questioned, for example in the first edition of this book, why we were still catering for high levels of predicted household growth in the Wirral, Cheshire and Warwickshire when the housebuilding was fuelling migration from the adjacent conurbations? The forecasts of modest household growth in these urban areas in the 1990s compared to the surrounding rural counties caused housebuilding to be concentrated in the latter which inevitably meant that these suburbs further increased in population while the urban areas continued to decline. In this way the 'predict and provide' approach to household growth was the real cause of the depopulation of urban areas not the fact that people didn't want to live there.

This also raised questions about the targets for the proportion of homes built within urban areas. In the early 1990s the government wanted 60% of new homes to be built within urban areas and yet continued to allocate housing to suburbs and rural districts least able to meet this target. We suggested that there was a need to grasp the nettle and to redirect household growth back into the larger urban areas where the capacity was to be found. The government had in fact already recognised this point by the time this book was first published. John Prescott's announcement in February 1998 ditched the predict and provide approach to housing allocations. Since that time housing allocations have been increased substantially and some rural areas (such as those in the rural North West) have seen a moratorium on new housing. This change in policy removed the inbuilt bias in the planning system and has allowed preferences for urban housing to be fully expressed.

The result has been an economic renaissance in many of the UK's urban areas. It had been argued that the loss of population from cities was the result of economic decline. As unemployment rose people followed Norman Tebbit's advice to get on their bike and find work elsewhere. However this was also a circular

COIN STREET COMMUNITY BUILDERS

Coin Street is an important example of both community-sponsored regeneration and urban brown field development. Coin Street Community Builders were formed in 1984 when they bought 13 acres of land on London's South Bank.

Since that time they have created a mixed-use urban neighbourhood in the heart of London. This grew out of a campaign to stop the area becoming a mono-functional office area and a belief that it should be a mixed residential area affordable to London people. The scheme includes a small park – Bernie Spain Gardens, a riverside walkway, the Gabriel's Wharf craft market, a range of housing developments and the mixed-use refurbishment of the Oxo Tower Wharf. An annual festival is also organised to animate the area.

The Broadwall scheme (below) was designed by Lifschutz Davidson Architects. It includes 27 units managed by Palm Housing Co-op in a four-storey block and a nine-storey tower. The flats face west but large areas of double glazed Low E glass maximise passive solar gain. The flats also incorporate gas stoves vented through stainless steel stacks up the face of the building.

The adjoining Oxo building has been refurbished at a cost of £20 million for a mixture of shops, cafés, design workshops and flats along with a rooftop restaurant and performance area. It includes 36 designer/maker workshops and 78 flats managed by the Redwood Housing Co-operative.

The scheme shows that it is possible to create attractive high-density mixed-use neighbourhoods that are attractive to a wide range of people including social housing tenants.

165

argument since depopulation was both a result and a cause of urban economic decline. The argument had been made by Jacobs in her book the *Economy of Cities*[63] where she pointed out that population decline is always correlated with economic stagnation and that economic development is only possible if population first start expanding. The reason is that increasing population expands the size of local markets, generates more people capable of starting new economic activity and widens the choice of workforce for employers. It is also true that when population declines it tends to be the most able and motivated who leave, the very people that local economies can least do without.

This can be illustrated with the example of Liverpool which has lost more than 250 000 people since 1961, say 100 000 households. If we assume that the average household income of these households was a modest £15 000 per year, it would mean that the city is losing £1.5 billion of 'turnover' a year as a result of population loss. While only a proportion of this would be recycled in the local economy it would dwarf the public subsidy which currently flows into the city. This is as poorly understood today as it was in Jane Jacobs' time. It does however suggest that the repopulation of our urban areas has been an important prerequisite for economic regeneration, not something that has resulted from it.

The crime, poverty and social problems which have come to be associated with residualised urban populations, like economic decline, are also a symptom as well as a cause of urban depopulation. As able people fled the inner city, it became a repository for those members of society least able to escape. A vicious circle was created since people would not be attracted back into urban areas until they could see more people like themselves living in these areas. This has to an extent been overcome for childless households but remains a problem for families because of the problem of urban schools which is a microcosm of the wider urban condition. Children in inner city schools are still less likely to succeed and parents cannot be expected to sacrifice their children's education for an ideal of urban living. The search for better education is therefore one of the most important aspects which causes people to leave cities. Once more urban repopulation is a prerequisite if we are to break down the social stigma which has become attached to some inner city neighbourhoods and their schools. This is where far less progress has been made since the pioneers and settlers attracted back to urban areas still tend to leave when they have children.

In this chapter we have argued that there are good reasons for repopulating towns and cities. This brings environmental benefits as well as injecting new life into areas which have declined as a result of population dispersal for much of the 20th century. The urban housing capacity exists, particularly in the north, to accommodate the projected growth in households and the traditional concerns about town cramming and lack of demand have largely been overcome. Much of the debate about these issues in the 1990s was driven by absolutist positions. The 'decentralists' reacted against a perception that containment would force people to live in dangerous overcrowded urban areas or a nostalgic and impossible vision of the Italian hill town. In contrast the 'centralists' recoiled in horror from the prospect of green and pleasant pastures being consumed by the hated suburban semi. Neither position was very helpful and the debate was really about the relative balance between urban development, suburban expansion and new settlements. As Breheny said at the time, 'Does the answer have to lie in one extreme or the other? Will town or country only survive under decenterist or centralist regime? Could they survive satisfactorily under a middle line, a compromise?' It is possible to argue that more housing should be built in urban areas without suggesting that all housing should be built there. However whereas the English have always been pretty good at developing suburbs we lost the knack of building urban areas. Attracting more people to live in towns therefore requires the development of new models for urban living, which is what we turn to in the next three chapters.

Chapter 10
The eco-neighbourhood

Each element of the Sustainable Urban Neigh-bourhood represents an important principle. Sustainable refers to the ability of the neighbourhood and wider urban systems to be sustained over time and to minimise their environmental impact. Urban refers both to the location of the area and to its physical character whilst neighbourhood relates to the social and economic sustainability of the area, the community ties which hold it together and its relationship to surrounding areas. In simple terms our aim is to create urban areas which will endure. In this wider sense the term sustainability can be applied to economic and social as well as environmental systems. It relates to urban areas that minimise their impact on the environment and which can also be sustained economically and socially in the future – urban areas which will not require public investment and wholesale redevelopment in the future, unlike many of the urban areas built in the 20th century. Urban character and the importance of the neighbourhood will be described in the following chapters. Here we will focus on the concept of environmental sustainability.

What is urban sustainability?
If by urban sustainability we mean towns and cities which sustain themselves without any adverse impact on wider natural systems then the sustainable urban neighbourhood is an impossible goal. The last human settlement to be sustainable in this respect, in Europe at least, was probably the small medieval town dependent on its local hinterland. A truly sustainable city may therefore be impossible. However the way we plan human settlements has an important role to play in increasing the sustainability of human activities and it is the responsibility of those who shape towns and cities to minimise their unsustainability and their impact on the natural environment.

It is important to be clear what we mean by environmental sustainability in the urban context. To some sustainability implies self-sufficiency. This is something which has been achieved by pioneers like Robert and Brenda Vale in small-scale developments[1]. They have developed individual homes and small groups of houses which are entirely self-sufficient, producing their own energy, recycling waste and collecting and treating water. The key to achieving this has been to reduce the resource requirements of the buildings to a point where they can be supplied from natural sources such as sun and rain and from the wastes produced by the building. The Vales would argue that all housing could be built like this and produced a number of autonomous housing schemes; some for housing associations within very tight cost constraints[2]. This is however a long way from the development of a self-sufficient neighbourhood town or city.

There have been attempts to build self-sufficient villages often in remote rural areas.

These are described by the Gaia Foundation as 'human scale, full featured settlements which integrate human activity harmlessly into the natural environment'[3], a worthy goal for any urban neighbourhood. There are more than a hundred such settlements in Sweden alone and the Eco-Village Foundation has members in twenty-one countries across Europe, Russia, India, Australia and the US. These settlements – like Findhorn in Scotland which is probably the best-known British example – grow their own food, generate their own power, and recycle their waste; coming as close as it is possible to an environmentally benign human settlement. They are however small in scale, rarely exceeding a population of 500, and demand time and commitment from their members. To many people they may offer an attractive way of life but only the most extreme environmental fundamentalist would suggest that the majority of the population should or could live this way.

There are precious few examples of eco-village ideas being applied in the urban context. Two early examples were Christania in Copenhagen and Kreuzberg in Berlin (before the fall of the Berlin Wall). Both were established as squatter settlements. Christania was originally a military camp and was taken over by squatters in the 1970s and has since become grudgingly accepted by public authorities. Kreuzberg[4] was a district isolated by a loop in the Berlin Wall which fell into decline and was colonised by squatter communities in the 1970s and 80s. Before German reunification transformed Kreuzberg from a backwater into a desirable district at the heart of the new German capital, it was probably the nearest urban equivalent to the rural eco-village. Like their rural counterparts the Kreuzberg squatters were driven by environmental ideals given added edge by the practical realities of squatting buildings which lacked basic services. There was, for example, a block in Kreuzberg which created a vertical reed bed with a series of oil drums down the side of a building through which sewage would filter and be purified. Other blocks incorporated wind turbines, solar panels and food growing. Kreuzberg was the subject of a major regeneration

Kreuzberg: A mixed-use social housing block in Kreuzberg, Berlin

programme from 1987 under the auspices of STERN, which can teach us much about what they called 'careful urban renewal', but even at its most ambitious it could not be described as a self-sufficient neighbourhood.

Something of the kind has been researched by the Martin Centre for Architectural and Urban Studies in Cambridge. Through their work on Project ZED[5] (Zero Emissions Urban Development) with architects and academics in the UK, France and Germany, they have developed theoretical models for self-sufficient urban blocks. Like the autonomous house and the eco-village these blocks do not rely on external services. However at present they only exist in a computer to create models of urban resource systems. The practical implications of Project ZED are being explored by architects, including Future Systems, who are working up schemes for sites in London, Toulouse and Berlin.

However as we saw in Chapter 5 the only full scale attempt to create a zero carbon neighbourhood in the UK is BedZED in London. Through the use of solar power, biofuel-powered Combined Heat and Power and a bioworks water treatment system this would have been a zero carbon development, if, that is, the systems had worked. As we describe in the case study in Chapter 5, the technical aspects of the scheme have however experienced problems.

Sustainability and the city

The development of autonomous houses, villages and even urban blocks may be a possible if complex task. However this complexity is nothing compared to the issues raised by addressing the sustainability of a whole neighbourhood or indeed city. As Robert and Brenda Vale state[6]: 'Green Architecture must encompass a sustainable form of urban development. The city is far more than a collection of buildings, rather it can be seen as a series of interacting systems – systems for living, working and playing – crystallised into built forms. It is by looking at these systems that we can find the face of the city of the future'. These systems are not easy

to pin down. They are not neatly confined to individual neighbourhoods or even to whole cities but operate on a regional, national and increasingly global level. It has been estimated for example that the eco-footprint of London[7] is equivalent to the entire land area of the UK although, of course, it is not neatly confined to these shores but stretches into every corner of the world. Cities use tropical hardwoods plundered from rain forests, import food from across the globe so that fruits and vegetables are never out of season, emit sulphur dioxide which kills forests thousands of miles away whilst their CO_2 collects in the atmosphere and their wastes pollute the world's oceans. Just as cities lie at the heart of global trading systems so they dominate global systems of resource consumption and pollution.

The traditional picture of UK cities and industrial towns with smokestack industries defiling the landscape may be fading but it has been replaced with an image of the fume-clogged, resource-hungry metropolis. Something of the scale of this can be seen from Herbert Girardet's Metabolism of London[8]. In this he estimated the annual resource consumption of London with a population of 8 million to include more than a billion tonnes of water, 20 million tonnes of fuel oil, 2.4 million tonnes of food, about 8 million tonnes of building materials and 1.2 million tonnes of metals. As a result of this London

Christania: Unofficial self-build housing on a former military base in Copenhagen, squatted since the 1970s, creates an alternative model for urban sustainability

produces 8.2 million tonnes of inert waste, 2.4 million tonnes of household wastes, and 7.5 million tonnes of sewage sludge. It also emits into the atmosphere 60 million tonnes of CO_2, 400 000 tonnes of sulphur dioxide and 280 000 tonnes of nitrogen oxide. London is not unique in this respect, indeed it is probably much better than many American cities. But it is still hard to look at the pall of pollution that hangs over the city on summer days, the barges carrying waste to landfill sites, the diminution of water resources and the congested streets and not to despair.

It is tempting to conclude that cities are environmental disasters and have no place in a sustainable future, that is until we consider the alternatives. More than half of the world's population now live in cities so that it is hopelessly unrealistic to postulate a city-free sustainable future. The reform of urban areas is unavoidable if we are to achieve sustainability at the global level. In doing this we may find that cities are part of the solution to global sustainability as well as part of the problem. We described in the last chapter how the repopulation of cities could help reduce transport energy use as well as protecting the countryside. This is only part of the story. It is possible that living in cities may be the sensible environmental choice for a number of reasons. This is because it is not cities which damage the environment but the people

who live in them. It is true that in the developing world cities attract people from self-sufficient rural economies leading to a huge increase in per-capita resource consumption. This is not however the case in the UK where people in rural areas are no less demanding in their desires for commodities and services. Because of the much lower population densities in these areas the resources required to serve these rural needs are far greater than they would be in the city. Rural dwellers travel twice the distance by car each year than do their urban counterparts[9], the distribution distances for goods and services are greater and the infrastructure required to provide basic services more extensive.

If London did not exist where would its eight million people live and would they consume any less resources or produce any less pollution? If these people and the thousands of companies and organisations based in the city were to be spread out at garden city densities across the south of England their environmental impact would be enormous. To the environmental balance sheet would have to be added the costs of distributing goods over much wider areas, the loss of public transport as it became less viable, the increased problems of recycling and transporting waste, the difficulty of heating freestanding buildings, the miles of road to be built, serviced and lit, the fact that postage and newspapers would have to be delivered by road, not to mention the hectares of green fields that would be developed. It may be that in a dispersed low-density polycentric settlement consumer habits would change and teleworking would reduce travel. However this is not dependent on decentralisation and would have an even greater environmental impact if it were to take place within a dense urban area.

It is arguable that the massive outward expansion of British cities means that the dispersed low-density model is already with us. The European cities to which Girardet compares London so unfavourably are built to much higher densities which explains the vibrancy of their streets and the fact that they can support a superior public transport system and have the density of demand to make services such as

Sustainability and the city region: An illustration from the Manchester 2020 project

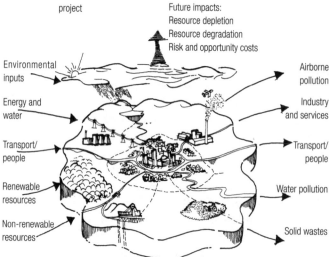

Future impacts:
Resource depletion
Resource degradation
Risk and opportunity costs

Environmental inputs

Energy and water

Transport/ people

Renewable resources

Non-renewable resources

Airborne pollution

Industry and services

Transport/ people

Water pollution

Solid wastes

recycling and local power generation more viable. Sustainability in its broadest sense is much more difficult to imagine in a dispersed settlement than in a compact city. The dense, walkable city may therefore be the most environmentally efficient form of settlement for the majority of the population. This was probably best summed up by Roger Levett, when he was at the Scottish Development Agency, when he said: 'with the exception of food-growing virtually everything can be done more greenly within cities'[10]. We will not secure a sustainable future for Britain simply by building eco-villages – we must rise to the challenge and reform our towns and cities.

To do this we must transform the metabolism of urban areas. At present this is a linear system with resources coming in at one end and waste being produced at the other. Increasing urban sustainability implies the transformation of these linear systems into circular systems whereby waste outputs provide the raw materials for resource inputs. It may not be possible, as with autonomous housing, to completely close the system but it is possible to do this to a far greater extent than we do now. We must look at the balance between resources imported into cities and their neighbourhoods and the wastes exported in order to reduce their contribution to the unsustainability of wider systems. Something of the kind was the subject of a ground-breaking City-Region 2020 project which has been researching the resource flows for the Greater Manchester Conurbation since the mid 1990s[11]. This work has formed the basis of the Centre for Urban and Regional Ecology (CURE) at Manchester University which has been exploring ways of bringing the impact of urban conurbations within the environmental carrying capacity of their wider area. This is a mammoth task and the final City-Region 2020 report ran to several volumes. As with many environmental initiatives, such a comprehensive approach to a mass of issues makes it difficult to draw out a clear message which can be used to influence action on the ground. The CURE team recognised this and suggested that the implications of their work be explored at a more local neighbourhood level

Project ZED: A concept scheme by Future Systems to create zero carbon urban buildings. This tower on Tottenham Court Road in London would have channelled wind through a vertical wind turbine

making reference to our work on the Sustainable Urban Neighbourhood.

Whilst it is clear that the practical implications of urban sustainability can become very complex, the principles are simple and apply to all sustainable development be it a house, a neighbourhood or a city:

Reduce inputs: The first principle is to reduce inputs to the system in terms of the resources and energy consumed. The Vales were only able to achieve autonomy in their housing by reducing the need for heat, water and power to minimal levels which could then be supplied by the house itself. Whilst the urban neighbourhood is unlikely to be able to reduce its resource inputs to a level which can be locally supplied, consuming less must be the starting point for any sustainable policy.

Use local resources: The second principle is to make maximum use of local resources such as the sun and the rain which falls on the roofs of the neighbourhood and the food which can be grown in its gardens and allotments. These local resources also include waste produced by the neighbourhood such as restored water which can be used for toilet flushing or composted waste which can nourish gardens and allotments. By minimising the input of resources and maximising the use of local

171

resources the neighbourhood can significantly reduce the level of resources imported into the area.

Minimise waste: The neighbourhood must also minimise the amount of unrecycled or unrecyclable waste exported from the area. The UK now recycles around 30% of its waste, a huge improvement on the 5% in the mid 1990s but still half the levels achieved in Germany. The sustainable urban neighbourhood should at least be reaching the continental levels by embedding recycling into the neighbourhood.

Make use of urban economies: However sustainability is about more than just the collection of waste for recycling, it is about the productive use of that waste to reduce the consumption of natural resources. This is the fourth principle of urban sustainability which is based on the role that urban areas play in trading systems. The first three principles are common to all sustainable development but the fourth is where cities come into their own. Environmental efficiency depends upon matching up supply with demand. Green consumer products, waste recycling, public transport etc. are only viable if they can find a market and it is in cities that the major markets exist. Even the most committed eco-community in the heart of the countryside is going to struggle to smelt its waste aluminium

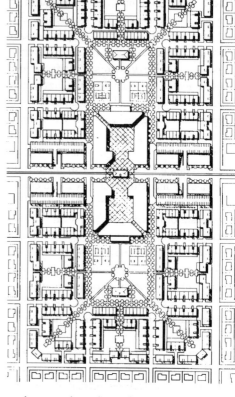

or glass or pulp and recycle its paper. It is going to struggle to support an efficient bus service or to manufacture low-energy light bulbs. Such activities require the sort of markets that only cities can provide. Thus urban areas as natural centres for trade have an important role to play in promoting more circular systems of resource consumption and waste reuse.

The eco-neighbourhood

If we are to discover the face of the city of the future we must explore the implications of these four principles on the design and planning of cities and the neighbourhoods within them. We must invent an urban equivalent of the eco-village. Concentrating, as many of the sustainability pioneers tended to do, on either the design of individual building or the broad sweep of national and international policy, misses many of the most crucial issues of environmental

New urban visions: Just as 19th century reformers produced Utopian visions for the city so should we. Examples include the US Pedestrian Pocket (above right) and the UK Urban Village (below)

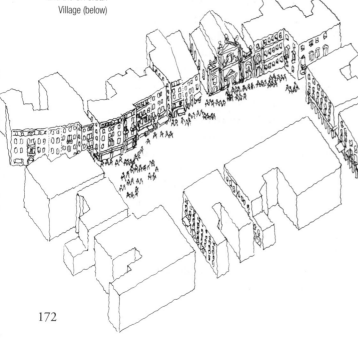

sustainability. The latter is too remote from actions required on the ground whilst the former has become a technical challenge, producing super-green buildings increasingly divorced from the standard product of most developers, or the condition of the existing built stock. There is much that can be achieved on the scale of the individual building, but surely now the challenge is not to push back further the frontiers of ecological building, but to raise standards across the board and to address wider issues such as car use, energy production and recycling. For this we need a wider canvas, and the neighbourhood is an appropriate level with which to work, large enough to address broader environmental issues but small enough to affect people's lives and to focus minds on the practicality of implementation.

The 19th century social reformers produced Utopian visions for the city. Should not the 21st century environmental reformers be doing the same? This is something that has started to happen. While there are many environmentalists who have continued to condemn cities as environmental villains, others have started to develop sustainable urban models. Concerns about car use, in particular, have led to an emerging consensus that the answer lies in dense walkable settlements around public transport nodes. There have however been two distinct schools of thought about how this should be achieved. The first adheres to the garden city tradition of relatively dense nodes of development within a general pattern of dispersal. This is the position of the UK Town and Country Planning Association, the original concept of the Urban Village[12] and the American Pedestrian Pocket movement[13]. It has been boosted in the UK by the government's announcement in 2007 of a programme of Eco-towns to encourage innovation and accommodate housing growth.

The second school of thought has favoured the repopulation (or compaction according to its critics) of existing cities by increasing densities and developing brown field land. This has become the position of the Urban Villages Forum and has also been the policy of

Ecocity Berkeley:
Is this a vision of the sustainable city of the future?

the UK government and European Union for more than ten years.

A vociferous debate has raged between these two schools, however both accept the need to increase development densities to make urban areas more sustainable. Both therefore require new models of urban development which respond to environmental concerns and are capable of accommodating higher densities. Both require a new vision for the eco or sustainable urban neighbourhood.

What will such environmentally sustainable urban neighbourhoods look like? Richard Register in his book Ecocity Berkeley[14] describes a Utopian vision for his home town which he envisaged being transformed into a dense mixed-use urban area with cascading terraced buildings covered with plants, '...like small mountains where greenhouse roofs and glass wind screens rise above the vegetation to shine in the blue sky'. He describes a city in which buildings are laced with alleys, passages, halls, atria, galleries and bridges between buildings, so pampered will be the pedestrian. This has overtones of some of the earlier Utopian visions and elements can be seen in communities such as Christania in Copenhagen. At the other end of the spectrum various architects have imagined sustainable high rise-blocks. The Project ZED research described earlier resulted in a number of architectural schemes. One of the most dramatic was Future Systems' tower proposal for the Tottenham Court Road in London (pictured on page 171). The shape of the structure funnelled wind through a central turbine, which together with photovoltaics would have made it energy self-sufficient. However somewhere between these extremes, a more common approach has been to see the sustainable settlement of the future as being similar to the traditional settlement of the past. Examples range from the evocation of the dense Italian hill town in the European Green Paper on the Urban Environment to the promotion of the traditional small American town by the US Pedestrian Pocket movement. As the Vales[16] have argued, since the city of the future will be based on the needs of the pedestrian its physical form is likely to be similar to traditional towns of the past which predate the car. From these various models we can start to postulate what the environmentally sustainable urban neighbourhood might look like.

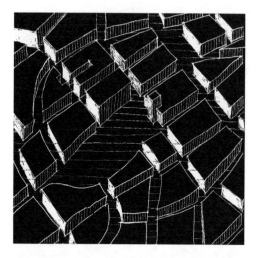

The walkable city: Traditional urban grids, whether formal or informal, encourage walking (above)

The walkable city

The reduction of car use is seen by many commentators as likely to be the most profound influence on future development forms. Just as the central location of the sustainable urban neighbourhood will reduce the need for car-borne commuting so its internal organisation should be pedestrian-centred. Most development in the last 50 years has done just the opposite of this. The pedestrian far from being 'pampered' has been subjugated to the needs of the car and forced into subways and over foot-bridges ostensibly for their safety but also lest they interrupt the free flow of traffic. Even away from main roads concerns about the car still dominate. Urban areas have been designed to exclude through traffic so that even the shortest journeys can involve lengthy detours, not a problem in a car, but an obstacle course for the pedestrian. At their most extreme, as in Los Angeles, such layouts make a car indispensable for virtually all journeys. In contrast to this in a sustainable urban neighbourhood, walking and cycling are the most convenient mode of transport for all local trips. This has a number of implications for design.

Permeability: The first implication is that the neighbour-hood should be permeable, at least to the pedestrian. Permeability as a term refers to the ease with which a liquid passes through a

The disconnected city: The plan below left shows how the layout of urban areas makes it impossible to walk and channels all traffic onto distributor roads. It is possible to reconnect the city as illustrated by the plan below right

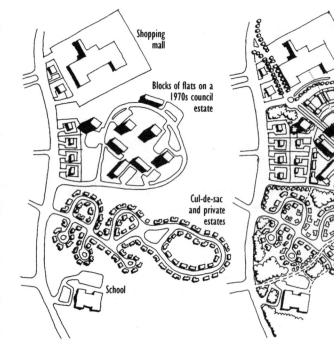

Shopping mall

Blocks of flats on a 1970s council estate

Cul-de-sac and private estates

School

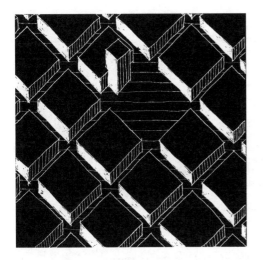

solid such as water through rock. In the urban design context it has come to refer to the ease with which people can move through an area by a choice of routes. Permeable layouts are those where each street leads to another street which in turn leads to another and so on. It also stresses the importance of avoiding long stretches of road without junctions and therefore dictates the size of urban blocks. Such streets may be attractive to highway engineers but they encourage traffic speed and reduce the choice of routes. Impermeable layouts are characterised by looping feeder roads which lead to cul-de-sacs and closes. In permeable areas all parts of the neighbourhood are accessible with particular emphasis on nodes of activity such as shopping centres. In impermeable areas the pedestrian is treated as a second-class citizen, large parts of the public realm are devoid of activity and the car is king.

Personal safety: Permeability, like many of the principles that we are promoting, has attracted criticism not least from the police who favour more 'defensible' impermeable layouts. Indeed in the 1990s concerns about security were probably the greatest threat to walkability in many urban areas. The problem is a vicious circle in which fears about personal safety mean that through routes are discouraged to keep strangers out. As a result streets become quieter and feel less rather than more safe. In response further barriers are erected leading eventually to the gated communities now so common in the US. The effect of this is to make walking even less convenient because direct routes are blocked. The safety within the gates is traded for a much less safe environment in the surrounding area where pavements are deserted and deprived of surveillance from surrounding buildings. This can lead to the absurd situation where pedestrians prefer to risk narrow pavements on heavy traffic routes rather than a deserted pedestrian route where they might be safe from cars but not from muggers.

CAR-FREE HOUSING: EDINBURGH

Edinburgh is home to one of the UK's first planned car-free housing schemes developed by Canmore Housing Association. The scheme on disused rail land consists of 120 flats and provide 'energy efficient homes in a car-free environment'. The scheme was completed in November 1999 and includes a range of sustainability features. However it grabbed the headlines because people wanting to buy or rent flats were asked to sign an agreement not to attempt to bring a car onto the estate. No parking facilities were provided and the intention had been to create a link with the Edinburgh Car Club. The land that would have been used for parking was to be used for terraced gardens, allotments and reed beds for grey water recycling. An independent evaluation of the scheme suggested that just 26% of households had a car compared to an average of 51% across the city, despite the failure of the Edinburgh Car Club. There was however a suggestion that the car-free nature of the scheme had affected sales, causing some of the homes for sale to be converted to shared equity. The 26% car ownership figure should also be seen in the light of the fact that the car ownership of households on Canmore's waiting list is just 17%. While this is an excellent scheme in many respects it shows the difficulty of innovating on car ownership in isolation.

POUNDBURY IN DORSET

Poundbury is being developed by the Dutchy of Cornwall as a planned extension to Dorchester. The initial phase provided for 244 houses and flats (35 for renting and 209 for sale), offices, retail space and workshops. The master plan by Leon Krier creates a mixed-use 'urban village' based on perimeter blocks and courtyards. Houses are built to the back of pavement in order to maximise urban form and street character and no two adjacent houses are by the same architect, ensuring a mix of styles. It is eventually planned that Poundbury should have a population of 6 – 8,000 developed over 25 years, so that the village and its community grows organically.

Taming the car: The plan incorporated a radical approach to the motor car developed by Alan Baxter Associates. Rather than seeking to calm or exclude traffic through engineering, it sought to civilise the car through the urban layout. The starting point was to create pleasing urban spaces which were human in scale. Only once this was

done were the pavements and roads fitted into these spaces. The highway engineering was therefore dictated by the building form rather than vice versa. Streets were shaped to avoid long vistas so reducing acceleration distances. Junctions also included tight radii and limited sight lines forcing drivers to stop rather than to glance and drive through. Parking was accommodated in wider streets and courtyards as well as being attached to individual dwellings. At the insistence of the planners the parking standards were however still very high with two places per dwelling plus visitor parking. Poundbury was the first scheme to introduce these ideas, subsequently incorporated into a government design guide, Places Streets and Movement, also written by Alan Baxter.

The development is regulated by a tight building agreement by which the Dutchy could render development rights forfeit if the scheme did not go ahead as intended. House buyers were also subject to restrictive covenants regulating maintenance and alterations to the homes. It is intended to eventually transfer these rights to a community controlled management company.

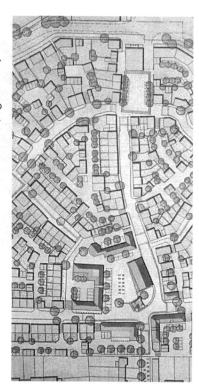

In permeable urban areas where walking is not a deviant activity the opposite happens. This seems to be counter-intuitive, you would think that a greater number of routes would serve to dilute and dissipate pedestrian activity. However permeable streets generate a virtuous circle in which walking is safer and more pleasant so that more people make short trips by foot so that pavements are populated and lively.

Legibility: Another important factor is the ease with which people understand the structure of a neighbourhood and are able to 'read' it as they walk around. Traditional urban areas are generally easy and pleasant to walk around. This relates partly to the variety of buildings and townscape. In areas with no landmarks, where everything looks the same, walking is monotonous and it is easy to get lost. Legibility also relates to the layout of the area. In traditional urban neighbourhoods main routes tend to lead to the centre and a grid of streets, whether formal or informal, makes orientation easy. If you miss a right turn it is normally

possible to take the next right and then turn right again to get onto your intended route. By contrast in modern developments a wrong turn can get you hopelessly lost in a maze of winding cul-de-sacs.

Taming the car: To many people a pedestrian-centred neighbourhood means the exclusion of the car. A number of car-free developments have been built in the UK and many city centres have successfully excluded cars. Indeed historic cities like Florence in Italy have excluded cars entirely from the old city bringing about huge improvements in air quality and the attractiveness of the street environment. However a pedestrian-centred neighbourhood does not always mean a pedestrianised neighbourhood. The experience of the last fifty years is a warning against creating the deserted pedestrian environments which characterise many inner city estates and indeed less successful town centres. The key to the pedestrian-friendly neighbourhood is to tame rather than to exclude the car. This means reducing traffic speeds and reclaiming much more of the street area for pedestrians but it does not necessarily mean removing cars entirely. Excluding cars and parking removes activity from streets making them feel less safe and therefore, ironically, less attractive to pedestrians. This was confirmed by research by Environmental and Transport Planning[17] which looked at the 'sociability' of streets and public spaces in nineteen towns in four European countries. They found no relationship between the extent of pedestrianised areas and the level of social and pedestrian activity. More important was the scale and familiarity of streets and squares – streets that were too wide or too tall did not encourage walking and the most positive reactions were to historic urban areas.

Active frontages such as ground floor commercial uses are also important in making streets feel safer and encouraging pedestrian activity. The urban character of an area may therefore serve an important role in promoting walking. This includes the mix of uses to create activity throughout the day and active frontages, a hierarchy of streets serving different functions and accommodating different levels of traffic and an urban form which creates a level of enclosure and intimacy without being claustrophobic. We will return to these aspects of urban character in the next chapter.

Creative congestion: The design and management of streets is also important in making areas pedestrian friendly. Colin Davies in his work for the Royal Fine Arts Commission[18] explored how streets can be made more attractive by widening pavements, providing cycle lanes and calming traffic. The latter need not be through chicanes, pinch points and speed humps. Just as effective and less intrusive can be limited sight lines, tight corner radii, narrow carriageways and street trees as designed by Alan Baxter Associates in Poundbury[19] and later proposed in their guide *Places Streets and Movement*[20] published in 1998 and originally intended as a replacement for DB32 the government's manual for the design of streets.

However one of the best forms of traffic calming is street activity, dare we say, a degree of congestion. Traffic lights, traditional cross roads, pedestrian crossings, on-street parking and turning movements all serve to reduce traffic speeds in traditional urban areas to a walking pace. It may seem perverse to suggest traffic congestion as an important characteristic of a pedestrian-friendly urban neighbourhood. However congestion is another name for vitality which is part of the attraction of urban areas and why many urban streets lose much of their character when traffic is excluded. Provided that heavy vehicles are restricted and generous space is given over to pedestrians and cyclists, this congestion need not undermine the quality of the environment. The result is not that the car dominates but that environments are created which are more pleasant for pedestrians. Motorists are not given the impression that they have free and unhindered right of way so that they are prepared for pedestrians and it is natural to drive slowly.

Since we first published this book the situation in the UK has changed significantly. After a number of attempts Design Bulletin 32 (which was the sources of many anti-urban street layouts) has finally been replaced by the Manual for Streets[21] which allows for more urban layouts. The Dutch-inspired Shared Space movement[22] has also gathered momentum based on the idea of streets where all road marking and traffic controls are removed. Take away traffic lights and cars have to negotiate a junction with such care that accident rates are reduced and pedestrians are safer. The irony it seems is that the paraphernalia of highway engineering, much of which has been provided over the years to protect pedestrians, seems to have made their lives more dangerous!

Indeed the creative use of congestion can also play a role in traffic reduction. We have argued through the SUN Initiative[23] that many traffic reduction measures suffer from the same weakness as road building. It is now widely accepted that a new road will increase highway capacity thereby making it easier to drive and encouraging more people to use their cars. The level of traffic therefore increases until the road system is once again congested when the

Tram systems: The Nottingham Express Transit (NET) opened in March 2004 and now carries 10 million passengers a year. It has contributed to a 20% increase in public transport use from the north-west corridor into the city centre

attractiveness of driving is once more reduced and traffic growth slows. This suggests that traffic will tend to increase to a level at or just below the saturation point of a given road system. The weakness of many traffic reduction measures is that they seek to reduce traffic without addressing the saturation point of the system. A park-and-ride scheme, for example, will be successful in taking a significant amount of traffic off a road. This will make it less congested and easier to use so encouraging other drivers to take the place of those using the bus. The only way of reducing total traffic volumes is to combine traffic reduction measures with a reduction in highway capacity (for example by allocating part of the carriageway as a bus lane) to reduce the saturation point of the system – in other words to maintain levels of congestion. The urban neighbourhood could do this by reducing the number and width of carriageways so maintaining traffic calming congestion with much lower volumes of traffic. In Copenhagen something similar has been done by giving over road space to bicycles and reducing car parking spaces by around 2% per year – sufficient to make a cumulative difference over time but small enough not to be noticed.

Density: A pedestrian-focused neighbourhood will also be dense so that distances between facilities are kept to a minimum. Both the Urban Village and Pedestrian Pocket are based on a maximum ten-minute walking time for the

majority of the population into the centre. To do this and still retain sufficient people and activity to animate streets and support local services and public transport we need to build to higher densities than has happened in the past. In fact since this book was first published the average density of new housing has almost doubled from 23 to 41 units/hectare[24]. Again there have been objections from those who believe that high-density development is synonymous with overcrowding and a reduction in internal space standards or a return to high-rise development. The reality is that much of the density gains have come as a result of apartment schemes some of which could be criticised in this way. There has however also been a change in the way housing is built following the government requirement in planning policy guidance that all housing should be built to a minimum density of 30 units/hectare[25]. Increasingly housing developers have heeded the words of the late Francis Tibbalds, who urged that we forget 'the spaced-out buildings of the past few decades, separated from each other by highways and leftover tracts of land and concentrate on producing intricate places related to the scale of people walking not driving'[26].

This goes hand in hand with the concept of mixed-use development since the facilities that people need should be located close at hand rather than being zoned into separate areas. This includes employment, shops, services, schools, and all other facilities needed by the community. Commercial activities should be mixed with the housing and focused on the main street and at or around nodes of activity to attract passing trade.

Public transport: The Sustainable Urban Neighbourhood should also be served by an efficient public transport system. In cities like Sheffield, Nottingham, and Manchester this may be one of the tram services developed in the last decade; however in many cases it will be the bus. The only place in the UK where buses have not been privatised is London and it is no surprise that this is also the only place where bus use has increased significantly. There is a need to reverse the decline in public transport by addressing the effects of deregulation and reduced subsidy. However it must also be recognised that the dispersal of development and the reduction of housing densities has also played its part. The Local Government Management Board[27] estimates that densities of 100 persons per hectare are required to support a viable bus service and 240 persons per hectare for a tram service. The average density of new housing development in the 1990s was just 22 units to the hectare which, at an average household size is barely half the minimum required for a bus service. Such low-density developments mean that even where services exist many people are forced to walk long distances to stops. Bus usage is therefore low and the service struggles to survive. The sustainable urban neighbourhood must counter this trend. It should be organised around public transport so that the maximum number of people can walk easily to stops which are safe and easily accessible. This generally means that all housing should be within 400m of a bus stop. In this way the neighbourhood can tip the balance away from the car by giving people a convenient public transport alternative.

Energy use

Another major environmental issue that will play an important role in shaping our cities is the reduction of energy use and CO_2 emissions. Much of the work on energy efficiency has concentrated on the technical aspects of building construction, something that we do not propose to dwell on here. Much less attention has been given to the implications of building type, location and urban design.

The energy use of buildings needs to be considered at different stages of its life cycle. The construction of a building accounts for more than 10% of its total energy use. Energy is then used to service and heat the building, to maintain it and to refurbish or demolish it when it is no longer required. In each of these areas urban buildings have a contribution to make. In terms of construction urban buildings potentially use less materials as apartments and terraces share foundations, roofs or party walls unlike detached dwellings. Against this must be set the need to use energy intensive materials such as steel in larger structures. However construction systems can be used, such as that used in the Greenwich Millennium Village which have low embodied energy values and can also be dismantled and recycled. More significant in terms of energy used in construction is infrastructure. Urban development can make use of existing roads, services and facilities so avoiding the resources that would be required to provide them on green field sites. The higher density of urban development also reduces the length of roads and service runs required which has both cost and environmental benefits.

Urban house types are also potentially more energy efficient in use than detached and semi-detached forms. Heat is lost through the roof, walls and floors of buildings. Since flats and terraced houses have less exposed wall area and, in the case of flats, often no heat-loss roof or floor, they are far more energy efficient than detached dwellings for the same level of insulation. This is also true of mixed-use buildings where workspace and shops below housing will lose less heat than single-storey structures. Urban buildings are more likely to be sheltered by surrounding buildings (unless they are towers). The sheltering effect saves energy when calculating domestic energy use[28].

With district heating or combined heat and power systems, terraced forms also mean that pipes can run within houses so minimising heat loss. In an urban street pattern it may not always be possible to maximise solar orientation to reap the maximum benefits of passive solar gain and natural lighting as the rather unsuccessful layout of BedZED illustrates (see case study on page 96). However passive solar gain accounts for just 15% of the heating needs of the average home in the UK and only rises to 25% in south-facing dwellings. The Martin Centre in Cambridge has developed a measurement of 'Sky View Factor' to assess the impact of shading[29] which can be used as a design tool to minimise the problem. With improved window designs which are both airtight and use low emissivity glass to reflect heat back into the home, the energy efficiency of windows has in any case been improved so that housing can be less sensitive to orientation. Having said this, the practice of creating double-loaded apartments with single-aspect north-facing units cannot be defended however good the windows are. There is much that we can learn from Tony Garnier and his high-density housing in the Cité Industrielle with its east-west streets along the contours of south-facing slopes maximised both densities and orientation.

Urban buildings can also be more efficient in their reuse and refurbishment. Much of the early urban housing that was been created in the 1990s was in former commercial buildings such as historic mills. This illustrates how urban buildings are flexible enough to be converted to different uses so that the resources used in construction are recycled. The Georgian Terrace

is an excellent example of this, originally built for a family with servants, many were subsequently converted to flats or hotels and have since been converted back to single family homes. New urban buildings can be designed with such reuse in mind, which is one of the principles that guided the Crown Street redevelopment in Glasgow[30].

Power generation: The main source of energy use and CO_2 in a well-insulated building is not heating but lights and appliances reliant on electricity. Great strides have been taken in recent years with the widespread adoption of low-energy light bulbs and the energy rating of appliances. However even the most efficient appliances are being powered with electricity generated in power stations that, in some cases, are only 30% efficient.

In the past power generation was locally based. Urban power stations run by councils or small companies were located in the very heart of cities. While they may have caused problems in terms of pollution they were well suited to serve the needs of their local market and to respond to local peaks of demand. They also had the advantage that their waste heat could be used to heat local buildings. Until recently there was a power station huddled within the warehouses of the Whitworth Street area of Manchester which had ceased to produce electricity but was still used as a district heating plant providing hot water through steaming pipes running along the canal to the surrounding buildings.

With the nationalisation of the electricity industry many of these urban power stations were seen as uneconomic, out of date and polluting. They were therefore replaced with huge stations able to buy coal in bulk and capable of serving whole conurbations. The 'super' pit in Selby in Yorkshire was part of a system serving the power stations at Ferrybridge, Eggborough and the massive Drax which together make up 12% of the UK's generating capacity. It is hard to believe but the pit was closed down in 2005, less than 20 years after it was sunk, when it was priced out of the market by cheap Polish and South African Coal. The three massive power stations

---

ST. PANCRAS HOUSING ASSOCIATION AND CHP

St. Richards House and Hillwood House managed by St. Pancras Housing Association near to Euston Station in London were one of the first to be fitted with CHP systems in the 1990s. The blocks include 95 flats plus an elderly person's community centre and ten commercial units. The building had a communal heating system originally served by two boilers. When these boilers were due for renewal it was decided to replace them with 54 kWe CHP unit. This now provides heat and light to commercial and residential units resulting in primary energy savings of 650 000 kWh/year, a 20% reduction in CO_2 emissions and a 25% cut in residents' energy bills. The system cost £268 000 compared to the cost of replacing the existing boilers of £80 000. This gave a payback period of 7 years although the scheme did benefit from an existing district heating system so didn't have to cover the costs of pipework.

now run on imported coal. It is no wonder that Drax has been the target of demonstrations by climate change protesters.

While this may make short-term economic sense, by any other measure it is madness. Rather than being used for heating, waste heat is squandered through cooling towers which become huge cloud machines. These large stations also find it difficult to respond to peaks and troughs of demand and losses also result from the transmission of electricity over long distances through the national grid. The waste implicit in this system largely undermines the impact of electricity-saving in buildings. It means that electricity is the most environmentally damaging form of power, even when it is used in electric vehicles which have so many other environmental benefits.

An important prerequisite for efficient power generation is therefore to bring it back to the local level so that it is more responsive to demand, distribution losses are minimised and waste heat can be put to good use. This has been made possible in the UK by the same deregulation of the electricity market that has led to the nonsensical situation in Selby. Deregulation has meant that a range of smaller companies and even individuals can generate electricity and sell it to the national grid. The initial effect of this was a massive switch to gas as the primary fuel for power generation. Unlike coal or oil which must be transported by road or rail, gas can be piped into urban locations through the existing distribution network. Improved pollution control also means that power stations can operate in urban areas with virtually no harmful emissions. So for example in London the Corporation of London in partnership with British Gas have built a 30 megawatt power station in the heart of Smithfield Market. This is able to supply the power needs of much of the city and also produces heat for the market and local buildings. This was an early example of Combined Heat and Power (CHP)[31]. At one extreme this includes the sort of local power station that has been built in London which provides heat to the local area. At the

other it can involve individual home CHP units that heat the house and sell surplus electricity to the grid so that it is possible to have a negative electricity bill. More common however are block CHP systems serving hotels of communal blocks such as the St. Pancras Housing Association example[32]. CHP systems convert up to 80 % of the fuel energy into a usable form compared to just 30 % for traditional power stations and so have the potential to make a major impact on energy use and the environmental consequences of electricity.

The sustainable urban neighbourhood can therefore have its own locally-controlled power station producing environmentally-friendly cheap heat and electricity. This would be linked to a district heating system so doing away with the need for individual domestic boilers. This is now commonplace in Scandinavia, indeed 65 % of buildings in Copenhagen are served by CHP. In the UK district heating systems have had a poor image because of the experience of the 1970s when they were widely used on council estates and regarded as unreliable and inefficient. The problem was lack of control and metering so that residents often had to keep their windows open even in winter to control the temperature of their homes. They also had little incentive to conserve energy because they paid a flat rate charge regardless of the amount of heat they used. These problems can now be overcome with improved thermostatic controls and heat meters which measure the difference between the temperature of water entering and leaving the home so that bills can reflect usage.

The only factor holding CHP back in the UK has been viability. The cost of the plant along with heat distribution pipes and heat meters (which can cost as much as a small domestic boiler) has compared unfavourably with individual heating systems. This is particularly true for well-insulated buildings where the heat load is so low that heating is hardly required. The initial schemes were therefore confined to situations where a district heating boiler needed to be replaced. This was the basis of the St. Pancras scheme and has also been done on the

Alexandra Park estate in Moss Side, Manchester. The viability problem has however been solved by financing the capital costs of the system from the revenue collected from residents for heat and electricity rather than from the development costs of the scheme. Specialist companies like Thameswey – that was set up by Woking Council – have emerged and will finance and operate CHP systems for developers based on the income from utility bills. Such Energy Services Companies or 'Escos' as they are called offer a practical solution to this type of local energy generation. There remains some resistance from residents about being tied into a communal system[33] and under UK law they are, in any case, free to change electricity suppliers. The schemes that have come forward have therefore been priced slightly below the market giving residents an incentive to stay with the system.

A further problem with CHP is that heat and electricity loads differ. On a warm summers day there remains a need for electricity but there is no need for heat. This is generally overcome by running the system to meet the heat load of the area and importing or exporting electricity as required. The national grid is therefore used as a giant battery 'storing' electricity in times of surplus and buying it back when the needs of the heat load are insufficient to meet electricity demand.

The density of development can increase the market served by the plant without huge distribution distances. Indeed the CHP association has identified 'heat densities' as one of the most important factors influencing viability. A mixed-use area can also help to even out energy demand since commercial premises use energy in the daytime and housing largely in the evening. Efficiency is also improved because in urban development forms such as terraces and flats, distribution pipes are shorter and can run within buildings so that heat losses are reduced along with the need to insulate pipework buried underneath pavements.

Once the control of power generation has been wrested to the local level it also becomes possible to consider alternative forms of power supply to supplement CHP systems. One possibility is to link the CHP system to a domestic waste incinerator as has been done in Sheffield where the municipal waste incinerator generates power and feeds a district heating system that serves city centre apartments, offices and both universities. However incinerators are controversial because they can produce harmful emissions and are often fiercely resisted by residents. It is also questionable whether incineration is the best way of using domestic waste compared to recycling and reuse.

It is however possible to use renewable energy sources linked to local CHP systems. Wind turbines have been used in urban areas. However in Energy World in Milton Keynes the turbine had to be switched off because of the noise it generated[34]. As an alternative a new generation of silent vertical turbines can be incorporated into the design of buildings. However a better option may be solar power which is readily available even in the UK's overcast climate. This has been widely used in the past for water heating although this has the problem that the energy tends to be most available when there is least demand for the heat. An alternative is photovoltaic technology which uses sunlight to generate electricity. This is more compatible with CHP systems because it generates electricity to fill the gap in capacity caused by low summer heat loads. The German and Japanese governments have invested heavily in photovoltaic technology both aiming to create a million photovoltaic roofs through a partnership between developers, consumers and manufacturers. Even oil companies like BP have made a corporate decision to change the emphasis of their business from oil to solar power. The hope is that over time volume production will mean that the cost of photovoltaic panels falls and that it will become possible to use them to replace traditional roofing and cladding materials. Unfortunately at the moment (2008) in Europe, the demand from Germany is such that it has actually pushed prices up.

There are further ways of fuelling CHP plants. One option is biofuel manufactured from crops. There are concerns at present because biofuels are being substituted for food crops or even grown on cleared rain forest! They also require a lot of energy to manufacture so that the CO_2 saving is minimal. However in the future it should be possible to manufacture biofuel from agricultural and food waste at which point biofuels will come into their own. It is also possible to use methane from sewage treatment or waste tips. Technologies such as hydrogen storage and fuel cell generation will also become more viable. Surplus solar heat in the summer is used for the electrolysis of water to create hydrogen and oxygen. The hydrogen is burnt for heat or reacted with oxygen in a fuel cell to generate electricity. Using this technology a government-sponsored house in Freiburg, Germany has supplied all of its heating and electricity needs from solar power since 1992.

These technologies hold tremendous potential for the reduction of energy use and CO_2 emissions. The impact however will be limited if we focus only on the scale of individual buildings. Instead we must rethink the way that energy is used and supplied at the neighbourhood scale. In the UK this point has been emphasised by the introduction of the Code for Sustainable Homes and the target that all new homes should be zero carbon by 2016[35]. Indeed through its Carbon Challenge Programme[36] English Partnerships are promoting a series of Code 6 (zero carbon) schemes across the country as we write in 2008. There are many developers who believe that it is not possible to do this in the current housing market. Indeed as we described in Chapter 8, it could add £30000 to the cost of a medium-sized home. The only way to get around this is to address energy issues at the neighbourhood scale and to use the investment that an Energy Service Company can bring to avoid the additional cost falling on the developer.

Urban recycling

A key issue if linear resource systems are to be made circular is the recycling of domestic and commercial waste. When we first produced this book the UK, unlike the continent and parts of North America had hardly reached first base in recycling its waste. Recycling remained little more than a middle-class fad, yet even then the volume of material collected sometimes outstripped the capacity of the recycling industry to cope with it. In an article at the time for the SUN Initiative journal Keith Collins[37] described the British attitude to recycling as like raising a child, feeding it, clothing it, putting it through school and university only to say, when it left its first job that there were just two options – incineration or burial. At the time most UK recycling took place through public recycling 'bring' points and research suggested that the environmental benefits of recycling were probably cancelled out by the environmental impact of driving to recycling points.

Since the late 1990s municipal segregated waste collection has been introduced throughout the UK and the recycling rate has risen from around 5% to just over 30%. The method of segregated collection varies across the country. Some areas have up to five separate wheelie bins, collected at different times for paper, glass, green waste, cans and general waste. The drawback of this is that people are very poor at segregating their waste, get confused about the times of collection and so fail to put the right bin out. They also lack the space to store so many bins so that the neighbourhood becomes cluttered with them. An alternative is a Green Box system where householders put all recyclables into a box and the waste is sorted by the waste authority at the point of collection. This is the system used in much of the US. However when it was first introduced into London the 'road rage' which resulted from refuse vehicles waiting in busy narrow urban streets while waste was sorted into containers was sometimes so bad that the vehicle had to flee the scene. As a result this form of segregated collection in London was around three times more expensive than it had proved to be in American suburban environments. However the London system was amended to make it suitable for urban environments by introducing electric hand carts so that the segregation took place on the pavement and the segregated waste was left at accessible pick up points to be collected by the main refuse truck. This not only brought costs down to American levels, it even proved as cost-effective as unsegregated waste collection.

The choice of system can have an impact on the design of urban areas. Space for the storage of waste bins needs to be provided around new homes. Since bins cannot be bought through the house, this needs to be at the front of terraced housing. The space requirements of wheelie bin systems can be virtually impossible to accommodate, particularly if there is also a requirement for cycle storage as there is in some authorities[38]. This is causing planners to question whether terraced housing is possibly leading to a retreat into more suburban forms.

One solution to this is to provide local 'bring points' such as the system used in Holland. Large underground containers are installed beneath ordinary looking waste bins so that the system is unobtrusive and can be located within easy reach of all homes. In some places in Holland a key code and scales have been incorporated into the top of the bins so that people can be rewarded for recycling and charged for the weight of unsegregated waste that they throw away.

The next stage in the process is to establish systems to reuse the waste. Here we have made much less progress in the UK. The reality is that much of the waste that we are collecting for recycling is being shipped to places like China and India for processing. This may meet the recycling target in the UK but raises questions about the common sense of shipping waste half way around the world to save the environment. Not only are there the carbon implications of transportation, but the environmental consequences are visited upon poor communities. Urban systems need to be established in this country to close the resource loop by making use of waste. Much of the work on this has focused on the industrial scale and the activity of councils. Examples include paper mills set up to recycle newsprint which can also use substandard material to produce cardboard or even ferment it to produce ethanol as a fuel. It includes the composting of household and garden waste to sell back to householders as is

KERBSIDE RECYCLING IN HOUNSLOW

The London Borough of Hounslow was at the forefront of the introduction of recycling in the 1990s. It recognised the limitations of communal recycling points so that when waste collection contracts expired in 1996 the council introduced a self-financing kerbside collection service. Segregation collection was put in place serving 68 500 households including 1 500 low-rise and 200 high-rise flats. Each home was given a green box (below left) which was used to collect recyclable waste. This was then segregated by operatives into sacks on handcarts (below centre) which were left at pick-up points for collection (below right). The contract was awarded to a not-for-profit company and assistance was provided with capital costs. This system has since been adopted by many authorities across the UK and is potentially better suited to urban areas than wheelie bin systems.

Communal recycling bins in Almere New Town Holland. The small bins sit above large underground containers and can be fitted into tight urban streets

happening in Ludlow[39]. In the first issue of this book we featured Urban Mines[40], a project in Yorkshire which was seeking to use recycling as a spur to economic development and employment creation by creating an eco-industrial park. The idea was to create a cluster of recycling and remanufacturing industries that would process waste but also feed off each other so that the waste from one plant would become the input to its neighbour. Ten years later the scheme has planning permission for a site near Wakefield but is not in operation. Like a number of other similar initiatives the project has proved difficult to get off the ground.

However the industrial scale or even municipal segregated collection is not the only way that recycling takes place. Cities are great recyclers of materials as anyone will know if they have watched an urban skip for a few days. As soon as a skip is delivered to a street it starts to fill with rubbish – much to the consternation of the person who hired it – as people take the opportunity to off-load bulky items. However other people in the street will often claim some of this rubbish, finding a use for an old chair or table or reclaiming the waste wood. Over the days the rubbish in the skip will constantly change as a result of this informal exchange of materials.

This system has been formalised in the squatters' community of Christania where a compound is specifically set aside for this exchange of goods. The process was copied by the Homes for Change Housing Co-op (see Chapter 13) which provides space on the staircase landings for people to leave things that they think others might find useful. This is where the chair that I (DR) am sitting on as I write this comes from. This is a good example of a neighbourhood scale recycling activity, but there are many others such as local composting to feed gardens and allotments which in turn produce food for local people. It can also include community furniture projects which take cast-off furniture and refurbish it for sale to poor households, creating local employment.

On a larger scale this recycling of materials is an important part of urban economies. As Jane Jacobs points out[41] this is an area where cities have tremendous environmental and economic potential. Indeed it was Jacobs who first used the metaphor of cities being the 'urban mines' of the future, citing an advert for a paper recycling company with a picture of New York and the slogan 'our concrete forest'. Rather than extracting resources from finite natural sources she envisaged a future where we will mine urban waste for many of the raw materials we need.

This already happens to a much greater extent than one might imagine. In addition to the conventional recycling systems there are charity shops which recycle cast-off clothes, antiques shops, scrap yards, and architectural reclamation yards. Warmcell, a company in Wales, makes domestic insulation from old newspapers, others recycle photocopier toner drums, manufacture concrete from power station fuel ash, or generate power from old tyres. These are all examples of economic activities based on mining the waste of cities. As Jane Jacobs points out, these activities are driven not by environmental consciousness but by the commercial dynamism of urban areas. As such they illustrate the potentially rich vein of economic activity which could do much to revive the moribund manufacturing base of urban areas.

Using water wisely — Kolding in Denmark

As part of the renewal of 40 properties in three and four-storey blocks containing 129 dwellings it was decided to explore a number of ecological measures. Some of the most radical measures related to water consumption.

Rainwater from roofs in the scheme is directed into a pond in the centre of the scheme. This is kept fresh by being circulated over a cascade and stream and is pumped to the flats for use in washing machines and toilets. However pride of place is given to the bioworks, a 13m high glass pyramid at the centre of the courtyard which treats all of the waste water on the site. Waste is first collected in tanks where sludge settles and it is treated with ultraviolet light and ozone. It is then fed through a series of tanks containing algae, plankton, and mussels/fish. The water is then used to provide nutrients to 15 000 flats as part of a commercial operation which covers all of the running costs. The bioworks is warm and humid and filled with plants and insects and therefore seen as an asset by the surrounding residents rather than as a local sewage works.

Water and sewage

Water, like many of the resources used in urban areas, is drawn from a wide area. The cities of Birmingham and Liverpool import their water from Wales whilst Manchester draws its supplies from the Lake District. The purification and transport of this water is costly and consumes large amounts of energy as does the treatment and disposal of this water after it is used. This is a classic linear system and, as with other linear systems, there is the potential to close some of the loops to create circular systems at the local level. Yet most cities do not even make good use of the rain which falls on their roofs and streets only to be channelled directly into the sewers.

These systems can be closed at a number of levels. We may not want to return to the night-soil men who provided a service by collecting the waste of out-houses in the Victorian cities to supply market gardens. However as Herbert Girardet[42] recounts, in the middle of the last century two systems were considered for the disposal of London's sewage. One involved a system of sewers, like the spokes of a wheel, feeding the sewage out to composting plants which would then be used on a ring of market gardens surrounding the city, the other (which was eventually chosen) involved the construction of sewage works and the disposal of treated effluent into the river. As a result the city consumes the fertility of agricultural land only to dump it into the sea rather than to replenish it with compost. However this circle can be closed. He describes a facility in Bristol which turns domestic sewage into pellets which can be used to fertilise and reclaim derelict land and would be available for agricultural use once they have devised a system to deal with the industrial pollutants in the waste.

These loops can also be closed at the neighbourhood level. Many things can be done very simply such as water butts connected to gutters that can be used to water gardens. Permeable surfaces can also be used so that rainwater replenishes the water table rather than running-off immediately into rivers. Such concepts have been developed as Sustainable

Urban Drainage Systems (SUDS) designed to collect water before it runs into the drains. Stored water is then allowed to soak back into the water table or is released gradually into the river system reducing the risk of flooding. Most systems use holding ponds and reed beds. However urban alternatives are possible using permeable underground storage tanks.

It is also possible to recycle water from baths and sinks for toilet flushing. This is known as grey water restoration and involves the collection of waste water which is then filtered and pumped into storage tanks. This was explored in some detail as part of the Homes for Change project that we describe in Chapter 13. In this case the capital costs of meeting the requirements of the local water board meant that it was not viable on a scheme of fifty flats. This was partly because of the fact that it doubled the amount of plumbing in the scheme. However the main reason was the structure of water charging in the UK that meant savings for residents were minimal. As a result the capital costs would have translated into rent increases of £4 per week while the savings on water bills would have been no more than £2.50. This situation has not changed as quickly as we hoped it might. Water charges have risen and in parts of the South water supplies have become seriously depleted. The introduction of water metering on new housing has given an incentive to save water. However the grey water systems that have been marketed for individual homes for only a few thousand pounds have not taken off even in the modest way that solar panels have.

At the other end of the scale, systems serving whole neighbourhoods could benefit from economies of scale as illustrated by the case study of Kolding in Denmark. Such systems need not confine themselves to grey water but could even become local sewage treatment facilities. Most of the eco-housing that has addressed sewage treatment has used reed beds or composting toilets. Notwithstanding the vertical reed beds in oil drums in Kreuzberg, this is not really practical in an urban setting. However the intensively managed bioworks

system is ideal for urban areas resembling, as it does, a humid, verdant greenhouse rather than a traditional sewage works. The output water from the bioworks is of bathing, if not drinking, quality and can be used either to supply grey water systems or, as in Kolding, to support a horticultural business. This was tried unsuccessfully in the BedZED scheme in London where a bioworks was installed but was never fully operational because once more the charging system for water makes it unviable.

Green space

There is a great deal of confusion about green space and sustainability. Part of this revolves around the idea that green spaces are the 'lungs of the city'. Yet as Robert and Brenda Vale[43] have pointed out, Milton Keynes may have a million trees but the layout which makes this possible generates levels of car use which produce vastly more CO_2 than the trees are able to absorb. Indeed Jane Jacobs ridicules the concept of green space being the 'lungs of the city' pointing out that three acres of woodland is required to absorb the CO_2 produced by just four people. This, of course, is not the only reason for green space in urban areas. Green lungs are important psychologically to city dwellers as can be seen by New Yorkers' devotion to Central Park. Green space is also an important contributor to biodiversity encouraging flora and fauna. Indeed in the last few decades the biodiversity of cities has risen significantly and the numbers of many species are recovering in urban areas at a time when they continue to decline in the countryside. A study by Manchester University[44] suggested that a 10% rise in tree cover in a city could cool urban temperatures by 4°C while documenting that street trees have a proven effect on house values.

However as we saw in Part 1 of this book, the assumption in much postwar planning is that green open space is a good thing and the more of it that is created the better urban areas will be. Not true! Too much green space reduces the density of urban areas lessening the viability of public transport and increasing walking distances. Its maintenance can be a drain on public resources and at night it can be deserted and unsafe. Urban green space needs to be carefully designed and planned to maximise its contribution to the environment of urban areas while minimising its negative aspects.

This is what we have failed to do in many of our cities. In Manchester in the 1990s, for example, it was estimated by the planning department that a third of the city's land area was open space, not including land which was vacant or derelict. Much of this open space was parks and playing fields which are rightly protected from development. However the majority of it was neither vacant nor parkland. It was the result of past planning dogma which regarded open space as a good thing in its own right so that everything from shopping centres to housing estates had been marooned in great savannas of council-maintained grass land which contributed

little or nothing to biodiversity recreational amenity or social cohesion. Many of the main roads in Manchester run through landscaped corridors, some originally reserved for future road widening but most with no other function than to protect surrounding development from the road. As a result the high streets that were once lined with shops and provided a focus for local communities are now hostile barriers between estates hidden behind landscaped mounds. In recent years in Manchester and other UK cities this profligate landscaping is disappearing as estates are redeveloped and landscape strips along roads are developed. To some people this may represent an erosion of the environmental quality of the city. However if it is properly managed it need not reduce either the psychological or biodiversity benefits of urban open space.

Sustainable urban areas are not necessarily those with the largest amount of

URBAN OASIS

The Apple Tree Court Tenants' Association formed a management company in 1996 to take over the management of the tower block from Salford City Council. As part of the agreement the land around the block passed to the tenants who decided that it should be put to productive use both to grow food and to provide a focus of the community in the flats.

The land has been fenced and developed with organic gardening, an orchard, a pond, wild flower meadow and seating areas. It has used horticultural principles imported from the Middle East through a partnership with the Arid Lands Initiative and has been implemented by local people along with community service offenders. As a result the residents of the flats are almost self-sufficient in fruit and vegetables and there have been spin-off benefits in terms of the management of the block.

Future plans include the recycling of waste heat from the flats to heat polytunnels, the collection of rainwater to remove reliance on mains water and composting of domestic waste as well as a geodesic conservatory and a café.

The project has attracted national interest after it won the BT/WWF Partnership Award and is being established to provide a food crop for the wider inner city for the elderly and people in high-rise flats. A tree growing kit has been used in over 500 schools and an Urban Oasis pack is being produced to help people replicate the project elsewhere.

---

open space. It is quality not quantity which counts. The sustainable urban neighbourhood may not therefore have large tracts of open space but it should nevertheless maximise the opportunities for wildlife and biodiversity. Indeed in Richard Register's vision of Ecocity Berkeley, the metropolis is a haven for wildlife and a net contributor to biodiversity. This it can do through street trees, parks, squares, balconies, window boxes, courtyards, private gardens and green roofs. The Homes for Change scheme (see Chapter 13) includes 75 flats and 16000 square feet of workspace on just 1.3 acres of land, yet incorporates extensive planting in its courtyard, three roof gardens – some of which are used for food growing – and many of the flats have balconies. Thus despite the density of the scheme the area of green space is equivalent to around half of the site area and the opportunity for greenery is maximised. When viewed on aerial photographs some of our older urban areas like Toxteth in Liverpool or Moseley in Birmingham are virtually obscured by tree cover and mature gardens. Such urban areas provide homes for all manner of wildlife from foxes, hedgehogs and owls to birds, insects and wild plants, and yet often have very little designated public open space. This is the sort of environment that we should be creating in new urban areas and is not at all incompatible with high-density development.

Large areas of public open space are, of course, important in urban areas. These can include wilderness areas like Hampstead Heath but just as important are urban parks, play areas, and sports facilities. If these areas are to work as successful, safe public spaces they need to be designed along the same principles as successful streets. They need to be overlooked by surrounding buildings or supervised by activity. The early parks like Sefton Park in Liverpool were financed by the development of up-market housing around the periphery which benefited from the views over the park. This meant that the park was supervised and clearly part of the public realm. By contrast many modern public open spaces are bounded by the back gardens of houses and therefore become abandoned to gangs of dissolute youths.

One of the parks that I (DR) use regularly illustrates the point. Alexandra Park in Manchester (pictured overleaf) is a large Victorian park which adjoins the Alexandra Park estate, historically the most dangerous and notorious part of Moss Side. Yet the park is well used and suffers from none of the problems of the surrounding area, indeed it has lower levels of vandalism than some of the parks in more prosperous parts of the city. This is because it is active throughout the day with dog walkers, fishermen, cyclists, children at play, people playing football, cricket or tennis and parents taking their children to the play centre in the middle of the park. It is surrounded by roads so that, while it may not be the most tranquil park in the city, no part of it feels isolated, despite its size. It is also bounded on two sides by large Victorian property, much of it subdivided into

Alexandra Park, Moss Side, Manchester

flats. This, along with the resident park keeper, gives the impression that the park is overlooked even though the mature tree cover means that for most of the park this is not the case. There is much that we can learn from such Victorian parks about the way that green space and landscaping can be successfully incorporated into urban areas.

Open space can also be put to productive use through the use of gardens and allotments for food growing. Urban agriculture is a traditional part of urban areas and is actually increasing in scale. It is also an important use for recycled waste, be it composted organic household waste or the product of locally treated sewage. Urban food growing can reduce the food miles associated with imported food, provide fresh produce for low income groups, and reduce travel to large supermarkets[45]. The Diggers self-build housing scheme in Brighton uses grass roofs to house beehives and the Springfield Community Garden in the heart of Bradford provides seven acres for organic food growing along with employment training, education and recycling workshops. In New York encouragement by the municipality has helped to create over 700 such

community gardens which together produce around \$100 000 of fruit and vegetables a year[46]. Such projects can also be linked to permaculture initiatives as in Apple Tree Court in Salford where the Urban Oasis project has transformed the land around a tower block into an organic food-growing area.

In this chapter we have reviewed the factors which taken together have the potential to significantly reduce the environmental impact of the Sustainable Urban Neighbourhood. In doing this the neighbourhood could play an important role in the wider task of greening the city. Yet most of what we have suggested is based upon existing technology, is practical and could be easily implemented without major increases in costs. These principles may be based on the lessons from eco-communities but they are appropriate for the urban context. Indeed many require an urban context since they are based upon a density of people and activities to make systems viable. In the next chapter we discuss in more detail this urban context and the characteristics which lie behind successful urban areas.

Chapter 11

Urban building blocks

In the last chapter we described the impact of environmental sustainability on urban development. Here we explore the meaning of the word 'urban'. This is first and foremost a description of the location of development, the fact that it takes place within existing towns and cities. However it also relates to the character of the neighbourhood, its physical form and its relationship to urban traditions which have endured for thousands of years. In Britain and other parts of the world these traditions are being rediscovered. This is partly driven by environmental issues as we saw in the last chapter and a concern to promote urban areas based on walking rather than driving. However it is also based on the belief that traditional urban forms have stood the test of time and are more attractive, functional and less likely to fail than many of the other ways that we have devised for planning and designing cities in the recent past.

In the 20th century British towns and cities were transformed from the sort of dense urban settlements that we still admire on the continent to sprawling low-density conurbations. This drained away the viability and vitality of many of our urban areas. It created an outer ring of affluent suburbs, out-of-town shopping and business parks and left an embattled town centre surrounded by inner city decay. In short we largely destroyed our urban society in favour of a suburban society.

The logical conclusion of this process can be seen in the rampant sprawl of American cities. Indeed the nightmare of US urbanism with its socially and racially divided cities was one of the factors driving a realisation that something had to change in the UK. Were we really prepared for our society as well as our cities to follow the American model? Did we really want the centres of British towns and cities to become nothing but tourist attractions and speciality shopping districts? Were we prepared to abandon our inner cities as no-go areas with burgeoning crime and social breakdown? Did we want to live and work in isolated 'edge cities' where social contact is limited and no journey is possible without a car? This is the reality of most US cities as so graphically described by James Howard Kunstler in his book *The Geography of Nowhere*[1] and is worse than ever today despite 20 years of Smart Growth and New Urbanism. The first edition of this book was written in the hope that this nightmare could be avoided in the UK. This looks more likely now than it did then. However if we are to achieve this on a lasting basis our task is nothing less than to reinvent the British town and city.

We were not alone in recognising a need to reinvent urban areas. HRH Prince Charles, in his book *A Vision for Britain*[2], urged that we should learn from traditional urban areas. This is something that the urban design profession has been doing for years. Writers like

Kevin Lynch, Francis Bacon, Gordon Cullen, Spiro Kostof, Francis Tibbalds, Ian Bentley and Harley Sherlock[3] have all sought to distil from the Italian hill town, the renaissance city, Georgian Bath or Napoleonic Paris the principles of successful urban planning. These writers generally agree on what makes urban areas work and from their writings we can draw a set of principles to guide the development of the sustainable urban neighbourhood which is what we do for the rest of this chapter.

The importance of the street

The first and most important principle is a rediscovery of the importance of the street as the central organising element of urban areas. The idea that urban areas should be based on streets seems self-evident. It is the way that traditional towns work and remains the way that most town centres are structured, at least

where they avoided the redeveloping zeal of the postwar planners. Yet on the ground the notion of developing new housing and commercial uses along traditional streets has been far from obvious to many people including developers and planning authorities. Better the cul-de-sac to remove through traffic and provide defensible space than the noisy dangerous old street that Le Corbusier so detested. Better the business or retail park with its secure perimeter fence and ample parking all in one ownership than the congested, diverse urban area with all its dangers and distractions.

We have lost faith in the traditional street just as we have lost faith in the city. Indeed before the days of high-rise council estates social problems manifested on street corners and in back streets. Ne'er-do-wells hung out on street corners, prostitutes were called streetwalkers, and gang violence was called

The traditional street:
Roupell Street in Waterloo is now something of a rarity in our urban areas. It is tightly defined by its houses with a shop or pub on every corner. Such streets were once seen as at the root of many urban problems

street-fighting. The location was confused with the problem so that the street came to be seen as the cause of many urban evils and was swept away in slum clearance and redevelopment areas. However the streetless council estate has fared even less well than the terraced streets that survived redevelopment. Removing the arena of the street did not sweep away urban problems, it just pushed them into staircases, walkways and parking lots or into the generous areas of landscaping provided to 'humanise' new estates. Here the problems have proved much more difficult to control and much more threatening to the inhabitants of the area. Should we therefore reconsider our negative view of the street? Is it possible that streets are a civilising influence which ameliorate rather than exacerbate the problems of urban life? This was not the view of the developers and planners of the 1990s who continued to replace streetless high-rise estates with streetless low-rise suburban estates based on the cul-de-sac. Many of these have been no more successful than their high-rise predecessors.

To understand both the potential benefits of the street and why it has, and in some cases continues to be, so resisted we must understand a little more about its nature. The street brings together two quite different functions. It is both a route for movement through an area and a focus for a local community. These are functions that postwar planning has regarded as incompatible but which compliment each other to create the magic of successful streets. A cul-de-sac can provide a community focus but only its residents and their visitors have reason to be there. A street by contrast will serve more than just its residents and will welcome and accommodate strangers. Yet for many years the stranger has been seen as the enemy in urban areas, someone who causes noise and disturbance and leads to crime and congestion. This is why, since Parker and Unwin designed the first garden suburbs, we have been so attracted to the cul-de-sac. However an area without strangers is an area which cannot support shops, which is deserted for large parts

of the day and where there are few passers-by to deter the criminal. The cul-de-sac may be ideal for the leafy suburb where such things are less of a problem but it is less well suited to the town and city where one expects to find more vitality and where crime is an unfortunate fact of life.

A street is more than a road since, as well as being a route from A to B, it is a place where people meet and interact and hence where the public life of the town or city is played out. An important principle of postwar planning has been that routes carrying anything but the most local of traffic need to be separated from residential and other types of development. Engineering guides were drawn up with road hierarchies in which all 'distributor roads' were to be kept free of frontage development. This was partly out of concern that traffic noise would damage the amenity of residents, but mostly to avoid curtilage access to individual properties interrupting the free flow of traffic. As a result our towns and cities are blighted with roads and roundabouts bounded by green swathes of landscaping and shunned by the buildings which would traditionally have sustained them.

The street by contrast can perform an equally important role as an artery for movement and a place defined and animated by its buildings. It is on streets that the public life of the city is played out. There are still many unappreciated streets that throng with life throughout the day, that nourish lively communities and support diverse commercial activity. At their best they are the 'great streets' described by Allen Jacobs but at the more mundane level they are what makes all urban areas work.

It could be argued that the idealistic notion of streets as public meeting place and artery is no longer possible in the modern city. The car and bus have filled the once civilised street with their noise and fumes, undermining its role as community focus. What is more, the idea of urban places where local people and strangers mix in harmony is at odds with the reality of modern city life. Streets may be the stages on which the drama of urban life is played out but people no longer wish to be part of the play alongside the mugger and the drug dealer[4]. This however is a counsel of despair. We must tame and civilise the worst aspects of urban life if cities are to be repopulated. In this task the traditional street is likely to be our most potent weapon.

Take for example the issue of traffic discussed in the last chapter. The road which is free of frontage development is designed to increase traffic capacity whereas the environmental impact of the car means that we should be doing just the opposite. Cars need to be discouraged from coming into towns so road capacities must be reduced and speeds checked, which is exactly what traditional streets do.

In terms of fear and crime, the street has also been wrongly accused. The flight of the middle classes may mean that the city today is more dangerous than it was between the wars. Yet is it more dangerous than the London described by Dickens? Cities have always been dangerous places, yet in no other age has this caused people to abandon the concept of streets or indeed to abandon cities. The street is the way in which cities have dealt with crime and allowed civilised life to continue. Good urban streets create a robust delineation between the public and the private realm protecting the latter and ensuring the former is surveyed by windows and passers-by. Suburban forms lack both of these properties. This is largely because, in suburbs with their low levels of crime and emphasis on family life, it is possible to blur the distinctions between the public and the private. It would however be a mistake to believe that because the suburbs have less crime, suburban forms will reduce crime in the city, as many crime prevention officers would have us believe[5]. The use of the more robust traditional street may therefore be a prerequisite for attracting a broader range of people back into urban areas.

What then are the practical implications of building urban streets? If a street is to fulfil the role of a route from A to B it must clearly lead somewhere. This relates to the concept of **permeability** as described in the last chapter. This simple rule means that all streets connect at both ends to other streets – the first important characteristic of an urban street. The route need not always allow through access for cars but pedestrians should normally be able to use the street as a route. Permeability is central both to the concept of a pedestrian-friendly neighbourhood and to its urban character. It has the effect of reducing walking distances because it makes it possible to reach your destination without major detours. This also has the effect of increasing activity on streets to support a wider range of economic activity and to make the area feel safer. In impermeable urban areas, where large housing estates or business parks allow no through routes, fewer journeys are possible on foot. Furthermore, trips by car are concentrated on a few main routes which become unbearable because of the volume of traffic. The approach of the highway engineers can therefore create the twin evils of congested high streets where life is impossible and deserted side streets which can sustain nothing but housing. This further discourages walking, creating a vicious circle of car dependency. Evidence for this has been provided by Bill Hillier through his studies of urban space syntax[6]. He has illustrated that areas with low levels of connectivity (another word for permeability) have low encounter rates (the frequency at which you meet other people) and also higher rates of domestic burglary.

Permeability does not mean, as many developers fear, that the cul-de-sac is outlawed. Urban areas have always included cul-de-sacs, or at least their urban equivalent, the mews court. These are essential to open up sites within urban blocks or land along railway lines and rivers. However it is important that cul-de-sacs, where there are used, should be short and should not predominate so that ease of access through the area is maintained. What we should avoid is the dendritic layout of suburban estates made up of branching cul-de-sacs from a single point of access.

Permeability also relates to traffic which is where the dual role of the street as a route and a community focus is thrown into sharpest focus. One need only watch forty-tonne juggernauts lumbering through streets built when the horse was the main form of transport to understand the appeal of the bypass. It should however be remembered that the shops and facilities on these streets are there precisely because of the volume of traffic and passing trade. Excluding through traffic, or pedestrianising the street runs the risk of cutting off its commercial life blood in all but the busiest streets. It is noticeable travelling through Britain by car that you rarely pass through the centre of a British town. As you approach the outskirts of the town you are channelled onto a ring road or bypass, no doubt much to the relief of local people. In France by contrast the National routes channel traffic through the heart of each town, along the main shopping streets and through the town square. Highway engineers no doubt consider France to be a very backward country. Yet it is no coincidence that many French town centres prosper despite the rumbling juggernauts whereas their British equivalents struggle to retain their vitality.

If this is true of major streets it is even more the case with smaller shopping streets. These streets depend for their success on a flow of activity to create a degree of vitality to provide surveillance and to support services. This can rarely be achieved outside town centres solely with pedestrian flows – traffic is important. However to a highway engineer this implies rat runs, pedestrian/vehicle conflict and a loss of control over where the traffic goes. We must not, however, give in to the traffic engineer's desire to exclude through traffic but must design these streets to accommodate it. Streets must be designed to accommodate traffic without squeezing out pedestrian life or becoming urban motorways. In this way permeability can be maintained for both pedestrians and cars without allowing the car to dominate.

This means widening pavements and reducing carriageway widths. It also means grasping the nettle and removing all of the railings and street furniture designed to separate cars and people. This is not easy and, as with all highways issues, the problem is liability for accidents and deaths that could result from any change. No one ever got sued for following the manual, however a highway engineer who innovates can become personally liable for accidents, which is why highways manuals are so difficult to change.

In London some important work was done by Terry Farrell in 2002[7]. He was asked to look at Euston Road which connects Euston, St. Pancras and Kings Cross Stations and feeds the traffic from the M40 into central London. The road is an important gateway to the city for millions of rail passengers and also contains a series of important institutions like the British Library, the Welcome Institute, Regents Park and the Royal College of Music. It carries 60 000 vehicles a day and over the years efforts to accommodate this traffic have turned it into an urban motorway, particularly at its junction

The Urban Mews:
Orchard Street in Bristol (below) shows how 'cul-de-sacs' can have a place in urban areas. Left: Chronos Buildings in London, a modern interpretation of the Mews by Proctor Matthews Architects

Kensington High Street: A pioneer in the UK following the removal of all of the paraphernalia of high-way engineering. The result is that accident rates have fallen and the shops have revived

with Tottenham Court Road where the Euston Underpass creates a major barrier to pedestrian movement. Terry Farrell's work compared Euston Road with international examples such as the Avenue des Champs-Élysées in Paris which carries almost twice the traffic and yet remains an attractive place.

Farrell's proposals for Euston Road are yet to be implemented. However some of the ideas have been put into practice on Kensington High Street[8]. Here the politicians were fed up with the street being dominated by traffic and asked their highways department to take out all of the railings and to widen the pavements. The engineers, while sympathetic to this, felt unable to take professional responsibility for such an untested approach. Eventually a compromise was reached and the professionals agreed to write a report recommending that the politicians <u>not</u> do this, and the politicians agreed to ignore this recommendation, thus absolving the professionals of legal liability. The changes to Kensington High Street have now been in place for a number of years and monitoring shows that it still accommodates nearly 40 000 vehicles a day but accident rates have fallen

and the shops have thrived. Emboldened by this the Borough of Kensington and Chelsea implemented a similar scheme for Exhibition Road (which links the Victoria and Albert, Natural History and Science Museums). This has a fully shared surface with traffic separated from pedestrians by just a row of bollards.

At a more local level even more radical solutions are being proposed by the Shared Space movement that advocates the removal of all traffic signals and markings. The idea is that if cars realise that they don't have priority it will change their perception of risk and cause their behaviour to change. In Scandinavia and Holland traffic signals and kerbs have been removed on quite significant junctions with the result that cars creep across the space at walking pace and the whole area becomes safer and much more pleasant for everyone. In the UK some moves have been made in this direction by pioneering engineers such as Ben Hamilton-Bailey[9] and in addition to Kensington, schemes have been implemented at Seven Dials in Covent Garden and in Brighton. However it is still very difficult to get local highways authorities to accept that people should come first.

The magic of successful streets:
A street in Bucharest which is a route
for movement, a place to spend time
and a focus for a local community

197

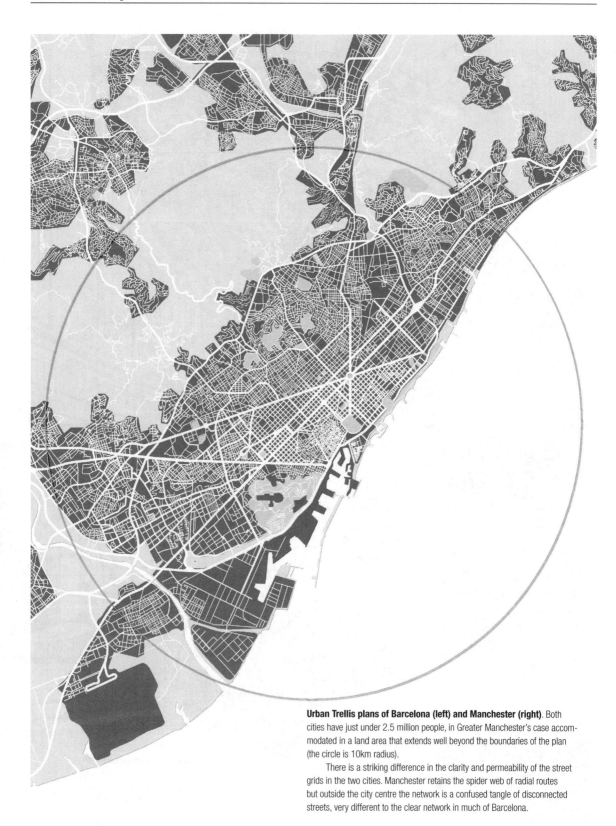

Urban Trellis plans of Barcelona (left) and Manchester (right). Both
cities have just under 2.5 million people, in Greater Manchester's case accommodated in a land area that extends well beyond the boundaries of the plan
(the circle is 10km radius).

There is a striking difference in the clarity and permeability of the street
grids in the two cities. Manchester retains the spider web of radial routes
but outside the city centre the network is a confused tangle of disconnected
streets, very different to the clear network in much of Barcelona.

Street networks: Figure ground plans of continental and British towns illustrating how continental towns are based on a strong network of streets defined by buildings. This network can be organic or based upon a grid iron such as Turin (3), New York (6) and Glasgow (9). Many UK cities like London (7), Edinburgh (8) and Glasgow (9) retain a strong street network although in the case of Glasgow this has broken down around the edges as a result of the ring road. This is more pronounced in other UK cities such as Barnsley (10) where a traditional structure has been undermined and Coventry and Bracknell (11 and 12) where comprehensive redevelopment or new town planning has meant that it has been entirely lost.

Full list: 1. Bordeaux, 2. Naples, 3. Turin, 4. Palma, 5. Dublin, 6. New York, 7. London, 8. Edinburgh Old Town, 9. Glasgow, 10. Barnley, 11. Coventry, 12. Bracknell Numbers 1-8 courtesy MBLC Architects.

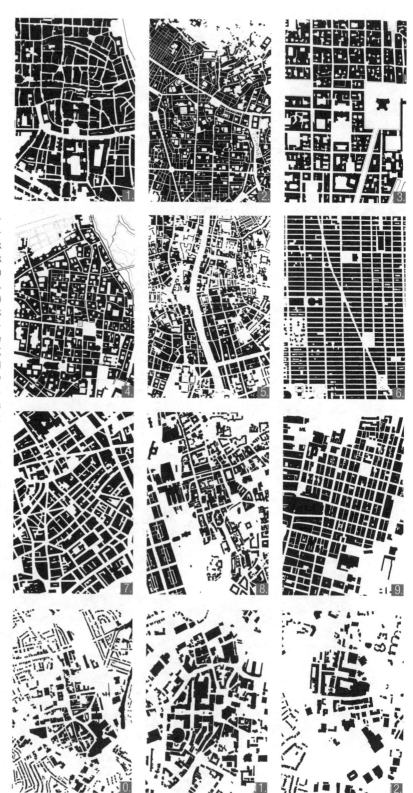

A framework of streets

The simple rule that all streets should join at either end to other streets creates the second important characteristic of urban areas – that they are based on a framework of streets. This framework is far more than just a movement system, it is a central organising element of any urban area. This framework of streets is the trellis on which the vine of the city grows giving it its form and structure. It is also the central nervous system carrying movement and communications (from bus routes to services and telecommunications under the pavements). Street frameworks can take many forms, however there is a clear difference between the planned and unplanned city. In the former the framework of streets is planned in advance and is generally geometric in form. This is most commonly an orthogonal grid as in Roman towns, New York, Barcelona or even more recently the 'super grid' of Milton Keynes. However planned towns can also be circular or hexagonal as in many fortified cities. The other type of street network, and the one which characterises most British cities, is the organic or unplanned grid. The organic grid has grown naturally over time and often resembles a spiders web. It is based on a series of radial routes which converge on the centre of town. Over time new roads are built to open up the land between these routes in a process described by Christopher Alexander in his book *A new theory of urban design*[10] (we will return to the importance of grids to the process of urban development in Chapter 14).

One of the most damaging aspects of modern town planning has been its failure to recognise the importance of this framework of streets within a town. This can be clearly seen by comparing the figure ground plans of British and continental towns. In the British examples the remnants of organic street plans can be seen with major streets converging on the centre of town. However the development of ring roads and the existence of a band of ill-defined development around the core means that the grid soon breaks down. This is in sharp contrast

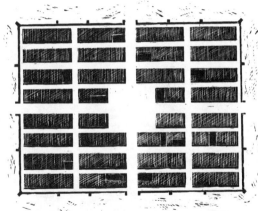

to many continental towns where traffic has been accommodated within the original street framework rather than by abandoning it in favour of the ring road.

One important effect of a grid is to make it easy to find your way around, the concept of **legibility** which was also covered in the previous chapter. A New Yorker could be dropped anywhere in the city and know immediately from the shape of the city blocks and the numbering of the streets exactly where he or she was. The same is true of many old cities where orientation is possible because you know that all major streets lead either to the centre or one of the city gates.

Hierarchies

This leads to the next important urban characteristic – hierarchies. The internal structure of all urban areas is based on an interconnected series of hierarchies. Uses, buildings and open space all have a hierarchy developed over time and reflecting the democratic organisation of the area. The most important of the hierarchies from which all others are derived is the hierarchy of streets. Street networks are never uniform, some streets are more important than others. In small cities there is a simple hierarchy with the most important streets leading to the centre. In larger cities the hierarchy is more complex as the centre is divided into a series of sub-areas and complemented by a range of satellite centres. The most important streets tend to be the radial routes and the streets linking the sub-centres. This creates a hierarchy of streets and this

Street hierarchies: The standard form of many Roman towns with primary routes, converging on a central square surrounded by four quarters each bisected by secondary and tertiary streets

**THE A6 CORRIDOR –
MANCHESTER**

A6 corridor (the Stockport Road) in
Manchester is one of the city's great
high streets passing through the districts of Longsight and Levenshulme
and is also an important transport
route between the city and Stockport.
Like an number of streets in the city
it has been the subject of environmental improvements and economic
development. Levenshulme in particular had declined and lost much
of its retail role. The strategy sought
to reconcile the regeneration of the
centre with the needs of through traffic by promoting new uses such as
the evening economy and antiques,
creating a new public space, while
slowing down traffic, creating bus
lanes and providing short-term cus-
tomer parking.

hierarchy determines the nature of development
along each street. The street hierarchy is central
to the structure of many urban design guides
such as those produced by Andres Duany and
Elizabeth Plater-Zyberk in America[11]. It was
also used in the *Hulme Guide to Development*[12]
(see Chapter 13) which has at its core a simple
hierarchy of streets:

High Streets: At the top of the food
chain are high streets which are the busiest
streets in any area and the most urban in
character. They tend to be the original radial
routes into the city, the routes linking sub-
centres and the main shopping streets within
each centre. Indeed many developed from
the country lanes that linked the town to its
neighbours when it was still a village. In the
heart of shopping centres the high street will
often be pedestrianised but elsewhere it is
an important route for through traffic, cars,
pedestrians and public transport. The high
street will thus be the shopfront of any city, since
it will be the most visible street to the largest
number of people. It will also be the focus for
surrounding communities. In the past people
would have gone 'up the high street' to do

their shopping, to visit the bank, to meet other
people and to worship. Unfortunately such
high streets, in Britain at least, are increasingly
rare. Many were lost in the redevelopments of
the 1960s. Hulme in Manchester lost its High
Street (Stretford Road) and in the process lost
thirty pubs and more than two hundred shops.
They were replaced with eight shops in a new
precinct, a new church, pub and health centre
designed to serve the needs, and no more, of
the planned population of the area. Thus was
lost the magic that sustains a good high street
which, because of passing trade, supports a
far wider range of services and specialist shops
than would be justified by the size of the
local community. Such high streets often pass
through deprived areas and play an important
role in preventing them becoming ghettos as
happened in Hulme when its high street was
lost. As we see in Chapter 13, Stretford Road
has now been rebuilt and there has been some
success in bringing back shops. But it will never
achieve its former vitality, once lost that is gone
forever.

The high streets which survived the
1960s are not however out of danger. Even

today high streets are being destroyed by road widening schemes and others are choked with traffic. In an effort to deal with this traffic local councils are removing on-street parking (such as the Red Routes in London), fencing in pedestrians on narrow pavements, creating bus and cycle lanes and restricting turning movements to and from side streets. The result is to ease traffic flow, for a time at least, but to undermine the viability of high street uses as their customers can no longer park or cross the road (other than at designated crossing points). The environment becomes even more dominated by moving traffic which can be much more intrusive than slow-moving congestion. Traditional functions such as shopping, leisure and even churches therefore move away from the street which is left deserted and lined by struggling shops and the ubiquitous hot food take-aways shuttered during the day. In the past high streets were the main economic thoroughfares along which everyone in the city

passed. They were lined with lively commercial frontages and often served to hide the adjacent slums from the eyes of passers-by. The opposite is often true of the modern high street where vacant, decaying commercial frontages can hide quite successful residential areas. The impression that this 'shopfront' to the city gives is that it is dirty and dangerous and closed for business. An important task in rebuilding urban areas is therefore to rediscover appropriate economic roles and design models for the high street.

Primary distributors: In the modern city we cannot escape the fact that there is another type of street at the top of the hierarchy, the primary distributor. They are a product of the motor age and would not have existed in tradition towns but, until major reform takes place in our car-based culture, they will remain important for the free flow of traffic. These are normally dual carriageways and are kept free of frontage development and are therefore the least urban element of the

SOUTHALL GAS WORKS

URBED worked for five years on a master plan for a 30ha site in West London which unfortunately will not be built. This was a former gas works that had never been incorporated into the surrounding city. The first task of the master plan was therefore to establish a street hierarchy.

At the centre of this is the creation of a new boulevard designed as

both a high street for the scheme and a relief road for Southall. The street was designed as a boulevard which accommodated a lane of traffic in each direction, a bus lane, a street tree margin, a service road with on-street parking, and wide pavements. This allowed it to accommodate a significant amount of traffic as well as being a shopping high

street for the area.

The boulevard was at the centre of a street hierarchy with secondary and tertiary streets that provided a structure for the 4000 homes master plan which also included a secondary school and health centre (on the boulevard) and offices.

Ayres Road Stretford
A rare example of a really good secondary street

hierarchy. It is however possible to give these primary distributors an urban character as demonstrated by the boulevards of Paris. The Champs Élysées, after all, has six lanes and accommodates a huge volume of traffic yet still operates as a street. This it does by providing very wide pavements and small feeder roads off the main carriageway to accommodate on-street parking and servicing. Two rows of trees protect the buildings from traffic noise, allowing the pavements to accommodate street cafés and activity. This however only works because of the scale of the buildings which face onto the Champs Élysées which creates a strong sense of enclosure despite the width of the street. It is probably unrealistic to expect that we can recreate such great streets in modern urban areas but it is important that we develop modern versions of the boulevard so that these main traffic routes do not undermine and isolate the character of urban neighbourhoods.

Secondary Streets: There can be a number of rungs to the hierarchy below the high street. Secondary streets are similar, in many ways, to high streets. They provide the main circulation routes within, rather than between, neighbourhoods and generally include a mix of uses including local shopping parades, small businesses and services such as doctors and schools. However the balance on these streets tends more towards a residential environment. In major cities secondary streets are characterised by specialist shops, cafés and other uses which thrive away from the cut and thrust of the high street. However smaller towns and declining urban areas often find it difficult to sustain lively secondary streets. This can be exacerbated by the efforts of highway engineers to prevent these streets being used as 'rat runs' which often leads to through traffic being blocked, further undermining their viability.

Residential or Tertiary Streets: Below this is the residential or tertiary street which accounts for most streets in an urban area. These streets carry only a small amount of traffic and are therefore seen by few people other than those who live and work there. These tertiary streets serve as the focus for local communities. They also accommodate parked cars and local servicing as well as community activities and even children playing on the street. In traditional urban areas these minor streets tend to be narrower and more intensely urban in character. However because they are not seen by so many people it is also possible to relax the urban form in places to allow for different building types such as larger houses or workshops. It is however important to maintain the permeability of these areas and also to retain, where possible, their mixed-use nature.

Reconciling the needs of cars and pedestrians is equally important in the local street. Here the concept of Home Zones has been developed as a form of Shared Space that has proved to be more acceptable to the highways profession in the UK. Based on the Woonerf concept developed originally in Holland is a street where pedestrians and cars share the same surface and vehicle speeds are reduced to a walking pace. The first Home Zone in the UK developed under a government pilot scheme was the Northmoor scheme in Longsight Manchester. The concept has since been enshrined in a government circular[13] effectively meaning that Home Zones have become part of the rule book. As the example from Groningen below shows, freed from the geometry of highways it is possible to create a much tighter, more intimate street scene.

There can sometimes be levels of the urban hierarchy below the residential street. In Georgian areas, such as the district around Hope Street in Liverpool, the main houses face onto the residential streets and to the rear they have stable blocks and servants' quarters facing onto back streets. These back streets can form a parallel street network allowing services such as refuse collections and deliveries to be kept off residential streets. On a smaller scale this is true of the back alleys which characterise areas of by-law terraces which were originally designed for the collection of 'night soil'. In Sunderland these back alleys are wide enough for a car and a refuse truck to pass and are therefore still used for refuse collection and parking. The modern equivalent might be the off-street parking area and there are occasions where there may still be a role for back streets.

This street hierarchy plays a central role in structuring urban areas. The frequency of high streets increases towards the centre and residential streets predominate on the periphery. It can also play an important role guiding urban regeneration. Traditionally urban areas expanded along radial routes and only later was the open land between these routes built up, often for poor quality residential development. As a result people moving in and out of the city were unaware of the open land or poverty just behind the high street frontage. Yet urban regeneration often starts in the back lands where the worst problems exist whilst ignoring the high street. As a result, people passing in and out of the city see only the problems and are unaware of the improvements behind the decaying high street frontage or landscaped buffer zone.

Home Zones:

Left: A street in Groningen, Holland and Right: One of the first Home Zones in the UK in Northmoor, Longsight Manchester

CROWN STREET – GLASGOW

The redevelopment of the Gorbals in Glasgow was at the forefront of the development of a new approach to urban design in the UK. The 19th century Gorbals was characterised by closely packed tenements. It had once been a respectable mixed community but deteriorated into one of Britain's most notorious slums. Redevelopment in the 1960s with monumental blocks, some designed by Sir Basil Spence and Robert Mathew, did nothing to dispel this image.

A comprehensive redevelopment scheme in the 1990s replaced all but two of the 1960s blocks with a series of three and four-storey courtyard blocks covering forty acres. The concept was to return to the original tenement pattern although at lower densities. The population after redevelopment was 20 000, a fifth of that of the original Gorbals.

A master plan was prepared for the development by Piers Gough following a nationwide urban design competition. This was not a blueprint, but enabled outline planning consent to be secured and provided the basis for infrastructure works and development phasing. The master plan accommodated

almost 1 000 new homes, a local shopping centre, hotel, student housing and a new local park. It is based on a grid of streets which defined building plots to be developed with continuous frontage perimeter blocks. Storey heights were varied along with front gardens, and 'necking' (a setback in the building line) to create variety and interest in the public realm.

Family maisonettes have been created on the ground floor of blocks with separate back gardens backing onto communal open space at the centre of each block. The flats above are accessed by communal staircases. The planners insisted on higher levels of parking than car ownership levels would have suggested and negotiations only succeeding in reducing levels from 130 % to 115 %. As a result the new streets are dominated by parked cars.

The project has sought a high level of investment in the external environment (said to account for 10–15 % of development costs in Northern Europe but less than 1 % in Scotland). Traffic calmed streets with on-street parking have helped to integrate the area with the outside world where it used to be cut off by heavy traffic routes and functionless open space.

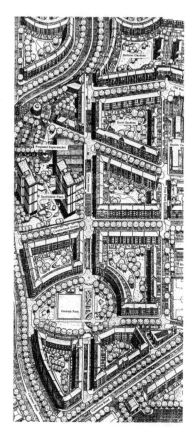

The urban block

Having established the framework and hierarchy of streets we have also created the main building component of an urban area – the urban block. Today the street tends to be seen as a means of gaining access to a site whereas in traditional cities streets were the way in which the boundaries of sites were defined. Once a framework of streets has been established, and in many urban areas it already exists, the streets naturally define a series of development plots. In urban areas these sites are then developed with buildings placed around the edge of the site facing onto the surrounding streets. There are many forms of urban block, some with tiers of secondary and tertiary accommodation in the heart of the block and others with levels of public circulation through the block. However the principle remains the same, the separation of the public front of buildings facing the street

from the private rear facing into the block.

The urban perimeter block may conjure up an image of a continuous terrace of buildings such as blocks 3 and 4 on the left hand plan opposite. The principle however is more fundamental than this and is appropriate to many forms of development including suburbs (Block 6). Indeed if you look at early suburban layouts such as Welwyn Garden City, not to mention interwar suburbs, both council and private, they are largely based on the perimeter block principle. The housing faces outwards onto the streets while cul-de-sacs are used only sparingly to open up large sites. In the context of existing urban development this can seem so obvious that it is hardly worth explaining. Yet it is entirely at odds with much recent practice, as illustrated again on the right hand plan opposite. This shows how development has been laid out for recent housing, commercial and industrial development. A distributor road is kept free of frontage development and feeder roads open up each development site. These single access points then branch out into a series of cul-de-sacs serving small clusters of housing or individual buildings. As a result many of the houses back onto the main road which would normally be regarded as a high street in a traditional hierarchy. This type of suburban development is the inevitable result of development undertaken without framework that creates a street network of the area. As individual developers buy sites they have neither the incentive nor the means to do other than to build a road to service their site. In existing urban areas a street network may have survived into which development can be accommodated. However even here and on larger brown field sites suburban forms have often been transplanted to urban areas. While the initial impetus for this type of built form probably stems from highways guidance and the desire to keep traffic routes free of curtilage access, by the end of the 20th century it had become the accepted model for many developers. It gave the illusion of privacy and security and proved popular with house buyers and commercial developers. However the new roads within such areas play no role in a wider framework

of streets and are thus deserted for most of the time while the distributor road is forced to carry all traffic and is therefore congested and dangerous. The orientation of the houses can also make them vulnerable to burglary and means that they present a blank frontage to the main streets which in turn makes it dangerous and unattractive to pedestrians.

The left hand plan shows an alternative approach to the development of the same area. This has a similar mix of development, albeit at higher densities, and is based on the principle of perimeter blocks. It also shows how this form of development is appropriate for a variety of uses and can even accommodate semi detached housing. Research by the surveyors Savills[14] has compared the values on a series of new developments including examples of a 'conventional approach' (right plan) and new urbanist approaches (left plan) and found that in all cases the latter created more value.

The practicalities of development influence the size and shape of urban blocks. In order to maximise the development potential of land, buildings tend to back onto each other. With housing this normally means a minimum distance between the backs of the buildings of 20 metres. If the width of the buildings is added to this along with a setback from the

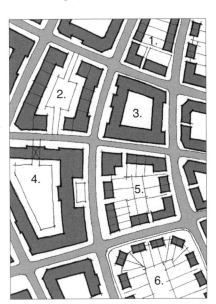

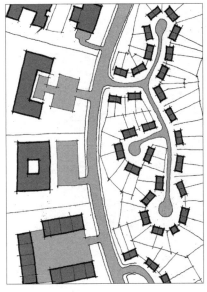

Alternative urban forms: These two plans show the same mix of uses developed in very different ways. The plan to the left shows a new urbanist approach where uses are accommodated in urban perimeter blocks. The plan to the right shows the same mix of uses being developed in isolation with access taken from a distributor road. The latter was the favoured approach of developers in much of the 20th century and was also the solution required by planning and highway authorities

street (which is not always necessary) it creates a typical block depth of 40–50 metres for housing. This dimension also holds true for dual-aspect apartments and even for offices (14–18m deep floors with a 10m arium).

There are other forms of development emerging which alter the width of urban blocks. One of the most influential schemes of the 2000s has been the Borneo Sporenburg development on Amsterdam's waterfront. Based on a master plan by West 8 the development creates a series of long thin urban blocks based upon a wide range of courtyard housetypes. These terraced houses are built around an internal courtyard, often with a roof terrace and share a party wall with the property to the rear (another form of back-to-back housing). Such housing can be built into plots as little as 25m

The Perimeter Block:
An illustration from the Urban Villages Forum

Amsterdam:
Courtyard Houses in Borneo Sporenburg

deep. For this reason there has been a lot of interest in their use as part of the redevelopment of terraced housing areas. By-law housing tends to be built on a 25–30m block structure so that redevelopment with perimeter blocks is not possible without grubbing up the roads, an expensive proposition.

The length of an urban block is limited by the permeability of the area and the optimum is probably somewhere in the region of 90–120 metres. Shorter than this and the development yield falls because there are too many roads. Longer and people are forced into long detours. The ideal arrangement is for the shorter edge of the block to front onto a high street. This creates regular links from the main circulation route so maximising permeability. This however runs counter to the philosophy of the highways engineer who will generally seek to limit the number of roads joining a high street to minimise traffic conflicts. Indeed engineers may insist on at least 90 metres between junctions onto a main road which can only be achieved if some of the side roads are pedestrian only.

Throughout history there have been many variations on the urban block. In medieval cities block sizes tended to be smaller. In the UK medieval towns are often based on burgage plots – long thin strips of land along the high street which would originally have accommodated a house facing the street with workshops to the rear and a small holding behind that as can be seen on the plans of Guildford.

In cities where apartments rather than houses predominate there is more flexibility in block layout. In Barcelona New Town the blocks are 115m square – big enough to accommodate the cathedral on a single block. Originally these were developed as 25m deep perimeter blocks of apartments with light wells. In the centre of the block were communal gardens (since filled with car parking), or in the poorer neighbourhoods warehousing and manufacturing uses.

In Paris the blocks tend to be 40-50m wide by 90–120m long. However they are developed much more intensely with apartments around the perimeter of the block and further apartments in the heart of the block accessed via small courtyards. Berlin is also based on courtyards although on a much larger scale. Berlin blocks are typically over 100m wide with a series of interconnected courtyards in the heart of the block that provide a tertiary circulation system, some of which even support shops and bars. In London the centres of the blocks are also used. Originally the servants quarters for the large town houses that make up much of London were located in the centre

of the block accessed by a mews court.

Elsewhere in the UK the urban block fell out of favour in the second half of the 20th century. However the typical 40–50m by 90–120m block is once more becoming common for new housing development outside city centres. Typically individual homes are used along the sides of the block in a structure that is flexible enough to accommodate a wide range of housing. The plan and illustration of the Chelmer scheme by Taylor Woodrow in Chelmsford is a good example of this new

Perimeter blocks: A housing development by North British Housing Association in Hulme showing the use of urban perimeter blocks

Medieval blocks: The plan of Guildford today (right) is still based on the long thin medieval burgage plots that can be seen on the historic plan of the city (left)

Chelmer: A modern housing development by Taylor Woodrow based on perimeter blocks (right)

Hulme: Two approaches to closing the corner of a block – Top, a block of 6 flats by Miller Homes, Bottom, a courtyard house by Places for People (below)

approach to housing design. The aesthetic is very much that of a village and the housetypes are now all part of Taylor Woodrow's standard range. It may not be to everyone's taste but it is street-based urban development and is able to integrate into surrounding development.

One of the problems with this type of development has been how to close the corners. The Chelmer scheme uses a number of special

housetypes to do this. In more urban locations the solution is often to use apartments. This has been assisted by the increase in demand for flats from smaller households. The photograph below shows one of the first instances of this by Miller Homes in Hulme, Manchester. This may not look a radical scheme but the use of the three storey block to close the corner was the crucial step in achieving an urban development.

The situation with new city centre apartment development in the UK is also changing. Most large UK cities experienced a building boom in the early 2000s based on apartment blocks. The traditional form of apartment in the UK as on the continent and indeed the US has been the 'walk-up' block. In this an entrance gives access to a staircase serving 2–4 flats on each landing. With careful design it was often possible to allow most of the flats to be dual aspect. A variation of this was the 'deck-access' apartment with a staircase giving access to a walkway serving the flats which could all be dual aspect. Both of these apartment forms can be wrapped around a perimeter block.

However in recent years the economics of apartment development has changed. Disabled access requirements have meant that flats need to be served by lifts. It has not been economic to install a lift for just a handful of apartments so that blocks have got bigger and internal corridors introduced. Higher standards of thermal efficiency have also increased the

cost of external walls. The game has therefore been to maximise the amount of saleable floor space with the minimum area of external wall and the fewest number of lifts.

The result is the 'double-loaded' apartment block – a rectangular slab with single-aspect apartments off either side of a central corridor. Because the apartments only have one aspect, they need to be well spaced to give them light and to avoid overlooking. The tendency has therefore been to plan them as east-west slab blocks 20m apart or alternatively as towers. If this is reminiscent of the council housing of the 1960s it is not surprising because it is driven by the same set of considerations. Potentially this is a very anti-urban form of development and in some modern apartment developments is creating an urban form little better than a 60s council estate.

Urban grain

It is important not to confuse the urban block with the urban building plot. This is a mistake which has been made in many recent urban developments in the UK. The early redevelopments in inner city areas found it difficult to attract developers particularly for urban mixed-use schemes which the development industry regarded as risky. This meant that only large developers were willing to take on the risk. Most of Hulme, for example, was developed by just four main developers, two housing associations, a private housebuilder and a commercial developer. As a result each developer took on very large sites. Variety was introduced by undertaking development in phases and using different architects for each phase. Yet even these phases generally included a number of urban blocks with the result that the development has a feeling of uniformity or artificially introduced variety. This is one of the reasons why these developments have failed to capture the true character of traditional urban areas.

The grain of most urban areas is much finer than this. A typical urban block in a great city like London, it is made up of a variety of buildings built at different times by different

Urban grain: The scale of building plots is much smaller in traditional urban areas like Siena to create a fine grain of development

developers with different designers. There is value in the unity of Paris or Bath but even here it is rare for an architect to have control over an entire block. It is this variety created by a fine grain of development that gives character to most traditional urban areas. However carefully an architect seeks to introduce variety into a large scheme it always looks artificial. True variety comes from the development of small plots and individual buildings by different developers.

The other aspect to urban grain is the size of urban blocks. In traditional cities blocks become smaller towards the centre. This means that streets become more frequent and permeability increases. This both accommodates and promotes a greater level of pedestrian activity and also means that the density of development and the mixture of uses increases towards the centre. However while this increase in grain through decreasing block sizes can be seen in most traditional towns it is rarely incorporated into new development.

Places not spaces

So far we have said nothing about buildings yet, unlike a road, a street without buildings cannot exist. If a street is to play the dual function of a route and a focus for the community it must be framed by buildings and enriched by their activity and life. The street network of a city along with its squares, parks and other public spaces makes up the public realm. This can be likened to a stage on which the public life of the city is acted out. Yet a stage is nothing without a back drop and in urban areas the back drop is made up of buildings. In this context the most important role of buildings is to frame and define the public realm. As Francis Tibbalds said in the first of his ten commandments for urban design, 'spaces are more important than buildings'[15]. The quality of spaces within urban areas is what determines their success yet too often this is ignored by planners, architects and engineers, concerned about buildings as objects.

In the medieval city only the cathedral would have been treated as an object to be viewed from all sides and even that would have very little space around it. Other buildings from the grandest merchant's palace to the lowliest hovel were joined to their neighbours and architectural expression was confined to the street façade. In the 20th century the modern movement has taught us to see buildings as pieces of sculpture to be viewed from above in the architect's model, or from the moving car, rather than experienced as a pedestrian. Such buildings do little to enclose and enliven the public realm and are surrounded by space designed as a setting for the building which is, as a result, formless and lacking in human scale. Think of any great city and you bring to mind a few great buildings, the cathedral, town hall, perhaps a palace or a museum. However the majority of the buildings will be nondescript, and walking around its streets you probably do not even notice the upper floors. Yet these nondescript buildings do not detract from the quality of the urban space, they enhance it. Quality buildings provide landmarks and their value is increased by scarcity. A city made up of nothing but landmarks would be too rich a meal to digest.

We have recently prepared urban design guides for the cities of Bradford[16] and Nottingham[17] in the UK in which we developed this idea. The guides include the concept of 'Star' Buildings and 'Supporting Cast' buildings. The rules in the guide relate largely to the supporting cast to ensure that they play their part in enclosing the streets and spaces of the town. The Star buildings, subject to a number of conditions and the agreement

Bradford City Centre: An image from URBED's design guide for Bradford. This establishes a set of rules for the 'supporting cast' buildings of the city centre. The transparent buildings in the image show the effects that these rules could have on repairing the urban fabric of the centre

Goose Gate in Nottingham: A typical winding medieval street looking towards the marketplace

of the planning authority, are free from all of the rules. The idea is that in certain limited circumstances freedom from the rules is needed to create something really special.

It is however probably more important to concentrate on the ordinary rather than the extraordinary when considering urban buildings. It is also important to focus on the space that buildings create as much as their design. Much of the official literature on urban design in the UK has focused on 'quality' design rather than 'urban' design. This was done originally to build consensus. Who, after all, was going to object to the notion of 'quality' at a time when many people had issues with the term 'urban'? However the two terms are not interchangeable. It is possible to have 'quality' suburban and rural development just as it is only too easy to have poor quality urban development. We should certainly be promoting quality, however we should also be ensuring that development

follows the good manners which should shape all urban buildings. These are ground rules which determine the position, height and form of buildings and if they are followed then even a poor building will not detract from the quality of the public realm. These rules are outlined on the following pages.

The building line: The first rule of urban etiquette is that buildings should follow a building line. This is the line created by the main front face of the building, ignoring projections and setbacks as illustrated in the plan below. There has been a tendency in modern urban design to introduce variety in the position of buildings by staggering buildings. However in most urban areas the building line is continuous even if it is not always straight. The distance between the building lines defines the width of the street far more than the carriageway or pavements. It therefore determines the scale, proportion and

213

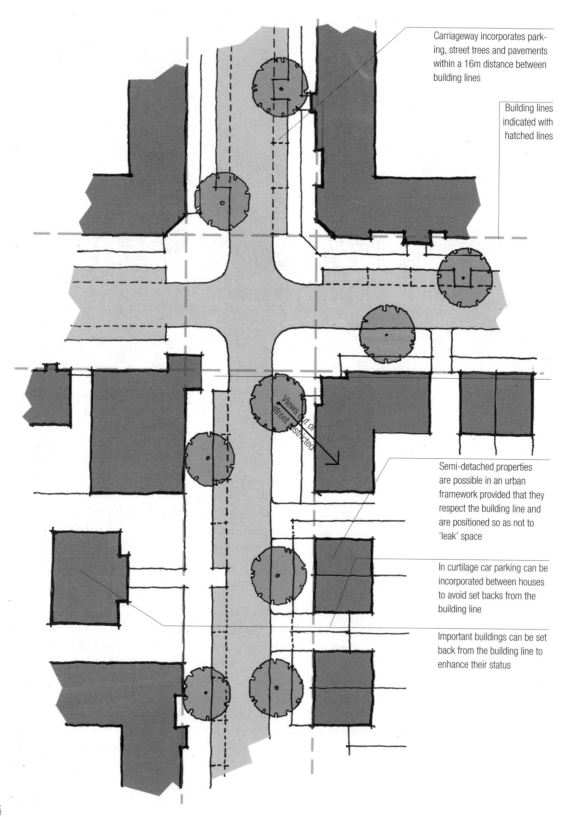

Carriageway incorporates parking, street trees and pavements within a 16m distance between building lines

Building lines indicated with hatched lines

Views out of street restricted

Semi-detached properties are possible in an urban framework provided that they respect the building line and are positioned so as not to 'leak' space

In curtilage car parking can be incorporated between houses to avoid set backs from the building line

Important buildings can be set back from the building line to enhance their status

character of the street, characteristics which will soon be lost if the building line is broken or ignored. On most urban streets the building line is already well defined by existing buildings and planning authorities are usually careful to ensure that new development does not project forward of this line so as to interrupt views along the street. However the tendency with many modern development forms is to set buildings back from the building line to create space for car parking. This can be seen in housing developments where planners or developers insist on a driveway to park the car off the street. It is also the case with retail developers who like car parking to be visible to passing motorists. While it is possible for buildings to be set back from the building line, as was often the case with churches, if this is done too often the integrity of the street as a space can be undermined.

Enclosure: If a street is to work as a place it must be enclosed by its buildings. In simple terms this means that as you walk down a street or through a square you should not be able to see out other than into other defined spaces. Good urban space, like water, needs to be contained and if you leave a hole it soon drains away. In most urban areas this is achieved by using terraced building forms. Indeed in Dutch new towns one of the few ordinances regulating development is that all buildings should have party walls with those on either side. It is however also possible to contain urban space with detached and semi-detached buildings provided that the gaps between buildings are small and do not leak space when you look along the street (see the plan on the previous page).

The junction between the building and the street: In suburban layouts buildings stand within a landscape but in urban areas it is important to consider the way in which they address the street. Because of the proximity of urban buildings to the public life of the street there is a need to create a transitional zone, however small, to protect the interior life of the building. In Victorian terraces this was often little more than a doorstep and recessed doorway. With larger buildings like the American brownstone tenement or the Georgian terrace, the main entrance is accessed via a flight of steps thus creating a type of moat and drawbridge. The footpath is framed by railings behind which

Addressing the street:
A cross section of Roslyn Place in Pittsburgh (above), the street described by Allen Jacobs (see Chapter 7). This shows an enclosure ratio of 1:2.5 and also the transition between the private life of the home and the public life of the street
New urban housing in London (above right) which employs the traditional technique of steps up to the ground floor and a half basement. This however creates problems with disabled access. An alternative is to use small front gardens and street trees (bottom right).

1:0.33 – The medieval street or downtown Manhattan. The buildings are three times higher than the street is wide. In this case five-storey buildings on a street which is 5m wide.

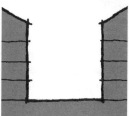

1:1 – The ratio of many Victorian commercial streets. In this case four-storey buildings on a street which is 10m wide

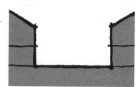

1:2 – An urban residential street such as many of the terraced housing areas in Britain. With modern two-storey buildings this implies a street width of 10m which is too narrow in many cases to meet highway requirements

1:3 – This is probably the maximum ratio possible while maintaining the character of an urban street. With modern storey heights it implies a street width of 15m for two-storey property, however the street could be wider if the height of buildings was increased

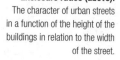

Enclosure ratios (above): The character of urban streets in a function of the height of the buildings in relation to the width of the street.

Brighton: The Lanes in the medieval heart of Brighton illustrates just how tight street enclosure ratios can be

is a light well opening up a half-basement. In the early suburbs in Britain and in the suburbs of continental cities the relationship is even more complex with an avenue of street trees, a wide pavement and a significant boundary wall. However the character of an urban street is retained. While the houses are set back they follow a common building line and are of sufficient scale to relate to the street.

Scale and proportion: If buildings are to define the public realm they must be large enough to enclose the space. This is defined by the enclosure ratio of a street which measures the height of buildings against the width of the street (between the building lines). In a street with an enclosure ratio of 1:1 the buildings on either side are as high as the street is wide. In many medieval cities and the urban canyons of New York, or indeed Victorian Manchester, the enclosure ratios are far greater than 1:1 as indeed should generally be the case in central commercial and retail areas. However in residential areas it is often neither possible nor desirable to achieve such a high level of enclosure. In these areas enclosure ratios can drop to 1:3 on streets and as much as 1:10 around parks and along boulevards. Enclosure ratios apply to all levels of the street hierarchy. A high street will be much wider than a residential street but its buildings should be correspondingly higher. A residential street which is 12 metres wide can adequately be enclosed by two-storey buildings whereas a high street, 25 metres across, will require buildings of at least five storeys.

There are two main problems today in achieving urban enclosure ratios. The first is the fact that modern buildings are much lower than those in the past, something which is obvious if you look at a modern house standing next to a Victorian property. Modern residential storey heights and level ground floor access mean that a two-storey property is little more than five metres high to the eves. A Victorian property in contrast will often have a half basement and storey heights in excess of three metres so that a two-storey house is as high as a modern three-storey building. This means that a modern street needs to be 15 metres wide to achieve a 1:3 enclosure ratio whereas a Victorian street could be 22 metres wide and achieve the same level of enclosure. This leads to the second problem since the demands placed upon the street by the transport engineer have increased since Victorian times so that modern carriageway widths, footpaths and parking do not easily fit within a 15 metre street. Nor indeed does the planning requirement for privacy distances of up to 22 metres between facing properties. The tightness of the engineering of such streets is illustrated on the table on the previous page which is taken from the *Hulme Guide to Development* in Manchester[12]. Here the residential street width is set at 15.5 metres and the suggested eaves height is increased to 5.8 metres to achieve a 1:2.5 enclosure ratio. The latter is achieved by raising the ground floors of properties slightly above ground level (providing ramps for disabled access) and also hiding the roof behind a parapet to increase the apparent height. However even this leaves little scope for on-street parking. In reality what happens is that a strip is created between the footpath and the road which accommodates street trees, visibility splays at junctions and parked cars, although if junctions are frequent parking can easily be squeezed out.

Active frontages: The final ground rule for urban buildings is that they should interact with the street rather than turn their back onto it. This is naturally achieved with mixed-use development where the ground floors are used for retail and commercial development. The frontage of the building is made up of shop fronts interspersed with doors giving access to housing or offices on the upper floors. This is the predominant building type in most continental cities but, other than in Scotland and central London, has been less common in the UK where residential areas cannot generate the demand to sustain ground floor retail uses. There is however much that can be done with single-use buildings to ensure that they

contribute to the life of the street. They should firstly face onto the street and take their main access from it, rather than from a car park to the rear. They should have windows which provide 'eyes onto the street' and along the street there should be entrances at regular intervals. Most important of all, they should not create dead frontages as so often happens with modern retailing and industrial development which minimise the number of windows to maximise usable floor area.

These ground rules create an envelope for buildings in urban areas. They define the position of the front wall, the orientation of the main entrance, the height of the building and its relationship to adjacent buildings. These parameters are set by the context that is the existing buildings surrounding a site and by the position of the street within the urban hierarchy.

The ground rules: The technical guidance from the Hulme Guide to Development which sets down some basic rules for street widths and enclosure

	High Streets	Secondary Streets	Residential Streets
Recommended distance between building lines	21m(max)	17.5m(max)	15.5m(max)
Recommended building height to eaves	9m	7.6m	5.8m
Number of storeys on footprints over 100m²	4–6	3–5	2–3
Carriageway width	10m max	7m	6m
Minimum footway width	2.5m	1.8m	1.8m
Cycle lane where appropriate	2m	2m	Within carriageway
Additional margin for street trees	1.2m	1.2m	1.2m
Design speed limit	30mph	30mph	<20mph
Kerb radii	10m	6m	3m
Visibility splays	2.4x70m	2x60m	2x33m
Minimum distance between junctions	60m (same side) 30m (opp. side)	60m 30m	30m 15m
% of frontage complying with enclosure ratio	90%	80%	60%

Source: Guide to development, Hulme – Manchester City Council

Stroget in Copenhagen:
Now considered to be one of the world's great streets, Stroget was once a major traffic route. It is difficult to imagine today but in the 1960s much of Copenhagen was clogged with cars. Stroget was the worlds first pedestrianised street and the predestrian zone has since been extended to cover much of the city core. Longitudinal work by Jan Ghel has documented how pedestrian activity has revived as the cars have disappeared.

They are also now set out in a wide range of design guidance, an early example of which was the *Manchester Guide to Development*[18] and the UK government published *By-Design*[19], both of which establish a simple set of rules for urban development. There are still those – usually architects – who believe that these guides trespass onto territory which should rightfully be left to them. Yet these rules are not really optional. They were once implicitly understood by all designers and developers but were forgotten or ignored for much of the 20th century. Far from constraining the designer, these ground rules should be seen as a liberation. If the rules are followed then there is less need to control the design of the building and to meddle in the detail as has become the habit of the development control planner.

These rules are well illustrated by the illustration of Stroget in Copenhagen on the previous page, one of the finest medieval streets in the world. While the buildings that make up the street are not of great architectural merit they create a public space of the highest quality by following a defined building line, creating a well proportioned space, curving gently so that new vistas are constantly opened up and

enlivening the street with active frontages. We find such great streets so difficult to recreate today because we have lost an understanding of the etiquette or good manners which should guide their development.

The identity of urban areas

Whilst it is vital for buildings to follow these rules of urban etiquette, a city or neighbourhood is more than the sum of its parts. It also has an overall unity and identity which results from the layout of its streets and the cumulative impact of its buildings. To understand this we must discuss well-established urban design concepts such as landmarks, vistas and focal points. These are the elements that allow you to locate

The use of landmarks:

Above: Blackburn where a modest commercial building creates a landmark terminating the vista of the street

Below: Corn Street which runs through the medieval heart of Bristol and is terminated by landmark towers at either end

220

yourself within an urban area, provide points of orientation, and linger in the memory when you leave. They can be found in both planned and unplanned cities suggesting that they need not be imposed by the city planner but are part of the natural organisation of urban areas.

Focal points in urban areas are established by the urban hierarchy. The main focal points are the town or city centre and sub-centres and these are generally marked with public squares and landmarks. This can be seen most clearly in the medieval city with its market square in front of a cathedral which dominates the town's skyline. On a smaller scale centres can be marked with sculptures or fountains. In the medieval city the streets leading to the centre were generally curved so that there were few views into the main square increasing the sense of arrival on entering the space. However in planned cities it is common for vistas to be created which terminate in a landmark. Perhaps the grandest example of this is the Champs Élysées which provides visual links through the heart of Paris to the landmarks of the Place de la Concorde, the Arc de Triomphe, and more recently the grand Arche de la Defense.

UK city planners rarely have the powers to make such grand gestures. It is however extraordinary how often the vista down an urban street is terminated by a landmark, be it a church spire or a tower. A fine example is Corn Street in Bristol (left) which has a tower at either end to terminate vistas along the street. This happens far too often for it to be pure chance even in cities which have not been planned. This suggests that the creation of landmarks and vistas is part of the urban etiquette that we have already discussed. When landmark buildings are planned they are placed so that they can be seen from a distance along a vista and are often associated with a public space. Alternatively when planning the development of an urban block certain points can be emphasised such as the corners and points which terminate the vista of adjacent streets as in the illustration of Blackburn (above left). This was well understood in the development

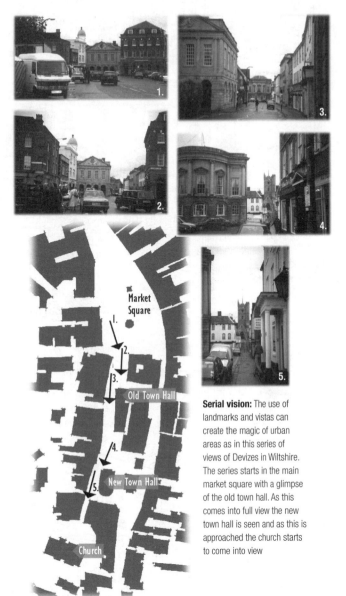

Serial vision: The use of landmarks and vistas can create the magic of urban areas as in this series of views of Devizes in Wiltshire. The series starts in the main market square with a glimpse of the old town hall. As this comes into full view the new town hall is seen and as this is approached the church starts to come into view

of the Crown Street neighbourhood of Glasgow where detailed briefs[20] were drawn up for each development site showing the position of buildings and the points to be emphasised with landmark features.

The importance of landmarks and vistas has also been used in the regeneration of Barcelona. Here a policy which roughly translates as 'point and line'[21] was used to regenerate large areas around the edge of the city. The process started with the identification

221

of a series of focal points, marked with public sculptures and landmarks that has led to the improvement of 150 small public spaces. The streets (or lines) between these points were then improved creating a network of visible improvements which permeated into the surrounding areas.

There are two further aspects to urban areas that we should discuss in this chapter, both of which are central to the concept of the walkable city, namely density and a mix of uses.

A critical mass of activity

As we discussed in the first part of this book, density has been a bugbear of planners and other urban professionals. Density has been associated with all manner of urban evils and used to justify clearance and redevelopment. The same is true today as witnessed by the fear that the development of more housing within urban areas will lead to 'town cramming'. This is an emotive phrase but we are yet to see a satisfactory definition of what it means. If town cramming means congested streets then most of our towns and cities are already crammed. If it means overcrowding the solution is to build more not less housing. If it means a loss of privacy and overshadowing then the answer lies in better design. As we suggested in Chapter 9, town cramming will only occur if we seek to introduce more housing into cities without rethinking the design of urban areas, if we do nothing but pack the suburban semi more tightly or put more traffic onto streets without promoting a shift to walking and public transport.

The urban framework described so far in this chapter need not mean higher density development. If urban blocks are large, streets widely spaced and the predominant building form detached and semi-detached then urban development can take place at relatively low densities. Indeed the early garden city developments like Hampstead Garden Suburb share many of the urban characteristics described so far in this chapter. However urban

areas have the potential for much greater densities as illustrated by the density gradient on page 161. Whereas suburban areas start to squeak if net densities rise much above 37 units to the hectare (fifteen to the acre), with urban layouts much higher densities are possible without undermining the quality of life. Jane Jacobs[22] refers to ideal urban densities of almost a thousand persons per hectare (more than 400 people to the acre) and that in areas which also contained a range of other uses. In Kowloon densities rise as high as 1250 dwellings to the hectare and yet still the city functions. It is therefore clear that the design and layout of urban areas will determine their ability to accommodate a higher density of population. As we suggested in Chapter 9, architects since the 1960s have known that three and four-storey perimeter blocks around squares and open spaces are the optimum form to maximise density while protecting the amenity of residents. This is very similar to the terraced perimeter block with a mix of housing and flats on the corners that we have described in this chapter. This may not achieve Jane Jacobs' benchmarks for ideal urban densities but it should comfortably achieve densities of 60–120 dwellings to the hectare (25–50 to the acre).

Density is not a necessary evil that we must tolerate in urban areas. Density is essential to the social and economic life of cities. If urban areas are not built to high densities they will not sustain a range of economic activity and shops, their streets will not be nourished by activity and public transport will not be sufficiently viable to provide an alternative to the car. In the low-density neighbourhood the streets will be congested with cars whilst the pavements are deserted, whereas in the high-density neighbourhood the streets may be equally congested (but no more so because of the limits set by highway capacity) and the pavements will bustle with life.

The importance of density can be illustrated by reference to public transport. Net densities of 100 persons per hectare are required to sustain a good bus service[23]. This

Density but not cramming: Attractive neighbourhoods such as Edinburgh New Town illustrate that high-density areas can be attractive and need not feel crammed

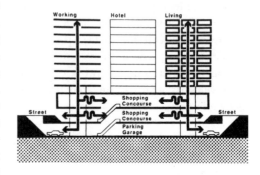

corresponds to 25 dwellings to the hectare is we assume an average dwelling size of four bed spaces. However if we use instead the current average household size in the UK we would need 40–50 dwellings per hectare to sustain a bus service. This is above what can be achieved with suburban development but would be quite comfortable with the urban development forms described in this chapter.

It should also be remembered that the figures that we quote here are net densities and relate only to the site where the housing has been built. The density across the whole neighbourhood is referred to as the gross density and can be substantially lower than the net densities if the neighbourhood includes large areas of open space or existing low-density development. It may therefore be that to achieve gross densities capable of sustaining and animating an area net densities will have to be further increased to compensate for existing low densities elsewhere.

Within urban areas densities are not even. Densities traditionally increase towards the town or city centre and around local centres. This is a natural result of the street hierarchy which dictates that buildings should be taller on high streets and secondary streets. This increased density ensures that the centres remain

The mega-structure approach: A diagram from a handbook on mixed-use development published in the late 1970s

lively and also sustains the public transport which runs along these arteries.

A rich mix of uses

Our discussion of density has so far been confined to housing development. However an important characteristic of successful urban development is that it contains more than housing. If people are to walk to work, to school and to the shops, these uses must also be located within the neighbourhood, which leads us to the concept of mixed-use development.

Mixed-use development has become a much used concept in recent years partly because it has been so loosely defined. The huge city centre retail developments in Britain and America in the 1970s were called mixed-use schemes as indeed they were since they contained a mix of retailing, offices and often hotel and residential accommodation. In the 1980s schemes like Canary Wharf and Chiswick Park were referred to as mixed-use since they incorporated some other uses alongside the predominant office use. But is this really what we mean by mixed-use development? As Alan Rowley has pointed out[24] 'the term mixed-use development is in danger of degenerating into a slogan for a product that is a pale imitation of traditional mixed-use areas'. These schemes owe little to the European tradition of small-scale development with active ground floor uses and housing on the upper floors which is what many people bring to mind when thinking about mixed-use development.

These very different concepts of mixed-use development highlight the different

TESCO/PEABODY – HAMMERSMITH

Large shops are a fact of life and they can be difficult to accommodate in urban areas. The Crown Street redevelopment team in Glasgow in the 1990s planned to develop a back of pavement supermarket with parking on the roof but experienced resistance from operators. Another option was to wrap housing and other uses around a supermarket or to build on the roof. This was first done by Peabody in association with a Tesco supermarket in Hammersmith. Tesco have since been looking at the airspace above their London stores as residential development opportunities

roles that it can play. If our sole concern is the accommodation of different uses in proximity to each other to create activity throughout the day and to promote walking rather than car use, then the form of development matters little. Andy Coupland[25] suggests that most of these benefits can be achieved by mixing uses horizontally within streets, blocks or neighbourhoods. However if our concern is to create a building type which is appropriate for the urban streets that we have described in this chapter then we need to take the concept a stage further by mixing uses vertically within buildings. This is what traditional developers have found so difficult. Indeed when we were preparing the first edition of this book the Deptford High Street scheme in London and the Gloucester Green scheme in Oxford (described below) were two rare and celebrated examples of a form of development which was bread and butter to continental developers and has since become much more common in the UK. For much of the 20th century the property industry was allergic to mixed-use development for many of the reasons that we described in Part 1 of this book. The English in the 20th century shunned the flats and apartments which are an inevitable result of mixed-use development. The planning system also sought to separate uses to avoid conflicts and therefore has tended to deter mixed-use development. Developers have also tended to specialise so that different firms would build shops, offices and housing and were reluctant to dabble in uses they did not fully understand. This was reinforced by the different way in which residential and commercial property markets operated. Homes were either built for sale or rental with secure tenancies which means that the developer and investor lost control of the completed development. Commercial development, by contrast, takes place on the basis of twenty year leases often with the intention that

---

DEPTFORD HIGH STREET

Deptford High Street in East London is a busy market street. However like many streets of its kind in the 1990s, it was declining, many of its buildings were dilapidated and the upper floors were largely vacant. In the late 1990s a small developer, First Premise, undertook a series of four innovative mixed-use developments which be-

came a model that inspired many other developers.

- 164–168 Deptford High Street: seven workshops and a studio on the ground floor totalling 3829 sqft with fifteen one and two-bedroom flats on the upper floors.

- 133 Deptford High Street: Six flats above a pair of shops, a large stu-

dio/workspace and a church hall.

- 210–212 Deptford High Street: two shops with five one and two-bedroom flats on the upper floors.

- 46–50 Deptford High Street, a corner site which First Premise developed for another owner. This included two blocks of flats around a small paved court at first floor level with two shops and a row of garages on the ground floor.

In total the four sites provide 50 flats along with just over 10 000 square feet of workspace and shops. The flats were all for private leasing and were funded with a combination of City Grant and private finance from the Unity Trust Bank. The residential and commercial property was successfully let and the schemes encouraged other development on the High Street.

In many respects, the most remarkable aspect of these schemes is the amount of attention that they received. This is the sort of development that has become common but was so rare in the 1990s that these schemes were used as an exemplar of mixed-use development for years after they were completed.

the building will be redeveloped or refurbished after that time. If this commercial space is beneath residential accommodation the options for the developers and investors are limited, making the development less attractive as an institutional investment. This is compounded by concerns about security, particularly from the tenants of social housing, and very practical issues such as what happens when someone lets their bath overflow and floods the commercial property below. The last point was such a concern to Tescos in the example on the previous page that they insisted on a pitched roof being built between the supermarket and the concrete platform on which the housing has been built.

All of these problems can be overcome as illustrated by a new breed of mixed use developers who have emerged in the 2000s. Even specialist housebuilders have overcome their reticence often by setting up joint ventures with commercial developers such as Isian (Amec and Crosby Homes) and BASE (Barratts and Artisan). Experience since the first edition of this book suggests that the problems of mixed-use buildings can be overcome. Indeed it is sometimes hard to see what all the fuss was about.

We have in this chapter described the importance of a framework of streets in giving structure to urban areas. We have discussed how this framework is ordered by a hierarchy of streets, how it defines urban blocks and how the buildings on these blocks are subject to an urban etiquette which ensures that they contribute to the public realm. We have explored how unity and a sense of place can be created on these urban streets and how a critical mass of development can be accommodated with a mix of uses to sustain the social and economic life of the city. In doing so we have described the characteristics of urban as opposed to suburban design. This is both a description of how cities were built in the past and a prescription for how they must be built in the future. As environmental pressures and social and demographic change herald a rediscovery of the importance of urban living these techniques of city building are being rediscovered. But urban development will not, on its own, make a district into a neighbourhood. We therefore turn in the next chapter to the social context of the urban neighbourhood.

Wind Street in Swansea: A medieval street with many of the qualities of the Stroget in Copenhagen but for years dominated by cars and blighted by a number of important gap sites. The street today is unrecognisable, traffic has been reduced, gap sites filled and the street now throngs with bars and restaurants

Chapter 12
The sociable neighbourhood

Environmental sustainability goes hand in hand with social sustainability. Towns and cities are first and foremost places where people live and work, not just as individuals but as communities. If urban areas do not provide civilised places for people to live and for communities to prosper then it will not matter how 'green' they are, they will not be sustainable. We must therefore widen our definition of the sustainable urban neighbourhood to include social as well as environmental concerns. We need to draw upon the concept of neighbourliness or being a good neighbour which is potentially far stronger than the more widely used term community.

It was Ruskin who said 'when we build let us think that we build forever'. This, on the whole, is what we have striven to do in the UK. The Japanese may treat buildings like automobiles, to be discarded when tastes change, but in Britain our intention at least has been to build to last. Yet we have failed lamentably in this task over the last half century. Many neighbourhoods built since the war have failed the most fundamental test of sustainability and have been demolished only a few decades after they were built. Their only legacy is the debt charges which will continue to burden the local tax payer for years to come. To this economic cost must be added the environmental cost of resources squandered and the social costs of communities uprooted and destroyed and people consigned to life on estates which rob them of their health and dignity.

It is the nightmare of any urban planner and architect – that they are unwillingly repeating the mistakes of their predecessors. However persuasive the arguments may seem for one new model of development or another (like the sustainable urban neighbourhood) we can be sure that they are no more persuasive than were the argument for the deck-access estate or the tower block. Yet there are neighbourhoods that have endured and it is from these that we must learn when planning new neighbourhoods.

In the 1990s the problem of failing estates seemed to be history, albeit very recent and rather uncomfortable history. At the time the high-rise council estates of the 1960s and 70s were problems to be sorted out but most people were comforted by the fact that at least they would never be built again. They were an aberration and never again would we play fast and loose with architectural innovation and allow planning dogma to ruin the lives of vulnerable people. Our lesson had been learnt and we would, in the future, build traditional buildings with traditional bricks. It may not be exciting but at least it would last. Innovation had become a dirty word and British housebuilding retreated into an arcadia of leafy suburbs and semi-detached housing. Everything else that we had tried in the century had failed. Better to stick to the housing forms that we are good at – Britain's only successful housing model, the suburban estate.

It was therefore all the more disturbing when in the mid 1990s new estates built to suburban designs started to fail as disastrously as their modernist forbears. As we described in Chapter 4, David Page wrote in 1993 'There is now evidence that the process of rapid decline of large social housing estates, which some had thought peculiar to council housing, can also apply to the stock of housing associations'[1]. These housing associations had not been building architectural flights of fancy, they have been building traditional suburban estates. They were indeed often located in the suburbs and had built in partnership with private housebuilders using their standard house types. Identical estates were doing a perfectly good job serving the needs of first-time buyers, but in the social housing sector decline was sometimes swift and merciless. As Page pointed out, whereas deck-access council estates had taken more than twenty years to decline, some housing association estates built in the 1980s and 1990s have fallen apart in as little as four years.

It was therefore an illusion to believe that the key to social and economic sustainability

lay in bricks and mortar as opposed to concrete and steel. In our haste to condemn the despised housing of the 1960s we had overlooked some fundamental questions about what makes an area socially sustainable.

The challenge of creating sustainable communities

The challenge of social sustainability is to build neighbourhoods which last not for twenty or even two hundred years but which are immortal. This, after all, is what sustainability means – somewhere that can be sustained. This is not to say that the buildings of the neighbourhood will last forever. It does however mean that change will take place naturally and gradually over time without the need for radical redevelopment. There are neighbourhoods in ancient cities like Naples that have lasted for more than two thousand years. Their function may have changed many times and their buildings will have been demolished and rebuilt time and time again but the neighbourhood has endured. In this respect successful neighbourhoods are like great forests which outlive even their most ancient trees. Like

The immortal neighbourhood: Ancient towns like Cirencester have existed since before Roman times. While there are few Roman buildings left in the town, its street patterns and neighbourhoods are the result of an unbroken chain of evolution and change since that time

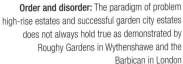

Order and disorder: The paradigm of problem high-rise estates and successful garden city estates does not always hold true as demonstrated by Roughy Gardens in Wythenshawe and the Barbican in London

great forests, they develop naturally rather than being artificially planted, they are constantly renewed by new growth and they contain a rich variety of species. The buildings of a sustainable neighbourhood, like the trees of a forest, are not all of the same type or age. They will not all reach the end of their natural life at the same time or be decimated by some external change – be it Dutch elm disease in the case of the forest or the obsolescence of a particular industry in the case of the neighbourhood. These are some of the issues that we explore later in this chapter.

But social and economic sustainability is about more than mere survival. We should be aiming higher than this. We should be creating neighbourhoods which enhance the quality of social and economic life of their citizens, which are a joy to live in, to work in or to visit. This, at its root, is the key to a sustainable neighbourhood. Places that are popular will attract people and investment and will be constantly renewed. Unpopular neighbourhoods, by contrast, will be places from which people seek to escape, where people live and work out of necessity rather than choice and where what is now called 'social exclusion' takes root. However to advocate popular neighbourhoods is one thing, to build them is

quite another. Overcoming social exclusion is now seen by government as a key priority yet there is still considerable confusion about the best way to tackle it.

In the first edition of this book we made the statement that the social sustainability of neighbourhoods at its most basic – the survival of the neighbourhood – was something which largely related to social housing. At the time there had been a few private housing estates that had failed but they were rare. This was before the widespread abandonment of private Victorian terraced housing neighbourhoods in Northern England became such an issue in the early 2000s – we will come back to this in a moment. At the time we were working on the first edition of this book it seemed that owner-occupation served to inoculate neighbourhoods from drastic decline by giving people a vested interest or stake in the success of their neighbourhood – if it declined so did the value of their home. At the time the Joseph Rowntree Foundation held a conference to discuss failing council estates at the Barbican Centre in London[2]. The irony was not lost on delegates that the concrete towers surrounding the conference hall bore a striking resemblance to the council estates that they were discussing.

Yet the Barbican has not failed, it is one of the most desirable addresses in the City of London and the flats in its concrete towers change hands for hundreds of thousands of pounds.

In social housing areas by contrast decline could be rapid and unforgiving. Some years ago we undertook work in an area of Wythenshawe on the southern edge of Manchester[3]. As described in Chapter 2, Wythenshawe was developed in the 1930s and designed by the garden city architect Barry Parker. It housed families decanted from slum clearance areas in the city and has over the years nurtured many strong communities. We however were asked to look at a close of fifty council houses which had been destroyed in less than six months. The problem had started when a small number of vacancies started to appear. These had been passed by the council to a housing association for refurbishment as short life property. There were delays in the work taking place, by which time other voids had appeared which were also passed to the housing association. All of the properties on the close except for two were subsequently vandalised and gutted by fire, including those refurbished by the association so that within a few months the area resembled a war zone.

It transpired that the problems stemmed from two warring 'problem' families one of which lived in a council house and the other, which had been allocated to one of the refurbished properties. These families had systematically intimidated all of the other tenants out of the area and their children had dismantled and burned all of the houses. This may be an extreme example but it is not unique and cannot be put down to design since the close had survived more than sixty years without problems.

At about the time this book was first published something similar started to happen in the private Victorian terraces of East Manchester and the West End of Newcastle that had been though to be insulated from decline. This process was described by Anne Power and Katharine Mumford in their 1999 report[4], the *The Slow Death of Great Cities?* The process started with the councils responding to the sort of problems

that we found in Wythenshawe by cracking down on problem tenants many of whom lost their tenancies. However the Council remained responsible for finding housing for these people and many ended up in the private rented sector with their rent paid by Housing Benefit. A breed of unscrupulous landlords emerged who practised a form of slash and burn letting. They would put one of these families into a terraced street. All the management skills of the council had failed to control these families so that it was hardly surprising that, left to their own devices, they caused havoc in the tight-packed streets of these Victorian neighbourhoods. Housing prices tumbled and the landlords were able to pick up more property at knock-down prices. More families would be moved in and those who had ruined their first house were moved on. In Beswick in East Manchester this process caused houseprices to collapse from around £30 000 to just over £1 000 in just six months. In desperation residents abandoned their homes or sold them to landlords for a fraction of what they still owed on their mortgage. Within a year the neighbourhood had been demolished.

Similar problems of abandonment started to appear across northern England in 2000. A study by the Centre for Urban and Regional Studies at Birmingham University highlighted failing housing markets across northern England and as far south as Stoke and Birmingham[5]. This study led to the launch of the UK government's Housing Market Renewal Programme in 2002 which allocated £500 million to nine 'Pathfinder' areas and charged then with finding solutions to failing housing markets.

The process of collapse in these neighbourhoods, once triggered, was similar to that described in Benchill and Beswick. Once an area reached a tipping point decline accelerated and more often or not the result was abandonment and demolition. Fortunately not all areas with weak housing markets suffered such catastrophic collapse. However the work done by Brendon Nevin[6] and others on the reasons for decline show that they were not so different from the

Abandonment:
A street of fine houses in Anfield, Liverpool that had been almost entirely abandoned, except for the poor person trying to sell their home. This street has since been saved, and has been refurbished for first-time buyers

problems that had affected council estates. In some places neighbourhoods simply emptied out. As traditional industries closed in the towns of East Lancashire, the mining towns of Yorkshire and the Potteries in Stoke on Trent, the towns depopulated and the least popular neighbourhoods bore the brunt. In other areas like Oldham and Rochdale the housing simply deteriorated for lack of maintenance while remaining fully occupied, normally with ethnic minority communities.

However some of the most dramatic market collapse took place in places like Newcastle and Manchester, cities that were thriving at the time. The reason for this was a trend that we described in the first part of this book. People had been trapped in certain neighbourhoods for years and when, at last, the improving economy gave them the chance to find work, they used their new-found economic freedom to move to a new neighbourhood. Economic boom can therefore lead to market failure especially when a housing boom is flooding the market with affordable new housing.

Such problems of social sustainability go to the heart of the sustainable urban neighbourhood. Why is it that the concrete towers of the Barbican prosper while good quality social housing fails? Why is it that terraced streets in East Manchester are abandoned while houses in similar streets in South Manchester sell for a quarter of a million pounds? The breakdown of social structure in small areas, like the parts of Wythenshawe and East Manchester described above, are extreme examples of the problems facing all neighbourhoods that find themselves at the bottom of the hierarchy of desirability.

In the 1980s the Conservative government believed that the answer to these problems lay in home ownership. The 1980s saw a huge increase in the level of owner-occupation which was extended to households which, never before, had been given the opportunity to own their own home. Right-to-buy policies in particular transformed many council estates as council tenants bought their homes and ploughed money into home improvements.

Putting aside for a moment the political

issues about right-to-buy and the concerns about negative equity and repossession, it is clear that in many areas this policy has been successful. There is little doubt that the 'magic' of home ownership has contributed greatly to the sustainability of many council estates such as Kirkby in Liverpool. There are however some signs of emerging problems as the first generation right-to-buyers move on or die and property passes into private renting[7]. The programme, by denuding the stock of social housing of many of its best properties, has also focused the problems of social sustainability more sharply on the remnants of the sector as well as the most vulnerable sections of the private sector. As the amount of social housing declined in the 1990s it was rationed to those in greatest need. We warned of the danger that this could mean that social housing became welfare housing and a council or housing association tenancy a badge of disadvantage. On the whole this has been avoided as the management of social housing has improved. However this has only served to focus problems further on the private rented sector.

We did not always have such problems with social housing. When Peabody and Guinness started building social housing in the middle of the last century and when council house building started in earnest in the 1920s the housing was let to the 'upper' sections of the working class[8]. The theory was that these new tenants would be responsible, could pay the higher rents and would release their previous private rented homes so that poorer people could also improve their housing conditions creating a 'ladder of opportunity'. Today we shy away from such notions of 'deserving' and 'undeserving' poor but politically-correct policies that lead to social breakdown benefit no one. At the end of the 1920s a council or housing association home was a matter for pride whereas today anything other than owner occupation is considered a mark of failure. This is no basis on which to build a sustainable community. It has been suggested by a number of studies for the Joseph Rowntree Foundation[9] that new social housing should not be let to the most needy but rather to established tenants wishing to move and

with the capacity to establish a new community. These tenants would then vacate property within established communities which would be let to those in greatest housing need. Even with recent improvements to social housing we are a long way from accepting this idea.

A good deal of progress has been made in overcoming the stigma of some inner city areas and social housing estates. As we have seen, private developers have been attracted into inner city areas and former council estates and they have succeeded in selling their homes to people attracted back to the city and others who would otherwise have left. However we are still a long way from building socially sustainable neighbourhoods. If we are to consolidate these recent gains we must learn to build communities rather than just housing which means following some simple principles:

Continuity

One of the most important factors in the creation of sustainable communities is time. Just as a derelict site, left for long enough, will become a haven for wildlife so people left to their own devices in urban areas, barring disasters, will create communities. It sometimes seems that the recipe for a sustainable neighbourhood is to build whatever you want and leave to stand for a hundred years. Yet to build an instant community from scratch is almost impossible however carefully conceived. This has often been the tragedy of large-scale redevelopment over the last forty or so years. The terraced communities swept away by the slum clearance of the 1960s did not survive being transplanted to the overspill estate and high-rise block. In these new and often hostile environments the communities took years to regenerate. But regenerate they did only to be swept away once more by the redevelopments of these estates in recent years.

Today as in the 1960s the value of these communities, or even their very existence, is not always recognised. Professionals may talk at length about the value of community but, as we described in Chapter 7, these rough edged urban communities rarely correspond to the cosy notion of community held by planners and architects. Yet they are the glue which holds urban areas together and, like listed buildings, they should be subject to preservation orders. When problems occur in urban areas, as they always will, we must resist the urge to wipe the slate clean and start again. We must instead tap the capacity of existing communities to address local problems. In extreme cases where redevelopment is inevitable communities can still be preserved. Their housing can be left standing until new housing is complete, they can be involved in the design and neighbours can be given the opportunity to move together. In this way we will, at least, not destroy what we have. But we must do more than this, we must strengthen communities and we must promote social sustainability where it does not exist.

Balance

We must therefore analyse the nature of socially sustainable urban areas. To many professionals the key to sustainability is an arithmetic balance of tenures and social groups. Housing associations are now encouraged to incorporate private homes in their estates and planning policy requires private developments to include an element of 'affordable' housing. But what do we mean by balance? True, the iconic village and urban communities described in Chapter 7 are socially mixed. However many communities thrive on shared rather than diverse interests. Communities work in miners' villages as they do in suburban closes because people like living with people like themselves. Mixing the two very different communities so that they become more 'balanced' would not be a recipe for strengthening either.

There are however benefits to mixed communities. The unspoken aim of some of those who advocate mixed communities seems to be that owner-occupiers will exert a civilising influence on social housing tenants. We would not go so far, but there are benefits in avoiding the stigma to social housing estates. Residents are also able to buy a home or trade-up without having to leave the area. Schools also benefit from being able to draw on children from a range of

backgrounds and the area can support a wider range of shops.

However creating mixed communities is far from easy. It may be part of the human condition to seek out people like yourself and to fear those who are different. At its most ugly this can manifest in the racial self segregation happening in many northern towns. However it can also be seen in campaigns against gentrification (homes for yuppies) in working-class communities and nimbyism against social housing in middle-class areas. These are powerful forces working against the creation of balanced communities. The danger is that social divisions are redrawn at a more local level with protected enclaves of private housing built side by side with social housing. This can be seen in America where a large proportion of new private housing is being built as gated communities[10] protected by walls and security guards from the surrounding area. So while mix may have a role in overcoming stigmatisation it is not the whole answer and must be reflected in the design, layout and management of the area.

Hidden communities: They may not be recognised but communities thrive in many problem housing estates and are as worthy of preservation as listed buildings

BRISTOL TEMPLE QUAY

URBED were appointed to master plan the Temple Quay area of Bristol following a design competition. The master plan was undertaken for a commercial developer Castlemore Securities working in partnership with the South West Development Agency. Broadly the scheme has 500 homes and 500,000 sq feet of office space. To the rear is a deprived neighbourhood called the Dings and previous schemes had retained the tall listed wall that separated the site from this area. We argued that the wall should be removed in sections allowing us to create an integrated neighbourhood that linked the new development in to its surroundings. The radiating vistas also mean that all of the area benefits from views of the Floating Harbour. The scheme is now largely complete and the new development has been coordinated with a Home Zone scheme for the Dings so that the two areas feel like one neighbourhood (photo top right). The scheme is also a good example of the Outline Planning application approach to masterplanning that we describe in Chapter 14.

Neighbourhood-based development

One way of doing this is to think about development at the neighbourhood scale. The neighbourhood as a concept has fallen out of favour and today we deal in housing or industrial *estates* or business and retail *parks*. In a more confident age the neighbourhood was the natural unit for the planning of urban areas from Perry's plan for New York to Abercrombie's plan for London. But now we rarely think beyond the bounds of the site under development. Planners may claim that they no longer zone uses but the truth is that they do not have to. The development industry became so specialised in the 20th century that different developers became specialists in housing, commercial and retail development. Their interest was to seek out sites for single-use development and their normal practice was to develop these sites as estates. Like their distant relative, the country estate, these estates were self-contained and inward-looking. They had a single point of access and were likely to be surrounded by a high wall or fence. It is this form of development which has made balanced communities so difficult. Mixing tenures and uses within estates tended to lead to conflict whereas developing them as separate estates reinforced divisions.

The urban principles described in the last chapter imply a very different kind of development. Rather than being zoned into estates, uses and tenures are integrated into the urban fabric and linked by a common street network. Urban neighbourhoods tend to be fine grained and complex so that developments are small and different classes are accommodated within a shared framework of streets. This can still be seen in many traditional urban neighbourhoods like Chorlton in Manchester, Moseley in Birmingham, Hackney in London and even Toxteth (despite its reputation) in Liverpool. Such districts have found a point of balance between gentrification and decline and contain streets of desirable housing cheek by jowl with bedsits, council housing and new housing association development. Their residents can therefore relate to the neighbourhood that they share rather than the stigmatised social housing estate. So-

cial divisions will not of course be abolished. In even the most balanced neighbourhood, certain streets will acquire good or bad reputations. But these divisions will be blurred and ill defined on the ground. They will also be fluid as decline is followed by regeneration in a process which has always characterised urban areas. There are now good examples of neighbourhoods being rebuilt in this way. The two earliest examples, Hulme in Manchester and Crown Street in Glasgow, have shown that it is possible to build private and social housing side by side to create one community. This does however require an urban approach to development, which is the next principle of social sustainability.

Robust urban development

Mixing uses and tenures at the neighbourhood scale will not work unless the design of the area is sufficiently robust. We hesitate to suggest that the design of urban areas has an important role to play in the creation of sustainable communities. There is a long and largely discredited tradition of designers who believed that communities could be created on drawing boards; they clearly cannot. However the design of an area must have an influence on the lives of its residents.

It is tempting to believe that suburban designs are the most effective at creating communities. This is partly based on the sustainability of suburban communities but also on the fact that many inner city residents express a preference for suburban design when consulted on new housing. However the success of the suburb is due in part to its location in areas where crime and other social problems are less prevalent. In the city and in social housing areas, the benefits of suburban design are less clear-cut.

The reason for this is that suburban areas are sustained by a fragile framework of social and economic pressures which do not always exist in urban areas. Freedom from the petty and sometimes intrusive values of the middle-class suburb is, to many, one of the attractions of urban living. Yet in many respects it is these values which make the suburb work. They work as a check on antisocial behaviour

Robust urban development:
Social housing in Brixton creates a clear definition between the public realm of the street and the dwellings

Robust urban development: Social housing in Brixton creates a clear definition between the public realm of the street and the dwellings

and ensure that gardens and properties are well maintained. The criminologist Barry Poynter has pointed out[11] how in middle-class areas boundary fences are maintained and houses are rarely left empty because people do not move out until their house is sold. This is not the case in social housing where maintenance is the responsibility of the landlord and there are inevitable delays in reletting property. Empty units can be vandalised and give access to the rear gardens of surrounding property. As in the Wythenshawe example this can lead to an escalation of problems and in the worst cases can undermine the sustainability of the area.

It is also questionable whether suburban designs can foster urban communities. We have long abandoned the idea that grouping housing into small courts creates communities but the suburban close still holds a powerful attraction. It can work, as in the Old Eldonians Housing Co-operative in Liverpool where a strong urban community has been created in what is essentially a suburban estate in the heart of the city. It is however likely that the success of this community has more to do with the co-operative structure

of its tenants rather than its design. Other examples such as Arkwright town in Derbyshire have been less successful[12]. Arkwright was a mining village of some four hundred people based in tightly-packed terraced streets with a pub, post office, local shops, school and church. Due to the leakage of methane from mine workings British Coal agreed to rebuild the village in a safer location. Following extensive consultation the residents opted for a suburban design based around semi-detached housing. Work by Gerda Speller, a research psychologist, has charted the effect that this has had on the residents. Despite a vast improvement in housing conditions people soon felt that the community had been lost. 'A lot of them asked for privacy but now they are finding that privacy isn't really how they want to live. They are keeping themselves to themselves and now they are isolated'. This illustrates the danger of uprooting communities but also suggests the importance of urban form. Urban communities are very different to suburban communities and demand a very different approach to design.

We therefore believe that in urban areas the design principles outlined in the last chapter have an important role to play in promoting social sustainability. The perimeter block with its clear delimitation between the public realm of the street and the private realm of the house and garden is far more robust than the suburb. The street expands opportunities for socialisation rather than confining them to the dozen or so houses on a suburban cul-de-sac. It makes civilised life possible in neighbourhoods where there will always be strangers and crime is an unfortunate fact of life. Indeed fear of crime is one of the most important issues of urban sustainability and is dealt with below.

Secure places

There have always been two faces to the city, one associated with culture, civilisation and wealth, the other dark, dangerous and full of unseen threats. To some this may be part of the excitement of urban living but to the majority it is the most important reason for shunning cities[13]. If it is to succeed the sustainable urban neighbourhood must therefore tackle the issue of crime. Yet some of the most powerful arguments against the urban forms that we describe have come from the police and institutional investors who believe that far from reducing crime, urban forms will make the problem worse[14]. The widely promoted principles of Secured by Design (see insert) have tended to promote the type of estate-based suburban development that we believe undermines social sustainability in urban areas.

Much of the theoretical framework for Secured by Design is based upon the writings of academics like Oscar Newman[15] and Alice

Coleman[16]. Newman, for example, argued for the elimination of routes through residential blocks, something which has been adopted by Secured by Design and is used as an argument against permeability. He also developed the idea of defensible space which is used to justify a preference for estate-based layouts and cul-de-sacs. Yet if you go back to Newman's original writings you find that he also argued for small urban blocks and the type of fine-grained perimeter block that we described in the last chapter. In a similar vein Coleman states 'as cul-de-sacs have multiplied so have deaths and serious injuries to child pedestrians… (we) recommend traditional street plans'. Those who argue from a Secured by Design perspective against urban layouts would therefore benefit from a rereading of the original sources.

One of the main critics of Secure by Design is Bill Hillier. This is based upon his space syntax studies[17] in which he has correlated the extent to which streets are connected to other streets with the level of pedestrian activity or 'encounter fields'. In his studies of modern housing estates he shows that 'the daytime encounter field in estates turns out to be like the night time in ordinary urban streets. In terms of their naturally available encounter fields, people on these estates live in a kind of perpetual night'. Hillier goes on to demonstrate a correlation between encounter fields and domestic burglary and suggests that permeable layouts may help to reduce crime.

Research evidence for the effect of urban layouts on crime reduction is sparse and we would hesitate to suggest that urban layouts

---

SECURE BY DESIGN PRINCIPLES:

- Houses should be clustered in small groups and estates should have clearly defined boundaries.

- Rumble strips, pinch points or changes in road texture should be used at the entrance to the estate to give the impression that the estate is private.

- Public access should be restricted to as few routes as possible so as to avoid unnecessary public access.

- Communal areas such as playgrounds should be open and supervised by surrounding houses.

- Good lighting covering all parts of the estate will deter intruders and reduce fear of crime.

- House frontages should be open so that views are not obstructed by planting and high walls or fences.

- In-curtilage parking is preferred but if communal parking is required it should be in small groups open to view and well lit.

- Commercial development should create a defined perimeter to increase 'natural surveillance'.

Paraphrased from Secured by Design Guidelines published by the Home Office Prevention Centre 1994.

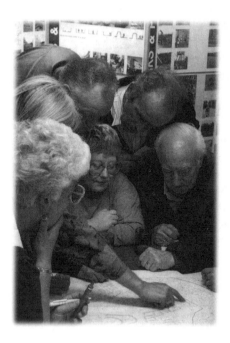

Design for Change

The tenant workshops in St. Wilfred's in Hulme (above left) were the first time that we used a series of consultation techniques that have since been developed into the Design for Change workshop process. This started with a request from the Glasshouse Foundation and the National tenant Resource Centre in Chester to develop a training course for tenants facing the redevelopment of their estates. This became two residential courses, one dealing with masterplanning and the other with housing design. We have run-three day courses for the tenants of more than a hundred estates (such as Coventry below) as well as running courses on site such as the Greater Village in Belfast (above right).

The training course has since been developed into a consultation technique called Design for Change that has been run across the UK. This involves taking residents through a masterplanning process including the analysis plans, site visits to exemplar schemes and a masterplanning exercise using plasticine. The resulting plans are remarkably good and in places like Anfield have been converted directly into the master plan that is being taken forward.

are the whole answer. However if we are to build sustainable urban areas we must move away from what the Safer Neighbourhoods Unit[18] have called 'a drawbridge strategy protecting the most stable and prosperous communities against the criminally inclined residents of poorer, less stable neighbourhoods.' To do this we must focus not only on the design of the neighbourhood but the attitudes of people living there. Having windows as 'eyes onto the streets' is of little value unless the people behind those windows feel some level of stewardship over the area and a willingness to get involved.

Community and stewardship

This leads to the final principle of social sustainability. The most important challenge of the sustainable urban neighbourhood is to engender in its residents a feeling that they belong, a pride in the area, and a sense of responsibility for it. In other words to create neighbourhoods where the word neighbour means something. This challenge is greatest in social housing and in inner city areas where the process of marginalisation and stigmatisation has corroded these community values. However it is possible to engender pride and stewardship through the way that housing is planned and managed.

An important element is community involvement in design both of new housing and refurbishment schemes. For this to be effective residents need to be identified in advance and given the time and skills to work alongside planners and architects as in the BO 100 example in Sweden. Once the housing is complete there is also a role for resident involvement in management. In this way local people can be given both the responsibility and the power to address local issues, rather than regarding them as someone else's problem. Tenant involvement in design and management has come back onto the agenda as a response to the problems experienced in social housing development. Yet while social housing providers may have started to respond to this issue, the fact is that most social housing is now built by private developers as part of planning agreements and there is no opportunity to involve people in the design process. We still have a long way to go just to get back to the level of consultation that went into the council house building of the late

Communities taking control: Left, an urban self-build scheme in Berlin where the building frame was erected by contractors and fitted out by residents. Right, the award-winning Diggers self-build scheme in Brighton using the Segal fabrication system

1970s and early 1980s following the Skeffington Report[19]. One of the highest profile schemes from this era was Ralph Erskine's redevelopment of the Byker estate in Newcastle (see page 73). The success of Byker over many years stands in stark contrast to the deck access estates built at the same time which failed so disastrously. Yet even today there are few redevelopments which can claim the level of involvement achieved in Byker.

The involvement of residents can raise difficult issues about the design of housing. Indeed, as we have suggested, many residents when asked what sort of housing they would like to live in will, like the residents of Arkwright, opt for something suburban. How do we square this with our advocacy of urban development forms? Rod Hackney[20] was prominent in the late 1980s as an advocate of community architecture which he saw as a means to puncture the pomposity of architects and designers who for years had inflicted their Utopian ideas on vulnerable people.

However community architecture does not mean that architects can abdicate responsibility for design. This is illustrated by the example of St. Wilfred's in Hulme, Manchester (see page 118). Unlike most parts of Hulme this area was home to a traditional ageing community many of whom had lived in the terraced housing which had been cleared in the 1960s. The area was redeveloped by North British Housing Association in the mid 1990s who put a great deal of effort into the involvement of local residents. At the same time the city council were developing a vision for the redevelopment of the area as an urban neighbourhood as we describe in the next chapter. The problem was that the plan which had been developed with strong community involvement was at odds with the council's vision for the area. Of most concern was the fact that, despite most of the housing being terraced, the estate had been designed with one access road and three cul-de-sacs. A local community architecture project led by Charlie Baker was therefore asked to work with tenants to redesign the plan that they had already agreed. The starting point was to show the tenants a series of slides of different types of

BO 100 – MALMÖ, SWEDEN

One of the most striking early examples of tenant involvement in the development of housing can be found in Malmö. In 1987 the city commissioned

the architect Ivo Waldhör to undertake a radical experiment in social housing. An initial meeting brought together 70 tenants and a development company was established with a tenant majority on the board along with the city, the developer and the Swedish Architectural Institute. Ideas were developed through detailed interviews with tenants and a boskolan (living school) was established to teach tenants the basics of building and design with a view to each of them producing a 1:20 model of their ideal flat. At the same time the tenants learnt about the area's history, planning policy, and infrastructure to inform the development of the whole building.

Design and construction lasted four years with tenants moving in the summer of 1991. Of the thirty-nine households who moved in eighteen had been involved from the start and a further eight had been involved for more than two years.

The five-storey building which has resulted contains an enormous variety of flat types and detailing. Whilst some standardisation was introduced by the architects – the number of window types was reduced from 150 to 48 – tenants were able to change elements throughout the design and construction process both to individual flats and to the whole building following a vote at the general meeting. This resulted in party walls which do not line up with the walls below and kitchens and bathrooms which fail to line up for soil stacks and services. The scheme also includes communal facilities – unusual in Swedish social housing – such as a community room, a sauna and a guest room on the roof along with a hobby area in the basement.

The scheme cost some 25 % more than comparable social housing. It has also been incredibly demanding on the time of everyone involved, not least tenants. However the participatory design process has produced a strong and characterful building occupied by a community which has been created through the process and is committed to both the building and to each other.

urban development elsewhere from which they picked the ones that they liked. They then dug out old street plans of the terraced housing that many of them had lived in before the 1960s and discussed what it was that they liked and disliked about the old housing. It transpired that most of the negative points related to the interior of the home and most of the older residents had fond memories of the terraced streets while the younger tenants could relate to terraced housing areas which still stood in adjacent districts.

As a result of this process the tenants suggested that the new development should be based on the original street pattern which had existed in the area. This made a great deal of sense since many of the underground services still followed the old street patterns. They then experimented with models to decide on the character and width of streets and developed a plan based upon perimeter blocks. The estate has since been completed and is very successful. It demonstrates that the key to successful community involvement in urban development is not to give the residents a blank sheet and to ask them what they want but to treat them as a designer would treat any client. This involves explaining to them the constraints on development, including the policy context, and giving them a full range of options of what is possible within this context.

If taken to its logical extreme, community involvement can promote stewardship by empowering local people to take control of their neighbourhood though housing co-operatives, self-build groups, co-housing projects, estate management boards or community-based housing associations. These can provide exceptions to the rule that sustainable communities cannot be created from scratch. When groups of people commit years of their life to building and managing their own housing they are also building a community and have an incentive as strong as any owner-occupier to ensure that the community is successful. Within weeks of the completion of the Homes for Change scheme in Manchester (see Chapter 13) the community spirit was tangible. People felt able to leave their front doors open and populate the walkway

outside their flats with plants. Yet in physical form, Homes for Change is very similar to the demolished deck-access blocks in Hulme which had never managed to generate this level of community spirit. The difference was not so much the design of the housing but the fact that through the co-operative the members of Homes for Change felt that the building belonged to them, had been designed in partnership with them and was their responsibility.

Balanced incremental development

We have suggested in this chapter that sustainable communities, like good wine, need time to mature, that they should include a balance of tenures and uses and should be organised as neighbourhoods rather than estates. We have argued that they should be urban in character to promote community and to reduce crime and should engender in their residents a feeling of ownership and stewardship. These are the things that successful urban areas seem to achieve almost effortlessly and yet which constantly elude us when we try to build new urban areas. One of the reasons for this is that, like the forest that we described earlier in this chapter, urban neighbourhoods are almost never successfully built from scratch. They rather evolve naturally over time through the accretion of small-scale development and redevelopment. This balanced incremental approach to development is something which we have been promoting in our urban regeneration work for many years and is also the key to successful urban development.

Comprehensive development or redevelopment is a risky business. It puts all your eggs in one basket and means that if mistakes are made they will be big ones. As we have seen with many system-built estates, a simple problem such as the wrong mix of concrete or a poorly specified construction detail can mean that hundreds of properties have to be consigned to the wrecking ball or subjected to expensive remedial works. Balanced incremental development by contrast suggests a fine grain of development with large numbers of small sites being developed over time by different developers. When this is done the inevitable mistakes which are made will be small and easily fixed. If a particular development type fails it can be demolished or refurbished without the disruption of the whole area. Similarly when schemes prove to be successful they can be identified and replicated through a process of natural selection. It is also impossible to predict what will happen in the future in terms of demographic, social and economic change. Many deck-access estates were built for families with children in manual employment and were unable to adapt to a time when the manual employment had disappeared and the families were moved away. Contrast this to the traditional Georgian street which was originally built for well-to-do families with servants, subsequently was subdivided into flats and bedsits and is now being converted back into desirable homes for the urban middle classes. Fine-grained diverse urban areas can adapt to such change and in this way we can build neighbourhoods which will evolve and adapt over time rather than being cast in concrete and steel. This is the key to building the 'immortal' neighbourhood and will be the focus for the final chapter of this book. But we will first explore the implication of these ideas on a model neighbourhood in Manchester.

Chapter 13
A model neighbourhood?

There is no better place than Manchester to explore how cities might change in the future. The city described by Disraeli in 1844 as 'the most wonderful city of modern times' was, after all, the birthplace of an economic model of industry and urban form which was to reverberate around the world. The Manchester School of 'laissez faire' economics provided the foundations for modern capitalism and the city is a textbook case of how the forces of industrialisation and economic growth have shaped urban areas ever since.

Back in Chapter 1 we described how the origins of suburbanisation in the UK can, in part, be traced back to the flight of the merchants of Manchester in the first half of the 19th century. In setting up the early suburbs, merchants like Samuel Brookes abandoned the polluted, overcrowded city and leapfrogged an area of low-lying marshy land to create suburbs like Whalley Range and Victoria Park. The marshy nature of the land that they crossed lives on in names like Moss Side, Rusholme and Hulme. Less than twenty years after these suburbs were established this low-lying land was also being developed, not for exclusive suburbs but for working-class housing. As wave after wave of suburbanisation swept out from the city, these working-class areas declined into what was to become known as the inner city. This too has since expanded outwards to engulf the original exclusive suburbs. Thus was created in Manchester the classic 'doughnut' shape of the 20th century western city.

Manchester along with Glasgow and Liverpool declined further and lost more population than any other UK cities. These cities however have also led the way in showing how cities can reinvent themselves for the 21st century. It is too early to be certain, but it is possible that Manchester is once again leading the way in the transformation of British cities. Just as Whalley Range was a fundamental turning point in the 1830s so the neighbouring district of Hulme could come to be seen as equally significant in the future. The Hulme area is one of the most important redevelopment projects in the UK. While flawed in many respects it provides a model for the sustainable urban neighbourhood. In this chapter we therefore use the Hulme area as a test bed to illustrate how the sustainable urban neighbourhood might be developed.

The development of Hulme

As Manchester boomed in the middle of the 19th century the Hulme district, immediately to the south of the city centre, was one of the first districts to be developed, starting in the 1850s. The housing in Hulme was of a poorer quality than the later bylaw development in Moss Side and had become a notorious slum by the end of the century. In 1923 there were 130000 people living in Hulme. At a time when the average population density of Manchester was 34 people per acre, in Hulme it was 136 persons per acre rising to 196 persons per acre in the north of

Stretford Road: in the 1950s when it was one of the city's prime commercial routes (right)

Hulme pior to redevelopment: The Naval Brewery stands on the site which has been developed by Homes for Change (far right)

A brave new world: The Crescents under construction in 1970 (below)

the area[1]. Hulme was declared Britain's largest clearance area in 1934.

However Hulme was also a vibrant urban area. Until its closure in 1965, Stretford Road, which ran through the heart of Hulme, contained the largest selection of shops outside the city centre including, what was later to become, the Debenhams department store. The area contained churches designed by Pugin and Charles Barry as well the extraordinary St. Mary's Church by Crowther which still boasts the tallest spire in the city. Hulme was home to more than sixty pubs, three breweries and two music hall theatres. It was a mixed-use areas with large factories such

as the Dunlop rubber works and Gaythorn gas works as well as hundreds of small workshops, with specialities like gold beating and sign writing, including one where the engine for the first Rolls Royce was designed.

The clearance and redevelopment of Hulme took place in a piecemeal fashion from the 1930s onwards but it started in earnest in the 1960s. The housing was subject to compulsory purchase orders and was cleared. Eventually all that was left was the Stretford Road which was closed in 1965 leaving only the churches by Pugin, Barry and Crowther and a handful of pubs. The redevelopment of the area was planned

by the city architect incorporating many of the principles described in Part 1 of this book[2] (see the illustration on page 45). The area was dissected by a series of major roads designed as grade separated dual carriageways. These roads divided the area into a series of neighbourhoods each to be served by a local shopping centre. Stretford Road was pedestrianised and its shops were replaced with a large covered shopping centre and a series of local centres. The housing was redeveloped with thirteen tower blocks and six deck-access housing estates, the last and most impressive of which was The Crescents designed by Wilson and Warmersley Architects. The Crescents were modelled on Georgian Bath and included four, nine-storey deck-access blocks named after the architects Charles Barry, William Kent, Robert Adam and John Nash. By the early 1970s there were 5 000 properties in Hulme and its population had fallen from 130 000 to around 12 000.

This massive investment in slum clearance only served to make the problems of Hulme worse. When you talk to the older residents of the area it is clear, as in other slum clearance areas, that there was a short honeymoon period in which they enjoyed their large comfortable flats with internal toilets and central heating. However it did not last long. Following an accident in the mid 1970s when a child fell to his death from an upper walkway the council resolved to move all families out of the area and its decline accelerated.

The reputation of the area rapidly deteriorated and it suffered all of the typical problems of urban decline: poverty, crime, drug use, and unemployment. However the easy availability of large flats in the area and its proximity to the University meant that Hulme gradually became a magnet for young people many of whom would stay in the area for a few years before moving on. Over the years Hulme became a focus for Manchester's subculture. Many of its residents were squatters living as single people in flats designed for families and pressing spare bedrooms into service as offices, workshops and even recording studios. At one point the *Ethical Consumer,* a national magazine, was published

from a Hulme flat and employed eight people. In another part of the estate three flats had been knocked together to create the Kitchen Night Club. A major government-sponsored report on the area in the late 1980s (The Hulme Study[3]) found that 30% of the population had higher education qualifications, more than Manchester's most affluent suburb. However another 30% of the population had no qualifications at all and unemployment rates were the highest in the city. Despite, or perhaps because of its reputation the

The hidden community: While the Crescents deteriorated into a notorious slum they were home to a strong if unconventional community. Their demolition was celebrated by a local performance group, the Dogs of Heaven (below)

young community which adopted Hulme thrived in the area and many fought hard to prevent the area being redeveloped.

Manchester City Council had quite different views about Hulme and had been working on redevelopment since the mid 1980s. The area had originally been planned as one of the first Housing Action Trusts, something which was fiercely resisted by local people in a campaign which was eventually successful. Following a further study by Price Waterhouse[4] in 1991, the Housing Corporation allocated funds for the redevelopment of two of the deck-access estates and the following year Hulme was designated as one of the first round City Challenge projects. The redevelopment plans were widened to include all six of the deck-access estates. Around 2 500 deck-access properties have since been demolished to be replaced by 1 026 housing association properties

and about twice that many homes for sale. Stretford Road has been reopened and the covered shopping centre has been redeveloped with a new supermarket and market hall. A range of other facilities have been created including workspace, local shops, community and cultural facilities and a new park. The City Challenge project came to an end in March 1997 although work will continue on the redevelopment of Hulme for many years to come.

The initial redevelopment was undertaken by a handful of developers. The social housing was all developed by two housing associations, North British (since renamed Places for People) and the Guinness Trust. A large part of this social housing was subsequently transferred to six local housing associations for management including a community-based association and a housing co-operative (Homes for Change). The majority of the early private housing was developed by Bellway Urban Renewal and the shopping centre redevelopment was undertaken by Amec in partnership with two further private housebuilders.

There is little doubt that Hulme has been transformed by this process. The first £100 000 home was sold in 1999 in an area where home ownership was, until a few years earlier, inconceivable. But not everyone was impressed. There has been ongoing protest from parts of the community who feel alienated from the increasingly commercial focus of development. Some of their concerns were shared by the Urban Task Force following a visit to the area in 1999. The Task Force's reaction was however probably more disappointment that Hulme failed to live up to its own hype. Expecting a redeveloped mixed-use urban quarter the Task Force were disappointed to find that parts of Hulme are quite suburban in character. The question is whether Hulme should be criticised for falling so far short of what it could have been, or praised for being so much better than similar schemes elsewhere. In our view it deserves some credit for the latter. The neighbourhood provides a good starting point to explore the implications of building a the sustainable urban neighbourhood.

The great urban experiment

Traditionally cities in the UK have compared themselves to their nearest competitors. In the past Manchester would have to looked to cities like Birmingham, Leeds and Glasgow to gauge its success. However as the Hulme redevelopment was being planned Manchester was bidding to stage the Olympics and was therefore seeking to compete on an international rather than just a national stage. As part of the Olympic bidding process, senior politicians from Manchester spent time in Barcelona, host of the 1992 games. Manchester had always seen itself as one of Europe's great provincial cities alongside cities like Barcelona, Milan and Frankfurt yet the politicians were shocked by the contrast between Manchester and Barcelona. It was clear that while Manchester had been doing well enough in comparison to other British provincial cities it had fallen a long way behind its European counterparts in terms

of their economy, culture and sheer urbanity. Manchester's leaders concluded that if Manchester was to take its place as a leading European city it would need to transform itself and a central part of this project was the transformation of its urban environment. Hulme was to be the test bed for this transformation.

The leader of the Council, Graham Stringer, pledged that Hulme would be redeveloped as a vibrant mixed-use urban quarter, although it must be said that few people in the city understood what this meant at the time. Initially a master plan was commissioned from a Canadian architect, Joe Berridge, although this failed to live up to the politicians' expectations. Following this a local architect, George Mills, was commissioned to develop an urban code similar to those of Duany and Plater-Zyberk in the US. While George was to play a central role as urban design advisor to the council throughout the redevelopment the

Hulme V:
A development by North British Housing Association. The streets are well-proportioned but the area looks artificial since all the buildings are of the same design

A new urban vision: One of the illustrations from the Hulme Guide to Development (above) and below the Hulme Arch, a major new landmark in the area

code proved difficult to understand and failed to overcome the resistance of many of the key players in the area. It was therefore decided to commission a written urban design guide[5] from a local designer and activist Charlie Baker who at the time was running the Hulme Community Architecture Project. This written guide, which was eventually co-written with myself (DR), set out a series of principles for urban development and codified these into a set of simple rules covering:

☐ **Streets:** The development of streets which are more than traffic routes but which promote sociability, community and natural surveillance.

☐ **Integration:** The promotion of a rich variety of uses within an integrated pattern of streets.

☐ **Density:** The creation of sufficient density of people and activities to animate streets, to support public transport, and to sustain a wide range of shops and services.

☐ **Permeability:** The development of a neighbourhood with strong links to surrounding areas,

which is easy to move around.

☐ **Routes and transport:** The accommodation of the car without allowing it to dominate by reducing traffic speed.

☐ **Landmarks, vistas and focal points:** The use of existing and new buildings along with public art to create interest, excitement and character.

☐ **Definition of space:** The creation of an attractive well-proportioned public realm defined by appropriately scaled buildings.

☐ **Hierarchy:** The organisation of uses and buildings within a recognisable hierarchy of streets reflecting the organisation of the area.

☐ **Identity:** The encouragement of diversity in the design of buildings and spaces to create a strong sense of place.

☐ **Sustainability:** The promotion of development which is sustainable environmentally, socially and economically by encouraging energy efficiency, recycling, public transport and urban ecology and allowing the area to adapt to future change.

There was nothing particularly original about these principles. They were being promoted by the Urban Villages Forum[6] and had been part of the Crown Street development guide published the previous year in Glasgow[7]. However initially the Hulme guide was fiercely resisted. The housing developers said that it would make their housing expensive and unpopular. The housing associations complained that it could not be achieved within their regulatory framework or cost yardsticks. The police argued that it would increase crime, the traffic engineers that it would lead to accidents and the institutional investors that it would reduce the returns on their investment in an area which was already high risk. These objections were thrashed out in hours of negotiation with these different parties. The most difficult discussions were those to reconcile the guidance with local and national highways standards[8]. Arguments can become very difficult when you are arguing principles of urbanism and your opponents are accusing you of risking children's lives by creating unsafe highways.

The guide came through all of these discussions remarkably intact and was adopted by the Council in June 1994. The reason for its survival was the fact that it was being pushed not by professionals but politicians. A council sub-committee had been established to deal with all planning applications and land disposals in Hulme. This was chaired by the leader of the council and included the key politicians in the city including Richard Leese who was to become leader of the council and David Lunts, then chair of housing, who went on to head the Urban Villages Forum and to become head of urbanism for the GLA. Because the committee had planning and land ownership powers it was able to exert a huge influence on development. Whereas a planning committee rarely spends more than a few minutes considering a planning application, the Hulme committee would spend several hours pouring over the detail of applications and quizzing architects and developers even before the guide to development was adopted. Virtually none of the schemes in Hulme were approved at the first meeting as developers were sent away – much to their frustration given funding deadlines – to reconsider detailed elements. In the process the politicians became even more convinced that this was the way forward for the city and learnt a great deal about urban development. They increasingly began to question the professional advice from their own officers in departments such as planning and highway engineering leading to considerable internal tension within the council.

While many council officers welcomed what was happening in Hulme, others were very concerned and comforted themselves with the thought that at least these ideas were not being applied to the whole city. There was therefore consternation when a resolution was passed by the Council applying the Hulme guide to the whole city. It was rightly pointed out that many of the items in the guide were not enforceable through planning legislation and were of questionable relevance to the more suburban parts of the city. However the application of the Hulme guide to the whole of the city was only ever an interim measure and the Council set about developing a city-wide guide which could be adopted as statutory planning policy. Because there remained considerable concern about the willingness of parts of the Council to take on this new agenda an external panel was convened to develop the Manchester Guide. We were lucky enough to take part in this panel alongside leading professionals from private practice in the city as well as developers and academics. The work on the Manchester Guide to Development revisited many of the conflicts and negotiations in Hulme. While a large measure of agreement was reached quickly, detailed concerns remained about highway engineering, crime, investment and its enforceability through the planning system.

A draft guide was published for consultation and elicited hundreds of responses both within the city and nationally. There was a particular problem with the police's architectural liaison officer which was only resolved after a meeting between the leader of the council and the Chief Constable. Articles also appeared in the property press[9] accusing Manchester of being irresponsible and risking the loss of inward investment into the city by insisting on permeable street layouts. These were sensitive issues since large parts of the city's functional area fall outside Manchester City Council's administrative boundaries – Salford and Trafford councils actually adjoin parts of the city centre. The danger was not therefore that the city as a whole would lose investment but that it would slip over the border into neighbouring districts which were not promoting urban development thus

Urbanising the city: Mixed-use student housing developed by Manchester University illustrating the application of urban principles to other development in the city

undermining the impact on the city. These issues were brought into focus by a major application to develop a large student hall of residence on the edge of Hulme. Manchester Metropolitan University was concerned that the perception of the city as a dangerous place was putting off parents who might otherwise send their offspring to the university. They had proposed an inward-looking compound which involved the closure of part of the Stretford Road which the Council was putting so much effort into reopening. This went to the heart of the debate over permeability. The University argued that a permeable street layout would give criminals access to their accommodation, putting students at risk. The Council countered by contending that street life and activity created by a large student population would make the area safer. A compromise was agreed and the street was retained for pedestrian use. Elsewhere in the city the politicians made clear that they would stand firm on the urban principles, arguing that any negative impact on the city would be short-lived and outweighed by the long-term benefits.

The *Manchester Guide to Development* was completed in 1997[10] (and republished in

A guide to development in **Manchester**

revised form in 2006[11]) and was appended to the city's statutory local plan as Supplementary Planning Guidance. Despite all of the concerns, once the guidelines were adopted they were largely accepted by the development industry and the results can be seen in much of the development that has taken place in the city since that time. Following the adoption of the guide a series of training sessions were organised for development control officers in the city to explore the impact on their work. Three recent redevelopments in the city, a housing scheme, a commercial development and a retail park were used to demonstrate how the approach to design would be altered by the new guidance. All of those involved in these sessions were shocked by how far-reaching the impact was. Guidelines which, in their written form, seemed innocuous or motherhood and apple pie actually involved a complete reversal of many of the principles which had guided the planner's work for many years. The housing scheme which had been designed as an inward-looking cul-de-sac was turned inside-out as the houses were made to front the surrounding streets and the internal roads were driven through to link to the surrounding street network. The commercial development, rather than being an isolated block in the centre of a large area of landscape, became a perimeter block with an internal courtyard and the retail scheme was moved from the back of the site to the front with parking to the rear. In fairness to the planners who took part, the majority were very enthusiastic about these changes and their work to apply these principles has had a significant positive impact on the city.

The enormity of the transformation attempted in Manchester should not be underestimated. Through the Hulme redevelopment and the adoption of urban design guidance for the whole city an attempt was made to reverse urban trends and planning theory which had held sway for more than a century. It may be that Manchester's remarkable economic renaissance since the mid 1990s has nothing to do with urban design. In that time the city's economic power has outstripped rivals such as Birmingham and Leeds. However while design may only have played a small part, urbanism in the form of the repopulation of the city and the revival of its city centre has been absolutely crucial to its economic success. The significance for other UK cities is enormous as are the implications for urban repopulation and the development of a new urban vision in Britain.

A model neighbourhood?

The development of Hulme has not been without its problems. When the redevelopment started Hulme was seen as a huge risk for developers and investors so that only organisations with the financial muscle to take this risk were able to get involved. Development sites were parcelled up into very large chunks which only large developers could take on. The result is that the area looks artificial which is not entirely due to the fact that it is so new. This approach also shut out smaller developers and created a very course grain of development with little diversity. The scale of the area cleared for development was huge as an attempt was made to develop a new urban neighbourhood from scratch. As we have already suggested this is almost impossible and most successful neighbourhoods tend to grow organically. This has also meant that at the end of the City Challenge process almost half of Hulme remained undeveloped leaving islands of high-density urban development marooned in a sea of future building sites. Even ten years later when many of these sites have been developed the area still lacks the benefits of diversity, street life and safety that the design guide sought to promote. It will be many years before the urban vision for Hulme is fully realised and the hope is that the area will survive in the interim.

We were fortunate to play a small role in the redevelopment of Hulme. This experience informed this book and the development of the idea of the sustainable urban neighbourhood. However because Hulme has a number of weaknesses we decided in the late 1990s to hypothesise what the area might look like if it were completed along the lines that we are suggesting. The result is illustrated on the plan on the following pages[12]. This is based on the central

part of Hulme and includes the new developments that had been completed at the time that it was drawn as well as a number of existing buildings in the area. It did not however represent the plans that the Council had for the area, some of which have since been completed. The intention was not to develop an alternative plan for this part of Hulme or indeed to critique the development that was planned. Rather we wanted to use the area as an example of a place where a sustainable urban neighbourhood would be appropriate and which was typical of many of the sites created by the redevelopment of council estates or indeed brown field land formerly in industrial use. The result is an illustration of what the sustainable urban neighbourhood might look like.

In developing the plan we sought to incorporate all of the principles described in Part 3 of this book. The aim was to create a high-quality urban environment with well-proportioned buildings and attractive streets, squares and parks. The public realm is human in scale but urban in nature and designed to promote interaction and to accommodate the diversity of urban life. The plan is based on a clear framework of streets designed to serve both as routes and as public places supervised by the occupants of surrounding buildings. This street framework contains a density of different uses, buildings and tenures to create a balanced community, to reduce car travel, to animate streets and public places, to sustain shops and other public facilities and to foster activity and security throughout the day. The plan is also based on a high degree of permeability so that there is a choice of routes through the area. It also avoids the development of housing and workspace as defined estates but rather mixes them up and blurs the boundaries between them.

The plan covers an area of 45 hectares (112 acres) and includes up to 2500 housing units, 45 000 m^2 of commercial space plus a 75 000 m^2 supermarket and could accommodate a population of 4 – 5 000 people. A wide range of uses have been incorporated into the plan including different types of housing, local shops as well as office accommodation and light industrial workspace.

251

Live/Work accommodation: Units which can be jointly used for living and business (see page 111)

Workshop units: One of the problems with much urban development is that it does not make provision for small-scale manufacturing yet this is often more appropriate to the skills of urban communities

Student housing: Student populations are increasing rapidly in many urban areas and represent an important source of demand for new urban housing

Public facilities: Public facilities such as a health centre, library, pub, an existing church and local shops are located at the junction of the two high streets as an important activity node served by public transport

Urban park: There is a tension in urban areas between the desire to create large amounts of open space and the need to maintain densities. Whilst urban communities will often fiercely resist development on land which has been landscaped, the reality is that these areas are a drain on resources, often a target for fly tipping and can be dangerous at night. A better solution is the more intensively used and overlooked urban park linked to a network of green spaces, including back gardens and green roofs, to support a range of urban flora and fauna

High streets: Many important routes through urban areas were closed off in the 1960s or turned into formless dual carriageways. Here the high street has been recreated with existing landmark buildings supplemented by four and five-storey development to recreate the character of an important street

rban edges: An important principle of the sustainable urban eighbourhood is to maximise the number of links between nd through areas. Railways or motorways can make this fficult. The solution is to treat the barrier as you would a er bank with the equivalent of an embankment street so at local traffic can circulate without conflict with the main ad traffic

Combined heat and power plant and recycling point: The recycling point has been located on the edge of the area so that it can be accessed by lorries. The CHP plant is located away from housing because of the noise generated and to al- lay public concern about emissions. It is also linked to the recycling point to allow it to be powered by a waste incinerator. This would be linked to a district heating and a power distribution system serving the area

Supermarket: Large shops are a fact of life and can be difficult to accommodate in urban areas. One option is to wrap housing and other uses around the supermarket or to build on the roof. This has been done by Peabody in association with a Tesco supermarket in Hammersmith (see page 224). The plan shows a similar solution with a landscaped car park to the rear

Shopping high street and market square: Many inner city shopping areas have declined as trade has been diverted to supermarkets. This can even happen around inner city supermarkets as shoppers travel to the supermarket by car and never leave its territory. By linking an urban supermarket to an outdoor market shoppers are offered a wider range of goods and can support a range of small shops

Leisure and recreation facilities: An attempt has been made to integrate leisure facilities into the local shopping centre. The main building is therefore brought to the back of pavement on the high street with outdoor activities to the rear

Bus routes: The bus routes are based on exist- ing routes running through the area selected for this exercise. The white circles are 160m in diameter representing a 2 minute walk time (in a straight line). This illustrates that all buildings in the area will be within five minutes walk of a bus stop on one of these routes

Dense mixed-use development: One of the principles of urban areas is that the grain of development should increase around activity nodes. This means a greater density of mixed-use buildings and decrease in block size, as in the picture of Deptford High Street. (See page 225)

Existing buildings - Redevelopment areas generally contain a variety of existing buildings. Some like the old institute illustrated here can be refurbished as landmarks. Others like the school and old people's home to the rear are of less architectural quality and contribute little to the urban fabric. These have been framed by more substantial buildings to create a boul- evard with the lower buildings in the centre

Educational facilities: Like business and retail uses there is a tendency to develop educational facilities on campus. This illustrates how a university depart- ment of a college extension could be integrated into an urban area

Main illustration by Jonathan Polley formerly of Build for Change

The concept of the sustainable urban neighbourhood is based on the principle that neighbourhoods are more sustainable environmentally, economically and socially when they include a mix of uses and are built as part of a city to high densities, so contributing to the vitality and walkability of urban areas. But what are the implications of putting these ideas into practice? As we have already described it has been argued that compact development will lead to 'town cramming' and that cities are such dirty, congested and dangerous places that people cannot be forced to live in them. Critics have also questioned the benefits of compact development, suggesting that it is impossible to increase densities to the level required for even a small reduction in energy use or car travel. These arguments turn on circumstances at the most local level. What sort of urban areas are created if we increase densities? What are the walking distances to facilities and to public transport? How viable is waste recycling and combined heat and power? These are questions that we have sought to answer through the hypothetical neighbourhood.

KEY TO PLAN ON PREVIOUS PAGE

1. The Hulme Arch – see photograph on page 248
2. Mixed-use development by North British Housing Association
3. Princess Parkway – the main route out of Manchester to the south and the airport
4. Homes for Change
5. The Junction Pub, one of the handful of pubs to survive the redevelopment of the 1960s
6. This area is currently being developed as Zion Square and Hulme Park, although not to this design
7. The Zion Institute recently converted to an arts centre
8. Royce Primary School
9. The Hulme Playhouse and Hippodrome – two listed music hall theatres. The Playhouse was converted to an Afro-Caribbean cultural centre which has recently closed
10. The Chichester Road housing scheme by Triangle Architects for North British Housing Association
11. St. Mary's Church
12. Loretto Sixth Form College

Density: One of the main bones of contention about urban development is density which, to its critics, is synonymous with overcrowding and town cramming. As the *UK Strategy for Sustainable Development* suggests, intensification should be a 'dynamic process, but the limits and thresholds must be understood… for the city to be sustainable'[13]. The hypothetical neighbourhood seeks to test these limits. It is based on net residential densities of 62 to 124 units per hectare (25 to 50 per acre). These densities are measured to the centre line of the surrounding streets and therefore equate to the standard density measure used by most local authorities. Indeed the densities are broadly comparable to the standard set in the *Hulme Guide to Development* which includes a density guideline of 86 units per hectare (35 to the acre).

The plan explores the implications of building at these densities. It is clear that 62 units to the hectare can be achieved with a mix of terraced housing and flats on the corners or above commercial premises (Site C). However to achieve 124 units per hectare requires the predominant use of flats as in sites A and B. These sites also include a range of other uses which further increase the density of development and activity. The potential housing yield of the area has been calculated by applying these two density levels to the developable land in the area. This would produce 1 225 units at 62 to the hectare and 2 450 units at 124 to the acre. The quality of the residential environment created is a matter of personal taste. However we would suggest that the plan and indeed the completed developments within Hulme illustrate that densities of this level are consistent with a high-quality residential environment, albeit not the sort of suburban environment that has come to be seen as the norm in recent years.

However plot densities have little meaning when considering issues such as walkability. We have therefore looked at the gross residential density of the neighbourhood. The area covered by the plan is 45 hectares so that the gross residential densities across the area would be

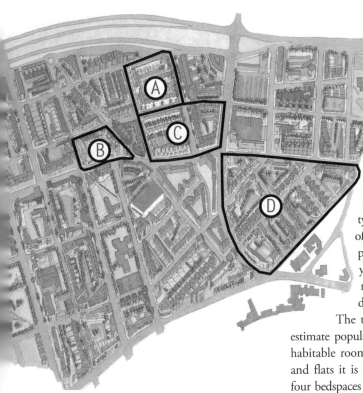

It is also important to realise that the number of units to the hectare is less important than the number of people. Indeed one of the problems with falling household size is that the population density of many urban areas is falling even though all of the housing remains fully occupied. Jan Gehl has pointed out[14] that a typical urban block in the centre of Copenhagen has ten times fewer people living in it than it did 100 years ago despite the fact that none of the buildings have been demolished.

The two measures generally used to estimate population density are bedspaces and habitable rooms. In an area of mixed houses and flats it is probably reasonable to assume four bedspaces per dwelling. This however will only translate into population density if all of the properties are fully occupied which is very unlikely. We have therefore also used a measure

between 27 and 54 units to the hectare which is less than half the net residential densities. This is a point which is often missed in the discussion about density. At net densities of 62 units to the hectare the gross residential density across a mixed-use urban neighbourhood can fall to the equivalent of a single-use suburban development. This clearly depends where the boundaries are drawn. In the illustrated neighbourhood, for example, the area includes a park, a school and other institutional buildings. However the fall in gross density is also due to the area devoted to the street network (just over 17 hectares) and there may be value in increasing the size of blocks or reducing the width of streets to reduce the gap between net and gross densities. At present if the housing in the area was built to traditional garden city densities of 30 units to the hectare (12 to the acre) the gross densities across the area would fall to just 12 units to the hectare (5 to the acre) and the yield to just 588 homes. This illustrates the danger of using net densities to assess urban land capacity and the viability of services such as public transport and recycling.

ANALYSIS OF DENSITIES AND HOUSING YIELDS

Neighbourhood area	112	45	
Developed area	69	28	Excluding roads
Area developed for housing	49	20	Excluding non-residential uses
DENSITIES			
Assumed net densities			
units/acre	12	25	50
units/hectare	30	62	124
Gross densities			
units/hectare	13	27	54
Bedspaces (net)			
per hectare	119	247	494
Bedspaces (gross)			
per hectare	52	108	216
Persons (net)			
per hectare	71	148	296
Persons (gross)			
per hectare	31	65	130
Housing Yield	588	1 225	2 450

**ANALYSIS OF EMPLOYMENT
DENSITY AND YIELDS**

	Floor area m²	m²/job	Total jobs
Retail space	11 250	40	281
Supermarket	7 500	40	18
Workshops (B2)	11 250	50	225
Warehousing (B8)	6 750	80	84
Office space (B1)	15 750	25	630
Total	52 500		1 407
Employment density/hectare			31

of people to the hectare based upon an average household size of 2.4 people. This was the average household size across the country in the 1990s and while it is about right for much of the development in Hulme, the growth in single-person households may mean that it is an overestimate for new development.

It is also important to take into account employment uses since three of the sites that we looked at include significant commercial floor-space reducing the net residential density. Density guidelines generally do not take into account non-residential uses and so are difficult to apply to mixed-use schemes. Yet the density of people working in an area is just as significant when considering the viability of public transport and the vitality of areas. We have therefore estimated the number of people employed in the area. This is illustrated on the table above which shows a total of 52 500 m² of employment floorspace, a workforce population of 1 400 producing employment densities of 31 workers per hectare.

Urban transport: The most common justification for mixing uses and building to higher densities is the reduction of car use and the promotion of walking, cycling and public transport. Some commentators have questioned research[15] which suggests that people living and working in dense urban areas make less use of their car. However, as we have suggested, car use will inevitably be reduced by regulation, taxation or sheer congestion. The question is therefore not whether the design of urban areas will reduce car

use but whether urban areas can be designed to accommodate a less car-intensive way of life. If this is to work it is vital that the alternatives to the car such as walking, cycling and public transport are available. It is therefore important to design urban areas which ensure that alternative forms of transport are practical, attractive and viable.

The viability of public transport and the walkability of urban areas both impact on urban form. The maximum distance that people are prepared to walk is generally considered to be around 2 000 metres although the optimum is 800 metres (a comfortable ten-minute walk)[16]. Indeed in shopping areas developers use 400 metres as the distance that people will walk with shopping. This means that, to promote walking, distances within the neighbourhood need to be short. The example neighbourhood is approximately 1 000 metres from north to south by 740 metres from east to west so it would take no more than fifteen minutes to walk from end to end and everywhere within the neighbourhood would be easily accessible on foot by all residents. Given that the neighbourhood includes shops, schools, a park, significant employment and other public facilities it should therefore be possible to meet most of their daily needs without using a car.

The second criteria is public transport. The Local Government Management Board's sustainable settlements guide[17] suggests net densities of 100 persons per hectare to support a good bus service. As the table on the previous page shows, this could be achieved with suburban densities if the bedspaces measure is used. However it is also important to consider gross densities across the area and the likely occupancy levels of the housing. The table illustrates how easily this can fall well below 100 persons per hectare even with relatively high net densities.

Energy use: We have also used the neighbourhood to model energy use. Whilst buildings can be made energy efficient wherever they are built, there are some inherent advantages of building within urban areas. Urban terraces and flats have fewer external heat loss walls so that the heat loss for any given level of insulation is lower.

They are also more likely to be sheltered by surrounding buildings. Against this should be set the possibility that they will be overshadowed and the fact that they are unlikely to optimise their aspect to maximise passive solar gain.

However the real advantages in terms of energy efficiency and emissions come with the introduction of Combined Heat and Power systems. We have therefore assumed that the neighbourhood will include a district heating system. This is likely to be more viable in dense urban areas which reduce the distances over which heat and power mains extend minimising thermo-dynamic losses and infrastructure costs. The mix of uses also helps to smooth out the demand profile over the day. Because there is just the one heat source for the neighbourhood, a district heating system would be more efficient than individual boilers in each building, particularly given improvements in heat metering.

However even greater savings could be made by linking the district heating to a Combined Heat and Power system. This would use gas to generate electricity and heat, increasing operating efficiencies to 80–90 % so reducing bills to local residents and businesses. Assuming net densities of 62 units to the hectare the total annual energy requirement of the area would be just under 10 000 MWh for electricity and 18 000 MWh for space and water heating. The CHP plant would be sized to meet the electricity requirement and would therefore require additional boiler capacity to meet winter heat loads. The calculations on CHP undertaken as part of the Sustainable Urban Neighbourhood Initiative[18] show the virtual elimination of SO_2 emissions and a potential reduction in CO_2 emissions of around 40 %.

It has been suggested that further savings could be made by linking the system to a waste incinerator so that a proportion of the heat is generated from locally-produced waste. However again the calculations that we have undertaken show that the calorific value of the waste generated by the housing in the neighbourhood would amount to little more than 2 000 MWh per year which is just 7 % of the district heating requirement. Taking into account the fact that incineration carries the risk of pollution and dioxin emissions and is likely to encounter local resistance, it appears that this is a less attractive option than the recycling of local waste.

Autonomous urban development

One of our concerns in the development of the *sustainable urban neighbourhood* is that too much emphasis has been devoted in recent years to the design and technical specification of individual buildings and not enough to planning at the neighbourhood scale. The model neighbourhood described above has therefore proved very useful in exploring issues such as density, transport and the economics of power use and CHP systems. However if it is to be built we must reconcile these neighbourhood issues with the practicalities of development. We have therefore explored a section of the plan in more detail as illustrated on the following pages. This examines the implications of sustainable urban development on the design of individual blocks. In doing so it starts to develop a new language for sustainable architecture as an alternative to the rural vernacular which has characterised much green architecture to date. At the time we did the work in the late 1990s we were able to show that zero fossil fuel urban development was theoretically possible if not at the time viable. However the government has now set 2016 as a target for all new housing to be carbon free and we have therefore continued to develop the autonomous neighbourhood model to show how this can be achieved. The main characteristics of the plan are described below:

Mixed-use development: The illustration shows a very broad mix of uses both within blocks and across the areas. Blocks 1, 2 and 4 which front main streets are vertically mixed-use with ground and first floor commercial or retail space below housing. Block 3 is an attempt to incorporate manufacturing space into urban areas – responding to a concern that office-based mixed-use development fails to create jobs that are well suited to the skill-base of many inner

Sustainable Urban Neighbourhood

Public transport: Proximity to local public transport routes allows for mobility beyond the neighbourhood without promoting the use of the car

Mixed-use: A mix of uses including housing, offices and workshops as well as potentially retail and leisure uses. Workshops are seen as particularly important to generate jobs for local people

Permaculture: Individual blocks use their communally managed courtyard space for food-growing using permaculture techniques to maximise yield. This would contribute to self-sufficiency, provide a cheap source of food and promote neighbourhood stewardship

Light manufacturing: A sustainable B2 business park based around 'green' entrepreneurship, which stimulates skills transfer and local enterprise, as well as developing markets for appropriate technology. Businesses could include grey water plumbers, solar or CHP distributors, a local recycling company, an organic food retailer, repair companies, or goods manufacturers

Training and enterprise c Skills development and in pa 'green' entrepreneurship are of the neighbourhood appro would form a focal point. Th be to train and educate loca sustainable business practic

Street Trees: Enhances urban microclimate, softens the street and strength-ens vistas and legibility

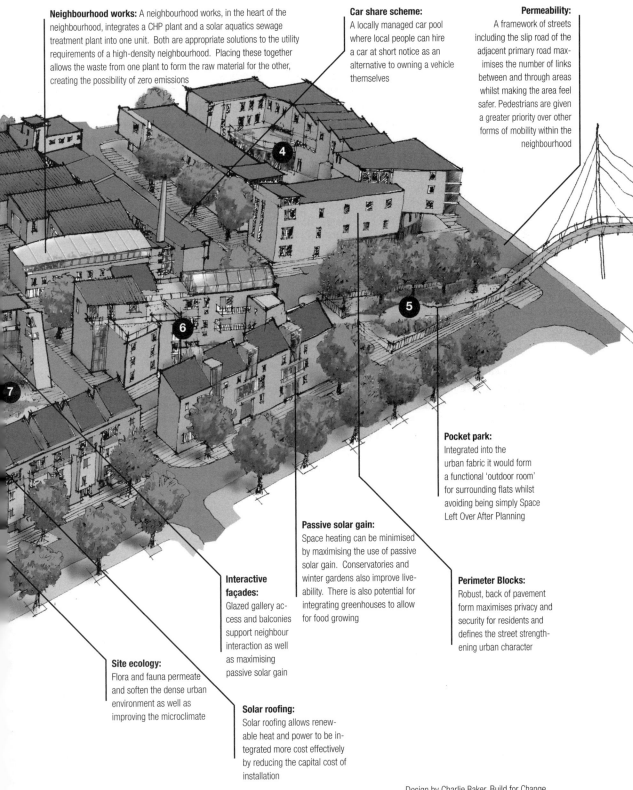

Neighbourhood works: A neighbourhood works, in the heart of the neighbourhood, integrates a CHP plant and a solar aquatics sewage treatment plant into one unit. Both are appropriate solutions to the utility requirements of a high-density neighbourhood. Placing these together allows the waste from one plant to form the raw material for the other, creating the possibility of zero emissions

Car share scheme: A locally managed car pool where local people can hire a car at short notice as an alternative to owning a vehicle themselves

Permeability: A framework of streets including the slip road of the adjacent primary road maximises the number of links between and through areas whilst making the area feel safer. Pedestrians are given a greater priority over other forms of mobility within the neighbourhood

Pocket park: Integrated into the urban fabric it would form a functional 'outdoor room' for surrounding flats whilst avoiding being simply Space Left Over After Planning

Passive solar gain: Space heating can be minimised by maximising the use of passive solar gain. Conservatories and winter gardens also improve liveability. There is also potential for integrating greenhouses to allow for food growing

Interactive façades: Glazed gallery access and balconies support neighbour interaction as well as maximising passive solar gain

Perimeter Blocks: Robust, back of pavement form maximises privacy and security for residents and defines the street strengthening urban character

Site ecology: Flora and fauna permeate and soften the dense urban environment as well as improving the microclimate

Solar roofing: Solar roofing allows renewable heat and power to be integrated more cost effectively by reducing the capital cost of installation

Design by Charlie Baker, Build for Change,
Illustration David Rudlin

city populations. The wider neighbourhood plan therefore suggests the incorporation into the area of manufacturing workshops and the autonomous neighbourhood plan explores their physical form. The concept is to create an urban edge of well-proportioned offices which backs onto a series of workshops within the block. The block also includes a training and enterprise area and a 'bioworks' as described below with the intention that it will be developed as a base for green businesses in areas like recycling and remanufacturing to tap the employment potential of sustainable development. Blocks 6 and 7 also include an element of live/work accommodation.

Urban green space: One of the concerns about urban development is that it lacks landscaping and urban green space. We have therefore used the plan to explore how vegetation and wildlife habitats can permeate the area. This includes a pocket park which is supervised by surrounding buildings and can provide an 'outdoor room' for residents and workers in the area. This however is only part of a wider network of green space which includes courtyards within each block and a variety of roof gardens at different levels as have been incorporated into the Homes for Change development. An important role is also played by street trees which are used throughout the area. A number of the blocks also include balconies, winter gardens and even roof-top greenhouses for cultivation and food growing.

Car use: The green space within the area has been achieved largely at the expense of car parking. We have opted not to go for an entirely car-free neighbourhood because of concerns about the viability of commercial space and also about the danger of deserted pedestrianised streets in inner city areas such as this. However there is no off-street parking other than that which was required by the planners as part of the completed phase of the Homes for Change scheme and service access to the workshops. The plan also incorporates space for a car pool which would ideally be locally managed and which would give residents and workers access to a hired vehicle as an alternative to owning their own.

Housing density: The incorporation of such a wide mix of uses and green space has an impact on the residential density across the area. The Homes for Change scheme achieves net densities of 124 units per hectare as well as being mixed-use and the other residential blocks (2, 4, 6 and 7) aim to achieve broadly similar densities. However the incorporation of the workspace and the park reduce the overall residential density of the area. The area covered is just over 3.6 hectares and it is estimated that the housing yield should be around 300 properties which will give an overall density of 83 units, 200 people or 300 bedspaces to the hectare.

Eco-design: The most radical aspect of the neighbourhood is however its environmental design. The aims are that it should achieve a net balance of CO_2 emissions, that it should eliminate fossil fuel for heat and power, that it should have a closed water system without reliance on the mains or external sewage treatment and that all recyclable waste should be recycled. This is not quite autonomous urban development since the area would still rely upon and provide services to the wider urban area. However it would reduce the neighbourhood's environmental impact to virtually zero.

In our hypothetical scheme this is achieved by wresting control of resources and waste flows to the neighbourhood level as we suggested in Chapter 10. Rather than rely on large centralised systems for power generation, water supply and waste treatment the neighbourhood is designed to provide these services at the local level. This has a number of advantages. It means firstly that full use can be made of natural resources such as solar energy and the rain falling on the site (which in Manchester could potentially provide the entire water needs of the development). Secondly it means that resource systems can be converted from linear to circular systems by using locally generated waste, such as heat, organic matter and domestic waste as resources to be used locally. Thirdly it means that the jobs and economic activity generated by resource consumption can be created locally rather than in distant power stations, or recycling plants and so are available to local people in areas of high unemployment.

At the heart of this local resource system is the combined bioworks and CHP plant illustrated in the centre of the scheme. These would be linked so that the waste from one would form the inputs to the other. This is similar to the system in Kolding in Denmark that we described on page 186. The bioworks is an intensively-managed, solar-aquatic local sewage works processing local waste through a series of controlled tanks in a greenhouse full of plants. It would be fuelled from the sun and also from the surplus heat from the CHP plant. The water from the bioworks could be used for food growing and can also produce compost and harvest methane to fuel the CHP plant. The bioworks and CHP plant are linked to the workshop spaces which would then be let to businesses able to use the outputs of the plant as well as other waste generated locally. The car pool is also part of the block and it is possible that the CHP plant could be used off-peak to recharge electric vehicles.

In addition to this, the neighbourhood incorporates a range of further environmental features. Many of the roofs are made up of photo-voltaic panels to generate electricity, possibly linked to hydrogen storage and fuel cell generation. These panels would help to overcome one of the problems of CHP systems which is that the electricity demand in summer is far greater than the heat load. While the technology is currently expensive, as volumes increase prices should fall and, by using the panels to replace traditional roofing, there is the potential to reduce the overall price by making savings elsewhere. The heat load is also reduced by ensuring that the buildings are highly insulated and by including features such as winter gardens and glazed access balconies on south-facing elevations. The closed water system is also made possible by grey water restoration linked to rainwater collection and it is possible that the water storage tanks could be used as heat stores.

Many of these suggestions remain at an experimental stage. While initial calculations suggest that they are capable of achieving zero carbon development, a non-reliance on fossil fuels and a closed water system, they remain some way from being affordable or viable.

SMITHFIELD – MANCHESTER

There has been a remarkable change in the last few years. The ideas that we have advocated in this book were until recently regarded as radical yet they are now being accepted by mainstream developer. Nowhere is this more apparent than in the illustrated scheme proposed by Ician, a joint venture between Amec and Crosby Homes in Manchester.

This includes buildings by most of Manchester's leading architects including MBLC, Hodder Associates, and Stephenson Bell. The scheme accommodates almost 250 residential units at 60 units to the acre yet most of the ground and first-floor floorspace is in commercial use.

The scheme is now largely completed although unfortunately without the planned environmental measures that had included CHP and a car share scheme.

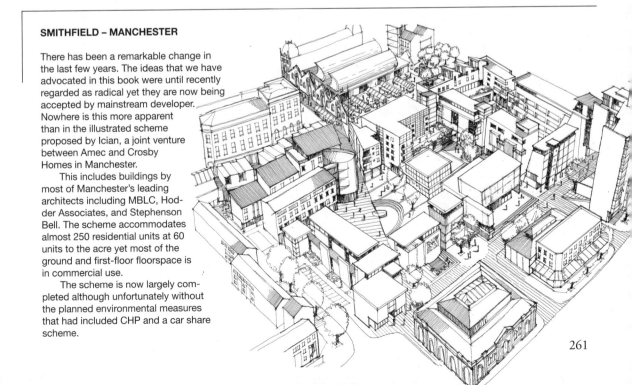

The sustainable urban block

We can be much more certain about one part of the neighbourhood because it has already been built. The first phase of the Homes for Change scheme (Block 1 on the plan) was completed in September 1996 and the second phase in 2000. This was one of the first mixed-use, high-density urban blocks developed in the UK and for more than ten years it has provided a living model of the sort of development that we are advocating. It is also a scheme that I (DR) know intimately since I was a founder member of the co-operative and its secretary for many years. It was also home to URBED's northern office and the Sustainable Urban Neighbourhood Initiative for five years until 2001.

The scheme was developed by the Homes for Change housing co-operative and a sister co-operative, Work for Change, which has developed the workspace. It is a product of its environment and a physical embodiment of the character of the Hulme community that created it. The building dominates the heart of Hulme and is to many a symbol of the area's rebirth. It is based on a recognition that, whilst the Hulme

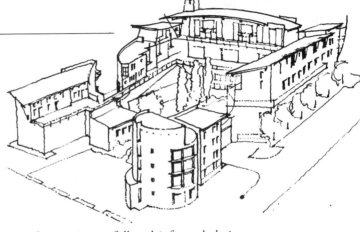

built in the 1960s may have failed, it nevertheless nurtured a strong if unconventional community. This community quite liked the old Hulme, the proximity to the city centre, the size of the flats, the tolerance of the community and the close networks of neighbours. These are the positive aspects of urban living that we are promoting and existed even in the heart of what was considered to be one of the country's most notorious system-built housing estates. With the launch of the City Challenge-funded redevelopment of Hulme, parts of the local community feared that these benefits might be lost and conceived Homes for Change as a lifeboat to preserve at least part of the local community. The co-op sought not to reject the past but to build upon it by rescuing the best points of the old estate. At the same time they used their very practical experience of its failings to ensure that these were not repeated in the new development. In doing this the co-operative created a model for the regeneration of other urban areas that many groups have sought to copy.

The relevance of the Homes for Change model is not so much the architecture of the building, striking as this is, but the process by which it was built. It illustrates that when local people are given a full and informed choice over their environment, the result need not be the blandness which has characterised so much community architecture. It has been suggested that the development is the result of a unique combination of circumstances and people. But the membership of Homes for Change is not untypical. They may have been young and largely childless when the scheme was conceived but so are 40% of UK households and more than 80% of the 4.4 million extra households predicted by the government. What is more, in the few years following the completion of the building the birth rate in the co-operative was phenomenal and the scheme's communal courtyard and roof gardens are now full of children!

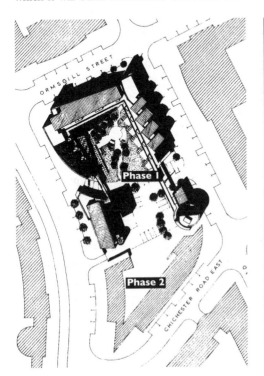

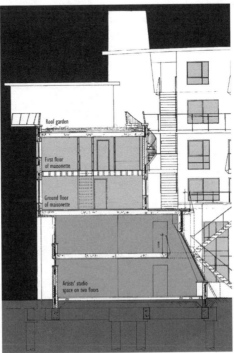

Homes for Change: A site plan showing Phases 1 and 2 of the scheme making a perimeter urban block (left). A section through the building showing the two floors of workspace below the housing and roof garden (right)

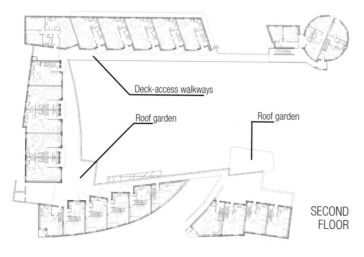

Deck-access walkways

Roof garden

Roof garden

SECOND
FLOOR

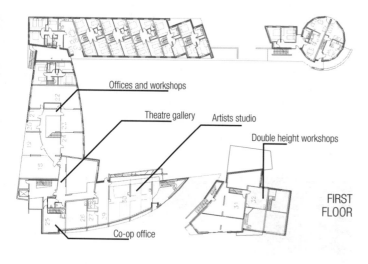

Offices and workshops

Theatre gallery

Artists studio

Double height workshops

Co-op office

FIRST
FLOOR

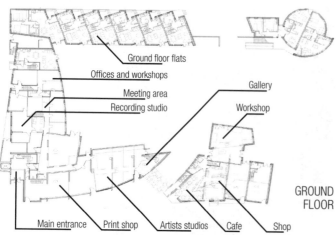

Ground floor flats

Offices and workshops

Meeting area

Recording studio

Gallery

Workshop

GROUND
FLOOR

Main entrance

Print shop

Artists studios

Cafe

Shop

The development of the scheme: The Homes for Change co-operative emerged from Hulme in the late 1980s. Its members spent almost five years working on a scheme to convert a former police station in Central Manchester to flats and workspace. Whilst this project did not happen, it did give the co-op a huge amount of experience. Crucially the co-op was registered with the Housing Corporation, something which few new-build co-ops have achieved since 1988. When it was announced that Hulme was to be redeveloped through City Challenge, Homes for Change was able to turn its attention to its home territory as an already established and recognised co-operative.

Homes for Change was accepted as one of the social housing developers in Hulme and following lengthy negotiations was allocated funding for 75 flats and a site in the heart of the area. However the Housing Corporation as the main funder made it clear that an untried co-operative could not take on what was to become a £4 million development. The members therefore selected the Guinness Trust as development partners. Under the terms of the partnership agreement Guinness was to undertake the development for the co-op whilst co-op members were given the right to be involved in all decisions and to take on ownership on completion if they could raise the necessary finance. This arrangement led to inevitable tensions, however to Guinness's credit, they gave the co-op real control as witnessed by the fact that the building is radically different to anything that a mainstream housing association would normally have developed.

The impetus for mixed-use development: From the start the co-op's vision has been of an urban mixed-use building. This was entirely in line with the strategy for Hulme but was particularly important to co-op members, many of whom were used to working from home and had developed businesses in the space provided by the old Hulme flats. There was a risk that these businesses would be destroyed by redevelopment unless affordable workspace could be provided. Homes for Change therefore planned to incorporate 1500 m² of workspace into the scheme and established a sister co-op, Work for Change, to develop and manage this space. Work for Change is organised like a housing co-operative and is run by its member businesses. It developed a concept of 'self-managed workspace' so that businesses put time into managing the space in return for a reduction in service charges. A feasibility study for the workspace was commissioned from URBED, and funding was secured from City Challenge, the Moss Side and Hulme Task Force and the European Regional Development Fund. As with the housing, there was also a borrowing requirement which is provided by the Guinness Trust until Work for Change is able to raise its own finance. Because the tenants of Work for Change had been members of the group for some time, the workspace was almost unique in being virtually fully let the day it opened.

The design process: After Guinness, the most important appointment was the architects. Whilst the co-op wanted a building which was both 'green' and collectively designed, they took the unusual decision of appointing architects who at the time were specialists in neither of these

areas. The Manchester practice Mills Beaumont Levey Architects were appointed for their design flair and because of their attitude to the co-op, not as a group to be consulted, but as a multi-headed client. The co-op were confident that they knew how they wanted to be involved and were concerned to find consultants who shared their vision and would not be constrained by conventional wisdom.

The design process which followed was one of the most participatory to have been undertaken in recent years. Day-long workshops took place every month for more than a year. In the early workshops members visited schemes around the country and plundered architectural journals to make up style sheets to illustrate the sort of building that they wanted. They made 1:50 Plasticine models of the scheme to explore building forms and worked with larger models to understand the space. The group even made up full-scale models of the flat interiors in a local church hall. Throughout there were disagreements; Guinness for example initially objected to the grass roofs and deck-access walkways, both of which were subsequently incorporated into the scheme. These disagreements were, however, resolved through informed debate within the partnership which took account of costs and management implications. This meant that when members had to drop elements they understood the reasons and in most cases took the decision themselves.

Environmental design: Co-op members were concerned that the building should incorporate

best practice in environmental design. The development became a demonstration project as part of URBED's *21st Century Homes* research for the Joseph Rowntree Foundation[19]. This provided funds to engage environmental consultants ECD, who worked with the group to draw up a range of environmental targets ranging from CO_2 emission to sustainable materials and waste recycling. These targets were monitored through the development process[20]. Seventeen of the targets were met in full and only two: embodied energy and water saving, were not achieved. As part of the development of the scheme a number of environmental features were considered which could not be incorporated into the scheme. These included a grey water restoration system which, because of the attitude of the local water board, would have added almost twice as much to rents as it saved in water charges. Similar problems were experienced with a passive stack ventilation system. The building is therefore 'green', certainly by the standards of the early 1990s when it was designed, but falls short of what many of the co-op members would like to have seen and what is possible today.

The perils of innovation: The Homes for Change scheme innovates on many levels. It is innovative in its layout, design and structure, the co-operative way in which it was built and managed, the mix of uses and its environmental specification. Innovation is always a risk and, when undertaken on this scale, is something that organisations with more experience probably would not have attempted. There were indeed problems, the tenders to build the scheme came in well over budget and savings had to be made quickly by the co-op and its architects. There were a range of problems on site and the scheme was completed over budget and behind schedule. There is always a cost to innovation and everyone involved has paid it heavily. To some this may reinforce the view that the scheme is a one-off. However innovation is only justified if it leads

to lessons being learnt. Phase II of the scheme completed in 2000 added a further 25 apartments to the scheme and was designed by Charlie Baker. This experienced far fewer problems and achieved higher levels of environmental specification. However since then there have not been any other schemes like Homes for Change built. True there have been many mixed-use buildings but none that contains such a mix of uses or that is co-operatively managed. Nevertheless the scheme continues to be visited by communities and students looking for inspiration.

Much of this book has been about the theory of urban development. Those of us who have been involved in the practice of development know that theory is all well and good but is difficult to relate to practical decisions made on the ground within tight timescale and funding constraints. The experience in Manchester, as described in this chapter, illustrates this tension and there are many aspects both of the overall development of Hulme and of the Homes for Change scheme in particular which fall short of the principles that we have been advocating. This is why we used the design exercise described in this chapter to roll forward the redevelopment of the Hulme area to illustrate the type of neighbourhood it could have become. The practical experience thus far does however show that while the principles that we have set out in Part 3 of this book can at times seem to be a statement of the 'bleeding obvious', they can be difficult to implement and their impact on the ground can be very radical. They involve new ways of working and thinking about urban areas and run counter to many powerful professional ideologies and commercial orthodoxies. It is therefore not surprising that they have encountered resistance and that mistakes have been made. However the lessons are being learnt and the impact of these ideas on the future development of Manchester and hopefully other UK cities has been significant.

Chapter 14
The process
of urban generation and regeneration

We may believe passionately in the importance of cities. We may even be able to describe and analyse the characteristics of an urban neighbourhood that make it successful. This we have sought to do in the third part of this book. However putting this passion and knowledge into practice in the creation and recreation of successful urban neighbourhoods is quite another matter. As Elizabeth Plater-Zyberk has said[1]: 'Our predicament is this; we admire one kind of place... but consistently build something very different'.

In this final chapter we therefore explore a process for the creation of successful urban neighbourhoods which can become the building blocks for successful cities. This relies crucially upon an understanding of the economic and social forces outlined in Part 2 of this book and the principles and characteristics described in Part 3. However the genius of city building lies not solely in a vision of physical forms and space but in an understanding of the process by which they are created.

There is a view that the rediscovery of successful urban planning depends solely upon the recognition of the 'timeless principles which underlie successful communities'[2]. Prince Charles in his introduction to the original Urban Village manifesto went on to say that these principles are 'manifest good sense and must surely be plain to anyone' regardless of planning or architectural qualifications. There is an irritation in his words – it is easy, anyone can

see it, why is it that professionals cannot create it? This however is like admiring a fine painting and bemoaning the fact that we have somehow lost the ability to create such masterpieces. We can analyse the qualities that make it great, the composition, execution, symbolism etc... but this knowledge and understanding does not allow us to create a masterpiece. If it did all art critics would be great painters. The creation of greatness requires more than analysis, it requires an element of genius. If the genius of great painting is rare how much more unattainable is the genius of great city building? This is the creation of not just one mind but of thousands and takes place not over days and weeks but over centuries.

Yet for thousands of years this mammoth act of collective genius has come naturally to the human race. People from all cultures have created cities and urban spaces of great beauty, complexity and functionality. What is more this has been achieved effortlessly, almost accidentally and often without the aid of planners and architects or even in some cases any coherent municipal government. The results could be seen as a happy accident if it were not for the fact that such 'accidents' can be found throughout the world and in most human cultures. Indeed many of their characteristics can still be seen in modern unplanned squatters' settlements. Such places can be chaotic and overcrowded with their narrow streets and tightly-packed buildings, but where they have been mellowed by the pas-

Organic development patterns: The natural process of city building creates similar patterns whether it be a squatter settlement in San Paulo (left) or a medieval Italian town

sage of time, as in the towns of northern Italy or the medieval streets of York or Chester, they remain some of our most enduring and popular urban environments. For many years planners and designers have analysed and plundered these historic cities and derived from them the principles of urban design. Yet as Elizabeth Plater-Zyberk points out it has proved almost impossible to apply these principles to modern cities. This is partly because of modern regulations, particularly those concerned with the car. However it is also because urban designers have concentrated on the physical form of these historic places and not the process by which they were created.

There are, of course, many very attractive towns and cities which have been shaped by the firm hand of state. The beauty of Rome and Paris owes much to the visionary plans of Pope Sixtus and Haussmann and cities as diverse as Edinburgh (New Town), New York and Barcelona are based upon strong master plans. However even these cities have been shaped as much by the process of organic growth as they have by the hand of the master planner. The plan has provided little more than the trellis up which the vine of the city can grow. It gives form to the whole and this form can enhance the beauty, function and coherence of the city. But

the trellis does not sustain the vine and many of the world's most beautiful cities have grown organically without such artificial support. The city planner may be able to guide and shape this process of natural growth but cannot replace it. Where this has happened, as in modern planned cities such as Brazilia and, closer to home, new towns in the UK, the result has been to create artificial, soulless places which have not proved popular. It is this process of organic growth that we need to study to rediscover the art of creating successful urban neighbourhoods.

This natural process of urban development has shaped settlements throughout human history until, that is, the 20th century. It is a sad indictment of 20th century planning in Britain that whilst it has been able to protect some of the urban areas of the past it has been unable to create any new urban areas of the same quality. In the 20th century we have created many fine buildings and some fine spaces yet it is difficult to point to any urban neighbourhood created since the birth of town planning which is likely to merit conservation in the future. The dead hand of planning, in its quest to ameliorate the worst excesses of urban development, has managed to eliminate the very characteristics which result from organic urban growth and which make urban areas work. We have sought to tame the city and bring order and logic where once there was confusion. In doing this we have ignored the fact that conflict is part of the very nature of the city. The operation may have been successful but unfortunately the patient has died.

The natural process of urban growth

The author who has done most to analyse and describe the natural process of urban growth is Christopher Alexander[3]. Through his writings he has described how humans have developed a 'timeless way of building' which guides this natural process of creating beautiful places and buildings. In his book *A pattern language* he describes the patterns which lie behind this process and in his book *A new theory of urban design* he applies them to the creation of urban areas. The overriding principle behind this natural process of urban development in Alexander's view is that every action undertaken should take place in such a way so as to heal the city and to make it whole. This wholeness – which can be experienced in urban areas when they feel 'right' – works at every level from the detailed design of buildings to the shape of the whole city. In order to achieve this Alexander suggests seven rules which are required to achieve 'wholeness in urban development':

Piecemeal growth: The whole is too complicated to be created in large chunks so that the grain of development and the time over which it takes place must allow room and time for wholeness to develop.

The growth of larger wholes: The creation of larger patterns and order from urban development develops slowly from the cumulative effect of local decisions rather than being imposed by a plan. When the process starts no one knows what the end result will be but gradually over time the process creates a natural form. Alexander is very uncertain about how this principle can be applied to new development but it is clearly the way that traditional settlements developed.

Vision: Each individual action within an urban area is guided by an 'authentic' or 'heartfelt' impulse of vision which can be communicated to others. This is based not upon consumer surveys or economic returns and cannot be decided by committee. It is rather a sense of what feels right and is intricately tied up in people's experience of an urban area and what is required to make it more whole.

Positive urban space: In making these decisions the natural process of development considers space as a positive quantity rather than the area left over after a building is created. In other words when people create buildings they are thinking as much about the quality of the public realm that they are creating as they are about the design and planning of the structure. In this way the public realm is understood and shaped by the individual decisions of developers which is the opposite of modern development where the roads come first, the footpaths second and the buildings third.

The design and structure of buildings: Rules five and six govern the design, internal layout and structure of buildings so that they too contribute to the creation of the whole.

The formation of centres: The final rule describes the character of centres and how a system and hierarchy of centres is created to give a wider form and structure to urban areas.

The timeless way of building:
An illustration from Christopher Alexander showing the results of a natural process of urban growth

269

In *The Oregon experiment* and *A new theory of urban design* Alexander describes the application of these principles to the design process for a building and an urban area. The latter is based on a site on the San Francisco waterfront where a simulated design exercise was undertaken over a five-year period with Alexander's students. The plan for the area was developed incrementally with individual decisions taken by students and mediated by Alexander based upon the principles outlined above. The result is an organic urban area which is remarkably similar to a medieval city and which has none of the artificiality of a single master plan.

We were involved in something similar in the development of the Smithfield scheme in Manchester (see Page 261). This was designed by a group of six architecture practices. Rather than undertaking an initial masterplanning exercise each practice was given a portion of the site and told to liaise with the designers of adjacent sites to

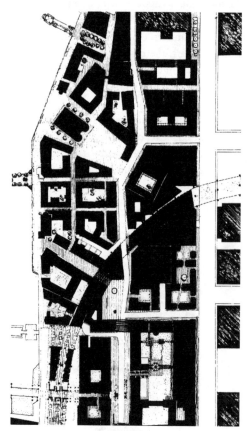

A new theory of urban design: The plan of the completed design for the San Francisco waterfront site developed by Alexander's students as part of a simulated design exercise over five years.

work out issues such as access and the relationship of one building to another. Models were produced for each building which were assembled on the plan of the whole site. Like unplanned development, the result was a scheme which was much denser than a master planner would have dared to create. It was also striking once the models had all been assembled that the scheme looked like a natural piece of the city rather than a master planned enclave. Since we completed the first edition of this book Smithfield Quarter of Manchester has been largely built (although not entirely without a master plan). Nevertheless the end result is a remarkably natural part of the city standing in stark contrast to some of the nearby developments masterplanned by a single architect.

Emergent cities

However, as Alexander admits, the process that he describes in *A New Theory of Urban Design* can throw up many difficulties when applied to the planning and creation of new urban areas. It may be that the theory is more useful as a description of the way in which urban areas were developed in the past than as a practical tool for their creation in the future. The reason for this is that Alexander describes a natural, organic process. Just as in ecology or medicine, our understanding of such processes does not mean that we can or should recreate them artificially.

When we were working on the first edition of this book we were not aware that what we were actually struggling with here is called complexity theory. The natural process of urban growth is explained by Steven Johnson in his 2001 book *Emergence*[4] which is subtitled '*The connected lives of ants, brains, cities and software*'. In this he shows how complex systems emerge from simple elements and in doing so links ant colonies with Jane Jacobs. An ant colony has no hierarchy or leader. Each individual ant is programmed to respond to around 10 pheromone messages from other ants – 'there is food over here', 'run away' etc. Complexity theory suggests that if you take a large number of ants, programmed with such simple instructions and leave them for many generations, the result will be incredibly complex structures and behaviour that will emerge as the process of natural selection is applied not to the individual but the colony.

Johnson applies this theory to the very city that we have used as our working model in this book – Manchester. He describes the explosive growth of Manchester in the first half of the 19th century, as we did in the first part of this book. So swift was this growth that Manchester did not have a municipal government until 1853 by which time it was, in Johnson's words, 'arguably the least planned and most chaotic city in the six-thousand year history of human settlements'. Yet when Friedrich Engels described Manchester in *The Conditions of the Working Class in England*[5] he found amid the insanity of the city a strange kind of order. He noticed in particular that the city had contrived to hide the atrocities of its poor neighbourhoods behind a veneer of respectable shops and houses along the main routes into the city. Engels suspected a plot by the merchants of the city, however as Johnson points out the city was in fact an example of an Emergent system: 'The city is complex because it overwhelms yes, but also because it has a coherent personality, a personality that self-organises out of millions of individual decisions'.

Johnson quotes Jane Jacobs from *The Death and Life of Great American Cities*: 'vital cities have vital innate abilities for understanding, communicating, contriving and inventing what is required to combat their difficulties' and adds himself 'they get their order from below, they are learning machines, pattern recognisers, – even when the patterns they respond to are unhealthy ones'. Complexity theory suggests that if Manchester had been left alone in 1852 it would have developed in a self-organising way over the intervening years to optimise its efficiency. This of course would not have made it a good, beautiful or equitable city (as any worker ant would tell you). However the problem with modern systems of city governance and planning is that they have failed to understand that they are dealing with a self-organising system. Because of this their actions undermine the feedback loops that keep the system working and self-correcting. This fundamental misunderstanding is possibly the one of thing that has done most damage to the modern city.

Self-organising urbanism

Is it possible to apply complexity theory to urban design? Alexander suggests that the feeling 'organicness' that we get from traditional towns is 'not a vague feeling of relationship with biological forms. It is not an analogy. It is instead an accurate vision of a specific structural quality which these old towns had… and have. Namely each of these towns grew as a whole, under its own laws of wholeness… and we can feel this wholeness not only at the largest scale, but in every detail; in the restaurants; in the sidewalks; in the houses, shops, markets, roads, parks, gardens and walls'. What he is saying is that this 'timeless way of building' is a benign self-organising system that shapes human settlements, just as it shapes termite mounds and ants nests. It explains why human settlements across the world are so similar, why the Egyptians, Aztecs and Chinese all developed cities that each would have recognised even though they were not aware of each others existence. In Alexander's view the pheromone signals that govern these self-regulating systems are his seven rules of wholeness, not applied by a remote planning authority but intrinsically understood by the people of a town, its authorities, businesses and its developers.

I (DR) find this easiest to understand by thinking about the French market town of Périgueux which is the home town of Hélène, my wife. I have been visiting Périgueux for more than 25 years and got a sense, in the early days particularly, of what it must have been like to live in a place where these rules were understood. It is a beautiful town about the size of Chester but unlike British towns seems to be 'owned' by its people. In my early visits all of the shops were independently-owned and most of the development was undertaken by local builders, for small-scale local developers. Even the local council seemed responsive to local people. This had something to do with the fact that many of the influential people in the

271

Périgueux where some elements of a natural process of urban development can still be seen

to an extent today, the application of Alexander's principles make much more sense.

It is clearly not the case that local developers in towns like this understand the seven principles of wholeness. They are expressed not as rules but as tradition, an understanding of the town, its people and its history and an empathy with the place. The developments, of course, have to be viable and the developer will be concerned to make a profit, but these will not be the only factors. One of the most powerful factors is peer pressure. Since developers are not faceless their buildings affect their reputation and standing in the town. A good scheme will emphasise their importance and wealth but the opposite is also true if a scheme is poorly built or badly designed. The effects of this process can be seen in the design of shopfronts which are of the highest quality (to emphasise the status of the shopkeeper) and yet respect a series of unwritten but universally understood rules and are entirely in harmony with the character of the town. This contrasts sharply with the situation in most UK towns where the rules of the conservation officer are often very specific and written down but the multiple stores with their corporate designs lack an understanding and empathy with the town so that their shopfronts jar and grate.

There was a time when this process applied to all development in all towns and cities. In the Victorian cities merchants would use local architects to build residences and warehouses for their own use and to emphasise their status. The unwritten rules which guided this development were widely understood and rarely transgressed. They could be seen as the good manners and etiquette of urban development. It is ironic that the understanding of these rules was lost with the introduction of the planning system which took these decisions off the developers and vested them with remote bureaucrats that we now refer to as 'they'.

An important aspect of this natural process of urban development, and the first of Alexander's principles, is incremental change as we advocated in Chapter 12. Traditional urban areas are based upon a continuous cycle of devel-

town lived in the centre including elected officials and council officers. In a British town things are done by faceless developers, national chains and remote councils collectively referred to as 'they'. Who 'they' are is never really specified but the word implies an external force beyond the control of local people. In Périgueux it was more common to hear conversations about what Monsieur X or Madam Y is doing. Monsieur X is building that apartment scheme and his daughter goes to school with W's son and his wife runs the local florist. Development is personalised, even when it is undertaken by the council where it is seen as the mayor's doing. In the new edition of this book I have changed the tense of this sequence because I'm not sure that Périgueux is like this any more although it may be that since the death of Hélène's grandparents and the closure of the electrical shop that they owned, I no longer move in the right circles. However more recently as member of the UK Academy of Urbanism I had the experience of assessing their 'Great Towns Award' and visiting Ludlow and St. Ives as the guest of the great and good of those towns[6]. In both cases something of the spirit that I first saw in Périgueux still exists. In towns such as this, particularly in the past, but still

opment, demolition and redevelopment and at each stage the urban good manners are followed. A continuous cycle of small-scale changes means that there is a fine grain of development and no one, not even the council, has the capacity to buy up large parts of the town for comprehensive re-development. This natural process of incremental change allows the town to evolve gradually in response to changing circumstances and economic conditions, so that it is constantly able to reshape itself, to self-correct, and to meet its needs while retaining a continuity of character.

This raises questions about our ability to conserve historic urban areas. We closely protect the environments which predate modern town planning, from medieval York to Georgian Liverpool and the Victorian splendour of Manchester, lest our incomprehension of the principles which made them would destroy the very thing that we cherish. Yet the principles which shaped these areas are not static but fluid. They are (were) based upon this constant cycle of demolition and renewal, and our efforts to protect them by conserving everything or insisting that new buildings are an artificial pastiche of their historic neighbours runs the risk of atrophying these areas and turning them into museum pieces cut off from the forces which have historically shaped them. The same lack of understanding of process lies at the root of our inability to build successful new urban areas.

How we lost the art of city building

The first part of this book was devoted to the reasons why we lost the art of urban development. We described how in the pre-industrial city there was a natural tendency for people and activity to gravitate towards the centre of towns and cities and how this created a rich, dense and attractive urban form. We looked at how the pressures created by the Industrial revolution placed intolerable pressures on this traditional form of city building and caused people to flee urban areas creating the engine of suburban sprawl. We also explored how many of the urban professions grew up to address the problems that the Industrial revolution created in towns and cities, such as overcrowding, insani-

tary conditions, pollution and congestion. These gave birth to the two main philosophies that have shaped urban areas in the 20th century, the garden city and the modernist Utopias. All of these factors contribute to our inability today to develop urban areas as we did in the past.

We have however argued that these trends are being reversed and that environmental, demographic and social pressures are leading us towards a rediscovery of the value and importance of urban living. We have also described the characteristics of sustainable urban neighbourhoods capable of responding to these trends and creating urban areas fit for people to return to. However we should not make the mistake of believing that there is one correct model for urban areas and that our troubles would be at an end if only we could discover it. The key is not to find the right physical model but to discover, or rediscover, the natural process of city building that we have been describing in this chapter that will enable a city to naturally work towards and to constantly reshape the physical model which best meets its needs. There are, however, many powerful barriers which block this natural process of urban development:

Planning policy: The first of these barriers results from the policies and attitudes which still live on in many parts of the planning system. As we have described in this book, while many of the Utopian models of 20th century planning have been discredited their legacy lives on in the minutiae of planning policy. These include policies on residential amenity, the promotion of public open space, the zoning of different uses and the creation of an efficient transport network. While taken individually these policies seem perfectly reasonable, their cumulative impact can be to undermine the character of urban areas and to distort the natural process of urban growth.

A fragmented approach: As Rob Cowan has suggested, one of the reasons why these attitudes are perpetuated is the fragmentation of the development industry. In his pamphlet *The Connected City*[7] he suggests that ever since the 'big bang' created by Ebenezer Howard and Patrick Geddes the professionals that deal with urban areas have been 'flying away from each other at unimaginable speed'. He writes that 'from their distant planets they [architects, engineers, developers, planners and politicians] now beam messages to the rest of the universe in the strange language that they have evolved and wonder why there is no reply'. Each of these players is responsible for a small part of the urban fabric and has evolved a professional philosophy which optimises its performance from their perspective. But they have no responsibility for the whole and a poor understanding of the motivation of other players. Engineers are concerned to ease congestion and reduce accidents, housebuilders to cater for the aspirations of buyers, developers to maximise the return on their investment and planners to minimise the impact of all this development. It is hardly surprising that this leads to conflict and makes it so difficult to develop a coherent approach to urban areas.

End-state plans: This is compounded by the way that we plan urban areas. There has long been a debate about the way that public policy should influence urban areas. There was a great deal of interest in the 1970s in the concept of cybernetics in which the process of planning and the process of urban development ran side by side with the former seeking to influence and guide the latter. However it is easier to think in terms of end-state plans be they an adopted local plan or a master plan drawn up for a development. Such end-state planning starts with a decision about how a process will end – what the area will be like in the future – and then works towards achieving this vision. If this master plan is confined to the trellis on which the city can grow, as in Haussmann's Paris, it can be positive, particularly if it creates confidence and certainty. However many plans tend to be much more prescriptive than this and define not only the framework but the type of uses and the design of buildings to be developed as part of the plan. Many very talented architects have produced 'exciting' master plans as if the master plan were a building that can be conceived

and built in a single building contract under the guiding hand of one designer. In the rare cases where this has happened it tends to lead to very sterile environments. However the size of most master plans means that they are implemented over many years by different architects and even by different developers. In such cases the prescriptive end-state vision is of limited utility and is almost inevitably undermined before it is complete. Such plans work against the natural process of urban development.

Negative planning: The final problem with the planning system is that it only really has the ability to say no. The planning system established by the 1947 Town and County Planning Act was based on the assumption that the majority of developments would be undertaken by the public sector. At the time four out of five new homes were being built by councils or in new towns. When the act created local planning authorities and required them to develop five-year plans for their area it was therefore assumed that they would also have the power to implement these plans directly[8]. At the same time development land rights were nationalised and private developers were required to apply to the local authority for permission to develop or change the use of land.

The situation since 1947 has changed radically and the vast majority of new development is now undertaken by the private sector. A system designed to deal with a small rump of non-public sector development has therefore become the main tool to shape the pattern of settlements. This has set up a conflict between the development industry and the planning system. The public and the development industry seems to regard planners as all powerful. While they do often wield considerable influence on the detail of development much of this influence is exerted through a process of persuasion and bluff using the threat of a refusal of planning permission to get the developer to comply. However when their bluff is called planners are exposed as having relatively limited powers of refusal because the risks of appeal means that only the very worst applications are refused. While the threat of refusal will persuade most small developers to comply with the planner's wishes this is less true of larger developers with the resources to take on the system. It also works less well in areas of decline where local authorities are keen to promote development and are therefore reluctant to refuse anything that brings investment into the area. Planning in the 20th century therefore became a negative process designed to prevent the unacceptable rather than to promote the best. It has proved itself lamentably ill-equipped to deal with the issues of urban good manners described above.

Attempts have been made to change this in recent years through the new planning system in England and Wales introduced through the Planning and Compulsory Purchase Act 2004. This replaced the Unitary Development Plans that all local authorities had been required to draw up for their area with a two tier system of more flexible *Local Development Frameworks* covering the whole district and more master plan-based *Area Action Plans* for areas of change. These reforms grew out of the work of the Urban Task Force and its faith in the value of masterplanning. Area Action Plans hold out the prospect of a welcome return to the age of Abercrombie when planners actually drew beautiful plans. However there is within the system a danger of end-state planning and it remains based on the stick of planning refusal that many local authorities remain reluctant to use.

We may by now have managed to irritate most of those involved in the planning and design of urban areas. But this is not an argument against planning or planning professionals. While the natural process of development that we have described could be seen as the product of capitalism unconstrained by planning law, we need look no further than the cities of the tiger economies that emerged in the 1990s to see that the commercial forces that created the medieval city or indeed Victorian cities like Leeds and Manchester are now so strong that they dwarf the capacity of even the greatest cities to control and shape

them. This is not a phenomenon confined to the Far East. Similar forces can be seen at work in the UK. In the 1980s the Conservative government introduced Enterprise Zones, part of which included a relaxation of planning controls on the assumption that the dead hand of planning was stifling entrepreneurship. The result was not well-mannered urban development but the excesses of Canary Wharf.

Something has changed and we can no longer rely upon the natural forces of development to produce successful urban areas. The developers, financial institutions and international companies who shape the modern city are very different to those who built the traditional city. They are rarely based in the city nor are the banks and financial institutions who provided the funds. Buildings are developed for occupation by others and, in a global market, international design styles rather than local character hold sway. It is not that the pace of change has accelerated because even today there is little to rival the explosive urban growth of the Industrial revolution. What has changed is the view that developers take of the future. Whereas in the past developers built monuments to themselves which they expected to last forever, today investors are concerned with the investment return over ten or, at most, twenty years so that the building becomes a disposable commodity.

This remains true although interestingly one of the positive aspects of Manchester's regeneration has been the emergence of a series of developers based in the city such as Urban Splash, Artisan, Ask and Igloo. These developers together with a strong group of local architects has led to a new confidence and pride in design in the city. This perhaps explains why Manchester has emerged from the market boom of the early 2000s with a better set of buildings than cities like Leeds and Birmingham.

Is planning the problem?

It is not easy to recreate the natural process of urban development. One day we might get back to a point where Alexander's rules are understood and respected – at which point maybe we won't need planners any more. Indeed in the first edition of this book we postulated that one way of creating a dense mixed-use urban area would be to establish a street network, divide each of the urban blocks into small plots of say a quarter of an acre and to auction these blocks while removing the requirement for planning permission. The idea was that the urban form of traditional places is not the result of planning controls but the constrains imposed by the site. If sites are small and hemmed in by other buildings and land is valuable then there is little option but to build densely and to the back of pavement if development is to be viable. If these circumstances were recreated artificially there may be less need for planning controls. The auction of a series of small sites within an existing street framework could do this. The size of sites would create a fine urban grain, would promote a variety of development and allow a range of smaller developers to

Small sites tend to promote high-density development:
The size of sites and the way that they are hemmed in by development in many traditional towns and cities makes urban development almost inevitable as in Mychull House near the Cathedral in Manchester

participate. It would also create the robustness discussed in Chapter 12 since any mistakes that were made would be small and easily repaired.

Since the first edition of this book was published something of the kind has been tried in various places. In a number of Dutch new towns free planning zones have been created where small plots have been sold to developers with minimal planning controls. Developers are required to respect the building line and to join their building to those on adjacent sites but can otherwise build whatever they wish. In Borneo Quay in Amsterdam a similar process was used to create a row of houses, each of which is different and which looks remarkably like a traditional Amsterdam waterfront. In Manchester Urban Splash is trying something similar in its Tutti Fruitti scheme as part of the New Islington development. A row of plots is being sold off to individuals to design and build their own home although they will still need to apply for planning permission.

The assumption behind such experiments is that urban form cannot be imposed through rules but will emerge naturally from the parameters that developers face. If the parameters are carefully prescribed, urban form will just sort of appear. This is of course what happens in existing urban areas, when a particular site comes up for development. The size of the site and the constraints imposed by the surrounding buildings mean that developers have little option but to build a well mannered urban building. The difficulty is when there is no built context or constraints as in comprehensive redevelopment areas or urban extensions. Here the planning-free approach would be a considerable leap of faith. The examples in Amsterdam and the Urban Splash scheme in Manchester rely on careful orchestration by the developer and may have limitations if applied more widely.

The problem may in any case not be the concept of rules but the type of rules that have been used. Ever since the introduction of bylaw housing, the planning system has been writing practical rules about how urban areas should function; how to get sun to the homes, to

allow parking for cars, to provide access for the fire engine and bin truck and to create amenity space for the residents etc. The physical form of the neighbourhood was an accidental and even unintended consequence of all of these practical rules – more often than not it was the suburban cul-de-sac. We cannot set aside these rules – bins still need emptying, cars need parking, fires need putting out and developers indeed cannot always be trusted to be concerned about the amenity of residents. However we do need to stop these rules undermining urban quality, indeed we need to make them subservient to the rules of urbanism.

The rules of modern planning currently make it impossible to built the sort of urban environments that we find in say York or Périgueux. Yet in these places which break all the rules, the bins still get emptied, fires are put out and, while not all of the cars can be parked, the residents are happy to make do. In such historic urban areas it is not that the practical rules have been set aside, they have simply become subservient to the urban form of the area. Life goes on,

services are supplied, people get by. Life may not be quite as convenient as it would if all of the practical rules were optimised but it is richer and more interesting.

New rules

As we have said, there may come a day when the rules of urbanism are so ingrained that they don't need to be written down. Until that day rules are going to be necessary, something that has been pursued in recent years through urban design guides. The *Hulme Guide to Development*[9] that we described in the last chapter was one of the first to be produced in the UK and it is worth dwelling in a little more detail on its potential as a new approach to planning. One of the most important aspects of the Hulme redevelopment was that it was decided not to have a master plan thereby avoiding the pitfalls of end-state planning. Instead a framework of streets was established (the vine on which development could grow) with development being brought forward incrementally within this framework. However,

Borneo Quay in Amsterdam:
A terrace of houses each designed by a different architect but respecting a set of simple rules

without a plan, there was a problem of how new development could be made more urban in character. In existing urban areas the principles of development are implied by the buildings and public spaces that surround a site. These will, for example, set the building line, the position, height and massing of the new buildings and thus their contribution to the public realm. In a redevelopment area like Hulme where no built context existed, the role of a design guide is to artificially recreate this context. The Hulme guide contains ten core principles which are developed into 53 guidelines. These are stated in simple but specific terms such as 'all streets should terminate in other streets' or 'doors onto streets should be at no more than 15 metre intervals'. The guide goes into far more detail than is possible through traditional planning control and could only be enforced in Hulme because the council had land ownership and grant-making as well as planning powers. It was initially seen by many developers as over-prescriptive and a potential disincentive to development. However the experience of implementing it on the ground has been that this was not the case. The guide, for example, says nothing about the architecture of buildings, the materials to be used or their elevational treatment, all areas normally of concern to develop-

The Duany Plater-Zyberk approach: The regulatory plan (below) sets a framework for different development types. Detailed guidance is set out in a series of graphic codes (facing page).

ment control planners. It establishes instead an envelope into which buildings must fit in terms of their position, height and orientation. If this is done then developers, in fact, have more freedom of design and detailing than they would be given by traditional development control as testified by the very wide variety of traditional and modern buildings that have been developed in Hulme.

A similar approach has been adopted by the new urbanists in the US through the work of Duany and Plater-Zyberk [10]. They have developed a system of urban ordinances and codes which have come very close to recreating traditional urban form. As they state: 'In a town built without the benefit of centuries or a diversity of founders, the codes encourage variety whilst ensuring the harmony required to give character to a community'. This method is based on a master plan but only to illustrate the way that the settlement might develop and to determine the location of the centre and sub-centres as well as the network of streets. The master plan is developed into a street plan showing a hierarchy of different streets as well as defining building plots which are small enough to ensure that buildings face onto these streets. Each of the streets is drawn in section showing the width between building lines and the character of each space. The next stage is to develop a regulating plan which designates each building plot for a particular type of development. This does not refer to the land use of the site but to the form of development, its height and position. A series of detailed guidelines are then set out as graphic codes which specify everything from the design of streets to the height, massing and position of buildings down to the detailed design and materials to be used. These codes are presented as matrices (above) so that each street and building type can be related to the different areas designated on the regulating plan.

This 'paint by numbers' form of urban coding is much more prescriptive than the Hulme Guide but it is nevertheless very different to a traditional master plan. Compare it, for example, to the plan by Ralph Erskine for the Millennium Village in Greenwich (see page 134). In the case of Greenwich we knew from the plan

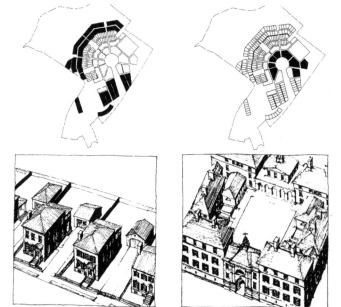

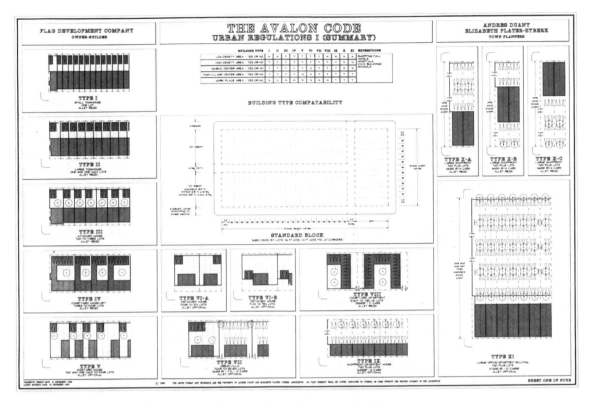

what would be built where, when it would happen and how it would look. The Duany Plater-Zyberk approach by contrast creates a framework which can be developed gradually by a wide range of small developers over a number of years. This is actually very similar to the traditional way in which parts of Victorian London were developed, as described in Chapter 4. In developing estates like Bloomsbury, landowners would commission a master plan, lay out the streets and then write a series of rules for development that would be imposed through the leaseholds sold on each of the sites. I (DR) own a house in the Whalley Range suburb of Manchester (see Chapter 2) that was developed in this way. The deeds to my house still include the rules written for the neighbourhood – such as a prohibition in erecting any structure within 15ft of the pavement (to protect the building line) – that are still binding on me 170 years after they were written.

The only application of the Duany Plater-Zyberk approach in the UK was the development of Poundbury in Dorset (see page 176)

where it was made easier because the land was owned by the Duchy of Cornwall. Its strength in the US has been that the plan and code is developed in close partnership with the local community through a week-long *Charette*. This involves the establishment of a team on site who work closely with local architects, developers and other professions and run a series of intensive workshops with local people. In small town America this means that the whole community is able to influence the plan, can understand why it has been done and can sign up to the vision that it contains. Given that the community in these small towns will also include the local developers a consensus is created which overcomes local resistance.

This may not work in the UK but urban design guide are playing an increasing role in creating a new role for planning. A number of design guides or codes have been produced in the UK, including the government's publication By Design[11], English Partnership's Urban Design Compendium[12] and various publications by CABE such as the Building for Life criteria[13]. Many local areas have also successfully used design guidance to shape development and the increasing use of design review panels.

The role of masterplanning

It is not however enough to change the rules. It is important to reconsider the way that development takes place. This happens at a variety of levels, from the planning of the entire city by the local authority to the masterplanning of urban quarters and the design of individual sites. The reform of the planning system is something that is being tried in the UK with the new system of Local Development Frameworks and Area Action Plans. It is too early to assess the success of this system, that will have to wait for a further edition of this book. However considerable progress has been made at the more local scale through masterplanning and site briefs.

Public sector masterplanning: As urban designers URBED have developed many master plans for local authorities. This can be a frustrating process because the plan may garner support but there is little understanding in the local authority of how they can be implemented. It is however still possible for local authorities to master plan in the way that the city planners of the past did – it is just not done very often. One of the rare examples was Crown Street in Glasgow[14] (see page 206). Here a master plan was commissioned from

the Architect Piers Gough, the role of which was to establish the street network and public spaces of the area. Once this had been done the area was divided into a series of development plots which, unlike Hulme, did not generally include entire urban blocks. Detailed briefs were written for each of these development plots. These briefs indicated a strip down the front of the site where the front wall of the building was to be positioned along with the positions of entrances and the points to be emphasised with landmarks. They also specified the height of the blocks and where parking was to be accommodated but otherwise said nothing about the design of the buildings. Like the Hulme guide this created an envelope for development without being prescriptive about design. The next stage was to hold a seminar with potential developers to explain to them the vision for the area. Then the sites were put out to competitive tender. Crucially this was on the basis of a fixed price and grant requirement. Hence the only factor determining which scheme was selected was the quality of the development which gave the tenderers a real incentive to invest in design. The successful developers were sold the site with conditions tying them to their winning scheme. The result in Crown Street works and is a worthy successor to developments from the past such as Edinburgh New Town.

This form of public sector masterplanning is however rare. At URBED we have tried to develop the process in a way that can be used

Detailed development briefs: An example of one of the development briefs from Crown Street and the completed development.

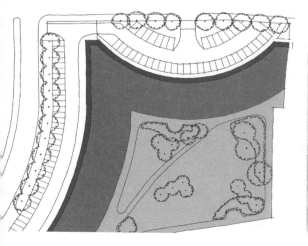

in the planning system. In Bradford, for example, (see page 212) we developed an Urban Design Guide for the city centre[15] that was based upon the master plan drawn up by Will Alsop[16]. The guide sought to establish a building line for the entire city centre and, like the Crown Street briefs, defined a three-dimensional envelop for development. This has been successful on some sites but the inevitable conclusion is that the UK Planning system is not well suited to this type of three-dimensional masterplanning. The only really successful examples of the 'new' rules being implemented have been where the local authority has the powers of land ownership – planning powers alone are not enough. It is therefore important to consider the private sector's role in using master plans.

Private sector masterplanning: There has been a tendency by the private sector to see masterplanning as big architecture. Developers have commissioned architects to develop plans who have approached the task in the same way as they would a single building. There can be a role for this, but it runs a number of risks. On the rare occasions where master plans are realised by a single architect – such as the More London scheme next to Tower Bridge by Norman Foster or Rem Koolhaas's Grand Palais around the Eurostar terminal in Lille – the result can be overbearing and even slightly dull. However more often than not, the master plan lacks the flexibility to respond to changing circumstances over the years that it takes to implement so that the original vision is undermined.

Masterplanning is not architecture and should not be left to architects. Listen to Koolhaas talking about Lille; 'the representation of the contemporary city is no longer determined by a ceremonial opening of gates, by the ritual of procession and parades, nor by a succession of streets and avenues. From now on architecture must deal with the advent of a technological space time'17. This is the sort of twaddle that creates disastrous master plans! Masterplanning is, or at least should be, a very different discipline to architecture, one that moulds and shapes the natural process of urban growth into

something beautiful, rather than surplanting it with the ego of an individual architect. This is what Haussmann did in Paris, Cerdà in Barcelona and Nash in various parts of the UK. As we have described, the historic master plans that they developed were based on a framework of streets and a set of rules for development which could then be allowed to come forward over time within the street framework. It is possible to apply this process to modern development. Indeed this is what we at URBED have been doing for the last ten years in a series of master plans for private developers. These include the Bristol Temple Quay scheme (page 234), the Southall Gasworks scheme (page 203), East Ketley Millennium Village in Telford, the Sheffield West Bar scheme (inside front cover), the Marshall's Mill in Leeds (inside back cover) and the Brighton New England Quarter on the next page. Each of these schemes has been developed through the outline planning application system in the UK. This establishes the principle of a development but doesn't consider detailed designs (which is considered in subsequent 'Reserved Matters' applications). There was a time when all developers had to do for an outline planning application was to draw a red line around the site and list the uses that they wanted to build. This is no longer possible and planning authorities need to see a master plan to show how the uses can be accommodated. The problem in the past has been that master plans drawn up as part of the outline planning process have not been binding and have been ignored in subsequent applications by developers.

URBED has developed a process for outline planning applications that is very similar to the historic process of masterplanning. We too start with an *Illustrative* plan that shows how the area could look and which is used to explore the scheme. This, however, cannot be binding because it goes into far more detail than can be fixed in an outline planning application. The Illustrative plan is therefore broken down into a *Regulatory* plan that covers only the issues to be fixed in the outline planning consent. This includes the position and status of the roads

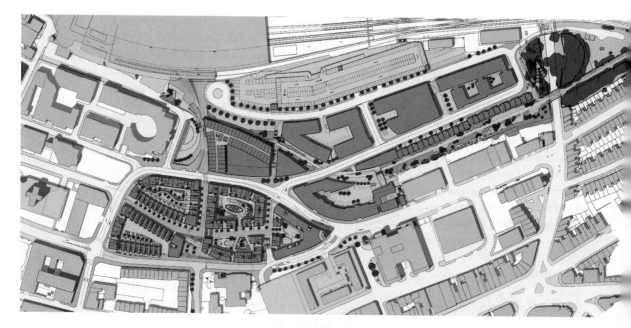

BRIGHTON NEW ENGLAND QUARTER

The former goods yards next to Brighton Station had lain vacant for 30 years. Plans in the late 1990s to build a superstore on the site were refused following a campaign by local people. One local group argued that the site should be developed as a Sustainable Urban Neighbourhood as advocated in the first edition of this book. Within a year we were asked to master plan the site, URBED's first major private sector master plan.

The master plan was developed over three years and incorporating the supermarket in the base of a residential block freeing up the rest of the site for a high-density mixed-use scheme. This included 261 residential units, a language school with accommodation for 400 students, a four star and a three star hotel, a training centre, health and fitness club, offices, workspace and community uses. Unfortunately the community opposition did not abate because of the continued presence of the supermarket.

The scheme was initially drawn up as an illustrative plan (top) which described the intention of the development. This was broken down into a regulatory plan (Centre) which fixed the key parameters of each building and was the basis for the planning consent. This process is designed for the Outline Planning system in the UK and is similar to the way that master plans were coded in the past. The resulting development (bottom) is remarkably similar to the approved master plan, something that is surprisingly rare in the UK

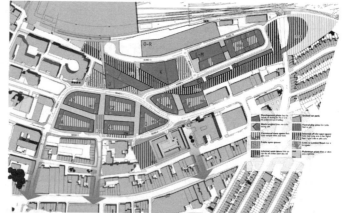

and public realm, the primary building line for each of the development plots, the means of access, the height and the use. These are the same rules that formed the basis for the masterplanning of Paris and Barcelona. The plan establishes a three-dimensional envelope into which future buildings can be built. However rather than fixing the rules in leasehold conditions, we have used outline planning consents. This allows each plot to be brought forward as individual reserved matters applications, preferably by different architects and even sometimes by different developers. Masterplanning is a long process by necessity. However the first two master plans that we developed in this way, Temple Quay in Bristol and The New England Quarter in Brighton, are largely complete and the process has worked. The master plan as prescribed by the outline planning consent has been robust yet flexible enough to respond to changing circumstances and the schemes have developed in a way that feels like natural pieces of city rather than artificial insertions.

New life for urban Britain

In the late 1990s when we produced the first edition of this book the great debate was about how to accommodate the need for 4.4 million homes over two decades without building on large parts of the countryside and in doing so also regenerate our cities. We argued that to achieve this the settlement pattern of the UK needed to change. This has happened to an extent far greater than even we expected. After a century or more of dispersal and suburbanisation, forces have been at work over the last ten years that have started to repopulate British towns and cities and to rediscover new forms of urban development such as the sustainable urban neighbourhood. In the first edition of this book we were mixing prediction with advocacy; we were describing trends that we could see at work but also advocating that these trends should be encouraged. Since that time there has been an extraordinary change in the UK – urban areas have been through a remarkable renaissance and the amount of new housing

build on green field sites has been drastically cut, particularly in the North.

It is too early to assume that this change is permanent, particularly as we enter recession. The fact is that green field housing was cut back to a greater extent than urban housing was expanded. As a result we have consistently built fewer homes than are needed to accommodate household growth. This in turn has led to housing shortages and has inflated houseprices. This housing price bubble, particularly with the city centre apartment market, has meant that the UK housing market has been particularly badly hit by the 2008 Credit Crunch as we work on this edition of the book. The worry is that the slump in prices, the difficulties faced by the housebuilding industry and the worries of government about housing shortages will cause the hard-won gains of the last ten years to be reversed. If so we will have been given a glimpse of the renaissance of urban Britain only to have it snatched away from us. Our hope is that something more fundamental has changed and that the underlying demographic, social, economic and environmental forces that we have described in this book will continue the transformation of Britain back into an urban nation.

It is just over a hundred years since Ebenezer Howard published *Tomorrow: a peaceful path to real reform*. The impact of this work, and the early garden cities that it inspired, on the public and professional consciousness cannot be underestimated. Howard saw cities as 'ulcers on the face of our beautiful island' and for much of the intervening hundred years people in Britain have tended to agree with him. Howard's ideas struck a resonant chord in the times in which he lived, but times have moved on. Since his time, towns and cities in Britain have changed out of all recognition. They are less crowded, less polluted, greener and support a quality of life undreamed of at the end of the last century. However the changes have not all been positive. Urban areas have sprawled over the countryside rather than been integrated with it as Howard proposed. As cities have expanded congestion and environmental degradation have spread and while the quality of life for the many may have improved a significant minority have been left behind. The urban evils of dirt, overcrowding and pollution may have been overcome but crime and poverty have proved more resilient to reform and new urban problems such as drug dependency, unemployment and economic collapse emerged in the inner city towards the end of the century, arguably caused by the trends that Howard set in motion. Howard was responding to the runaway growth of urban areas whereas at the end of the century our problem was to stem their decline.

We have tried to learn from the way in which the Garden City changed the way cities were built. Initial model settlements such as Bournville and Hampstead Garden Suburb were coalesced by Howard into a movement still championed today by the Town and Country Planning Association. The movement was endorsed by official reports and enshrined in government policy particularly with the early development of mass council housing in the 1920s. However what really made a difference was the change in the market responding to demographic, social and economic change which led to the explosion of suburbia in the 1930s.

We are mid way through a similar change: Our models have been built – Poundbury, Hulme, Greenwich Millennium Village

– our official report written (the Urban Task Force) and government policy has changed. But has the market changed? That might be slightly too early to call. Certainly housebuilders have changed the way they do business. They are no longer reliant exclusively on green field suburbia but have expanded into different markets and refocused their efforts onto urban sites. This however remains a policy response, they are building urban neighbourhoods because the government has made it difficult to do otherwise. If government policy were to be relaxed, as well it might if Conservatives win the next election, it is quite possible that the market and the housebuilding industry will slide back into its old ways. We are perhaps half way through the transformation that we predict and it is too early to declare the change permanent.

The ideas that lay behind the garden city were a powerful influence on the policies and professional attitudes which shaped our cities in the 20th century. As the world changes it would be a retrograde step to allow the recent renaissance of urban areas to unravel. The garden city has served us well but we need new models if we are to build the 21st century home. In this book we have described how this could take place and how new models could emerge, such as the sustainable urban neighbourhood, to give a new lease of life to urban Britain.

One of URBED's largest master plans for Liverpool's Knowledge Quarter including the city's two Cathedrals, three universities and the main hospital (masterplanned separately by Taylor Young).

The aim of the plan was to show the potential for large-scale urban repair and restructuring of the shatter zone that encircles much o f the city centre.

Epilogue
Nicholas Falk

Building Sustainable Urban Neighbourhoods

'A successful city neighbourhood is a place that keeps sufficiently abreast of its problems so that it is not destroyed by them.' Jane Jacobs[1]

'Three critical factors have determined the overall health of cities – the sacredness of place, the ability to provide security and project power, and last, the animating role of commerce.' Joel Kotkin[2]

The collapse of the housing bubble in 2008, the longer term effects of the 'credit crunch' and the emerging global recession will make it hard to keep the mission of building sustainable communities alive. There seems to be neither the finance nor the will to overcome the forces of inertia. Yet the need to improve and expand our housing stock is as great as ever. We have a growing population and one where half of people will be elderly. Unemployment is escalating. Properly planned, housing could be used to restart the economy and create a fairer society. It could also address the impact of climate change by helping to save energy and other scarce resources.

It is easily forgotten how Britain has led the way in the past. Between 1750 and 1800 Britain accounted for 70% of urban growth in the world. By 1881, when Arnold Toynbee coined the term the 'Industrial revolution', the majority of the population already lived in large cities (a position reached by the rest of the planet 120 years later). At the start of the 20th century the idea of the garden city was widely copied, as was the idea of new towns after the Second World War. But in the last three decades we have lost our way, despite urban White Papers in 1977 and 2000 which sought to provide direction. The figures for house building clearly show the failure of the private sector to take the place of government, once cutbacks started under the Thatcher government in the early 1980s.

We therefore need not only new products with wider appeal in what is now the age of the Internet, but also new models for delivery that can respond to local circumstances. Local government has become discredited as a result of the failures of large housing estates. The conventional British (and American) model of relying on the private sector to lead development has also clearly failed. Both governments and financial institutions are now widely distrusted to provide the necessary leadership. As a result our cities could easily sink into depression and lose the resolve to build again. Like leaking supertankers headed for the rocks, our cities are slow to respond to instructions from the bridge, and the waters are poorly charted.

This end piece to the second edition of Building the 21st Century Home therefore seems the right place to draw together URBED's experience of three decades of urban regeneration. Others have brought out the importance of the concepts such as 'emergence' through which ideas are spread, of the 'critical mass' needed before take-off, and of the 'tipping point' which stops things returning to equilibrium. However it is Jarel Diamond in his great study of why civilisations collapse[3] who warns us of the dangers of failing to adapt. To quote Jane Jacobs again, 'Cities have the capability of flourishing because and only when they are created by everybody.' It is therefore important to catch the tide. There are, in my view, three main waves that characterise the British experience over the last thirty years, the discovery of inner cities and urban regeneration; a shift towards urban renaissance in the centres of the largest cities; and the drive to build sustainable communities. We are now entering a fourth wave where we need to close the gaps with European cities by changing the way we procure development and engage communities in the building of urban neighbourhoods.

Urban regeneration discovered
Disillusionment with the results of postwar planning, as well as levels of productivity and investment that lagged far behind the rest of Europe, meant that there was little enthusiasm for cities when we set up URBED in 1976. There was a reluctance to raise funds for investment through increased taxation. The starting point for urban regeneration was therefore making better use of wasted resources such as empty buildings and waterfronts, and encouraging small enterprise to colonise abandoned areas. These ideas were first tested out in Rotherhithe in London's Docklands, and then set out in a Fabian Pamphlet on the Inner City. The pamphlet brought out the idea of a vicious circle of economic decline, physical decay and social polarisation. It called on local government to lead the process of regeneration by promoting local economic development[4]. It led to David (now Lord) Sainsbury backing the setting up of URBED, with initial projects in Covent Garden and then North Southwark.

Over the last three decades many inner city areas that once depended on local industry have found new roles. Agreements between central and local government focused additional resources on areas that had the highest levels of deprivation. Competitive bids for City Challenge provided sums of over £50 million for comprehensive programmes. There were some real successes in cities such as Leicester, with the expansion of universities into inner city areas. A combination of ethnic groups and middle classes have colonised the traditional white working-class resident areas. But the programme was scaled down and spread more thinly in the Single Regeneration Budget to make funds go further.

URBED was in the forefront of applying American ideas of adaptive reuse and waterfront revival. Everyone talked about the model of Baltimore without always understanding why it worked; our case study established the importance of timing; regeneration takes a generation and having the right driving force. In the first wave, many former textile mills and warehouses were turned into managed workspace for small and creative enterprises. Examples are regenerating the former Merchants Quarter known as Little Germany in Bradford (where David Rudlin joined us), and setting up Merton Abbey Mills as a joint venture with Sainsburys and Urban Space Management in South London. Local authorities recruited economic development officers, and set up regeneration programmes. Local community initiatives, including development and environmental trusts such as Groundwork helped bring derelict sites back to life. The idea of the asset based and community run development trusts started to take off along with the notion of local economic development as oppose to relying on inward investment.

However the bulk of the public money went not to local authorities or community groups but to government sponsored Development Corporations, particularly the London Docklands Development Corporation. American ideas of 'leverage' government sought to use public investment to mobilise much larger amounts of private investment, and relied on the private sector for ideas. If anything the community was seen as a nuisance, getting in the way of development. The overriding measures of success became the amount of physical development, and the bigger the better.

'Grand projects' like Canary Wharf were only achieved at a significant public cost in terms of tax incentives. They did little to improve the prospects for existing residents, as the benefits did not 'trickle down'. Major public investment had to be made in extending the Underground Railway to enable staff to reach the new offices. At the time it was heralded as a triumph for private enterprise, yet the American developers went bankrupt! Though attitudes to enterprise changed for the better, the legacies of the Thatcher Years were the abandonment of the national and regional planning system, the erosion of the role of local and independent authorities and three million unemployed. Markets were thought to know best. Europe was seen as a way of cutting government expenditure, not as a means of creating a fairer and more peaceful world.

Towards urban renaissance

By the middle of the 1990s, there was a huge swing back to Labour. The setting up of the Urban Task Force under architect (Lord) Richard Rogers marked a major turning point in thinking about cities[5]. For the first time design was seen as an important element of urban policy. Household growth was undeniable. Urban Renaissance, the second wave, meant people living in cities out of choice not necessity. Experts looked to European cities like Barcelona and Rotterdam for inspiration.

One immediate result of the Urban Task Force was the setting up of a national organisation, the Commission for Architecture and the Built Environment (CABE). British architects like Norman Foster and Richard Rogers achieved worldwide acclaim. A series of 'grand projects' celebrated the Millennium, and new public places, helped by the National Lottery, marked a shift away from the traditional British suburban lifestyle. An Academy for Sustainable Communities was formed to develop the missing skills needed to spread the urban renaissance.

URBED was commissioned by the Office of the Deputy Prime Minister to work with 24 towns and cities in the run-up to the first ever Urban Summit held in Birmingham in 2002[6]. The project report observed that 'Towns and cities are essentially organic and should not be seen as just a set of problems or machines to be fixed with a "toolkit" of short-term projects.' The full set of reports *Partners in Urban Renaissance* won a design award. We showed through over 60 case studies and workshops with citizens and property developers, that attitudes to urban living could be changed and that an urban renaissance was feasible. The report identified eight dimensions of urban renaissance, from community engagement to valued neighbour-hoods (subsequently taken up by the Egan Skills Review). Unfortunately a change of ministers and senior civil servants led to its recommendations for improving working together being forgotten.

High-density contemporary apartment blocks colonised our waterfronts and the edges of our city centres. This is because they were driven by developers out to benefit from a change of land use, and by investors who bought small flats to let out in the hopes of ever increasing property values, as demand outpaced supply. The design and media sectors flourished for a while, and 'social entrepreneurs' and the creative class emerged as forces for change[7]. It was thought that economic revival could be secured through retail led regeneration and the growth of the service economy. But before long government stopped using the term urban renaissance (though it continued to be used in the regions).

The Sustainable Communities Plan

The third wave was marked by the importance given to housebuilding in response to house price inflation, which had made even the smallest home unaffordable. While government relied on the Core Cities as the main 'engines for growth' the new focus became the city region. Gordon Brown set a target for building 3 million new homes or 240,000 a year, and went on to promote the idea of ten new Eco-towns that could show how to cut carbon emissions. Thames Gateway was prioritised because less opposition was expected there. The Treasury commissioned the Barker Review from an economist who put the blame on planning, and the unsatisfactory system for funding infrastructure, but neglected the role of financial institutions in pushing up prices. The plan was simply described by a civil servant as 'build them in the South, knock them down in the North'. The Northern Way was apparently born in a pub as a means of showing that the plan covered the whole country! However, Growth Areas were identified and supported with extra funds. A whole new set of partnerships were launched to overcome the deficiencies of local authorities by bringing in private sector expertise on short-term contracts. For a while housing led regeneration seemed feasible.

Though our work as masterplanners now, as well as regeneration consultants, we saw whole neighbourhoods transformed in stages particularly around city centres. The successful rediscovery and renaissance of once run-down inner city neighbourhoods like Covent Garden in Central London, the Jewellery Quarter in Birmingham, the Cultural Industries Quarter in Sheffield, have been complemented by whole new neighbourhoods such as Harbourside in Bristol or the New England Quarter in Brighton. These proved that mixed uses and denser urban forms in highly accessible locations around railway stations can be financially viable as well as physically attractive. As a personal example in moving from Hampstead Garden Suburb to a flat near Kings Cross, just a short walk from URBED's London office, we enjoyed the benefits of living at higher densities in a multicultural area with lots of facilities, and not spending several hours a day standing in a crowded train on the Northern Line!

Many people have changed the way they lived. Half of all flats in the South East have been built in the last two decades, and young people have come to rely on renting rather than expecting to buy a 'starter home'. Concepts like 'loft apartments' imported from the USA and promoted by entrepreneurial developers enabled young urban professionals (Yuppies) to gentrify inner areas (and a few older people to move back). Cities such as Brighton experienced an influx of young people as students and the growth of a creative economy, enabling mixed-use developments to be built. A 'renaissance' was under way, at least as far as the design and media worlds were concerned. Café culture was taking off everywhere it seemed, and both the quality of the air and eating out improved hugely (though 'vertical drinking' still predominated). While the quality of much new housing was criticised, few questioned the basic concept of relying on the private sector to achieve social goals, such as mixed communities where a third of the housing might be for households off the local authority waiting list.

However URBED research in 2005 revealed that the benefits were neither trickling down nor spreading out to the smaller towns and cities on the edge of urban conurbations[8]. A society once based on mass production has been replaced by one of mass consumption. The dependency culture has been reinforced by the removal of both housing and employment 'ladders'. Many of the suburban centres were in a very weak state, particularly where people no longer worked nearby. Money was channelled into out of town retail parks and superstores, and little got reinvested in improving the public realm[9]. The centralisation of funding led local authorities to compete with each other rather than collaborate, and to rely on Planning Gain to fund the improvements that were so needed in the public realm[10]. Tristam Hunt convincingly argues that the success of Victorian cities came from civic leadership, which has suffered when suburbs started to sprawl[11]. Local government's share of public spending went up from 32% in 1882 to 51% in 1905 but fell back to 28% in 1971 and 24% in 1998. The 1984 Rate Act centralised the proceeds of the Business Rate and made local authorities agents of central government.

Recent research has shown that despite ambitious government goals for building better homes, narrowing regional inequalities, and improving everyone's quality of life, gaps have often widened[12]. Though the physical achievements in the centres of our principal cities and historic towns are undeniable, and there are lots of new hospitals and colleges, the social results, such as increased mobility, have lagged behind. As jobs expand on the edge, and people who can move further out to find homes they can afford, we end up with 'fat cities' with arterial sclerosis. In the neighbourhoods that were targeted for renewal, social exclusion is still rife, with a 'non-working class' disconnected from the formal economy. Renaissance seemed to be only skin deep.

UNICEF studies suggest we have the most miserable children in Europe! Obese and antisocial children may have their roots in a way of life that sees people primarily as consumers and not as citizens or co-producers of communities, people who rely on the private car rather than going by bus or walking. Gambling and shows like Big Brother, binge drinking and fears for security, and low rates of turnout in elections, are all a long way from a nation that set up the world's first co-operatives and building societies. They point to communities that have lost both the solidarity of the old working class, and the sense of self-improvement that once marked the middle class. The forces of urban exodus and every man for himself are working against the urban renaissance ideal of places where people live out of choice not necessity. It is therefore high time to look again at the social democratic countries of Europe to see what can be learned.

Learning from Europe
The ideas behind the sustainable urban neighbourhood are about much more than simply building new homes or even improving the way cities look. As well as limited American examples of 'smart growth' and Transit Oriented Development such as Portland, Oregon, there are hundreds more European towns and cities that have invested in high-quality public transit schemes and local energy generation and distribution, and that have achieved higher growth rates and prosperity than their British equivalents[13]. Rather

than trying to go it alone in building zero carbon developments, Britain needs to catch up with Continental towns and cities in attracting people to live in town, reducing energy use, encouraging walking and cycling, and building sustainable urban extensions.

Our research for the Joseph Rowntree Foundation, Regeneration in European Cities, into regeneration success stories in Gothenburg, Lille and Rotterdam showed the benefits from making connections between different forms of investment, so that, for example, the run-down mill town of Roubaix is benefitting from the growth of neighbouring Lille, and its position on the European high speed rail system. The impact of expenditure on regeneration and development in the UK suffers from being made up of isolated projects funded through national decisions, rather through the working together of key players in the public, private and community sectors at sub-regional and neighbourhood levels. In other words, the structures through which power and resources are channelled are not fit for purpose. We are simply not being smart enough.

The importance of local leadership was further brought out in a study of exemplary European new settlements and the report Beyond Ecotowns[14]. Case studies of ten new communities in four different countries drew on comparative research. Study tours with practitioners[15], and subsequently councillors brought out common features that people liked. The new settlements were well-linked to jobs and services with easy walking and cycling routes and with first-class public transport systems. Social infrastructure like schools and meeting places was provided from the start, not as an afterthought. A balance of housing types and tenures as well as distinctive and attractive neighbourhoods created a pride of place without social tensions. Initiative like cogeneration and community energy saved on fuel and emissions, and made it possible to tap non-renewable sources like solar and wind power[16].

Local authorities lead this process instead of waiting until the private sector came up with proposals, and then running plans through exhaustive tests, and expensive and time-consuming public inquiries or complicated Section 106 agreements. The wider community was engaged in drawing up briefs. Once agreed, new settlements such as Vathorst in Amersfoort in the Netherlands or Vauban in Freiburg in Southern Germany are built much faster and to higher standards than in the UK. Development is combined with the provision of infrastructure so that many more small builders, including co-operatives, can get involved. Faster rates of growth and site disposals repay the initial investment in infrastructure and land. Public land assembly helps keep land costs down to 20–30 % as well as reducing the risks and hence the profit margin developers require. The cost of infrastructure is reduced by using low cost long-term public borrowing rather than expecting the private sector to take all the risks.

Urban Husbandry: A series of images from URBED's early work using the transformation of a derelict site into a productive orchard as a metaphor for urban regeneration

Resourcing sustainable urban neighbourhoods

The Sustainable Urban Neighbourhood goes beyond Howard's marriage of town and country by using higher densities to support higher quality infrastructure, and by using energy conservation as a means of climate proofing. Like the garden city, it depends on a better delivery mechanism that combines the lessons from the British New Towns with European best practice. The five steps to successful urban renaissance from our work with 24 towns and cities provide a simple framework, and one that could be used in reaching agreements[17]:

1. **Developing the vision:** Planning is essentially a collective process, and cannot just be left to experts. It is now common practice to work up visions for cities, using some form of the 'action planning process' which we first used to create a shared vision for the centre of Birmingham at the Highbury Initiative in 1988 over a weekend. The key to success is getting the various stakeholders to sink their differences and work together for a period of time. They are fired up by the energy that comes out of 'round table workshops'. Inspiration comes from surveys to reveal local concerns and priorities plus health checks that draw useful comparisons with other similar places.

The British planning system has become inordinately complicated and circular because it relies excessively on central government direction. The regions, which are the size of some European countries, are too large to plan strategically. We need to focus our efforts on accommodating growth within coherent sub-regions, and on linking infrastructure more closely with development. The vision needs to identify the best areas for regeneration and planned growth so that it is a proper spatial strategy, and not just a series of wish lists. The extra resources involved in doing strategic planning would be more than saved through reducing abortive work and studies that lead nowhere.

2. **Building a concordat:** Visions and plans have little value without the whole-hearted support of the different stakeholders. These need to include property owners as well as public agencies. While the UK has spawned a profusion of partnerships, most lack the authority or resources to make things happen, and are often criticised as being 'talking shops'. On the Continent we found that there is a much clearer relationship between central, regional and local government, exemplified by what the French first called Contrats de Ville or the VINEX ten year housing programme in the Netherlands. In the UK longer-term agreements need to bind together the expenditure plans of the main public agencies and provide the confidence for private investment. They need to integrate investment plans and not just land-use allocations and could be embodied in the Local or Multi Area Agreements that the Treasury's Sub National Review is rightly advocating. Once signed, these should allow local authorities or joint venture companies to borrow the funds for investment without having to rely on where individual projects stand in the national queue.

To help reach agreement, we came up with the idea of 'charters' or 'protocols' as a means of overcoming the barriers to building at higher densities[18]. URBED has applied the charter process to securing higher quality standards in growth around Cambridgeshire, and this has been shortlisted from an award from the RTPI[19] (as well as in work in Yorkshire, such as in Selby). With the aggravate rate of housing growth in the UK, the local authorities established Cambridgeshire Horizons as a means of tackling common issues and sharing experience. We organised a series of study tours 'looking and learning' from experience elsewhere, from Letchworth to Freiburg. Working with over 100 people we drew up a set of overriding principles under the themes of connectivity, community, climate proofing and character. By signing up to the charter, organisations declare their commitment to a set of shared principles. By working as a network, people are building the capacity to achieve what seems individually impossible.

3. Carrying out a phased strategy: Visions and strategies failed in the past when they concentrated on the 'end state' but neglected the route to get there. Because the future is so uncertain, it is important to be clear on the fundamentals, for example the street system or plot ratios, while leaving a degree of flexibility on the design (and even use) of buildings. This is one of the lessons from the Dutch and German planning systems, as most of the basic rules that govern the development of a place as complex as Vauban can be displayed on one large sheet of paper! There is much more complexity in the UK.

Pilot Projects such as festivals or interim uses should be used to build confidence, in the period before flagship projects take off. Arts, culture and entertainment have a crucial role to play as creative people can often be pioneers in areas that do not yet feel safe enough to attract large numbers of people to live in. In the process they can play a crucial role in changing an area's image, as the Royal Ballet did in moving from London to Birmingham. They may be used to 'brand areas' with a distinct identity, as has for example happened through opening up new canals in Dutch developments, and significantly the Vathorst Development Company established a foundation to involve artists in the community development process. Asset endowed development trusts can be an excellent way of building a community, and not just homes as in the Shenley Park Trust which we set up.

4. Orchestrating investment: Even during a period of housing boom the private sector was unable to fund the extra infrastructure that developments require. Relying on the Private Finance Initiative to fund schools and transport facilities is not going to work in a recession, and can double the cost. Approaches are now called for that channel resources where they will have most impact, rather than responding to the 'worst first' and that would avoid excessive complexity. As these often have to be political rather than technical decisions, it is important to bring decision making down to a sub-regional or neighbourhood level through delivery vehicles with a long-term mission. Business Improvement Districts that raise a supplement to the Business Rate will not work when businesses are seeing their turnover and profits fall. Nor will utilities invest in the upgraded local generation and distribution systems that are needed to match Continental performance, unless they can secure long-term benefits.

The solutions lie in using public funds, such as those handled by the Housing and Communities Agency in England, to reinforce and accelerate development in areas where the returns are going to be greatest, through some form of joint venture company. This means making the most of areas with under-used infrastructure, such as around many suburban railway stations, or where transport investment is being committed, such as new link roads and bypasses, The Vathorst Development Company in Amersfoort, to install the local roads and services including energy distribution, before selling sites on to builders (who include housing associations and financial institutions investing in rented homes). Local authorities can use assets to underpin investment, as in Croydon, for example. Long-term contracts secured by covenants that go with the land would justify higher levels of investment through Multi Service Companies. There is also scope to raise funding for investment in utilities and transport infrastructure through bonds[20], which would suit some pension funds and insurance companies. The uplift in land values can then be used to repay the bond. In the short-term borrowing against expected income from parking charges is a practical option. In the longer term local government needs to get back the power to raise funds through local taxation (for example by splitting the yield from the Business Rate).

5. **Maintaining the momentum:** In moving development ahead, delivery mechanisms are needed to sustain the confidence and support of both the public and private sectors, and overcome the hostility of community groups to change. While we have a mass of statistical indicators, the short-lived nature of most partnerships means we are not very good at learning from experience. Most authorities are too small to employ the necessary technical staff and political leadership, and too large to focus on a single area. Neighbourhood management is still poorly resourced despite the Egan Review of skills, the formation of regional centres of excellence, and several national academies, as well as host of conferences and publications. The public realm and community facilities tend to be most criticised in new developments and these are crucial to living together at higher densities.

The answers lie in developing a broader range of tenures to get away from the simplistic divide between owner occupation and social housing. In most places there are enough people to act as the 'eco pioneers', particularly if some form of community control is established (as was successfully demonstrated by Homes for Change in Hulme). Private renting currently accounts for only 11% of British households compared with 17% in Sweden and 49%

in Germany, while in the Netherlands, a third of the population live in housing provided by social landlords[21]. By starting with groups who want to live in different ways many of the risks associated with innovation and development can be reduced, which will make the whole process much more viable. The ongoing success of Letchworth Garden City shows the value of a community-based trust or foundation that has a property stake, as does our own experience with setting up the Shenley Park Trust for a new village in Herfordshire.

Conclusions

In the first edition of Building the 21st Century Home, we suggested it was time for a new model, and that that the Sustainable Urban Neighbourhood would appeal to a changing market by offering a much better quality of life. We put forward an 'organic' approved development, more like gardening than engineering. Since then initiatives URBED have been closely involved in, like the renewal of Hulme in Manchester or the New England Quarter in Brighton, have shown how to create places where people live out of choice not necessity.

The hope now is that the tangible symbols of urban renaissance in major British cities such as Manchester and Glasgow, Birmingham and Bristol, will spread to the smaller industrial towns and the suburbs. Building sustainable urban neighbourhoods need to be embraced as a practical solution to the current financial turmoil. There are also the imperatives of responding to climate change and rising energy costs, for building better and fairer cities. The alternative could be a return to the Dark Ages experienced after the collapse of the Roman Empire, when there was no longer sufficient security to maintain even the basic infrastructure.

Living in a more sustainable way could create a stronger economy and a better quality of life for all. The unresolved issue is whether central governments are willing to trust local authorities with the powers, as well as the responsibilities, to shape their futures and raise the extra income needed to upgrade the infrastructure. As the American inventor Benjamin Franklin said at the time of the American War of Independence, 'Gentlemen we either hang together or hang separately.'

Index

Notes and references

INTRODUCTION

1. **Department of the Environment** – Projections of Households in England to 2016, London HMSO, 1995
2. **The Urban Task Force** – Towards an Urban Renaissance: Department of the Environment, Transport and the Regions, Distributed by E & FN Spon 1999
3. **Department of the Environment, Transport and the Regions** – Our Towns and Cities: The Future – Delivering an Urban Renaissance – 2000
4. **Office of the Deputy Prime Minister** – The Sustainable Communities Plan – Building for the Future 2003
5. **http://www.cabe.org.uk/**
6. **Department of Communities and Local Government** – Planning Statistical Release, October 2008 (http://www.communities.gov.uk/documents/statistics/pdf/1005440.pdf)
7. **Alan Holmans** – Housing demand and need in England to 1991–2011, Joseph Rowntree Foundation, 1995
8. **Department of Communities and Local Government** – Green Paper on Housing (Homes for the future: more affordable, more sustainable, 23rd July 2007
9. **John Prescot** – Planning for Communities – Statement of The Secretary of State for the Environment, Transport and the Regions – Hansard – 23rd Feb 1998
10. See 2
11. **Northern Way Steering Group** – The Northern Way – September 2004
12. **Who says we have to slum it?** – Peter Hall – The Guardian – 5th February 1997
13. **David Page** – Building for Communities: A study of new housing association estates – Joseph Rowntree Foundation, 1993
14. **Robert Fishman** – Bourgeois Utopia: The rise and fall of suburbia, Basic Books, 1987
15. **John Burnett** – A Social History of Housing 1815–1985, Methuen, 1986
16. **Will Hutton** – The state we're in – Vintage Books – 1995

CHAPTER 1

1. See **Spiro Kostof** – The City Shaped and The City Assembled, Thames and Hudson, 1991 as well as Jane Jacobs – The Economy of Cities, Vintage Books, 1969
2. **Michael Breheny** – Urban Densities and Sustainable Development, Paper to the Institute of Geographers, January 1995

3. **Commission of the European Communities** – Green Paper on the Urban Environment, 1990
4. **David Morris** – The Return Of The City State, Resurgence Journal Issue 167, page 4, Nov/Dec. 1994
5. **W.G. Hoskins** – The Making of the English Landscape, Pelican, 1955
6. **Robert and Brenda Vale** – Green Architecture, Thames & Hudson, 1991
7. See Introduction note 14
8. **Peter Hall** – Urban & Regional Planning, Pelican, 1975
9. **Stefan Muthesius** – The English Terraced House, Yale University Press, 1982
10. See for example Mulholland Research Associates – Towns or leafier environments; a survey of family homebuying choices – Housebuilders Federation, Dec. 1995
11. There have been various reviews of urban depopulation. One of the best reviews is **Tony Champion** (ed.) – Counterurbanisation: The changing pace and nature of population deconcentration, London, Edward Arnold, 1989
12. **Professor Michael Parkinson et al.** State of the Cities Report – Office of the Deputy Prime Minister – March 2006
13. **URBED** – Vital and Viable Town Centres: Meeting the Challenge, HMSO, 1994
14. **Nicholas Falk & Haris Martinos** – Inner City; Local government and economic renewal, Fabian Society, London, 1975
15. **Brian Robson** – Inner City Research Programme: Assessing the Impact of Urban Policy, HMSO, 1994
16. **Paul Harris** – Eight miles of murder – The Observer, Sunday April 16 2006
17. **Joel Garreau** – Edge Cities, Doubleday, 1992
18. **Gregory Greene** (Writer and director) The End of Suburbia: Oil Depletion and the Collapse of the American Dream – Film released by The Electric Wallpaper Co 5 May 2004 (Canada)
19. **Donald J. Olsen** – The City As A Work Of Art, Yale University Press, 1986
20. **David Rudlin** – But would you live there? Shaping Attitudes to urban living – MORI, URBED and the School for Policy Studies at the University of Bristol for the Urban Task Force – February 1999
21/22/23. See note 2–4 Introduction
24. See Introduction note 11

25. Current versions of PPS6 http://www.communities.gov.uk/planningandbuilding/planning/planningpolicyguidance/planning-policystatements/
26. **The Urban Task Force:** Towards a Strong Urban Renaissance – November 2005
27. See note 12
28. **The Mayor of London** – The London Plan – The Greater London Authority – February 2004
29. **Richard Florida** – The Rise of the Creative Class – Basic Books – April 2002
30. **Jane Jacobs** – The Economy of Cities, Vintage Books, 1969

CHAPTER 2

1. The material in this chapter draws on a number of sources, the best two being: **Ian Colquhoun & Peter Fauset** – Housing Design in Practice, Longman Scientific and Technical, 1991, **Sim Van der Ryn & Peter Calthorpe** – Sustainable Communities: A new design synthesis for Cities, Suburbs and Towns, Sierra Club Books, 1989
2. **Ebenezer Howard** – Tomorrow: A peaceful path to real reform, 1898 (republished 1902 as Garden Cities of Tomorrow)
3. **Raymond Unwin** – The Art of Building a Home and Town Planning in Practice, 1909
4. **Peter Hall** – Urban & Regional Planning, Pelican, 1975
5. Consultancy work in Benchill North, Wythenshawe by URBED for Manchester City Council, 1994, Unpublished
6. **Tony Garnier** – Une Cité Industrielle, 1917
7. **L'Office Public Communautaire D'HLM De Lyon** – Musee Urbain Tony Garnier, November 1991
8. **Le Corbusier** – The City of Tomorrow, 1922 La Ville Radieuse, 1933
9. **Marilyn Taylor** – Unleashing The Potential: A review of the Action on Estates Programme, The Joseph Rowntree Foundation, 1995
10. **Hans M. Wingler** – The Bauhaus, MIT Press, 7th edition 1986
11. **Ludwig Hilberseimer** – The minimal home in a stairless house, From the Bauhaus Journal

CHAPTER 3

1. **Congres International de l'Architecture Moderne** – Charter of Athens, 1933
2. **Conference proceedings** – The Heart of the City, CIAM, 1952

3. **Clarence Perry** – New York Regional Plan, 1923

4. **Lewis Mumford** – The Culture of Cities, 1938

5. **Sir H Alker Tripp** – Town Planning and Traffic, 1942

6. **Sir Colin Buchanan** – Traffic in Towns, HMSO, 1963

7. **DOE/DOT** – Design Bulletin 32: Residential Roads and Footpaths; Layout considerations, HMSO, 2nd Edition 1992

8. **DETR** – Places Streets and Movement: A Companion guide to Design Bulletin 32 – Residential Roads and Footpaths, prepared by Alan Baxter Associates, September 1998

9. **Department of Transport** – Manual for Streets (written by WSP et al. Thomas Telford Publishing – 2007

10. **Raymond Unwin** – Nothing gained by overcrowding, 1912

11. **Sir John Tudor Walters** (committee chair) – Dwellings for the working classes, 1918

12. **J.B. Calhoun** – A Behavioural Sink: Roots of behaviour, Harper, New York, 1962

13. **Alice Coleman** – Utopia on Trial: Vision and reality in planned housing, Hilary Shipman London, 2nd issue 1990

14. **Jane Jacobs** – Death and Life of Great American Cities, Randon House 1961

15. **Patrick Abercombie with J.H.Forshaw** the chief architect for London County Council, published in 1943 and as a Penguin special edited by Arno Goldfinger

16. **Manchester City Council** – Plan for Manchester, 1949

17. **Jane Jacobs** – The Economy of Cities, Vintage Books, 1969

18 . Report to develop a cultural strategy for Milton Keynes (unpublished)

19. **DETR** – By Design – Urban design in the planning system: towards better practice – Thomas Telford Publishing – May 2000

CHAPTER 4

1. **Peter Gaskell** – Manufacturing Population of England, 1833, reprinted 1972

2. **John Burnett** – A Social History of Housing 1815–1985, Methuen, 2nd edition 1986

3. **Friedrich Engels** – The condition of the working class in England 1844, reprinted 1952

4. **Stefan Muthesius** – The English Terraced House, Yale University Press, 1982

5. **Donald Olsen** – The City As a Work of Art : London, Paris, Vienna, Yale, 1986

6. **Donald Olsen** – Town Planning in London: The 18th and 19th Centuries, Yale University Press, 2nd edition 1982

7. **H.J. Dyos** – Victorian Suburb: A study of the growth of Camberwell, 1961

8. **Gillian Tyndall** – The fields beneath, Granada Publishing, London, 1980

9. **Linda Clarke** – Building Capitalism, London, 1991

10. **H.J. Dyos and D.A. Reeder** – Slums and suburbs in the Victorian City; Images and Realities, Volume 1, 1973

11. Quoted in **John Burnett** – A Social History of Housing 1815–1985, Methuen, 2nd edition 1986

12. **Stefan Muthesius** – The English Terraced House, Yale University Press, 1982

13. **Sir John Tudor Walters** (committee chair) – Dwellings for the working classes, 1918

14. **Local Government Management Board** – Manual on the preparation of state-aided housing schemes, 1919

15. **Peter Hall** – Urban & Regional Planning, Pelican, 1975

16. **Earl of Dudley** – The Design of Dwellings, Report of the Design of Dwellings Subcommittee of the Ministry of Health Central Housing Advisory Committee, 1944

17. **Parker Morris** – Homes for Today and Tomorrow, Department of the Environment, 1961

18. **The RIBA/Institute of Housing** – Homes of the Future Group, 1983

19. **Valerie Karn** – British Housing Standards : Time for a new approach? Joseph Rowntree Foundation Enquiry into housing standards – 1994

20. **Tim Mars** – The good the bad and the ugly: Housing in Liverpool 8, Roof, Sept/Oct 1981

21. **Peter Bibby and John Shepherd** – Urbanisation in England: Projections 1991–2016, London, HMSO, 1995

22. **Martin Richardson** – Tower Block: Modern public housing in England, 1994

23. **Christopher Booker** – Writing in Building Design 15th April 1994

24. **Necdet Teymur, Thomas A. Markus, Tom Wooley** – Rehumanising Housing – Butterworths, 1988, Chapter 5, Bill Hillier – Against enclosure

25. **Oscar Newman** – Defensible space: People and design in the violent city, Architectural Press, 1972

26. **Ian Colquhoun and Peter Fauset** – Housing Design in Practice, Longman Scientific and Technical, 1991

27. **John Burnett** – A Social History of Housing 1815–1985, Methuen, 2nd edition 1986

28. **RIBA Client Focus; Housing** – RIBA Journal November 1994

29. **Tom Barron** – The challenge for the UK housing industry in the 1980s and the planning system, Construction management and Economics 1983

30. **Mark Stephens** – Housing policy in a European Perspective, Centre for Housing Research, Joseph Rowntree Foundation, 1994

31. **John Wrigglesworth** – Housing and Planning Review, February/March 1994

32. **Duncan MacLennan** – A Competitive UK Economy: The challenges for housing, Joseph Rowntree Foundation, 1994

33. **John Stewart** – Writing in the Housebuilder 1994

34. **John Wrigglesworth** – Housing and Planning Review, February/March 1994

35. **Savills** – Quarterly Residential Research Bulletin, FPD Savills Residential Research, Sept 1995

36. **Anne Power and K. Mumford** – The Slow Death of Great Cities? Urban Abandonment or Urban Renaissance – York Publishing Services – Joseph Rowntree Foundation – 1999

37. **Bank of England** – Monetary & Financial Statistics – September 2008

38. **Richard Wachman** – House building grinds to a halt – and sows seeds of next boom (reporting on a report from the Centre for Economic and Business Research) – The Guardian – Sunday August 3rd 2008.

39. **Adrian Coles** – Paper to NFHA Conference 1994

40. Salford Builds 200 at 25 % grant – Inside Housing news story 23rd Sept 1994

41. **Valerie Karn and Linda Sheridan** – New homes in the 1990s: A study of space and amenity in housing association and private sector production, Joseph Rowntree Foundation, 1994

42. **David Page** – Building for Communities: A study of new housing association estates, Joseph Rowntree Foundation, 1993

43. **Hamish McRae** – Writing in the Independent 24th March, 1994

CHAPTER 5

1. **William Rees and Dr Mathis Wackernagel** – Our Ecological Footprint: Reducing Human Impact on the Earth – New Society Publishers – 1996.
2. **Jane Jacobs** – The Economy of Cities, Vintage Books, 1969
3. **Rachel Carson** – A Silent Spring – Houghton Mifflin in 1962, and **Donella H. Meadows, Dennis L. Meadows, Jørgen Randers, and William W. Behrens III** – The Limits to Growth – The Club of Rome 1972
4. **Ulrich Beck** – Ecological politics in an age of risk, Policy Press, Cambridge, 1995
5. **Commission of the European Communities** – Green Paper on the Urban Environment, 1990
6. **Tony Aldous** – Urban Villages: A Concept for creating mixed use urban developments on a sustainable scale, Urban Villages Forum, 1992
7. **Peter Calthorpe** – The Next American Metropolis, Princeton Architectural Press, 1993
8. **Gro Harlem Brundtland** (Chair) – Our common future, World Commission on Environment and Development – NY Oxford University Press 1987
9. **DOE** – White Paper This Common Inheritance, HMSO, 1990
10. **Lord Stern of Brentford:** Stern Review on the Economics of Climate Change – UK Government – October 2006
11. **Commission of the European Communities** – 5th Environmental Action Plan, Towards Sustainability, Commission of the European Communities, 1993
12. **Son Nghiem** – NASA's Jet Propulsion Laboratory Jan 2007 – www.nasa.gov/vision/earth/lookingatearth/quikscat–20071001.html
13. **Energy Saving Trust** – www.energysavingtrust.org.uk/your_impact_on_climate_change/the_impact_of_climate_change_in_the_uk
14. **IPCC**, 2007: Climate Change 2007: Synthesis Report. Contribution of Working Groups I, II and III to the Fourth Assessment Report of the Intergovernmental Panel on Climate Change [Core Writing Team, Pachauri, R.K and Reisinger, A. (eds.)]. IPCC, Geneva, Switzerland, 104 pp.
15. **Ian Gazley** – The Office for National Statistics UK environmental accounts: air emissions and energy use Economic & Labour Market Review, vol 1, no 11 – 2007
16. **Agenda 21** – Action plan for the next century, UNCED NY, 1992
17. **The Kyoto Protocol** – United Nations Framework Convention on Climate Change 1997.
18. **UK Government** – Climate Change: The UK programme, HMSO, 1994
19. **Draft Climate Change Bill** DEFRA – 13 March 2007
20. **UK Climate Change Impacts Review Group** – Review of the Potential Effects of Climate Change in the UK, HMSO, 1996

21. **Aubrey Meyer:** Contraction & Convergence: The Global Solution to Climate Change (Schumacher Briefings, 5) Green Books – February 2001.
22. **Dr Alice Bows, Dr Sarah Mander, Mr Richard Starkey** – Living within a carbon budget The Tyndall Centre – Report for Friends of the Earth and The Co-operative Bank, July 2006
23. **David Malin Poodman** – Getting the Signals Right: Tax reform to protect the environment and the economy, Worldwatch Paper 134 – http://www.worldwatch.org/pubs/paper/134a.html
24. **DCLG:** Code for Sustainable Homes : A step-change in sustainable home building practice 2006
25. **DEFRA** – e-Digest Statistics about: Air Quality Emissions of Sulphur dioxide: 1970–2006 www.defra.gov.uk/environment/statistics/airqual/aqemsox.htm
26. **Savills** – The market for residential developments in the 1990s, Savills Residential Research, 1992
27. **Building Research Establishment** – www.breeam.org for details of all BREEAM Ratings, the residential rating (Ecohomes) waqs replaced by the Code for Sustainable Homes in 2007.
28. **DCLG** – The Code for Sustainable Homes: Setting the standard in sustainability for new homes – 27th February 2007
29. **DCLG** – www.homeinformationpacks.gov.uk/
30. **DfT** – National Travel Survey – 8 April 2008
31. **DOE/DOT** – Planning Policy Guidance: Transport, PPG 13, HMSO, 1994 and DETR – Developing an integrated transport policy, DETR, 1997
32. **DfT** – A New Deal for Transport: Better for everyone – White Paper July 1998
33. See 30
34. **DCLG** – Planning Policy Statement 3: Housing November 2006.
35. **Greater London Authority** – The Case for London, ISBN 1 85261 590 7, March 2004

CHAPTER 6

1. **DCLG** – House Building: January to March Quarter 2007 – Published 17 May 2007
2. **Mulholland Research Associates** – Towns or leafier environments; a survey of family homebuying choices – Housebuilders Federation, Dec. 1995
3. **Robson, Bradford and Deas** – The Impact of Urban Development Corporations in Leeds, Bristol and Central Manchester, DETR 1998
4. **John Burnett** – A Social History of Housing 1815–1985, Methuen, 2nd. Edition 1986
5. **Office for National Statistics** – Households: Rise in non-family households – www.statistics.gov.uk
6. **Andres Duany** – Paper given to the Connected City Conference, Liverpool Architecture and Design Institute, 1997
7. **Brian Lewis** – A Home for Life, Search 14, Joseph Rowntree Foundation, Dec. 1992
8. **The Joseph Rowntree Foundation** – Build-

ing Lifetime Homes, Joseph Rowntree Foundation Feb. 1997
9. **UK Building Regulations** – Part M Access and Facilities for Disabled People – 2007
10. **John Burnett** – A Social History of Housing 1815–1985, Methuen, 2nd. Edition 1986.
11. **DOE** – Projections of Households in England to 2016, London HMSO, 1995
12. **DCLG** – Projections of households for England and the Regions to 2029 – 2007
13. **Alan Holman** – Housing Demand and Need in England 1991–2011: The National Picture, The People – Where will they go? TCPA, Jan. 1996
14. **Office for National Statistics** – Editors: Abigail Self, Linda Zealey – Social Trends No. 37 – 2007
15. Henley Centre report described by **Ian Wray** – Can women save the city? Town & Country Planning Vol. 66 No 2 page 34, Feb. 1997
16. **Office for National Statistics** – Labour Force Survey – April 2008
17. **CIPD Chartered Institute of Personal Development** – Working hours in the UK – Originally issued December 2004; latest revision October 2007
18. **Will Hutton** – The state we're in – Vintage Books – 1995
19. **Richard Florida** – Who's Your City? How the Creative Economy Is Making Where to Live the Most Important Decision of Your Life – Basic Books – March 10, 2008
20. **Richard Florida** – Creativeclass.com/richard_florida/video/index.php?video=Authors_at_Google_presents_Richard_Florida_2
21. **S. Graham and S. Marvin** – Telecommunication and the City: Electronic Places, Urban Spaces, Routledge London, 1996

Chapter 7

1. **David Page** – Building for Communities: A study of new housing association estates, Joseph Rowntree Foundation, 1993
2. **Ian Taylor** – Private Homes & Public Others, British Journal of Criminology Vol. 35 No 2, Spring 1995
3. **Jane Jacobs** – Death and Life of Great American Cities, Randon House 1961
4. **Michael Breheny** – Centerist, Decenterists and Compromisers, Chapter in M. Jenkins, E. Burton & K. Williams (Eds) – The Compact City: A Sustainable Urban Form?, E & FN Spon, 1996
5. **David Rudlin** – But would you live there? Shaping Attitudes to urban living – MORI, URBED and the School for Policy Studies at the University of Bristol for the Urban Task Force – February 1999
6. **Allen Jacobs** – Great Streets, MIT Press
7. **David Popenoe** – The Suburban Environment: Sweden and the United States, University of Chicago Press, 1977
8. **Sheila Hayman** – Two-dimensional Living: Celebration, The Independent, 30th June 1996

CHAPTER 8

1. **DCLG** – Cost Analysis of The Code for Sustainable Homes – July 2008
2. **DCLG, EP and DTI** – Design for Manufacture – www.designformanufacture.info/home
3. **Sir Michael Latham** – Constructing the Team, Final report of the Government/Industry Review team on procurement and contractual arrangements in the construction industry, HMSO 1998
4. **David Olivier** – Energy efficiency and renewables: Recent experience on mainland Europe, Energy Advisory Associates, 1992
5. **Valerie Karn** – British Housing Standards : Time for a new approach? Joseph Rowntree Foundation Enquiry into housing standards – 1994
6. **John Wrigglesworth** – Housing and Planning Review, February/March 1994
7. **European Central Bank** – Fiscal Effects of Mortgage Debt Growth in the EU – Working Paper Series No. 526 / Sept 2005
8. **Philip Thornton** – UK mortgage debt soars through £1 trillion – The Independent – 30 June 2006
9. **Savills** – The market for residential developments in the 1990s, Savills Residential Research, 1992
10. **John Willoughby** – NHER Training Course, Energy Advisory Associates, 1993
11. **Colin Ward** – Grays Inn Road and its marble halls – T&CP August/September 1998 – Quoting from John McKean – Learning from Segal and from BBC Radio 4 on 13th August – 1997
12. **Ian Colquhoun & Peter Fauset** – Housing Design in Practice, Longman Scientific and Technical, 1991
13. **RIBA Client Focus; Housing** – RIBA Journal November 1994
14. From consultancy work by URBED work for the Threshold Tennant Trust in London
15. **Valerie Karn and Linda Sheridan** – New homes in the 1990s: A study of space and amenity in housing association and private sector production, Joseph Rowntree Foundation, 1994
16. **The Greater London Authority:** The London Plan – 10 February 2004.
17. **Sarah Monk, Tony Crook, Diane Lister, Steven Rowley, Christine Short and Christine Whitehead:** Land and finance for affordable housing: The complementary roles of Social Housing Grant and the provision of affordable housing through the planning system – Joseph Rowntree Foundation – 2005
18. **Conran Roche, Davis Langdon and Everest, Aston University** – Cost of Residential Development on Greenfield Sites, DOE, 1991
19. **David Rudlin and Nicholas Falk** – Building to Last: 21st Century Homes, The Joseph Rowntree Foundation, 1995
20. **PRP, URBED and Design for Homes** – Beyond Eco-Towns
21. **The Urban Task Force** – Towards an Urban Renaissance: Department of the Environment, Transport and the Regions, Distributed by E & FN Spon 1999

22. **Tia Cymru** – Technical Standards, Volume one: Development – The design and siting of housing, Tia Cymru, 1994
23. **Jane Jacobs** – The Economy of Cities, Vintage Books, 1969
24. **Agenda Housing Magazine** – Better ways to build homes – Japanese Industrialised Housing May 1997
25. **Michael Ball** – Housing and Construction: A troubled relationship, Joseph Rowntree Foundation, 1996

CHAPTER 9

1. **Champion (ed)** – Counterurbanisation: The changing pace and nature of population deconcentration, Edward Arnold, 1989
2. **Peter Bibby and John Shepherd** – Urbanisation in England: Projections 1991–2016, London, HMSO, 1995
3. **Commission of the European Communities** – Green Paper on the Urban Environment, 1990
4. **DOE** – Sustainable Development: The UK Strategy, HMSO, 1994
5. **UK Round Table on Sustainable Development** – Housing and urban capacity, Feb. 1997
6. **Breheny, Gent and Lock** – Alternative Development Patterns: New settlements, Department of the Environment, 1994
7. **DCLG** – Eco-towns Prospectus – 23 July 2007
8. **DOE/DOT** – Planning Policy Guidance: Transport, PPG 13, HMSO, 1994
9. See: www.communities.gov.uk/planningandbuilding/planning/planningpolicyguidance/planningpolicystatements/planningpolicystatements/
10. **Department of the Environment** – Projections of Households in England to 2016, London HMSO, 1995
11. **UK Government** – Our future homes: Opportunity, choice, responsibility, DOE, London HMSO, 1995
12. **UK Government** – Household Growth – Where Shall we Live?, DOE, London HMSO, 1997
13. **DOE** – Land use change in England – No. 11 Ruislip, Government Statistical Office, 1996
14. **Nick Raynsford** – Quality, Sustainability, Suitability, Town and Country Planning , Vol. 66, No. 3, March 1997
15. **Richard Cabon** – Interview on the Radio 4 Today programme, Autumn 1997
16. **John Prescot** – Planning for Communities – Statement of The Secretary of State for the Environment, Transport and the Regions – Hansard – 23 Feb 1998
17. **David Rudlin** – But would you live there? Shaping Attitudes to urban living – MORI, URBED and the School for Policy Studies at the University of Bristol for the Urban Task Force – February 1999.
18. **The Urban Task Force** – Towards an Urban Renaissance: Department of the Environment, Transport and the Regions, Distributed by E & FN Spon 1999.

19. **DCLG** – Our Towns and Cities: The Future – Delivering an Urban Renaissance 16 November 2000
20. **DCLG** – Sustainable Communities: Building for the Future (Summary, main document and regional action plans) – 5 February 2003
21. **Northern Way Steering Group** – The Northern Way – September 2004
22. **The Urban Task Force:** Towards a Strong Urban Renaissance – November 2005
23. **TCPA** – A series of papers were published as part of the national enquiry The People – Where will they go?' 1996
24. **TCPA** – Urban housing capacity and the sustainable city, A series of reports and a summary report published by the TCPA, 1998
25. **Michael Breheny and Peter Hall** – So where will they go? Summary of TCPA Enquiry, Town & Country Planning July/Aug. 1996   Vol. 65   No 2, July / Aug. 1996
26. **David Rudlin** – Tomorrow: A peaceful path to urban reform, Friends of the Earth, 1998
27. **David Rudlin and Nicholas Falk** – Building to Last: 21st Century Homes, The Joseph Rowntree Foundation, 1995
28. **DCLG** – Land Use Change in England: Residential Development to 2005 – (LUCS–21) – 20 July 2006
29. **Commission of the European Communities** – Green Paper on the Urban Environment, 1990
30. **Newman and Kenworthy** – Gasoline consumption and cities: A comparison of US cities with a global survey, Journal of the American Planning Association 55, 24–37, 1989
31. **Gordon and Richardson** – Gasoline consumption and cities: A reply, Journal of the American Planning Association 55, 342/5, 1989 plus Gomez-Ibanez – A global view of automobile dependence – Cities and automobile dependence: A source book, Journal of the American Planning Association 57 376/9, 1991
32. **ECOTEC** – Reducing transport emissions through planning, for the Department of the Environment, London HMSO, 1993
33. **P. Headicar & C. Curtis** – Strategic housing location and travel behaviour, Oxford Brookes University, 1995
34. **Michael Breheny** – The compact city and transport energy consumption, Institute of British Geographers NS 20 81–101, 1995
35. **Andres Duany** – Paper given to the Connected City Conference, Liverpool Architecture and Design Institute, 1997
36. Henley Centre report described by Ian Wray – Can women save the city? Town & Country Planning Vol. 66 No 2 page 34, Feb. 1997
37. **Tony Burton** – Urban Footprints, CPRE, 1996
38. Peter Bibby and John Shepherd – Urbanisation in England: Projections 1991–2016, London, HMSO, 1995
39. **David Rudlin** – Tapping the Potential: Best practice in assessing urban housing capacity – Report by URBED for DETR – July 1999 Summary published as an appendix to PPG3

1999 – Main report unpublished but available on www.urbed.coop.

40. **Michael Parkinson et al.** – The State of the English Cities – A Research Study – ODPM – March 2006

41. **Tony Champion** – Migration between metropolitan and non-metropolitan areas in Britain, Newcastle University, H507255132, 1996

42. **Michael Breheny** – Urban housing capacity and the sustainable city (Appendix 1 – Success in using urban land) TCPA/Joseph Rowntree Foundation, Dec. 1997

43. **DOE** – Survey of derelict land in England, London HMSO, 1993

44. **John Shepherd and Andris Abakuks** – The National Survey of Vacant Land in the Urban Areas of England – 1990, Planning research programme, London HMSO, 1992

45. **National Land Use Database** – Previously-Developed land that may be available for Development: England 2006 Published July 2007

46. **David Hall** – Housing capacity, how much and where is it? Town and Country Planning Vol. 66, No. 9, p230, Sept. 1997

47 **James Barlow** – Offices into flats: Flexible design and flexible planning, Policy Studies Institute, March 1994

48. **Herring Baker Harris Research** – Behind the facade, London, 1992

49. **Llewelyn Davies** – Sustainable Residential Quality: New approaches to urban living – LPAC, 1998

50. **Urban Initiatives & Chestertons** – Hertfordshire: Dwelling provision through planned regeneration – Hertfordshire County Council, 1995

51. **Empty Homes Agency** – Press release: England's empty homes, Feb. 1998

52. **Empty Homes Agency** – www.empty-homes.com/usefulinformation/stats/statistics.html

53. **Halifax Bank:** Action needed on 289,000 unoccupied homes – December 2007

54. **DOE** – The English House Condition Survey, DOE, London HMSO, 1991

55. **Llewelyn-Davies** – Providing more Homes in Urban Areas, for the Joseph Rowntree Foundation published by the Policy Press, 1994, also Llewelyn-Davies – Sustainable residential quality: new approaches to urban living, LPAC, January 1998

56. **Office for National Statistics** – Regional Trends 32, the Stationary Office, 1997

57. Quoted by **Kate Williams, Elizabeth Burton and Mike Jenks** – Achieving the compact city through intensification, Chapter in M. Jenkins, E. Burton & K. Williams (Eds) – Compact City: A Sustainable Urban Form? F & FN Spon, 1996

58. **Alan Hooper** – Housing Requirements and Housing Provision: The Strategic Issues, Background paper for The People: Where will they go? TCPA, Jan. 1996

59. **Brenda Vale and Ernie Scoffam** – How compact is sustainable, how sustainable is compact, Chapter in M. Jenkins, E. Burton & K. Williams (Eds) – Compact City: A Sustain-

able Urban Form? F & FN Spon, 1996

60. **Alice Coleman** – Utopia on Trial: Vision and reality in planned housing, Hilary Shipman London, 2nd issue 1990

61. **Harley Sherlock** – Cities are good for us, Paladin, 1994

62. **Michael Breheny** – Centerist, Decenterists and Compromisers, Chapter in M. Jenkins, E. Burton & K. Williams (Eds) – The Compact City: A Sustainable Urban Form?, E & FN Spon, 1996

63. **Jane Jacobs** – The Economy of Cities, Vintage Books, 1969

CHAPTER 10

1. **Robert and Brenda Vale** – The Autonomous House: Design and planning for self-sufficiency, Thames and Hudson London, 1975

2. **Robert and Brenda Vale** – Housing development at Cresswell Road Sheffield for North Sheffield Housing Association

3. **Eco-Village Foundation** – Proposal prepared by the Gaia Trust, May 1994

4. **The European Academy of the Urban Environment:** Berlin: Model project of ecological urban renewal in Berlin-Kreuzberg www.eaue.de/winuwd/79.htm

5. **Koen Steemers** – Project ZED: towards Zero Emission urban Development, The Martin Centre for Architectural and Urban Studies, Cambridge, 1998

6. **Robert and Brenda Vale** – Green architecture, Thames & Hudson Ltd. 1991

7. **Mathis Wackernagel & William Rees** – Our Ecological Footprint – reducing human impact on the earth, New Society Publishers, 1996

8. **Herbert Girardet** – From Mobilization to Civilization, Resurgence Journal , Issue 167, page 6, Nov/Dec 1994 and The Gaia Atlas of Cities, Gaia Books, 1992

9. **ECOTEC** – Reducing transport emissions through planning, for the Department of the Environment, London HMSO, 1993

10. **Roger Levett** – The Green City – What might it be? Planning Exchange Conference; Green Housing – Housing, planning, building and the environment, Feb. 1991

11. **Joe Ravetz** – Manchester 2020 – A Sustainable City Region Project, CER for the Town and Country Planning Association, Sept. 1995

12. **Tony Aldous** – Urban Villages – A Concept for creating mixed use urban developments on a sustainable scale, Urban Villages Forum, 1992

13. **Peter Calthorpe** – The Pedestrian Pocket Book – A New Suburban Design Strategy, Princeton Architectural Press, 1994

14. **Richard Register** – Ecocity Berkeley, North Atlantic Books, 1994

15. **Future Systems:** www.future-systems.com/architecture/architecture_19.html

16. **Robert and Brenda Vale** – Green architecture, Thames & Hudson Ltd. 1991

17. **Environmental and Transport Planning** – Streets as living space for the DETR, HMSO, 1997

18. **Colin Davis** – Improving Design In The High Street, Royal Fine Arts Commission, DOE,

Land Securities and Marks & Spencer, 1997

19. **Alan Baxter Associates** – Master Plan for Poundbury, Dorset, Dutchy of Cornwall, 1994

20. **Alan Baxter Associates** – Places, Streets and Movement: A companion guide to Design Bulletin 32: Residential Roads and Footpaths – DETR – 1998.

21. **DfT** – Manual for Streets – Prepares by WSP, published by Thomas Telford – 2007

22. **Shared Space** – Room for Everyone – A new vision for public spaces – www.shared-space.org

23. **David Rudlin and Nick Dodd** – Managing Gridlock: A sustainable transport policy, SUN Dial 5, URBED, Autumn 1997

24. **DCLG** – Land Use Change in England: Residential Development to 2005 – (LUCS-21) – 20 July 2006

25. **DCLG** – PPGS Housing – (Formerly PPG 3) Current versions available – www.communities.gov.uk/planningandbuilding/planning/planningpolicyguidance/planningpolicystatements/

26. **Francis Tibbalds** – Making People-Friendly Towns: Improving the public environment in towns and cities, Longman, 1992

27. **Hugh Barton, Geoff Davis, Richard Guise** – Sustainable settlements; A guide for planners, designers and developers, Local Government Management Board, April 1995

28. **John Willoughby** – NHER Training Manual, Energy Advisory Associates, 1993

29. **Peter Smith** – Sustainability at the Cutting Edge: Emerging Technologies for Low Energy Buildings – The Martin Centre Cambridge University Elsevier, 2007

30. **Elsbeth Wills, Mike Galloway, Piers Gough** – Crown Street Regeneration Project, Glasgow Development Agency, 1993

31. **Dr. Simon Minett** – Delta Energy and Environment – Time to Take a Fresh Look at CHP... Combined Heat and Power Association – October 2005

32. **Michael King** – The role of community heating in the sustainable urban neighbourhood, SUN Dial 2, URBED, Autumn 1996

33. **URBED** – Focus groups organised with MORI for Manchester City Council – Unpublished – 2000

34. **David Rudlin and Nicholas Falk** – Building to Last: 21st Century Homes, The Joseph Rowntree Foundation, 1995

35. **DCLG:** Code for Sustainable Homes : A step-change in sustainable home building practice 2006

36. **English Partnerships** – www.englishpartnerships.co.uk/carbonchallenge.htm

37. **Keith Collins** – Recycling: No longer just a middle-class fad, SUN Dial 5, URBED, Spring 1998

38. **URBED** – Masterplan for the East Ketley Millennium Community in Telford – Available www.urbed.coop.

39. **South Shropshire District Council and Greenfinch** – Anareobic Digestion Plant at Ludlow in Shropshire built with a DTI grant – 1998

40. **Urban Mines** – www.urbanmines.org.uk/

41. **Jane Jacobs** – The Economy of Cities,

Vintage Books, 1969

42. **Herbert Girardet** – The Gaia Atlas of Cities, Gaia Books, 1992

43. **Robert and Brenda Vale** – Green architecture, Thames & Hudson Ltd. 1991

44. **Susannah Gill, John Handley, Roland Ennos** – Adapting cities for climate change: the role of the green infrastructure – Built Environment, 33, 97–115 – 2007

45. **Tara Garnett** –Harvesting The Cities, Town and Country Planning, Vol. 65, No. 10, Oct 1995

46. **Levitt Berstein Associates** – Building Homes as if Tomorrow Mattered, The RIBA exhibition, Levitt Berstein Associates, June 1997

CHAPTER 11

1. **James Howard Kunstler** – The Geography of Nowhere: The Rise and Decline of America's Man-Made Landscape – Free Press – July 26th, 1994

2. **Prince Charles** – A Vision of Britain: A Personal View of Architecture, Doubleday, 1989

3. **Kevin Lynch** – Image of the City, MIT Press, 1975. **Francis Bacon** – Design Of Cities, Thames & Hudson, 1975. **Gordon Cullen** – Townscapes, Architectural Press 1961. **Spiro Kostof** – The City Shaped, Thames and Hudson, 1991. **Francis Tibbalds** – Making People-Friendly Towns: Improving the public environment in towns and cities, Longman, 1992. **Ian Bentley** – Responsive Environments – A manual for designers, The Architectural Press, 1985. **Harley Sherlock** – Harley Sherlock – Cities are good for us, Paladin, 1994

4. **Richard Sennett** – Uses of Disorder: Personal identity and city life, Faber and Faber, 1996

5. **Home Office Crime Prevention Unit** – Secured by design, Home Office, 1994

6. **Bill Hillier** – Against Enclosure, Chapter in: Necdet Teymur, Thomas A. Markus, Tom Wooley – Rehumanising Housing – Butterworths, 1988

7. **Terry Farrell** – www.terryfarrell.co.uk/ projects/moving/mov_maryleEuston.html

8. **CABE:** Case Studies – Kensington High Street London – www.cabe.org

9. **Ben Hamilton-Bailey** – Bid to ban clutter from streets – BBC News Thursday, 14 October, 2004, see also – **Shared Space** – Room for Everyone – A new vision for public spaces – www.shared-space.org

10. **Chistopher Alexander** – A New Theory of Urban Design, Oxford University Press, 1987

11. **Andres Duany and Elizabeth Plater-Zyberk** – Town and Town-making Principles, Rizzoli International Publications Inc. 1991

12. **Charlie Baker & David Rudlin** – Rebuilding The City : The Hulme Guide To Development, Manchester City Council, June 1994

13. **DfT** – The Quiet Lanes and Home Zones (England) Regulations – DfT Circular 02/2006 – 9th August 2006

14. **Yolanda Barnes** – Savills Research – The Value of Sustainable Urbanism – Presentation – November 2007

15. **Francis Tibbalds** – Making People-Friendly Towns: Improving the public environment in towns and cities, Longman, 1992.

16. **URBED** – Bradford City Centre Design Guide – prepared for Bradford Centre Regeneration and Bradford City Council – November 2005

17. **URBED** – Nottingham City Centre: Urban Design Guide – October 2008

18. **Manchester City Council** – A Guide to Development in Manchester, Manchester City Council, 1997

19. **DETR** – By Design: Urban design in the planning system: towards better practice – Thomas Telford Publishing – 2000

20. **Elspeth Wills, Mike Galloway, Piers Gough** – Crown Street Regeneration Project, Glasgow Development Agency, 1993

21. **Ajuntament de Barcelona** – Barcelona, Posa't Guapa, Ajuntament de Barcelona, 1992

22. **Jane Jacobs** – Death and Life of Great American Cities, Randon House 1961

23. **Hugh Barton, Geoff Davis, Richard Guise** – Sustainable settlements; A guide for planners, designers and developers, Local Government Management Board, April 1995

24. **Alan Rowley** – Mixed use development: Concepts and realities, RICS Books, 1996

25. **Andy Coupland** (ed.) – Rebuilding the city: Mixed Use Development, F & FN Spon, 1997

CHAPTER 12

1. **David Page** – Building for Communities: A study of new housing association estates, Joseph Rowntree Foundation, 1993

2. **Marylin Taylor** – Unleashing the potential: A review of the Action on Estates Programme, Joseph Rowntree Foundation, Dec. 1995

3. **David Rudlin** – Roughey Gardens, for North Cheshire Housing Association, Unpublished

4. **Anne Power and Katherine Mumford:** The Slow Death of Great Cities? Urban abandonment or urban renaissance – YPS in association with JRF – May 1999

5. **Brendan Nevin, Peter Lee, Lisa Goodson, Alan Murie and Jenny Phillimore** – Changing Housing Markets and Urban Regeneration in the M62 Corridor – Centre for Urban and Regional Studies – The University of Birmingham – 2001

6. **Ian Cole and Brendan Nevin** – The Road to Renewal: The early development of the Housing Market Renewal Pathfinder programme in England – Joseph Rowntree Foundation – Dec 2004

7. **John Harris** – Safe as houses – The Guardian Tuesday 30 September 2008

8. **John Burnett** – A Social History of Housing 1815–1985, Methuen, 1986

9. **Chris Bazlinton** – Mixed Blessings, Search 26 – the journal of the Joseph Rowntree Foundation, Winter 1996

10. **Sheila Hayman** – Two-dimensional Living: Celebration, The Independent, 30th June 1996

11. **Barry Poynter** – Paper to SUN Seminar, URBED, Unpublished, 1996

12. **Michael Simmons** – Out with the old, in with new, The Guardian, 3 Jan 1996

13. **Mulholland Research Associates** – Towns or leafier environments; a survey of family homebuying choices – Housebuilders Federation, Dec. 1995

14. **David Thame** – Fear is the Key – Manchester City Development Guide, Property Week, 21st Aug 1995

15. **Oscar Newman** – Defensible Space: People and design in the violent city, Architectural Press, 1972

16. **Alice Coleman** – Utopia on Trial: Vision and reality in planned housing, Hilary Shipman London, 2nd issue 1990

17. **Necdet Teymur, Thomas A. Markus, Tom Wooley** – Rehumanising Housing – Butterworths, 1988, Chapter 5, Bill Hillier – Against enclosure

18. **Steve Osbourn & Henry Shaftoe** – Safer Neighbourhoods: Successes and failures in crime prevention, Safer Neighbourhoods Unit, Joseph Rowntree Foundation, 1995

19. **Ministry of Housing and Local Government** – People & Planning (Skeffington Report) – HMSO – 1969

20. **Rod Hackney** – The Good, the Bad and the Ugly: Cities in Crisis, Frederick Muller, 1990

CHAPTER 13

1. **Peter Marcus** – Lessons from Hulme – Hsg. Summary 5, Joseph Rowntree Foundation, Sept 1994

2. **City Planning Department** – A new community: The redevelopment of Hulme, Manchester City Council, 1966

3. **Capita Consultants** – The Hulme Study, Commissioned by DOE and Manchester City Council, 1989

4. **Price Waterhouse** – Consultancy Study of Hulme which led to the establishment of City Challenge for Manchester City Council and the Housing Corporation, 1991

5. **Charlie Baker & David Rudlin** – Rebuilding The City : The Hulme Guide To Development, Manchester City Council, June 1994

6. **Tony Aldous** – Urban Villages: A Concept for creating mixed use urban developments on a sustainable scale, Urban Villages Forum, 1992

7. **Elspeth Wills, Mike Galloway, Piers Gough** – Crown Street Regeneration Project, Glasgow Development Agency, 1993

8. **DOE/DOT** – Design Bulletin 32: Residential Roads and Footpaths; Layout considerations, HMSO, 2nd Edition 1992

9. **David Thame** – Fear is the Key – Manchester City Development Guide, Property Week, 21st Aug 1995

10. **Manchester City Council** – A Guide to Development in Manchester, Manchester City Council, 1997

11. **Manchester City Council** – Guide to Development in Manchester – Supplementary Planning Document and Planning Guidance (SPD) – 11th April 2007

12. **URBED** – Illustrations first published in SUN Dial 4, SUN Dial 4, URBED, Spring/Summer 1997

13. **DOE** – Sustainable Development: The UK Strategy, HMSO, 1994

14. **Jan Gehl, Lars Gemzøe** – New City Spaces, Strategies and Projects – The Danish Architectural Press; 3 edition (May 15, 2008)

15. **ECOTEC** – Reducing transport emissions through planning, for the Department of the Environment, London HMSO, 1993. Michael Breheny – Urban Densities and Sustainable Development, Paper to the Institute of Geographers, January 1995

16. **Charles Fulford** – The Compact City and the Market, Chapter in M.Jenkins, E. Burton & K. Williams (Eds) – Compact City: A Sustainable Urban Form? p217–330, F & FN Spon, 1996

17. **Hugh Barton, Geoff Davis, Richard Guise** – Sustainable settlements; A guide for planners, designers and developers, Local Government Management Board, April 1995

18. **Nick Dodd and David Rudlin** – The Model Sustainable Urban Neighbourhood, SUN Dial 4, URBED, Spring/Summer 1997

19. **David Rudlin and Nicholas Falk** – Building to Last: 21st Century Homes, The Joseph Rowntree Foundation, 1995

20. **David Rudlin** – Homes for Change, SUN Dial 2, URBED, 1996

CHAPTER 14

1. **Andres Duany and Elizabeth Plater-Zyberk** – Town and Town-making Principles, Rizzoli International Publications Inc. 1991

2. **Prince Charles** – Introduction to: Urban Villages: A Concept for creating mixed use urban developments on a sustainable scale, Urban Villages Forum, 1992

3. **Christopher Alexander** – A Pattern Language, 1977. The Timeless Way Of Building, 1979. A New Theory of Urban Design, 1987, All Oxford University Press

4. **Steven Johnson** – Emergence: The Connected lives of ants, brains, cities and software – Allen Lane The Penguin Press – 2001

5. **Friedrich Engels** – The Condition of the Working Class in England with Victor G. Kiernan – Penguin Classics – 1987 (Originally published 1845)

6. **The Academy of Urbanism**, Edited by Brian Evans and Frank McDonald – Learning from Place – RIBA Publishing 2007 (Chapter 4 Towns – David Rudlin p46–65)

7. **Rob Cowan** – The Connected City, Urban Initiatives, 1997

8. **Peter Hall** – Urban & Regional Planning, Pelican, 1975

9. **Charlie Baker & David Rudlin** – Rebuilding The City : The Hulme Guide To Development, Manchester City Council, June 1994 and Manchester City Council – A Guide to Development in Manchester, Manchester City Council, 1997

10. **Andres Duany and Elizabeth Plater-Zyberk** – Town and Town-making Principles, Rizzoli International Publications Inc. 1991

11. **DETR** – By Design – Urban design in the planning system: towards better practice – Thomas Telford Publishing – May 2000

12. **Llewelyn-Davies** – Urban Design Compendium – English Partnerships the Housing Corporation – first published August 2000, Second edition September 2007

33. **CABE** – Building for Life; Delivering great places to live – CABE – November 2008

14. **Elspeth Wills, Mike Galloway, Piers Gough** – Crown Street Regeneration Project, Glasgow Development Agency, 1993

15. **URBED** – Bradford City Centre Design Guide – prepared for Bradford Centre Regeneration and Bradford City Council – November 2005

16. **Alsop/Big Architecture** – Bradford Centre Regeneration Masterplan – Bradford Centre Regeneration – 2003.

17. **Rem Koolhaas**, quoted in "Rem Koolhaas, Post-Nationalist Architect", The New York Times, September 11, 1994.

Epilogue

1. **Jane Jacobs** – The Life and Death of Great American Cities, quoted in Learning from Place 1, Academy of Urbanism/RIBA Press, 2007

2. **Joel Kotkin** – The City: A Global History, , Weidenfold and Nicolson, 2005

3. **Jared Diamond** – Collapse: How Societies Choose to Fail or Succeed – Viking Adult December 2004

4. **Nicholas Falk and Haris Martinos** – Inner City: local government and economic renewal, Fabian Society 1975

5. **The Urban Task Force** – Towards an Urban Renaissance: Department of the Environment, Transport and the Regions, Distributed

by E & FN Spon 1999

6. **URBED** – Towns & Cities: Partners in Urban Renaissance – ODPM 2002

7. **Charles Landry** – The Creative City – Earthscan 2000

8. **URBED** – Spreading the Benefits of Town and City Centre Renewal – for the Local Government Association and Sigoma – 2005

9. **Nicholas Falk** – Over the Edge? Town centres and the economy – North and West London Strategic Alliances – 2008 see also other reports on suburbs on urbed.co.uk

10. **Nicholas Falk** – Smarter Growth and Intelligent Local Finance – TCPA – 2005

11. **Tristram Hunt** – Building Jerusalem, The rise and fall of Victorian London – Holt Paperbacks – December 26, 2006)

12. **Dorling, D., Rigby, J., Wheeler, B., Ballas, D., Thomas, B., Fahmy, E., Gordon, D., and Lupton, R.** – Poverty, wealth and place in Britain, 1968 to 2005 – Bristol: Policy Press – 2007

13. **Professor Michael Parkinson et al.** State of the Cities Report – Office of the Deputy Prime Minister – March 2006

14. **PRP URBED and Design for Homes** – Beyond Ecotowns: Applying the lessons from Europe Report and Conclusions – Scott Wilson, The Guinness Partnership and Grainger plc – 2008

15. **Nicholas Falk and Peter Hall** – Learning from Dutch New Settlements – Towns and Country Planning – January 2009

16. **Nick Dodd** – Community Energy: Urban planning for a low carbon future – TCPA and the Combined Hear and Power Association, 2008

17. See 6

18. **URBED with research by PRP, Savills, Buro Happold and the LSE Cities Programme** – Better Neighbourhoods: Making higher densities – CABE and the Corporation of London – 2005

19. **URBED** – Quality Charter for Growth in Cambridgeshire – Inspire East and Cambridgeshire Horizons – September 2007 www. cambridgeshirehorizons.co.uk/qualitycharter

20. See 10

21. **Christine Whitehead and Katherine Scanlon eds.** – Social Housing – London School of Economics – 2008

Images and Illustrations

Building 1934–1939 the year book of the Building Employers Confederation

Page 69 **Tower block Sheffield**

Page 70 **Hyde Park, Sheffield**
Both images taken from Ten years of housing in Sheffield, published in 1962, reproduced by kind permission of Sheffield City Council

Page 72 **Byker, Newcastle** – David Rudlin

Page 75 **London Docklands** – David Rudlin

Page 76 **Werneth master plan and workshop photo:** URBED

Page 77 **Housing output by sector** – URBED based on data from JRF Housing Review 1996/97

Page 78 **Blackbird Leys, Oxford** – Ealing Family Housing Association

PART 2

Title **Figure ground plan Bordeaux** – MBLC Architects

CHAPTER 5

Page 83 **The earth** – Illustration Vibeke Fussing

Page 84 **Illustration of medieval Bristol**

Page 86 **Pedestrian Pocket** – Peter Calthorpe from Next American Metropolis, Princetown Architectural Press

Page 89 **Graph: Carbon Dioxide emissions** URBED, Adapted from Sustainability: the UK Strategy

Page 90 **Power station** – Vibeke Fussing

Page 91 **Car fumes** – Vibeke Fussing

Page 92 **Sewage outfall** – Vibeke Fussing

Page 93 **Land fill site** – Vibeke Fussing

Page 95 **The autonomous house** – Courtesy Robert and Brenda Vale

Page 96 **Photo BedZED** – URBED

Page 98 **Edinburgh New Town** – David Rudlin

Page 99 **Freiburg, Germany** – David Rudlin

CHAPTER 6

Page 102 **Warehouse, Manchester** – David Rudlin

Page 103 **Graph: Household composition** – URBED, adapted from ONS

Page 104 **Housing by McCarthy and Stone** – David Rudlin

Page 105 **The Wigan Foyer** – David Rudlin

Page 107 **Graph: Household growth is nothing new** – URBED adapted from Department of the Environment, Transport and the Regions

Page 108 **Graph: The nature of household growth** – URBED adapted from Department of the Environment, Transport and the Regions

Page 109 **The Smithfield Building, Manchester** – Stephenson Bell Architects, courtesy Urban Splash

Page 111 **The Westferry live/work scheme:** PCKO Architects courtesy Peabody Trust

Page 113 **The City of London** – David Rudlin

CHAPTER 7

Page 117 **Hallwood Park, Runcorn** – David Rudlin

Page 118 **St. Wilfreds, Hulme** – URBED

Page 119 **Moravian settlement, Ashton** – David Rudlin

Page 120 **The English Village** – David Rudlin, adapted from W.G. Hoskins in the Making of the English Landscape

Page 121 **Moseley Village** – David Rudlin

Page 122 **Roslyn Place, Pittsburgh** – Allen Jacobs taken from Great Streets courtesy of MIT Press

Page 123 **Bentilee, Stoke-on-Trent** – Levitt Bernstien Associates

CHAPTER 8

Page 126 **Social housing Lindenstrasse, Berlin** – Herman Hertzberger, courtesy 010 Publishers, Rotterdam

Page 128 **A safe investment** – Illustration by Gordon Harris published in House building 1934–1939 the year of the Building Employers Confederation

Page 131 **The Urban Splash Fridge** – Courtesy Urban Splash

Page 134 **Greenwich Millennium Village** – Photo URBED

Page 136 **Model plans from the Artizans', Labourers and general dwellings estate at Hornsey 1833** – Adapted by David Rudlin

Page 137 **Prefabricated housing** – Courtesy JT Construction

PART 3

Title **Figure ground plan Turin** – MBLC Architects

CHAPTER 9

Page 144 **Dickens Heath Solihull** – Barton Willmore Partnership

Page 148 **Density and travel** – URBED adapted from ECOTEC

Page 150 **The urbanisation of England** – URBED adapted from Bibby and Shepherd

Page 150 **Housing Land** – Graph created by URBED from Land Use Change Statistics for England 2007

Page 152 **The lost urban populations** – URBED adapted from ONS

Page 153 **The changing population of UK cities** – Graph URBED

Page 155 **Recycled land capacity** – URBED/Friends of the Earth

Page 156 **Derelict in England** – URBED adapted from Survey of Derelict Land in England 1993 – DOE

Page 157 **Infill housing Coventry** – David Rudlin

Page 157 **The Royal Free Hospital, Islington** Pollard Thomas and Edwards Architects and Levitt Bernstein Associates

Page 158 **Urban intensification, Hertfordshire** – Urban Initiatives

Page 159 **Living over the shop, Grantham**

– South Kesteven District Council

Page 159 **Cirencester urban infill** – URBED

Page 160 **The housing capacity of urban areas in England** – URBED/Friends of the Earth

Page 161 **The density gradient** – URBED adapted from various sources

Page 162 **Rye** – David Rudlin

Page 164 **Playing on urban fears** – Advertisement Milton Keynes Development Corporation 1970s

Page 165 **Coin Street Community Builders, London** – David Rudlin

CHAPTER 10

Page 168 **Kreuzberg, Berlin** – David Rudlin

Page 170 **Sustainability and the city region** – Adapted from the Manchester 2020 project courtesy Joe Ravetz

Page 171 **Project ZED** – Courtesy of Future Systems

Page 172 **The Pedestrian Pocket** – Peter Calthorpe from Next American Metropolis, Princetown Architectural Press

Page 172 **The Urban Village** – The Urban Village Forum

Page 173 **Ecocity Berkeley** – Richard Register courtesy North Atlantic Books

Page 174/175 – **The walkable city: Urban grids** – David Rudlin

Page 174 **The Disconnected City** – Phil Bonds reproduced from the Connected City courtesy of Rob Cowan

Page 175 **Car-free housing, Edinburgh** – Andrew Lee, Hackland and Dore Architect

Page 176 **Poundbury in Dorset** – Alan Baxter Associates

Page 178 **The Metrolink, Manchester** – Hélène Rudlin

Page 180 **St. Pancras Housing Association** – David Rudlin

Page 184 **Kerbside recycling** – Laurence Bruce/Friends of the Earth

Page 185 **Communal recycling bins:** Photo URBED

Page 186 **Bioworks, Kolding Denmark** – Courtesy Housing and Urban Planning Division, Statens Byggefor-skningsinstitut

Page 188 **Park Square, Leeds** – David Rudlin

Page 190 **Alexander Park Manchester** – Photo David Rudlin

CHAPTER 11

Page 192 **Roupell Street, Waterloo** – David Rudlin

Page 195 **Orchard Street, Bristol** – David Rudlin

Page 195 **Chronos Building London** – Photo Proctor Matthews Architects

Page 196 **Kensington High Street** – Photo Courtesy LB Kensington and Chelsea

Page 197 **Lively Street, Romania** – David Rudlin

Page 198 **Trellis Plan of Barcelona** – David Rudlin

Page 199 **Trellis Plan of Manchester** – David Rudlin

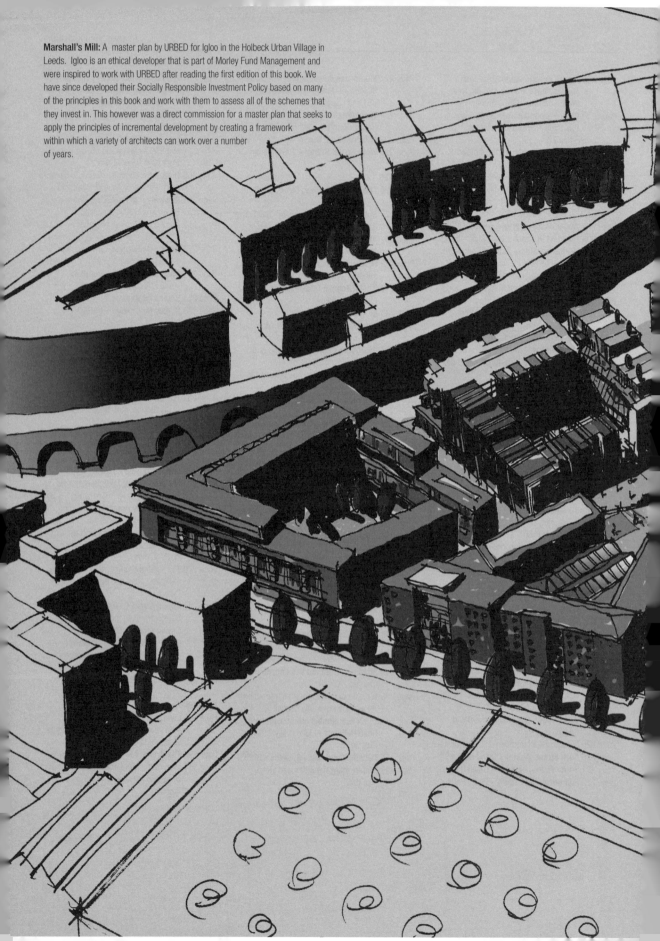

Marshall's Mill: A master plan by URBED for Igloo in the Holbeck Urban Village in Leeds. Igloo is an ethical developer that is part of Morley Fund Management and were inspired to work with URBED after reading the first edition of this book. We have since developed their Socially Responsible Investment Policy based on many of the principles in this book and work with them to assess all of the schemes that they invest in. This however was a direct commission for a master plan that seeks to apply the principles of incremental development by creating a framework within which a variety of architects can work over a number of years.

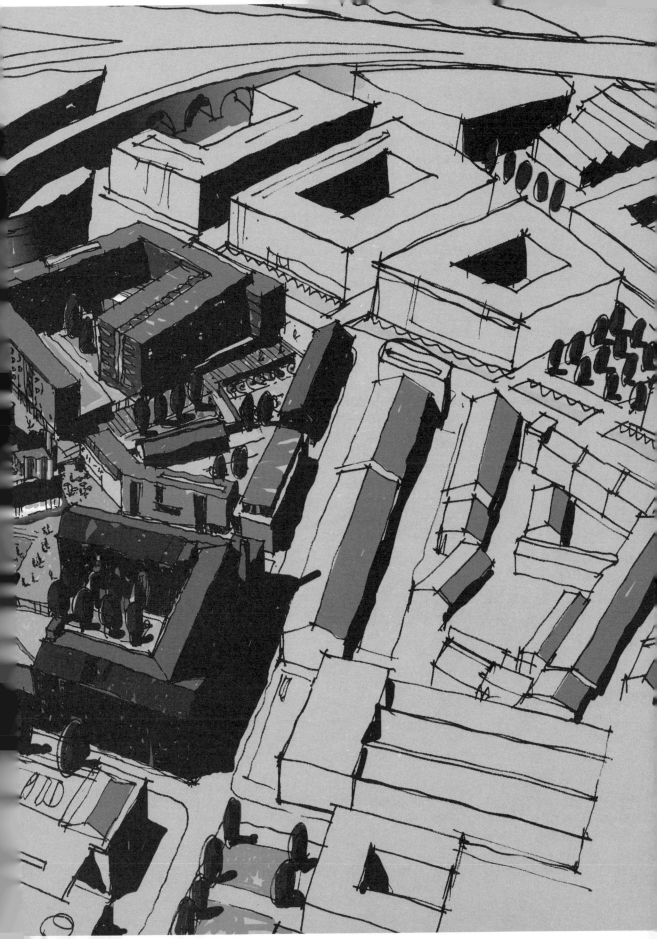

Sustainable Urban Neighbourhood explores the way that the UK's towns and cities are changing at the turn of the millennium. Previously known as Building the 21st Century Home, the second edition of this successful text describes the way that environmental and demographic change, economic pressures and the needs of community could change urban areas forever.

The first edition of this book predicted that just as the Garden City pioneers helped transform the urban society of the 19th century into the 20th century suburb, pressures for change could see an equally momentous change in the 21st century. Ten years later, this new comprehensively rewritten edition looks back at the momentous changes of the last few years and assesses progress.

Some of the arguments that were so contentious ten years ago are now widely accepted. Others rumble on, particularly after a property crash focused on urban apartments. The central point however remains; urban renaissance will not be achieved by coercion but by the creation of positive urban models. The book describes one such model, the Sustainable Urban Neighbourhood, mixed-use, medium-density urban development designed to minimise resource-use and maximise community.

This classic text has become essential reading for urban designers, architects and planners, indeed anyone involved in the development of new homes and the regeneration of towns and cities.

'Building the 21st Century Home is the best analysis I have read of the crisis of the contemporary British City... This book offers a chance to rethink our priorities, break the cycle of decline and to create sustainable cities suitable for citizens'.
Lord (Richard) Rogers

'This book says some good things and some things that in my view are quite misguided but all of it is interesting. Every British planner should read it forthwith'.
Professor Sir Peter Hall

'There are many books published now with a revisionist urban program... (this) is one of the best and most comprehensive'.
Joe Holyoak - AJ

'Leading protagonists of a burgeoning cult of the city... URBED know their subject intimately, put it across with lucid arguments, copious examples, fascinating statistics and attractive illustrations'.
The Land is Ours

'A reference to this book would have cut at least 100 pages from the Urban Task Force Report'.
Will Howie The HouseBuilder

'The authors have integrated a range of concerns into a well structured argument which will be hard to rebut – though one could easily think of some who will try to do so. The very weight and intellectually respectable nature of the book signifies a case to answer'.
Timothy Cantell - Royal Society of Arts Journal

'Those in the planning, housing and associated professions who see the need for new thinking would do well to read this book. Maybe even politicians of all shades might benefit from considering its message'
Anthony Goss Planning for the Natural and Built Environment